Few composers' posthumous reputations have grown as steadily as Shostakovich's. Yet outside the concert hall the focus of attention seems to have been on the extraordinary circumstances of his life rather than on the music itself. This book seeks to show that the power of his work stems as much from its craftsmanship as from its political and personal context. The theoretical chapters lay the foundation for a proper understanding of Shostakovich's musical language. The social context is not neglected, however, and alongside many new insights spread across the book a substantial and provocative chapter considers the issues surrounding the composition and reception of the Fifth Symphony. The eleven essays in the volume draw together some of the finest scholars of Russian music in Europe, Russia and America.

Shostakovich Studies

Shostakovich Studies

Edited by David Fanning
University of Manchester

CAMBRIDGE UNIVERSITY PRESS
Cambridge, New York, Melbourne, Madrid, Cape Town, Singapore, São Paulo

Cambridge University Press
The Edinburgh Building, Cambridge CB2 2RU, UK

Published in the United States of America by Cambridge University Press, New York

www.cambridge.org
Information on this title: www.cambridge.org/9780521452397

© Cambridge University Press 1995

This publication is in copyright. Subject to statutory exception
and to the provisions of relevant collective licensing agreements,
no reproduction of any part may take place without
the written permission of Cambridge University Press.

First published 1995
Reprinted 1997
This digitally printed first paperback version 2006

A catalogue record for this publication is available from the British Library

Library of Congress Cataloguing in Publication data

Shostakovich studies / edited by David Fanning.
   p. cm.
Includes index.
ISBN 0 521 45239 2 (hardback)
1. Shostakovich, Dmitriĭ Dmitrievich, 1906–1975 – Criticism
and interpretation. I. Fanning, David (David J.).
ML410.S53S52 1995
780.'92–dc20   95–39273   CIP   MN

ISBN-13 978-0-521-45239-7 hardback
ISBN-10 0-521-45239-2 hardback

ISBN-13 978-0-521-02831-8 paperback
ISBN-10 0-521-02831-0 paperback

Contents

	Acknowledgments	*page* ix
1	Introduction. Talking about eggs: musicology and Shostakovich DAVID FANNING	1
2	Public lies and unspeakable truth interpreting Shostakovich's Fifth Symphony RICHARD TARUSKIN	17
3	Form in Shostakovich's instrumental works YURIY KHOLOPOV	57
4	Russian theorists on modality in Shostakovich's music ELLON D. CARPENTER	76
5	The cycle of structure and the cycle of meaning the Piano Trio in E minor, Op. 67 PATRICK McCRELESS	113
6	Leitmotif in *Lady Macbeth* DAVID FANNING	137
7	From *Lady Macbeth* to *Katerina* Shostakovich's versions and revisions LAUREL E. FAY	160
8	*The Golden Age*: the true story of the première MANASHIR YAKUBOV	189
9	'And art made tongue-tied by authority' Shostakovich's song-cycles DOROTHEA REDEPENNING	205

10	A debt repaid? Some observations on Shostakovich and his late-period recognition of Britten ERIC ROSEBERRY	229
11	Shostakovich and Schnittke: the erosion of symphonic syntax ALEXANDER IVASHKIN	254
	Index	271

Acknowledgments

I wish to acknowledge the support of my colleagues at the University of Manchester during the preparation of this book and the University's provision of teaching relief during the final editorial stages. I also wish to thank Deirdre Donnellon for assistance with word-processing, Penny Souster at Cambridge University Press who suggested this book and fostered its development, Lyudmila Kovnatskaya of St Petersburg Conservatory who generously kept me up to date with developments in Russia, and John Cornish who made invaluable initial translations of the chapters by Kholopov, Yakubov and Ivashkin. I have fine-tuned these translations and must take responsibility for any inaccuracies in them, as also in Redepenning's chapter which I myself translated. Thanks are also due to the May 1994 St Petersburg conference, 'Shostakovich in a Changing World', organised by Lyudmila Kovnatskaya, at which versions of my *Lady Macbeth* chapter and Eric Roseberry's on 'Shostakovich and Britten' were read.

1

Introduction. Talking about eggs: musicology and Shostakovich

DAVID FANNING

What is a musicologist? Shostakovich offered his definition over breakfast: 'What's a musicologist? I'll tell you. Our cook, Pasha, prepared the scrambled eggs for us and we are eating them. Now imagine a person who did not cook the eggs and does not eat them, but talks about them – *that* is a musicologist.'[1] No doubt many would agree. Yet it should not be forgotten that among Shostakovich's closest friends and confidants was Ivan Sollertinsky – man of many parts, but primarily a musicologist – who probably did more than any other individual to shape Shostakovich's tastes and sharpen his intellect in his formative years; and his most extensive and revealing correspondence after Sollertinsky's death in 1944 was with Isaak Glikman, who, as a theatre historian, must count as another professional egg-talker.[2] There are even occasional words of praise for musicologists to be found in Shostakovich's writings, the most apparently sincere of them reserved for Lev (now Leo) Mazel', whose work on Shostakovich draws tribute from two contributors to the present volume.

---

[1] The joke was apparently passed on to him by his conservatoire piano teacher, Leonid Nikolayev. See Nikolai Malko, *A Certain Art* (New York, 1966), 180.

[2] Sollertinsky's writings have not been translated into English, with the exception of an extract of his 1932 Mahler book and his 1941 essay 'Historical types of symphonic dramaturgy', in Eric Roseberry, *Ideology, Style, Content, and Thematic Process in the Symphonies, Cello Concertos, and String Quartets of Shostakovich* (New York and London, 1989). A selection in German may be found in Iwan Sollertinski, *Von Mozart bis Schostakowitsch* (Leipzig, 1979). Extracts from the important correspondence between Shostakovich and Sollertinsky are published in Lyudmila Mikheyeva, 'Istoriya odnoy druzhbï' [The story of a friendship], *Sovetskaya Muzïka* (9/1986 and 9/1987); Mikheyeva (Sollertinsky's daughter-in-law) is currently seeking funds to publish a more comprehensive selection. Shostakovich's letters to Glikman, much referred to in the present volume, are in *Pis'ma k drugu* [Letters to a Friend] (Moscow and St Petersburg, 1993); French translation, with truncated editorial commentaries (Paris, 1994).

2   Introduction

But on the whole it remains true that Shostakovich had a low opinion of musicologists, not just because of their seemingly redundant and parasitical sphere of activity, but also because of the cowardice, even malice, he detected in some of them (above all in the doyen of Soviet musicology, Boris Asaf'yev).[3] Maybe, then, he would have been happy to know that musicologists outside the former Soviet Union have tended to shy away from his music: and maybe he would have looked with intense suspicion at the line-up of musicologists in this volume of *Shostakovich Studies*. Certainly, given the extent and significance of extramusical issues associated with Shostakovich, the value of traditional musicological commentary is questionable. This fact alone merits a longer than usual editorial preamble.

Recent published work on Shostakovich has been dominated by performers, personal friends or pupils of the composer, and the odd enthusiast.[4] I stress that none of those words carries a sneer, certainly not the kind of sneer that the shrillest of these recent publications reserves for musicologists.[5] But the kind of commentary these writers have favoured – anti-musicological, revisionist and casual in its ascribing of programmatic, usually subversive meaning – would probably have been no more to Shostakovich's taste than 'straight' musicology, as Richard Taruskin points out in his keynote contribution to the present volume, quoting the composer: 'When a critic . . . writes that in such-and-such a symphony Soviet civil servants are represented by the oboe and the clarinet, and Red Army men by the brass section, you want to scream!'

Taruskin's main project is to elucidate the background to and reception of the Fifth Symphony, the most significant watershed in Shostakovich's output and one of the most extensively and contradictorily commented works in the history of music. Taruskin dubs it 'a richly coded utterance, but one whose meaning can never be wholly encompassed or definitively

---

[3] For details see Krzysztof Meyer, *Dimitri Chostakovitch* (Paris, 1994), 99–101, and Elizabeth Wilson, *Shostakovich: A Life Remembered* (London, 1994), 112, 209, 304.

[4] Among performers see Vladimir Ashkenazy, 'Shostakovich was not an enigma', *DSCH Journal*, no. 20 (Spring 1992), 4–14; Rudolf Barshai, 'On ne boyalsya Stalina' [He was not afraid of Stalin], *Sovetskaya Muzika* (9/1989); Semyon Bychkov, interviewed in *DSCH Journal*, no. 19 (Autumn 1991), 15–19. For personal acquaintances and pupils see the statements collected in *Melos* (Stockholm), 1/4–5 (Summer 1993). For an eloquent and ideologically committed enthusiast, see Ian MacDonald, *The New Shostakovich* (London, 1990). The finest recent substantial contributions are from Elizabeth Wilson (primarily a cellist) and Krzysztof Meyer (primarily a composer) – see note 3.

[5] Ian MacDonald, *The New Shostakovich*, passim.

paraphrased', and he conducts his search for that meaning with as passionate an abhorrence for vulgarised programmatic commentary as the composer's quoted above. It has seemed to me right to let his polemical tone and content stand, even when they involve assertions I cannot personally endorse, because these assertions are founded on a scholarly grasp of Russian music in all its aspects which is unrivalled outside Russia (and possibly within Russia too). No one is better placed single-handedly to turn back the 'torrent of romantically revisionary, sentimental nonsense' which Taruskin finds characteristic of writing on Shostakovich in the eras of *glasnost'* and post-Communism.

It is not difficult to see how the urge for revisionism could have arisen. For Russians it is part of an ongoing process of de-mythologising their own history; more specifically it is an acknowledgment that Shostakovich's music provided an emotional safety-valve for tragic experiences which for decades could not be written about – indeed they could hardly even be talked about. In the West it is perhaps more a case of being tempted to make Shostakovich into the kind of hero we would like him to be, and in particular the mirror-image of the kind of hero former socialist-orientated commentators would have liked him to be. In both cases the risk is of replacing one mythology with another and still bringing us no closer to the experience of the music itself. As each provocative voice spawns new claims and counter-claims, and as anti-revisionism is added to the morass of conflicting opinions, Shostakovich commentators begin to seem rather like libel lawyers, with a vested interest in continuing controversy. And with such a profusion of 'evidence' on all sides there is every prospect of an endless cycle of appeals, new submissions and retrials.

Whether or not one agrees with Taruskin that the view of Shostakovich as dissident in the 1930s is 'a self-gratifying anachronism' (he urges us, in effect, to distinguish between dissidence and non-conformism), now at least there is an immensely scholarly and authoritative voice setting forth this view and supplanting such pioneer anti-revisionist efforts as Christopher Norris's.[6] It is a view that western writings on Shostakovich would do well to heed, especially if they seek to put an ideological slant on reception history[7] or analysis.[8]

---

[6] See his 'Shostakovich: politics and musical language', in the symposium edited by him, *Shostakovich: the Man and his Music* (London, 1982), 163–87.

[7] Günter Wolter, *Dmitrij Schostakowitsch, eine sowjetische Tragödie: Rezeptionsgeschichte* (Frankfurt am Main and New York, 1991).

[8] Karen Kopp, *Form und Gehalt der Symphonien des Dmitrij Schostakowitsch* (Bonn, 1990).

At the moment Taruskin's post-revisionism is a minority voice in writings on Shostakovich, but it finds echoes in other exasperated post-*glasnost'* Russian writings on the arts: 'The exposure of myths of the past threatens to grow into another mythology. The "Personality Cult" has much in common with "The Cult of Denunciation of the Personality Cult".'[9] In fact the richness of Taruskin's commentary consists not so much in its de-mythologising of Shostakovich as in its de-mythologising of musicology. For his deep soundings into the murky waters of Soviet criticism offer a timely reminder that identifying subtexts and ambiguities in Shostakovich's music is actually nothing new. Such insights, such unspeakable truths', were grasped, at least partially, in the first instance by those Soviet critics whose aim was to denounce the music. The same line was then adopted in more subtle fashion by post-Thaw Soviet musicologists, still well before westerners independently latched on to it and, encouraged by the appearance in 1979 of that arch-revisionist document, Solomon Volkov's *Testimony*,[10] all too often trivialised it.

There cannot be too many books on twentieth-century composers that have sold half a million copies, as Volkov claims.[11] There is no gainsaying *Testimony*'s influence on the public perception of Shostakovich's music – since the appearance of its curious mixture of rumour, fact and slanted reminiscence there is hardly a book, an article, a review, a programme note or a liner note on a major Shostakovich work which could truthfully claim not to have been influenced by it, at least outside Russia.[12]

It should be remembered that Volkov's well-known dishonesty about the provenance of the book says nothing about the truth or falsehood of its content. But whatever its status as a representation of the composer's views, it may be worth remembering that *Testimony* the book contains one of the best stories against testimony with a small 't'. It concerns Berg's visit to Leningrad in 1927 to conduct *Wozzeck*:

[9] Andrey Shemyakin, 'Malen'kaya pol'za' [Little use], *Seans*, no. 3 (1991). The article reviews S. Aranovich's film, *I was in Stalin's Apparat*, or *The Songs of Oligarchs*.
[10] Solomon Volkov (ed.), *Testimony: the Memoirs of Dmitri Shostakovich* (London and New York, 1979).
[11] 'Here a man was burned down', interview with Galina Drïbachevsky, in *Sovetskaya Muzïka* (3/1992), 10. Volkov candidly admits that, 'In fact there's much we don't know about Shostakovich' (*ibid.*, p. 5).
[12] The fraudulence of *Testimony* is documented by Laurel Fay, 'Shostakovich versus Volkov: whose *Testimony*?' *Russian Review*, 39 (1980), 484–93. The debate surrounding *Testimony* and Shostakovich's ideology has comparatively recently spread to the former Soviet Union. For a substantially pro-Volkov line see, for example, Lev Lebedinsky, 'O nekotorïkh muzïkalnïkh tsitatakh v proizvedeniyakh D. Shostakovicha' [On some musical quotations

Berg left two legends behind. The source of one legend was a critic and fan of Scriabin. Berg supposedly told him that he owed everything as a composer to Scriabin. The other legend came from a critic who didn't care for Scriabin. Supposedly Berg told *him* that he had never heard a note by Scriabin. Over forty years have passed, but both men still repeat with a thrill what Berg said to them. So much for eyewitness accounts.[13]

No doubt fascination with the question of Shostakovich's ideological standpoints will go on and on, and there is much to learn from the recent tide of reminiscences, correspondence and investigations into ideology, or Soviet cultural history, or any of the other recently aired biographical issues such as Shostakovich's relationships with literary figures, with fellow-musicians, and not least with women.[14] It is vital for our understanding of Shostakovich the man that much more Russian material should be available in translation and properly commented on by writers sensitive to the way Russian minds work. Furthermore, even the most intellectually disreputable commentaries may be of value if written with passion and genuine empathy, because they are a fact of reception history. What will do damage, however, is allowing Shostakovich's work to become no more than an arena for ideological mud-slinging.

Fortunately there is a strand of recent published work which is already taking a much more balanced view of the ideology question. Krzysztof Meyer's life-and-works study, originally published in Polish and German, was always one of the saner and more authoritative appreciations of Shostakovich; it has now appeared in French, updated and with many changes of emphasis from passages which were previously affected by (self)-censorship; and Elizabeth Wilson's documentary biography has gathered together a wealth of Russian reminiscence and epistolary material which provides a more finely nuanced, complementary version of the *Testimony* story (see note 3 above).

in the works of D. Shostakovich], *Novïy mir* (3/1990), 262–7, and Daniil Zhitomirsky, 'Shostakovich ofitsial'nïy i podlinnïy' [Shostakovich: official and authentic], *Daugava* (3–4/1990), 88–100; both Lebedinsky and Zhitomirsky were apostates of the proletarian line which was highly critical of Shostakovich's work around 1930. For an anti-Volkov riposte see Yuriy Levitin, 'Fal'shivaya nota' [A wrong note], in *Pravda* (11 November 1990), p. 3; Levitin was one of Shostakovich's first Leningrad pupils from 1937. For an attempt to mediate and point to a more fruitful way ahead, see Lev Mazel', 'K sporam o Shostakoviche' [On the Shostakovich controversy], *Sovetskaya Muzïka* (5/1991), 30–5; as noted above, Mazel' is one of the few musicologists whose work drew praise from Shostakovich.

[13] Volkov, *Testimony*, 32.
[14] For the last see Sof'ya Khentova, 'Zhenshchinï v ego zhizni' [The women of his life], in her book *Udivitel'nïy Shostakovich* [The Surprising Shostakovich], (St Petersburg, 1993), 89–170.

The appearance of these books is one reason why Taruskin's is the only article in the present volume which tackles the ideology issue head-on, though most of the other authors touch on it to a greater or lesser extent. But another more vital reason may be inferred from Taruskin's article itself, or rather from his original conclusion, amended by him without my suggestion but so pertinent that I want to take the liberty of citing it. Developing his approval of Liana Genina's remarks on cheap ideological inversionism he commented:

> She would like to see some attention paid to the music again, not in the spirit of the old escapist musicology, which practised analytical formalism as a way of evading risk, but in simple acknowledgment of the fact that Shostakovich was after all an artist, a composer. We might do well to heed her call, remembering that Albert Camus ended 'The artist and his time', the essay that more than any other proclaimed his commitment to political engagement, with a reminder that 'if we are not artists in our language first of all, what sort of artists are we?'[15]

All this is indeed a timely reminder. The bravest, the most subversive, the most socio-politically challenged, or the most politically correct composer, never gained immortality on those counts alone – witness the many unsuccessful attempts by western composers to commemorate the victims of the Nazi holocaust or the atom bomb. After all, Shostakovich's music speaks to listeners who have never heard of Stalin's Great Terror or read *Testimony*. And if the sources of that communication – in personality, experience and history – are undoubtedly an important concern, the very nature of music demands that the means of communication – the musical language itself – receives equal attention.

What the precise relationship is between the message and the language of music will always remain an elusive and fascinating question, and probably the best anyone working in this area can hope for is to examine its various facets one by one and leave the synthesis to the reader/listener. Such examinations must stand or fall by their own merits. But surely there is no more proper place for them than a scholarly series such as Cambridge's *Studies*. That is why two chapters in this book are predominantly theoretical (Carpenter and Kholopov) and two more predominantly analytical (McCreless and Fanning). The remaining five are more historical in emphasis. Two are single-work source-studies (focusing on primary sources in Laurel Fay's essay on the versions of *The*

---

[15] The Camus citation is from *The Myth of Sisyphus and Other Essays*, trans. Justin O'Brien (New York, 1955), 150.

Lady Macbeth of Mtsensk District, and on secondary ones in Manashir Yakubov's re-emphasis of the reception history of *The Golden Age*). Two are discussions of Shostakovich's relationship with his most significant contemporaries (Britten in Eric Roseberry's essay, Schnittke in Alexander Ivashkin's). And Dorothea Redepenning tackles broad issues of meaning and style in her discussion of the song-cycles.

One strand in Taruskin's essay provides an intellectual and critical context for the theoretical chapters. Writing apropos Shostakovich's post-Fifth Symphony works he asserts that:

> The changes wrought in him by his ordeals lent his voice a moral authority perhaps unmatched in all of twentieth-century music. But the impulse to communicate urgently in an atmosphere of threat did lead, at times, to an over-reliance on extroversive reference as bearer of essential meaning, and a correspondingly debased level of musical discourse.

'Extroversive' and its complementary opposite 'introversive' are terms common in literary theory and they apply here to fundamental areas of musical meaning – involving, respectively, references outside the musical work (to other musical works or to the world at large) and relationships within the work (the tensions and interconnections of its constituent elements). The distinction can be differently formulated – as semantic/syntactic, heteronomous/autonomous, or, as Patrick McCreless chooses in his chapter, extrinsic/immanent. Whatever the favoured terminology, it is the introversive side which has been so singularly neglected in recent writings on Shostakovich, and it is this neglect which it is one of this book's main aims to redress.

Not that there is no analytical literature whatsoever on Shostakovich. There is a vast amount of it in Russian, albeit mostly deficient in rigour and depth. And between them the non-Russian studies have a fair amount to say about formal design in the large-scale works and about thematic transformation.[16] This is not work to be sneezed at – large-scale

---

[16] A useful listing of Russian studies is in Laurel Fay's bibliography to the Shostakovich chapter in Gerald Abraham *et al.*, *The New Grove Russian Masters 2* (London, 1980). See also Ellon Carpenter, 'The theory of music in Russia and the Soviet Union, ca. 1650–1950', Ph.D. diss. (University of Pennsylvania, 1988), iii, 1369–92. Two extensive British Ph.D. dissertations in this field are Richard Longman, *Expression and Structure: Processes of Integration in the Large-Scale Instrumental Music of Dmitri Shostakovich* (New York and London, 1989), and Eric Roseberry, *Ideology, Style, Content* (see note 2 above). See also Laurel Fay, 'The last quartets of Dmitrii Shostakovich: a stylistic investigation', Ph.D. diss. (Cornell University, 1978), and Karen Kopp, *Form und Gehalt*.

form is after all the arena for Shostakovich's musical dramas, and thematic transformation is in many instances the powerhouse. But for discussions of this kind to enhance the reader's experience of the music they need to strike at least two careful balances: one between the various functioning elements of music, and another between its various temporal dimensions – short-, mid- and long-term.[17] And such discussions would carry fuller conviction if they were founded on a historical perspective. To provide such a perspective is the task that Yuriy Kholopov, the most prominent theoretical musicologist active today in Russia, has set himself. His essay ranges over most of Shostakovich's major works, and places its findings in the context of the pedagogical theory derived from Adolf Bernhard Marx which Shostakovich grew up with. The upshot is a persuasive demonstration of how Shostakovich adapted traditional concepts of form to his own aesthetic ends.

The most crucial lacuna in western understanding of Shostakovich's music concerns harmonic and tonal language. That commentators should have been perplexed in the face of a language which is sometimes tonal, sometimes modal, sometimes somewhere in between, and sometimes outside the bounds of either, is understandable. But the extent of downright false diagnoses in otherwise competent studies is still startling.[18] The stumbling block here usually concerns the question of mode. Fortunately this is an area in which Russian scholars have been active – so prodigiously active, in fact, that it is extremely difficult to distil their findings into a coherent and manageable unit; and the language barrier has further served to hide some valuable work from western view. Ellon Carpenter is the author of a huge dissertation on Russian theorists (see note 16 above) and her essay in the present volume is the fruit of her recent work on theories of mode in Shostakovich in particular. Her comprehensive survey offers for the first time a historical perspective on an important branch of musical theory, as well as an invaluable stimulus to a more accurate analytical understanding of Shostakovich's music.

For the most part Carpenter's essay is synoptic rather than critical, but she does conclude with an important caveat:

---

[17] This was in fact my main ambition in my study of the Tenth Symphony, *The Breath of the Symphonist: Shostakovich's Tenth*, Royal Musical Association Monographs 4 (London, 1989).

[18] For examples and discussion see my 'Writing about Shostakovich – performing Shostakovich', paper delivered at the conference *Shostakovich: the Man and his Age*, University of Michigan, February 1994, publication forthcoming.

Introduction

Modal language in Shostakovich's music has not been addressed in its totality, but only in part. Now that the unfolding of its diatonic basis has been examined, a more processive and all-inclusive approach needs to be applied, in order to reveal each piece's unique modal–tonal embodiment in and contribution to the thematic structure.

Quite. And this is easier said than done, of course. Nor is the modal angle the only theoretical one that merits exploration. It is also interesting to explore how Schenkerian insights and methods of presentation may complement the discussion. In the case of the first movement of the Fifth Symphony, for instance, I believe they can help to define the music's introversive qualities. This is all the more necessary, it seems to me, given that Taruskin's insistence on the necessity for 'interpretation' of this work could lead to the conclusion that it does not 'stand up' autonomously. Even Kholopov, whose focus is precisely on the introversive dimension, finds himself on the brink of extroversive description when it comes to the development section:

And so now begins the most important thing in sonata form, the development. But if all the strongest resources have already been exhausted, on what basis can the development exist when, according to the rules of the form, it should be an order of magnitude higher than the exposition? . . . In Shostakovich's movement if one considers all the harmonies prominently demonstrated in the exposition they will give an almost complete twelve-note chain, and moreover the main props are harmonies which are five steps away on the circle of fifths. Thus there is nothing left for the development.

Shostakovich's new solution as a twentieth-century composer consists of finding new effective means of contrast, an even higher order of dissonance. In the development section he now starts to place contrasted sound-layers one on top of another. The unity of the harmony in the vertical dimension is broken. The layers of polyharmony dissonantly contradict one another, as if the voices somehow are not listening to one another; in some places they even try to out-shout one another to see who can make the most noise. In places it becomes impossible to sense any tonality whatsoever. Supercharging the discordant mass of sound leads to a huge 'proclamation' at the beginning of the recapitulation, where uncoordinated shouting lines suddenly merge into a mighty unison.

Taruskin's and Kholopov's insights notwithstanding, I feel that at least in the middleground of the structure there are complex introversive forces at work which show a composer in full musical command of his material and which can be effectively presented in a Schenkerian light. The crisis-point in the development section, approaching fig. 30, is expressed harmonically rather than thematically – the return of the first subject in the trumpets is unaltered in intervallic and rhythmic structure but is placed in the key of the second subject (E♭ minor, and here Phrygian), while the surrounding ostinati proclaim the first subject's original tonic D minor (Ex. 1.1).

Ex. 1.1 Shostakovich, Symphony No. 5, first movement

This passage is not short of extroversive (specifically, intertextual) dimensions. Apart from those noted by other writers, the D minor bass ostinato is an astonishing, but almost certainly coincidental, recall of the battle-zone of the first movement of Nielsen's Fifth Symphony (Ex. 1.2).[19]

Ex. 1.2 Nielsen, Symphony No. 5, first movement

Another intertextual reference, to Beethoven's Ninth Symphony, may be more conscious (this is the very same work which Taruskin mentions in other connections with Shostakovich's Fifth). Compare the opening of Example 1.1 with Beethoven's famous 'Schreckensfanfare' which heralds his finale (Ex. 1.3).

Extroversive though this reference may be, Beethoven's fanfare and Shostakovich's crisis-point share a similar introversive function, namely

[19] There is no mention of Nielsen anywhere in Soviet musicological or critical writings of the 1920s or 1930s, and it is extremely unlikely that Shostakovich knew any of his music at this stage in his life. The Danish conductor Ole Schmidt recalls that in 1975 Shostakovich did claim acquaintance with Nielsen's work (personal communication, 24 February 1993).

Ex. 1.3 Beethoven, Symphony No. 9, fourth movement

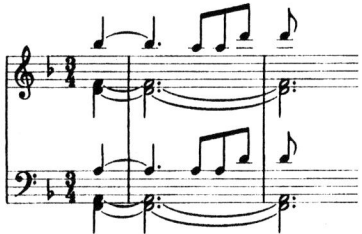

the crystallisation of large-scale tonal forces, involving an unorthodox relationship between the first and second subjects of their respective first movements.[20] In Shostakovich's case the relationship devolves from the first two notes of the work and from the modal peculiarity of the first subject (see Ex. 1.4); in Beethoven's it carries over into the key of the slow movement.

There are two ways in which the specific introversive force of Shostakovich's crisis-point, and thus its specific musical thrill, can be further defined. When each structural landmark in the movement is represented in terms of its basic modal pentachord, it is clear that they evolve diastematically (that is, as a large-scale upward motion in pitch rather than one functionally determined by sharpwards or flatwards movement). As well as being a summary of all the main preceding tonal and modal forces, the crisis-point is a negation of the hitherto rising bass *and* of the rising degrees between the modal pentachords at each landmark (Ex. 1.4).

Secondly, viewing the movement through a Schenkerian analytical lens, the background and middleground prolongations shown on Example 1.5 suggest an essentially static structure up to this point, reinforcing one's instinctive sense that the movement has not fundamentally progressed; the gradually stronger dominant progressions from the retransition onwards are sufficient to ground the structure effectively without ever unbalancing it.

If we imagine the pentachord structure of Example 1.4 and the Schenkerian middleground of Example 1.5 fused, this brings us close to the underlying musical forces at work in this movement and hence to the kind of forces which make us care about Shostakovich for more than his biography.

[20] For another instance of the same process see the first movement of Nielsen's Second Symphony, which crystallises its B minor – G major relationship into a dramatic superimposition at the beginning of the coda.

12 Introduction

Ex. 1.4 Shostakovich, Symphony No. 5, first movement

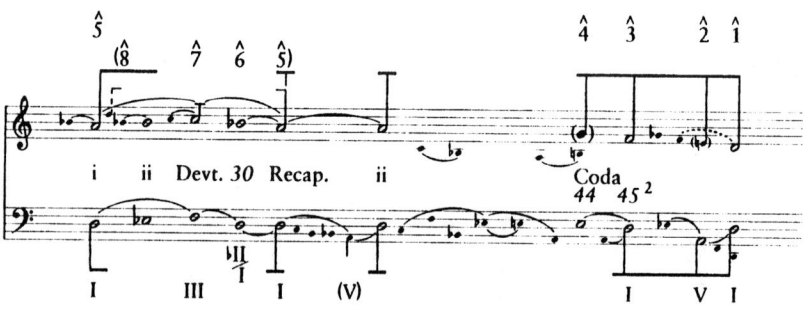

Ex. 1.5

In my own chapter on *The Lady Macbeth of Mtsensk District*, I start by looking at another possibility for Schenkerian analysis, this time more foreground-orientated and attempting to show the coherence of an apparently linear, non-tonal language. But the main thrust of my argument is to show that there are leitmotivic text–music associations at work in the opera (with all due respect to the composer's and others' denials of the presence of leitmotifs as such). These have been undetected hitherto, not least, perhaps, because many of them depend on the text of the original 1932 score for their identification.

Text–music associations are of course one way of keeping the introversive and extroversive sides of the equation in focus. But a more integrated approach is also possible, as Patrick McCreless shows in his chapter on the Second Piano Trio. As he succinctly observes, 'the music clearly demands a marriage of analytical and interpretative approaches', and his discussion of 'The cycle of structure and the cycle of meaning' sets out to do just that, laying bare the Trio's 'elegant and compelling musical argument that the conventional wisdom about the piece has discouraged us from hearing'. This is the chapter that most obviously rises to Liana Genina's challenge noted above (p. 6). What McCreless achieves might be summed up as a revelation of the expressiveness of Shostakovich's musical language *per se*. I am tempted to add that this is a lesson many Shostakovich commentators would do well to take to heart. But there has been enough self-righteous prescription in the field. It is time to let all who care about Shostakovich's music speak for themselves and in their own way.

Clearly most of the contributors to this book are committed to a revisionism of one kind or another. In her survey of the late song-cycles Dorothea Redepenning starts by noting that:

Songs and chamber music in general had a much lower ranking in Soviet musical life than imposing works such as operas or symphonies. That also meant that works with small forces figured less in the routine musico-political discussions and were less harshly judged.

Notwithstanding that, she proceeds to show how extremely important a thorough assessment of this repertory is in assessing Shostakovich's message, especially in the late works.[21]

---

[21] Redepenning is the author of an impressive two-volume survey of Russian and Soviet music: *Geschichte der russischen und der sowjetischen Musik, Bd.1, Das 19. Jahrhundert* (Laaber, 1994). I am particularly pleased to be able to include her contribution, as it has always seemed to me a shame that the extensive German contribution to Shostakovich scholarship has found so little echo on the English-speaking world.

Text-based works are peculiarly revealing of the inner life of a composer and the message-bearing capacity of Shostakovich's texts is obviously an important issue, not least for what they may reveal about other non-texted works. As early as the Krïlov Fables Op. 4, composed at the age of fifteen, something of Shostakovich's penchant for emotional ambivalence can be felt. When the moral is pointed concerning the ass's preference for the cockerel over the nightingale ('Deliver us, Oh God, from judgements of this kind') the coda embarks on a kind of pseudo-triumphalism which is powerfully echoed in the conclusion to the Tenth Symphony. Such clues to Shostakovich's inmost thoughts abound in his 100 or so songs, and at least since 1960, the year of his entry into the ranks of the Communist Party, the portrayal of a man weighed down by thoughts of death and the artist's responsibility is very close to the surface.

Revisionism of a more scholarly kind, yet not always pointing in expected directions, is one main aim of both Manashir Yakubov and Laurel Fay. Yakubov, for long curator of the Shostakovich family archives in Moscow, marshals an impressive body of evidence to disprove the standard wisdom that Shostakovich's first ballet score, *The Golden Age*, was a flop. This might provoke an intriguing anti-revisionist reflection that in 1930 Shostakovich's commitment to a vulgarly pro-Communist line may have been more whole-hearted than is often thought. Laurel Fay, author of the forthcoming Master Musicians volume on Shostakovich and the leading western expert on his life and career, shows the complexity of the issues surrounding the various versions of *The Lady Macbeth of Mtsensk District*. Drawing on a range of sources which includes unpublished scores and correspondence she reminds us that the toning down of the excesses of the libretto should not be put exclusively down to demands from above; it was already well under way during the early years of the opera's life, as part of the normal process of fine tuning which operas undergo in the course of rehearsal and production. And she concludes that we would be well advised to avoid the knee-jerk view that the *musical* revisions Shostakovich carried out prior to the opera's rehabilitation in 1963 as *Katerina Izmaylova* were carried out under ideological pressure either – or that they resulted in musical weaknesses.

Hardly a chapter in this book fails to mention the significance of Shostakovich's relation to musical tradition. It seems particularly appropriate therefore to conclude with two essays specifically devoted to that theme. 'Shostakovich and X' is a well-established scholarly

Introduction

gambit,[22] and the studies offered here are just two among many possibilities. The relationship between Shostakovich and Britten began with professional interest and flowered into a warm personal friendship, with a remarkable cross-pollination of ideas. From Britten's end the relationship extended over a forty-year period from the time he noted in his diary his enthusiasm for *Lady Macbeth*. Bearing in mind their shared interest in the music of Mahler and Berg, dating from their formative years, it is perhaps not surprising that Shostakovich and Britten's temperamental affinity should have shown up in extensive similarities of style and tone. Eric Roseberry, author of perhaps the most balanced non-specialist biography of Shostakovich,[23] documents these similarities, and commentates and speculates on the mutual responses of the two composers, covering some forty works.

Both Roseberry and Alexander Ivashkin in his chapter on 'Shostakovich and Schnittke' keep stylistic and ethical questions in judicious balance, in the process drawing together many threads from previous chapters in this book. Ivashkin is a cellist and musicologist with especially close connections to the generation of Russian composers who grew up in the 1970s and 1980s; he is the author of a book on Ives and of an extended essay on Schnittke.[24] He suggests that the many (often quite distinguished) Soviet composers whose style was close to Shostakovich's, whether as pupils of the composer or not, missed the more profound aspects of his art – notably its attitude to musical time and stylistic consistency. Schnittke, whose international standing in the 1990s is extraordinarily high, was among those who grasped that message and built on it in his own way. Indeed Ivashkin regards him as 'the real spiritual successor of Shostakovich's music'. At the same time this essay provides a salutary reminder of the dynamic and personal nature of responses to music. As Ivashkin says of Messiaen, 'the excessively slow tempi and disparateness of his language, which only recently seemed to be purely religious attributes of his music, are now, after the passage of just twenty or thirty years, perceived as organic elements of the musical language of the

---

[22] See, for instance, A. I. Klimovitsky, 'Shostakovich i Betkhoven', in *Traditsii muzikal'noy nauki* [Traditions of Musical Scholarship], ed. Lyudmila Kovnatskaya (Leningrad, 1989), 177–205; Krzysztof Meyer, 'Shostakovich und Mahler', in *Gustav Mahler*, ed. Ludwig Kolleritsch (Graz, 1975), 118–32; Rosamund Bartlett, 'Shostakovich and Chekhov', paper read at the conference *Shostakovich: the Man and his Age*.

[23] *Shostakovich* (London, 1982).

[24] 'Alfred Schnittke: la musica e "l'armonio del mondo"', in *Schnittke*, ed. Enzo Restagno (Turin, 1993), 81–243.

twentieth century'. Equally, without denying the importance of symbolism and interpretation, 'There is no doubt that the attitude to the music of Shostakovich and Schnittke has changed a great deal in recent years. Today we evaluate their music from objective positions, often not linking it with the social or cultural situation which has emerged.'

Well, perhaps not all of us do. But from whichever position we come to Shostakovich, the fascination of his art is unmistakable, as is its sheer importance to an understanding of musical history in his lifetime and in the twenty years that have now elapsed since his death.

What *Shostakovich Studies* offers, then, is not remotely a comprehensive coverage of Shostakovich's output, nor is it evenly spread across the various genres or eras. It leaves some major issues virtually untouched, notably on the biographical side, but also in such musicological fields as the difficulties of dealing with manuscript material. There remains huge scope for further research into this towering figure, and musicologists have to be as humble as anyone else in their search for the depths of his art. But if this book does not at least succeed in proving that musicologists have a role to play in enhancing the understanding of his message, then it will truly have earned the composer's scorn from the grave.

2

Public lies and unspeakable truth interpreting Shostakovich's Fifth Symphony

RICHARD TARUSKIN

Now that the institutions that supported him, and that he served to his incalculable personal cost, have at last been discredited and dismantled, I find myself reflecting with urgency on Shostakovich, the musical figure from the Soviet past who has the most meaning for us today, wondering why he does so, and what that meaning might be.

Urgency has mounted in proportion to revulsion at the torrent of romantically revisionary, sentimental nonsense about the composer that has inundated both the Soviet (or post-Soviet), and the western musical press since the mid-1970s, but particularly since Gorbachov's proclamation of *glasnost'* (airing-things-in-public) in the mid-1980s. Much of this literature has been motivated by an understandable but now pointless impulse to enjoy vicarious revenge. As long as the Soviet system and its institutions were alive and declaring themselves well, there was reason to do battle with them, reason to dwell on their hypocrisy, their criminality.

This essay was originally prepared for a conference organised around the theme, 'Soviet Music Toward the 21st Century', which took place on the campus of the Ohio State University from 24 to 27 October 1991. Between the planning and the convening, of course, the history of Soviet music came dramatically to an end. The conference, envisioned as a hopeful toast to *perestroyka*, celebrated not the meliorating continuity that Russian word implies, but instead a great historical divide fraught with peril and uncertainty. (Speaker after speaker at that unforgettable meeting mounted the podium to voice fears for the survival of institutions supporting the creation and performance of contemporary concert music in Russia, and some saw emigration as the only way to carry on with their lives.) My original assignment had been to narrate in detail the early history of the Union of Soviet Composers, now sketched briefly in the first section of the essay; the decision to focus instead on questions of interpretation was a reaction to the march of events. It was my own 'perestroyka' (the Russian for 'changing course midstream' being *perestroyit'sya na khodu*). For furnishing the immediate pretext to do a job that had been long simmering within me, and for generously allowing me to follow my impulse, I thank Margarita Mazo, the organiser of the conference.

But enough of that. *Poshlost'* – smug vulgarity, insipid pretension – has always lived and thrived in such accounts. Risking nothing, we excoriate the past to flatter ourselves. Our high moral dudgeon comes cheap. It is sterile. In fact it is nostalgic. We look back upon the Stalin period romantically, as a time of heroism. We flay the villains, as we define them, and enjoy an ersatz moral triumph. We not only pity the victims, as we define them, but envy them and wishfully project on to them our own idealised identities. Nor have we even given up our investment in personality cults, it seems; all we have done is install new worshipped personalities in place of the old. The new idolatry is as blinding as the old, just as destructive of values, just as crippling to our critical faculties. Shostakovich remains just as hidden from view as he was before, and efforts to make him visible are still roundly denounced, if from the other side.[1]

BACKGROUND: PERESTROYKAS AND PERESTROYKAS

The word 'perestroyka', perhaps needless to say, no longer describes what is going on in the lands of the former Soviet Union. The Communist institutions that were to undergo preservative restructuring have ceased to exist. The Union of Soviet Composers is one of them. Composers in the former USSR now face the same grave problems confronted by everyone else who (while complaining of its drawbacks) had become used to the illusive advantages of a command-driven, production-orientated economy, the economy the Gorbachov *perestroyka* had tried and failed to rescue. It is ironic, then, to reflect on the circumstances that attended the Union's creation. It was established by a decree of the Central Committee of the Soviet Communist Party, promulgated on 23 April 1932, entitled 'On the Restructuring [*perestroyka*] of Literary and Artistic Organisations'. Unlike Gorbachov's this was an entirely cynical *perestroyka* that had its origin in a political cover-up.

The first Five-Year Plan, Stalin's great push towards the building of 'socialism in one country', was inaugurated in 1928. An orgy of totalitarian coercion in which the country was forced headlong into urban industrialisation and rural collectivisation, it was a time of unprecedented political and economic violence, replete with show trials, mass arrests and punitive mass starvation, ceaselessly accompanied by a

[1] See Richard Taruskin, 'The opera and the dictator', *The New Republic*, 200/12 (20 March 1989), 34–40; Ian Macdonald, Letter to the editor, *Times Literary Supplement* (28 September–4 October 1990), 1031.

din of mass indoctrination that included the hardening of the Stalin personality cult. As part of the general effort, a cultural revolution was set in motion. In December 1928 the Central Committee passed a resolution establishing ideological controls over the dissemination of art and literature, and placing members of proletarian organisations in charge of the organs of dissemination and training. In music, executive power was concentrated by decree in the hands of the so-called RAPM, the Russian Association of Proletarian Musicians.

This was the period during which the Moscow conservatory was renamed the Felix Kon School of Higher Musical Education (*Vïsshaya Muzïkal'naya shkola im. F. Kona*), after the editor of the newspaper *Rabochaya gazeta*, the Workers' Gazette.[2] The composers Myaskovsky, Glière and Gnesin, stalwarts of the old, pre-revolutionary musical élite, were denounced and fired from the faculty. Grades and examinations were abolished, and admission restricted to students of acceptable class background. Ideologists of the RAPM like the young Yuriy Keldïsh consigned the composers of the past wholesale to the dustbin of history, excepting only Beethoven, the voice of the French revolution, and Musorgsky, the proto-Bolshevist 'radical democrat'. Tchaikovsky, virtual court composer to Tsar Alexander III, was a special target of abuse. Composers were exhorted to spurn all styles and genres that had flourished under the tsars and cultivate instead the only authentically proletarian genre, the march-like *massovaya pesnya*, the 'mass song', through which proletarian ideology could be aggressively disseminated. The only politically correct concept of authorship was collective, epitomised in the so-called Prokoll (*Proizvodstvennïy kollektiv* – Production Collective), a group of Moscow conservatory students who banded together to produce revolutionary operas and oratorios that were in essence medleys of mass songs.

The joyous declaration of a prematurely successful completion to the first Five-Year Plan was the leadership's way of retreating from a ruinous situation without admitting error. The country was in misery – a misery that could be conveniently blamed on local administrators and 'wreckers' in the case of the real tragedies such as forced collectivisation (hence the show trials), and on survivals of 'left' deviationism on the intellectual and artistic fronts. The reining-in of the proletarian cultural

---

[2] Juri Jelagin, *The Taming of the Arts* (New York, 1951), 188–90; Yuriy Keldïsh, *100 let Moskovskoy Konservatorii 1866–1966* (Moscow, 1966), 127–9.

organisations became necessary in order to regain the good will of an alienated intelligentsia, but especially in order to woo back *émigré* luminaries like Gorky and Prokofiev, who were fearful of proletarianist opposition. (Prokofiev, whose eventual decision to return to Soviet Russia had been sparked by the triumphant success of his first post-emigration visit in 1927, had been frightened off by the RAPM, which all but wrecked his second tour in 1929.) So the same Party that had installed the proletarianists at the beginning of the Cultural Revolution now suppressed them in the name of benign *perestroyka*. The RAPM and its sister organisations in the other arts were dissolved, and replaced by all-encompassing Unions of art workers. The Union of Soviet Composers was established at first in Moscow and Leningrad, and over the next sixteen years grew geographically and organisationally to encompass the entire country, becoming fully centralised just in time for the so-called Zhdanovshchina, the musical show trials of 1948.

At first the 1932 *perestroyka* was greeted with the same enthusiasm as (at first) greeted Gorbachov's. It was seen and touted as a liberalising move, for it meant the removal from the scene of the fractious radicals who since Lenin's time had hectored Soviet artists of the academic tradition (as well as their heirs, the élite modernists), and who had lately been allowed to tyrannise them. Now the radicals were stripped of power and their leaders forced to make satisfying public recantations.[3] Nominal power reverted to the old guard, from whose standpoint the 1932 *perestroyka* meant salvation from chaos and obscurantism – an obscurantism that was now officially labelled *levatskoye* ('left', for which read 'Trotskyite') and thus politically tainted.[4] The grateful old professors were called out of forced retirement, given back their classes, and installed as willing figureheads in the organisational structure of the

---

[3] See the article by two leading RAPMists, Lev Lebedinsky and Viktor Belïy (the latter the editor of the RAPM organ, *Za proletarskuyu muzïku*), entitled 'Posle aprelya: Sovetskoye muzïkal'noye tvorchestvo na pod'yome' [After April: Soviet music on the upsurge], *Sovetskoye Iskusstvo* (22/1933). Lebedinsky (1904–93) lived long enough to take part in the recent Shostakovich debates: see 'O nekotorïkh muzïkal'nïkh tsitatakh v proizvedeniyakh D. Shostakovicha', *Novïy mir* (3/1990), 262–7 (on Shostakovich's use of musical quotations and in particular about the meaning of the 'invasion theme' in the Seventh Symphony); the article was later attacked in *Pravda* by the composer Yuriy Levitin ('Fal'shivaya nota, ili Grustnïye razmïshleniya o delakh muzïkal'nïkh (11 November 1990), p. 3; Lebedinsky's rebuttal ('O chesti mastera: vozvrashchayas' k teme') was published in the issue of 19 March 1991).

[4] See 'Vïvodï po chistke yacheyki VKP(b) Moskovskoy Gosudarstvennoy Konservatorii v 1933 g.', *Sovetskaya Muzïka* (5/1933), 161–4.

Union – along, eventually (and very significantly), with the pupils of their pupils. To all appearances, the Composers' Union was a service organisation, even a fraternal club.

The real power, of course, lay elsewhere, and the real purpose of the organisation, though this was not immediately apparent, was to be a conduit of centralised authority and largesse. As the guarantor of its members' right to work, as the channeller of state patronage through commissions (*kontraktatsiya*, as it was called), and as dispenser of material assistance through the so-called Muzfond, the Union was ostensibly engaged in protecting the interests of composers, but by the same token it was implicitly endowed with the power to enforce conformity.[5] The Union's chief social functions were the so-called internal *pokazï* – meetings at which composers submitted their work in progress to peer review in the spirit of idealistic 'Bolshevik self-criticism'[6] – and open forums at which composers and musical intellectuals shared the floor discussing topics like Soviet opera, Soviet 'symphonism', or the state of music criticism, for eventual publication in *Sovetskaya Muzïka*, the Union's official organ, which began appearing early in 1933.

Acting through an Organisational Bureau set up to implement the 23 April decree, the Central Committee of the Communist Party installed one Nikolai Ivanovich Chelyapov (1889–1941) as chairman of the Moscow Union and editor of *Sovetskaya Muzïka*. He was not a musician. A jurist by training, Chelyapov was an all-purpose bureaucrat (what in Soviet jargon was called an *obshchestvennïy deyatel'*, a 'public figure') by profession. He functioned as a sort of middle manager, presiding at meetings, articulating official policy in his editorials and organising the Union's formal activities. From the beginning of 1936 he reported directly to the All-Union Committee on Artistic Affairs (*Vsesoyuznïy komitet po delam iskusstv*), a subdivision of the Sovnarkom, The Council of People's Commissars (later the Council of Ministers). Centralised totalitarian control of the arts was now complete. The command structure was in

---

[5] For organisational details see the report by Levon Atovm'yan, 'God rabotï soyuza sovetskikh kompozitorov', *Sovetskaya Muzïka* (5/1933), 131–41. A similar report for Leningrad, by A. Ashkenazy, appeared in *Sovetskaya Muzïka* (6/1934), 61–4.

[6] See Viktor Gorodinsky and Vladimir Iokhelson, 'Za bol'shevistskuyu samokritiku na muzïkal'nom fronte', *Sovetskaya Muzïka* (5/1934), 6–12, where the internal review of Shostakovich's *Lady Macbeth* is described in detail. (The authors express dissatisfaction at the lack of aggression on the part of the critics and at the lack of receptivity on the part of the composer.)

place. The next year Chelyapov, a superfluous Old Bolshevik, shared the general fate of his cohort. He disappeared into Lethe, not to be mentioned again in print until the 1960s.

For the new control system was one of the many harbingers of the coming storm, and the Composers' Union assumed the role for which it had been created. It all happened very dramatically. The February 1936 issue of *Sovetskaya Muzïka* opened with what editor Chelyapov called 'three historic documents', consisting of a TASS communiqué on a friendly conversation between comrades Stalin and Molotov and the creators of the opera *The Quiet Don* after Sholokhov's novel (composer Ivan Dzerzhinsky, conductor Samuil Samosud and director M. A. Tereshkovich), and two unsigned editorials reprinted from *Pravda*, both of them vilifying one composer, not yet thirty years old: 'Muddle instead of music' (*Sumbur vmesto muzïki*) attacked Shostakovich's wildly successful opera *The Lady Macbeth of Mtsensk District*, and 'Balletic falsehood' (*Baletnaya fal'sh*) denounced his ballet *The Limpid Stream*, then in the repertory of the Bolshoy Theatre. These articles were indeed historic documents. They were unprecedented, not because of the militant philistinism for which they are chiefly remembered, but because they are couched in terms of political denunciation and threatened violence, indistinguishable in diction from the scattershot attacks on the so-called 'Zinovievite faction' that had by then become ubiquitous in the Soviet press in advance of the great show trials of 1937 and 1938. Shostakovich was simultaneously accused of *levatskoye urodstvo* (left deformation) and 'petit-bourgeois' sympathies.

Needless to say, his Union offered Shostakovich the very opposite of protection. For what the *Pravda* editorials signalled above all was an end to even the semblance of public debate or discussion. The March and May issues of *Sovetskaya Muzïka* were devoted practically *in toto* to zealous ratification of the attack, in a manner exactly paralleling the unanimous endorsement of war-whoops against the 'Zinovievites' that had been appearing in *Sovetskaya Muzïka*, as in every other Soviet publication, since the middle of 1935.

The format of the old Union 'discussions' was retained, but only as a vehicle for a campaign of organised slander. Under the heading 'Against Formalism and Falsehood' (*Protiv formalizma i fal'shi*), the members of the Moscow and Leningrad Unions were marched to the rostrum one by one in the February days following the second of the *Pravda* editorials to deliver denunciations of their fallen colleague and fulsome praise of the historic documents. The mobilisation of such demonstrations of 'solidarity' would henceforth be among the Union's paramount functions. The dire period thus ushered in was hailed as a new *perestroyka*.[7]

Among the individual contributions to the 'discussions', two stand out as especially poignant and revealing. Maximilian Steinberg, Rimsky-Korsakov's son-in-law and successor as professor of composition at the Leningrad Conservatory, took the floor to declare that 'insofar as he was my best pupil . . . the drama of Shostakovich is my personal drama, and I cannot look with indifference upon what my pupil is going through in his creative work'. The tone is quickly modulated, however, into one not of defence but of personal exculpation and distance, illustrating the quintessential Stalinist theme: the fraying of the social fabric in the face of fear. 'The utmost expression of Shostakovich's "new" direction were his "Aphorisms" [for piano, Op. 13 (1927)]', Steinberg testified. 'When Shostakovich came to me with the Aphorisms, I told him that I understood nothing in them, that they were alien to me. After this he stopped coming to see me.'[8] In Moscow, the twenty-two-year-old Tikhon Khrennikov spoke for 'the rising generation of Soviet composing youth':

> How did the youth react to *Lady Macbeth*? In the opera there are some big melodic numbers that opened up for us some creative vistas. The *entr'actes* and a lot of other things called forth total antipathy. In general, our youth is healthy. A certain faction has succumbed to formalist influences, but this is being overcome; it does not represent any principal objective on our part.[9]

The oldest generation and the youngest were being deployed as pincers against the most vital one, as represented by its outstanding member, who had been chosen as sacrificial victim not only as a demonstration of the might of Soviet power but because his precocious fame and his phenomenal talent had made him the object of the greatest envy.

CODE WITHOUT KEY

That is enough about the phoney *perestroyka*. It is an ugly story and a much-rehearsed (if still under-documented) one, and I have recalled it

[7] 'Na visokom pod'yome', *Sovetskaya Muzika* (7/1936), 4–12.
[8] 'Protiv formalizma i fal'shi: Vïstupleniye tov. SHTEYNBERGA', *Sovetskaya Muzika* (5/1936), 38.
[9] 'Protiv formalizma i fal'shi: Vïstupleniye tov. KHRENNIKOVA', *Sovetskaya Muzika* (3/1936), 45.

only as preface to the *perestroyka* that is my subject, Shostakovich's own. That story is very much worth telling, because we do not fully understand it yet, and because its many repercussions still affect our lives.

We do not fully understand it, and perhaps we never will, because none of us alive today can imagine the sort of extreme mortal duress to which artists in the Soviet Union were then subjected, and Shostakovich more than any other. The only possible analogy is to the experience of condemned prisoners or hostages or kidnap victims. The nearest thing to it in the pre-revolutionary history of the arts in Russia was the case of Dostoyevsky, who, condemned to death for political subversion and granted a last-minute reprieve, became a fervent believer in the Russian autocracy and a religious mystic. The nearest parallel in today's world is the case of Salman Rushdie, whose response to dire death threats has included reconfirmation in the faith of his oppressors.

It is with thoughts like these in mind that I want to examine Shostakovich's Fifth Symphony, notoriously designated 'a Soviet artist's creative response to just criticism' and first performed in Leningrad on 21 November 1937, at the very height of the Yezhovshchina (named after Nikolai Ivanovich Yezhov, Commissar of Internal Affairs from 1936 to 1938), perhaps the bloodiest political terror the world has ever seen. Its tumultuous, ecstatic reception has become a legend. It led to the composer's rehabilitation – or would have, were it not that his forgiveness was surely just as foreordained as his fall. Thanks to the system of *pokazï* (peer reviews) and the need for securing performance clearance from the Committee on Artistic Affairs, Shostakovich's work was known on high before its public unveiling. Its status as apology and as promise of a personal *perestroyka* was a conferred status, bestowed from above as if to show that the same power that condemned and repressed could also restore and reward.

Shostakovich's rehabilitation became an opportunity for fulsome official self-congratulation. 'One feels that Shostakovich has been through and thought through a great deal', wrote Mikhail Mikhailovich Gromov, the polar aviator and Hero of the Soviet Union, who in a fashion so typical of the day was serving as all-purpose Party mouthpiece. 'He has grown as an artist. His growth, one cannot doubt, was abetted by stern, just criticism.'[10] 'Shostakovich is a great, truly Soviet artist', wrote the very

[10] M. Gromov, 'Zametki slushatelya (O 5-y simfonii D. Shostakovicha)', *Sovetskaya Muzïka* (3/1938), 29. (The quoted comment echoes the one attributed to the composer; see below, p. 34.) One can still find similar heartless claims in the literature on Shostakovich, though

partiynïy critic Georgiy Khubov on behalf of the Union in its official organ. He was at pains to note that Shostakovich's *perestroyka* went beyond mere style to the profoundest levels of consciousness.[11] The theme of ongoing personal *perestroyka*, beginning precisely with the Fifth Symphony, was sounded again a year later by Yuliy Kremlyov, writing in the official organ about Shostakovich's (first) string quartet.[12] The word continued to resound in Soviet critiques of the Fifth Symphony to the end of the Stalin period.[13]

The same critics who wrote about Shostakovich's *perestroyka* also wrote about his 'realism', which gives a clue to their meaning. By realism, of course, they meant socialist realism. The theory of socialist realism has always been an occult subject, especially when applied to music. The critic Viktor Gorodinsky had tried, soon after its coining, to explicate it theoretically in the very first issue of *Sovetskaya Muzïka* (1933),[14] only to have his waffling efforts derided by none other than Shostakovich in the days when the Union still functioned as something resembling a forum.[15] Over the next few years the idea had been roughly defined in practice. The recipe, to put it bluntly and oxymoronically, was heroic classicism.

That Soviet reality required a monumental scale and a high rhetorical tone for its proper celebration was an old proviso. It had been the topic of Chelyapov's first sermon as editor of *Sovetskaya Muzïka*. Distinguishing the Union's aims from the programme of the old discredited RAPM – no mean task, actually – Chelyapov fastened on scale. 'At a time', he sneered,

> now only in the uncomprehending West – cf. Malcolm Barry, 'Ideology and form: Shostakovich East and West', in *Music and the Politics of Culture*, ed. Christopher Norris (New York, 1989), 181:
>
>> If, for example, a substantial body of expert opinion declared that the revision [of *Lady Macbeth* as *Katerina Izmaylova*] was a finer work (based on whatever criteria), might there not have to be a revision of the critical commonplace about the reprehensibility of 'Chaos instead of Music'? Could it be that the intervention, brutal and traumatic as it was, might have been *helpful* to the *composer*, even within the context of a 'value-free' approach to the music *as such*?

[11] '5-aya simfoniya D. Shostakovicha', *Sovetskaya Muzïka* (3/1938), 14–28.
[12] 'Strunnïy kvartet D. Shostakovicha', *Sovetskaya Muzïka* (11/1939), 46–54.
[13] See, for example, Ivan Martïnov, *Dmitriy Shostakovich* (Moscow and Leningrad, 1946), 43.
[14] 'K voprosu o sotsialisticheskom realizme v muzïke', *Sovetskaya Muzïka* (1/1933), 6–18.
[15] 'Sovetskaya muzïkal'naya kritika otstayot', *Sovetskaya Muzïka* (3/1933), 120–1.

when proletarian literature was giving us great canvases of socialist construction, beginning with Gladkov's *Cement* and [Serafimovich's] *The Iron Flood* [*Zhelezniy potok*], continuing with *The Quiet Don*, [Panfyorov's] *Ingots* [*Bruski*] and so forth, . . . in the realm of music we were told: large forms are something for the future; now let us work on the small forms of mass song; first vocal works, afterwards we will get to writing instrumental music.[16]

One might say that the future of Soviet music, fated to preserve in a totalitarian aspic all the mammoths and mastodons of the western classical tradition – the programme symphony, the oratorio, the grand historical opera – was decided right here.

Except for his withdrawn Fourth Symphony, Shostakovich's Fifth was his first really heroic symphonic work. And while the unconventionally structured, maximalistic Fourth had been grandiose (as the composer later put it) to the point of mania, it was anything but 'classical' – which is exactly why it could not be performed in the aftermath of his denunciation. For it was precisely at this point, the very apex of political pressure, that Soviet composers were first directed to emulate '*russkaya klassika*' as a timeless model, signifying a return to healthy, 'normal' musical values after the excesses of early Soviet modernism.[17] With its ample yet conventional four-movement form, even down to an improbable minuet (as many have characterised the scherzo), its unextravagant yet sonorous scoring and its notable harmonic restraint, the Fifth Symphony amounted to a paradigm of Stalinist neoclassicism, testifying, so far as the powers were concerned, to the composer's obedient submission to discipline. It was time to reward him.

The immediate reward was an orgy of public praise (later there would be Stalin prizes and titles and honorary posts). It went on for months, to the point where Isaak Dunayevsky, the songwriter who was then president of the Leningrad Composers' Union, tried to put on the brakes. On 29 January 1938, the day of the Moscow première, he circulated a memorandum comparing the Fifth's reception to a stock speculation, a ballyhoo, even a psychosis that threatened to lead Soviet music into a climate of 'creative *laissez-faire*' in which the Union might not be able to

---

[16] 'O zadachakh zhurnala "*Sovetskaya Muzïka*"', *Sovetskaya Muzïka*, (1/1933), 5.
[17] See Anna Shteynberg, 'Pushkin v tvorchestve sovetskikh kompozitorov', *Sovetskaya Muzïka* (1/1937), 53–9. The Pushkin centenary, first marked at the Union of Soviet Composers with a conference on 11 and 12 December 1936, was the occasion for the earliest explicit exhortations to revive 'classical' models.

exercise its police function.[18] (It was inevitable that Shostakovich's Sixth Symphony would meet a hostile reception – and so his career would go on, yo-yo fashion, practically to the end.) Typical of the composer's official welcome back into the fold (and typical as well of the tone of grovelling civic panegyric that inevitably accompanied Soviet public rhetoric) was a pronouncement by the composers Anatoliy Alexandrov and Vasiliy Nechayev: 'A work of such philosophical depth and emotional force', they wrote, 'could only be created here in the USSR'.[19]

There were many, both at home and abroad, who willingly granted the last point, though not necessarily in a spirit of praise. The symphony's manifest philosophical and emotional freight, far more than its traditional form, made not only it but Soviet music generally seem backward and provincial to many western musicians in an age of burgeoning formalism. Many will recall how bitterly Igor Stravinsky mocked it in his Harvard lectures of 1939, later published as *Poetics of Music*. And he mocked it through the prism of the famous review by Count Alexey Tolstoy – 'a consummate masterpiece of bad taste, mental infirmity, and complete disorientation in the recognition of the fundamental values of life', as Stravinsky described it – in which the celebrated Soviet novelist attempted an inventory of that philosophical and emotional cargo:

Here we have the 'Symphony of Socialism'. It begins with the *Largo* of the masses working underground, an *accelerando* corresponds to the subway system; the *Allegro*, in its turn symbolizes gigantic factory machinery and its victory over nature. The *Adagio* represents the synthesis of Soviet culture, science, and art. The *Scherzo* reflects the athletic life of the happy inhabitants of the Union. As for the *Finale*, it is the image of the gratitude and the enthusiasm of the masses.[20]

'What I have just read to you is not a joke which I myself thought up', Stravinsky assured his audience. But this was true only to the extent that it had been thought up not by Stravinsky himself but by his ghostwriter, Pierre Souvtchinsky. Yet for over half a century now Stravinsky's

---

[18] Sof'ya Khentova, *Molodïye godï Shostakovicha*, ii (Leningrad, 1980), 192. The political threat was overt: referring to Leonid Entelis's remarks (see note 29 *infra*), Dunayevsky warned against any suggestion that 'the Party may have wrongly judged Shostakovich's work, that there had been no formalist high-jinks, no muddle, but just the innocent mistakes of youth'. (My thanks to Laurel Fay for Dunayevsky's text.)

[19] 'Vpechatleniya slushateley', *Muzïka* (26 November 1937); quoted in Genrikh Orlov, *Simfonii Shostakovicha* (Leningrad, 1961), 64.

[20] Igor Stravinsky, *Poetics of Music in the Form of Six Lessons*, trans. Arthur Knodel and Ingolf Dahl (Cambridge, Mass., 1970), 153–5.

joke has been believed, even though as fabrications go it is very crude, with the movements misnamed and in the wrong order.[21] Stravinsky has been believed not only because he was Stravinsky (hardly an assurance), and not only because one is ready to attribute any sort of statement about music to a literary man named Tolstoy, but because we accept the notion that Shostakovich's symphony not only invites but requires such an interpretation, if not this particular one. More than that, it is obvious that there is no way of rejecting the kind of interpretation Stravinsky derides (whatever we may make of the given reading), without rejecting the music outright.

So before addressing the vital matter of interpreting Shostakovich's Fifth, before examining past interpretations (beginning with Tolstoy's actual one) or proposing new ones, it is worth enquiring briefly just what it is that makes interpretation so necessary.

Like the symphonies of Mahler, with whom he is so frequently compared, and the late ones of Tchaikovsky (only recently rehabilitated in the Russia of the purge years, and shortly to be deified on his centenary), Shostakovich's Fifth Symphony self-evidently belongs to the tradition established in the wake of Beethoven's Ninth, whereby the music unfolds a series of components, gestures or events that are immediately recognisable as signs or symbols, but signs and symbols whose referents are not specified by any universally recognised and stable code (though they may, and obviously do, participate to some undeterminable extent in such codes).[22] Such signs are often said to exist on two broad levels, defined as 'syntactic' vs. 'semantic', or as 'introversive' vs. 'extroversive'.[23] Syntactic or introversive signs are those with referents that are perceived to lie within the boundaries of the work itself – in the case of music they include reprises, transformations and recombinations of previously heard events or gestures such as motifs and themes, culminating in broad sectional repeats and 'recapitulations'. Semantic or extroversive signs are those with referents that lie outside of

[21] James Billington actually reproduced Stravinsky's parody, accepting it at face value as 'Alexei Tolstoy's paean to Shostakovich's Fifth Symphony as the "Symphony of Socialism"', as a paradigm to illustrate 'the role of music in the Stalin era'. See *The Icon and the Axe: An Interpretive History of Russian Culture* (New York, 1970), 478.

[22] For a fuller discussion see Richard Taruskin, 'Resisting the Ninth', *19th Century Music*, 12/3 (Spring 1989), 241–56.

[23] For an extensive discussion of this distinction, which originated in the theory of Russian formalism, see V. Kofi Agawu, *Playing with Signs: A Semiotic Interpretation of Classic Music* (Princeton, 1991), chapters 2 and 3.

the work in which they occur. They cover a range all the way from primitive onomatopoeia to imitation of speech to metaphors, at times quite subtle, of physical motion or distance or modes of temporality (time-consciousness). Very often they invoke other music, whether by allusion to specific pieces or by more general reference to 'topics', genres and styles.

But this distinction – syntactic vs. semantic, introversive vs. extroversive – can be maintained only in theory. It is not usually possible, or even desirable, to distinguish them in practice. While thematic or motivic recurrences are in themselves defined as syntactic, their interpretation often depends on semantic codes. The climactic unisons in the first movement of Shostakovich's Fifth, for example, derive their significance equally from both perceptual spheres. Their loudness speaks – or rather shouts – for itself. At the same time, they remind us of the famous passages *all'unisono* in Beethoven's Ninth, with which Shostakovich's symphony shares its key. These are obviously extroversive references (or, to be precise, intertextual ones). But hardly less significant is the fact that the climactic unisons are a reprise of some of the quiet music from the first thematic group. That may be a syntactic feature, but the huge contrast in dynamics and texture asks to be read semantically, in relation to some mimetic or iconic convention. Another apparently syntactic observation concerns the tonal significance of the passage: it marks the arrival at the tonic key after a long series of modulations and an elaborate preparation. Yet when we recognise the effect as that of a sonata-form recapitulation, which we think is an introversive observation, we are instantly reminded of other recapitulations and of their expressive effect – semantics again.

To pick another example: surely the most conspicuous structural or syntactic peculiarity of the symphony as a whole is its use of a pervasive rhythmic cell, presented interchangeably as dactyl or anapaest, unifying all four movements. Yet the same feature is simultaneously a heavily laden intertextual reference to Beethoven's Fifth Symphony and its motivic 'dramaturgy', to use the Soviet jargon. Add to that an exceptionally wide-ranging panoply of suggestive generic or topical references (pastoral, rustic, military, religious) – again curiously paralleling those in Beethoven's Ninth – plus a network of specific allusions that includes conspicuous self-reference as well as more oblique yet still specific reference to passages in works by other composers, and it is clear that this symphony is a richly coded utterance, but one whose meaning can never be wholly encompassed or definitively paraphrased.

Given the conditions in Russia in 1937, this last was a saving, not to say a lifesaving, grace. It opened up the work to varying readings, which is precisely what made for the seeming unanimity of response at its première. Each listener could inscribe his or her own construction on the work's network of references. The process of continual, heavily fraught inscription and reinscription has gone on to this day, surely one of the circumstances that has kept the Fifth, of all of Shostakovich's symphonies, the most alive. The obvious questions: What constrains interpretation? What validates or invalidates a reading? What, finally, does the symphony mean? Answers cannot be asserted from general principles – at least, none I've ever seen – only deduced from practice and from the specific case.[24]

[24] Which is not to say that there is no relevant theoretical literature. In thinking about these questions I have found stimulation, though (I feel I must warn my reader) less guidance than I'd hoped, in two categories of literary/hermeneutic study, one dealing with the creation of art under conditions of censorship or persecution, the other more generally with the question of irony. Both stress sensitivity to internal contradictions (in style, tone or substance) and violations of stylistic or generic norms. In the first category are the pioneering study by Leo Strauss, *Persecution and the Art of Writing* (New York, 1952; rpt. Chicago, 1988), which after two introductory chapters focuses on Jewish writers publishing in hostile environments; and two books by Annabel Patterson: *Censorship and Interpretation: The Conditions of Writing and Reading in Early Modern England* (Madison, 1984) and *Fables of Power: Aesopian Writing and Political History* (Durham, N.C., and London, 1991). Hans-Georg Gadamer's passing critique of Strauss remains highly relevant not only to Strauss but to recent Shostakovich interpretation:

> Is not conscious distortion, camouflage and concealment of the proper meaning in fact the rare extreme case of a frequent, even normal situation? – just as persecution . . . is only an extreme case when compared with the intentional or unintentional pressure that society and public opinion exercise on human thought. Only if we are conscious of the uninterrupted transition from one to the other are we able to estimate the hermeneutic difficulty of Strauss' problem. How are we able to establish clearly that a distortion has taken place? Thus, in my opinion, it is by no means clear that, when we find contradictory statements in a writer, it is correct to take the hidden meaning – as Strauss thinks – for the true one. There is an unconscious conformism of the human mind to considering what is universally obvious as really true. And there is, against this, an unconscious tendency to try extreme possibilities, even if they cannot always be combined into a coherent whole. (*Truth and Method* (New York, 1982), 488.)

The most sustained recent study of the trope of irony is Wayne C. Booth, *A Rhetoric of Irony* (Chicago, 1974), whose guidelines for interpretations – bona-fide irony is necessarily (1) intended, (2) covert, (3) stable and (4) finite – have been sharply challenged from an antifoundationalist standpoint ('irony . . . is neither the property of works nor the creation of an unfettered imagination, but a way of reading') by

'ALL THAT I HAVE THOUGHT AND FELT'

The most obvious early constraint was the symphony's ineluctable relationship to the composer's recent life experience (viz., the 1936 denunciations), a connection almost immediately bolstered by the composer's public testimony, amounting to a plea – not to say a demand – that the symphony be read as autobiography. This 'conferred status', as I have called it, surely furnished Alexey Tolstoy – the real Count Tolstoy, not the one invented by Stravinsky – with the point of departure for his very influential critique. Solomon Volkov, speaking through his little puppet Mitya, has speculated that the article was ghost-written by 'musicologists . . . summoned to Tolstoy's dacha [who] helped him through the morass of violins and oboes and other confusing things that a count couldn't possibly fathom'.[25] In fact, the review, which avoids all technicalities, is just what might have been expected from a writer; combining the autobiographical assumption with what he must have taken to be the 'Beethovenian' mood sequence of the symphony's four movements (Beethoven, that is, construed in his 'revolutionary' guise), Tolstoy assimilated the music to a literary prototype: the Soviet *Bildungsroman*, a very popular genre of the period, exemplified by such prestigious books as Valentin Katayev's *I am the Son of Labouring Folk* (*Ya – sin trudovogo naroda*), on which Prokofiev would later base his

> Stanley Fish in 'Short people got no right to live: reading irony', *Doing What Comes Naturally* (Durham, N.C., and London, 1989), 180–96 (cited phrase on p. 194).
> For a rare attempt to formulate a theoretical framework for detecting or evaluating musical ironies in Shostakovich see the final chapter ('Conclusion: the language of doublespeak') in David Fanning, *The Breath of the Symphonist: Shostakovich's Tenth*, Royal Musical Association Monographs 4 (London, 1989), 70–6. While certain Boothian assumptions seem to persist – particularly insofar as the writer seeks explicit authorial confirmation (which, when found, eliminates the irony) – Fanning posits some useful musical analogues to the 'internal contradictions' literary critics have sought. One is incongruous thematic transformation, which he likens to 'a tragic speech delivered with merry inflections' (there are celebrated instances of this in the problematic finale of the Tenth); another is 'disjunction between gesture and immediate context', compared with 'a smile held beyond its natural duration – at first vaguely worrying, then more disturbing and finally frightening' (pp. 71–2). For a general broaching of the theme of Aesopian discourse in Soviet music see two overlapping articles by Joachim Braun: 'Shostakovich's song cycle *From Jewish Folk Poetry*: aspects of style and meaning', in *Russian and Soviet Music: Essays for Boris Schwarz*, ed. Malcolm H. Brown (Ann Arbor, 1984), 259–86; 'The double meaning of Jewish elements in Dimitri Shostakovich's music', *Musical Quarterly*, 71 (1985), 68–80.
> [25] *Testimony: The Memoirs of Dmitri Shostakovich as Related to and Edited by Solomon Volkov* (New York, 1979), 224.

opera *Semyon Kotko*, or Nikolai Virta's *Loneliness* (*Odinochestvo*), on which Khrennikov would base his opera *Into the Storm*, or – most famous of all – Nikolai Ostrovsky's *How the Steel Was Tempered* (*Kak zakalyalas' stal'*). These novels concerned the formation of new consciousness – personal *perestroyka* – on the part of 'searching heroes', honest blunderers whose life experiences teach them to embrace revolutionary ideals.

Tolstoy viewed the composer of the Fifth Symphony as such a one, and proceeded to paraphrase the work in terms of the catchphrase *stanovleniye lichnosti*, 'the formation of a personality (within a social environment)'. In the first movement the author-hero's 'psychological torments reach their crisis and give way to ardour', the use of the percussion instruments suggesting mounting energy. The second movement, a sort of breather, is followed by the most profound moment, the Largo. 'Here the *stanovleniye lichnosti* begins. It is like a flapping of the wings before take-off. Here the personality submerges itself in the great epoch that surrounds it, and begins to resonate with the epoch.' The finale is the culmination, in which 'the profundity of the composer's conception and the orchestral sonority coincide', producing 'an enormous optimistic lift', which, Tolstoy reports (and his report is corroborated), literally lifted the spectators out of their seats at the first performance, many of them before the piece was over.[26] That response, Tolstoy averred, was at once proof that his reading of the symphony was correct, and proof that the composer's *perestroyka* was sincere: 'Our audience is organically incapable of accepting decadent, gloomy, pessimistic art. Our audience responds enthusiastically to all that is bright, clear, joyous, optimistic, life-affirming.'

The whole review, in fact, is one enormous tautology, not only for the way the audience reaction is construed, but because it amounts throughout to a rehash of ready-made socialist-realist clichés. Compare, for example, a passage from a speech the former RAPMist critic (and Union boss) Vladimir Iokhelson delivered at one of the Leningrad meetings at which *Lady Macbeth of Mtsensk* had been denounced the year before. Socialist realism, Iokhelson proclaimed,

---

[26] 'Pyataya simfoniya Shostakovicha', *Izvestiya* (28 December 1937), p. 5. For descriptions of the reactions of the audience at the première, see Jelagin, *The Taming of the Arts*, 167–8 (thirty-minute ovation); A. N. Glumov, *Nestertïye stroki* (Moscow, 1977), 316, quoted in Khentova, *Molodïye godï Shostakovicha*, ii, 186 (rising from seats during finale); Isaak Glikman, '. . . Ya vsyo ravno budu pisat' muzïku', *Sovetskaya Muzïka* (9/1989), 48 (open weeping during the third movement).

Interpreting Shostakovich's Fifth Symphony 33

is above all a style of profound optimism. The whole historical experience of the proletariat is optimistic in essence. And we can and must affirm that optimism is intended as an obligatory feature of this style, its very essence. It is a style that includes heroics, but a heroics that is not merely tied to narrow personal interests. Here we mean a heroics of an individual connected with the mass, and of a mass that is capable of bringing forth such a hero. It is necessary that the connection between the hero and the mass be made intelligible.[27]

'A mass that is capable of bringing forth such a hero . . .' Tolstoy ended his review with a toast, not to Shostakovich, but to 'our people, who bring forth such artists'.

No wonder Tolstoy's review was influential. Its tenets were, to quote Iokhelson, obligatory. And no wonder, then, that the composer was among those it 'influenced', for Shostakovich was quick to seek (or to be granted) its protection. In an article that appeared over the composer's name in a Moscow newspaper shortly before the first performance in the capital – its headline, 'My creative response', became the symphony's informal subtitle – we read: 'Very true were the words of Alexey Tolstoy, that the theme of my symphony is the formation of a personality. At the centre of the work's conception I envisioned just that: a man in all his suffering. . . . The symphony's finale resolves the tense and tragic moments of the preceding movements in a joyous, optimistic fashion.' That man, the symphony's hero, is explicitly identified with the composer and his recent past: 'If I have really succeeded in embodying in musical images all that I have thought and felt since the critical articles in *Pravda,* if the demanding listener will detect in my music a turn towards greater clarity and simplicity, I will be satisfied.' A special effort was made to dissociate the symphony's 'tense and tragic moments' from any hint of 'pessimism':

I think that Soviet tragedy, as a genre, has every right to exist; but its content must be suffused with a positive idea, comparable, for example, to the life-affirming ardour of Shakespeare's tragedies. In the literature of music we are likewise familiar with many inspired pages in which [for example] the severe images of suffering in Verdi's or Mozart's Requiems manage to arouse not weakness or despair in the human spirit but courage and the will to fight.[28]

[27] 'Tvorcheskaya diskussiya v Leningrade', *Sovetskaya Muzïka* (4/1936), 5–15.
[28] 'Moy tvorcheskiy otvet', *Vechernyaya Moskva* (25 January 1938), p. 30. It is often stated that the 'subtitle' was Shostakovich's own, but near the beginning of this article there is a specific statement to the contrary:

Among the often very substantial responses [*otzïvï*] that have analysed this work [after its Leningrad performances], one that particularly gratified me said that 'the

In keeping with this last idea, Shostakovich's Fifth was assimilated to yet another factitious literary model. At a special performance for Leningrad Party activists, the musicologist Leonid Entelis first attached to it a phrase that would become another unofficial emblem, one that perfectly summed up the whole oxymoronic essence of socialist realism: recalling Vsevolod Vishnevsky's bombastic play about Bolshevik maritime heroism during the Civil War, Entelis declared Shostakovich's symphony an 'optimistic tragedy'.[29]

HERMENEUTIC FOLKLORE

Thus the official reading. The author of *Testimony* was of course at special pains to repudiate it, especially as concerned the 'joyous, optimistic' finale:

I think that it is clear to everyone what happens in the Fifth. The rejoicing is forced, created under threat, as in *Boris Godunov*. It's as if someone were beating you with a stick and saying, 'Your business is rejoicing, your business is rejoicing', and you rise, shakily, and go marching off, muttering, 'Our business is rejoicing, our business is rejoicing'. What kind of apotheosis is that? You have to be a complete oaf not to hear that.[30]

As a matter of fact, this was not news. People did hear that, and even wrote about it – but in private or obliquely. It, too, was a standard, if at first hidden, interpretation, which eventually reached public print in the Soviet Union around the time of the so-called post-Stalin 'thaw'. Volkov mentions Alexander Fadeyev, the head of the Writers' Union, whose diary, published posthumously in 1957, contains his reaction to the 1938 Moscow première:

A work of astonishing strength. The third movement is beautiful. But the ending does not sound like a resolution (still less like a triumph or victory), but rather

Fifth Symphony is a Soviet artist's practical creative answer to just criticism' (*pyataya simfoniya – eto delovoy tvorcheskiy otvet sovetskogo khudozhnika na spravedlivuyu kritiku*).

I have not seen this comment or review, nor (rather strangely, in view of its significance) has it been traced to its source in the huge subsequent literature. One might therefore suspect that Shostakovich coined his symphony's sobriquet after all, then cautiously attributed it to an unnamed reviewer or discussant. But to assume this would be to assume that Shostakovich was in fact the author of the article that appeared over his name, and that of course is a great deal to assume.

[29] Quoted in Khentova, *Molodïye godï Shostakovicha*, ii, 187.
[30] *Testimony*, 183.

like a punishment or vengeance on someone. A terrible emotional force, but a tragic force. It arouses painful feelings.[31]

Four years after this avowal appeared in print, the musicologist Genrikh Orlov, who has since emigrated from the USSR, came forth with the startling suggestion – of a type unheard of in Soviet criticism – that the composer's own commentary be set aside. 'It is well known', he argued, 'how often the objective results of a creative effort fail to coincide with the artist's subjective intentions. And if pretentious conceptions often lead to insignificant results, so, more rarely, a modest autobiographical theme may assume the dimensions of a broad generalisation about life.' Avoiding any awkwardly direct challenge to the veracity of Shostakovich's commentary, still less to its authenticity, Orlov none the less succeeded in challenging its relevance. The symphony's great strength, he asserted, lay in its ability 'to engrave in broad artistic generalisations the typical ideas, sensations, conflicts and hopes of its epoch'.[32]

That was letting in a great deal between the lines. Over the five years that had elapsed since Khrushchov's 'secret speech' at the twentieth Party congress, the 'epoch' of Shostakovich's Fifth Symphony had received a far more accurate – that is, a far harsher – public evaluation in the Soviet Union than was possible before. The subtext to Orlov's remarks was unmistakable. And there was more:

In the years preceding the creation of the Fifth Symphony, Shostakovich had grown not only as a master, but as a thinking artist-citizen. He grew up together with his country, his people, sharing their fate, their aspirations and their hopes, intently scrutinising the life around him, sensing with all his being its inner pulse.[33]

This places an altogether new and different construction on 'My creative response', with its famous allusion to 'all that I have thought and felt since the critical articles in *Pravda*'. Shostakovich's last Soviet biographer, writing under less liberal conditions than Orlov had enjoyed, went further yet, managing through a fleeting aside at once to enlarge the ambit of Orlov's interpretation of the symphony and to project it on to the early audiences. 'Shostakovich had created a universal portrait', wrote Sof'ya Khentova.

---

[31] *Za tridtsat' let* (Moscow, 1957), 891; quoted in G. Ordzhonikidze *et al.* (ed.), *Dmitriy Shostakovich* (Moscow, 1967), 43. The Ordzhonikidze collection also contains the 1966 memoir by Yevgeniy Mravinsky ('Tridtsat' let s muzïkoy Shostakovicha', 103–16) that occasioned the Brahms-like animadversion in *Testimony*; it will be quoted below.

[32] Orlov, *Simfonii Shostakovicha*, 68–9.

[33] *Ibid.*, 69–70.

'The people of the thirties recognised themselves, grasping not only the music's explicit content, but also its general feeling.'[34]

This was classic 'Aesopian' language, describing what was undescribable: a symphony that spoke the unspeakable. We can understand it only if we make the requisite adjustments, translating 'people of the thirties' as 'people in the grip of the Terror'; 'explicit content' as 'official interpretation'; 'general feeling' as 'unstated message'. And that is why they wept, then stood up and cheered, grateful for the pain. There are contemporary witnesses to this reaction, the most explicit, if somewhat tentative, from a defector, the violinist Juri Jelagin, who had attended the première:

> Later when I tried to analyse the reason for the devastating impression the Fifth Symphony made on me and on the entire audience I came to the conclusion that its musical qualities, no matter how great, were by themselves not enough to create that effect. The complex background of events and moods had to combine with the beautiful music of the Fifth Symphony to arouse the audience to the pitch of emotion which broke in the Leningrad auditorium. . . . The Soviet Government had set the stage for the incredible triumph of the gifted composer with long months of persecution and with the senseless attacks on his work. The educated Russians who had gathered in the auditorium that night had staged a demonstration expressing their love for his music, as well as their indignation at the pressure that had been exerted in the field of art and their sympathy and understanding for the victim.[35]

'The complex background of events and moods . . .' Jelagin, from his musician's perspective, construed it narrowly. For a fuller contemporary reading of the symphony's 'broad artistic generalisations', we must turn to what on its face seems the unlikeliest of all sources.

Georgiy Khubov's review, first delivered orally at an official Composers' Union 'discussion' on 8 February 1938 (eleven days after the Moscow première), was published in the March issue of the Union's official organ. Adopting the repellent tone and language of officious bureaucracy, the Union reviewer began by chiding those who had overpraised the symphony in their eagerness prematurely to exonerate the composer from all the old ideological charges. His overall strategy was to compare Shostakovich's actual musical performance with the Tolstoy-derived platitudes affirmed over his signature in the Moscow press, and to note the ways in which the music fell short of the stated goals. Pointedly, and very significantly, Khubov fastened on the 'static and drawn-out' Largo (which the author

[34] Khentova, *Molodïye godï Shostakovicha*, ii, 189.
[35] *The Taming of the Arts*, 167–8.

of 'My creative response' had called the movement that best satisfied him), protesting against the way other critics had overemphasised and overrated it. 'The problem of the *stanovleniye lichnosti*', Khubov pompously concluded, 'viewed from the point of view of genuine tragedy – that is, tragedy informed by a *life-affirming idea* – is in point of fact resolved in Shostakovich's symphony (the Largo and the finale) only *formally*, in any case inorganically, with great strain'.

The symphony, the critic declared, was an attempt to find a way out of existential 'loneliness' (again compare Nikolai Virta's *Bildungsroman*), a loneliness stated as a dialectical thesis in the first movement's first thematic group (dubbed the 'epigraph theme'). The masterly development depicts the composer's 'strenuous contest' with his alienation until a powerful proclamation of the epigraph theme – the massive unisons described above – temporarily stills the struggle. So far the critic entirely approves, as he approves of the scherzo, where in place of the composer's former manner ('specious urbanity, flaunting of cheap effects') there are 'new traits of fresh, hearty humour, naivety and even tenderness'.

Now the problems begin. Khubov calls the Largo a 'poem of torpidity' (*poema otsepeneniya*) in which 'a pallor of deathly despondency reigns'. According to the terms of Shostakovich's stated programme, this cannot be called tragic, 'since the truly tragic in art can only be expressed by great, inwardly motivated struggle, in which the high life-affirming idea plays the decisive role, determining the bright outcome through catharsis'. Complaint is piled upon complaint with unbelievable repetitiveness, the tone meanwhile turning sinisterly prosecutorial:

Precisely this is what the Largo lacks. And therefore, for all the expressivity of its thematic material, for all its crushing emotional impact on the listener, the third movement lowers precipitously the high level of symphonic development [attained in the first movement]. . . . The listener had a right to expect a further, even more determined dramatic development of the symphony's underlying idea. But instead the composer has revealed to the listener with naked candour a motionless little world of subjectively lyrical sufferings and . . . tearful apothegms. Instead of a great symphonic canvas . . . he has set out an expressionistic etching depicting 'numb horror'. . . .

Let us put it to the author outright: what does it say, where does it lead, . . . this numb, torpid Largo? Could it be an organic link in the process of the life-affirming *stanovleniye lichnosti*? Even the composer could hardly give an affirmative answer to this question. For what he shows with such expressionistic exaggeration in his Largo is torpidity, numbness, a condition of spiritual prostration, in which the will is annihilated along with the strength to resist or overcome. This is the negation of the life-affirming principle. This is clear to all and does not require any special proof. . . . What is the way out? What is the ultimate solution going to be?

The finale. The 'answer', as 'My creative response' had put it, 'to all the questions posed in the earlier movements'. The critic is obdurate:

> It breaks in upon the symphony *from without*, like some terrible, shattering force. . . . Having analysed the third movement, we understand that Shostakovich had no other choice; for there was no way to develop that mood of torpidity and bring it to life-affirmation. It could only be *broken*. . . . And this function the main theme of the finale fulfils. It definitely makes an impression, and no small one. But at the same time, precisely because of its unexpectedness, its lack of logical preparation, it *lacks conviction*. . . . And similarly lacking in conviction, therefore, is the loud coda with its hammering over a span of thirty-five bars at the opening motif of the main theme in D major! . . . A perceptive, attentive listener feels all the while that this theme is not the result of an organic development of the symphony's idea, that for the composer this theme is the embodiment of a superb but *external*, elemental, subjugating force. . . .
>
> And that is why the general impression of this symphony's finale is not so much bright and optimistic as it is severe and threatening.[36]

Solomon Volkov could not have put it better. Khubov, writing from the depths of the Stalinist freeze, leads his 'perceptive, attentive listener' to all the unmentionable truths adumbrated by Orlov and Khentova after the thaw, and stated outright (but to himself alone) by Fadeyev, all the while proclaiming their falsehood. By insisting on the probity of 'Shostakovich's' commentary, he exposes its untruth. He and Orlov have a common strategy; they both dwell upon the music's incongruity with the stated programme. Where Orlov could risk upholding the music, Khubov must uphold the muddle. But both rely on 'the complex background of events and moods' to right the score. I do not think it merely wishful to see in Khubov's bullying review – the work of a critic who remained a Party stalwart to the end, and who was widely suspected of having helped draft the *Pravda* editorials of 1936 – a rich vein of rhetorical ambiguity inviting readerly irony, in short, of doublespeak as classically defined.[37]

[36] Georgiy Khubov, '5-ya simfoniya D. Shostakovicha', *Sovetskaya Muzïka* (3/1938), 14–28, *passim*.

[37] Khubov was careful to conclude on an explicitly positive note so as to mitigate the risk of his review being read as a political denunciation (doubly an embarrassment if official approval, as suggested above, had been mandated): The symphony, despite its flaws,

> tells us that the composer has decisively thrown over all tawdry formalistic affectation and stunt, has made a brave turn on to the high road of realistic art. Sincerely, truth-

SOUND EVIDENCE

Confronted with two diametrically opposing perspectives on the symphony, the one public and canonical, the other a sort of folk tradition that could only be alluded to or hinted at, it is fair to assume that nowadays few will hesitate to choose the second. But is it only Kremlinological habit or bourgeois prejudice that so inclines us? Is there evidence to support the choice?

There is, of course, and Khubov even cites it for us. 'Numb horror' . . . 'spiritual prostration, in which the will is annihilated along with the strength to resist or overcome' – these were the dominant moods of the Yezhovshchina, as a whole library of *émigré*, samizdat, and *glasnost*'-inspired memoirs by now openly attests. Anna Akhmatova, in the prose preface she added in 1957 to the poem 'Requiem', which she began composing mentally in 1935, chose the very word that Khubov so conspicuously overused – *otsepeneniye*, 'torpidity' – to characterise the mood that reigned in the endless queues of women that gathered daily at the prison gates of Leningrad to learn the fates of their arrested loved ones.[38] The 'life-asserting principle' demanded by the theorists of socialist realism, and embodied in such exemplary musical compositions of the period as Dunayevsky's *Marsh entuziastov* (with which Shostakovich's symphony was often invidiously compared, incredible as that may seem) was the public lie. Count Tolstoy and the author of 'My creative response', writing virtually without reference to musical particulars, enthusiastically identified the symphony with the public lie. Khubov, whose ostensively chilly review is full of musical examples and precise descriptions, managed (wittingly or unwittingly – it matters not) to identify the work with the unmentionable truth.[39]

> fully, with great force of unfeigned feeling he has told his own story in the Fifth Symphony, the story of his recent doleful meditations and perturbations, of his inward, strenuous and complicated creative struggle (p. 28).

[38] The preface (actually titled 'vmesto predisloviya', or 'In place of a preface') in full:
> In the terrible years of the Yezhovshchina I spent seventeen months in the Leningrad prison lines. One day someone 'fingered' me. Then the blue-lipped woman standing behind me, who of course had never heard my name, roused herself out of the torpor [*iz otsepeneniya*] we all shared and whispered in my ear (everyone there spoke in whispers): 'But can you describe this?' And I said, 'I can'. Then something like a smile slid across what had been her face.

Anna Akhmatova, *Sochineniya*, 2nd edn (Munich, 1967), i, 361.

[39] A recent memoir by a friend of Shostakovich, the Leningrad theatre historian Isaak Glikman, seems to allege that the composer (reacting, perhaps, to its rhetorical camouflage

One could go much further with description – further than any Soviet writer before the officially proclaimed age of *glasnost'* dared go – towards identifying the Largo with publicly inexpressible sentiments. The movement is saturated with what, adopting the familiar Soviet jargon, we might call the 'intonations' and the 'imagery' of leave-taking and of funerals,[40] ironically disguised by the suppression of the brass instruments (anyone who has attended a Soviet secular funeral with its obligatory brass quintet will know what I mean). But that very suppression works together with multiple extroversive references to invoke the all-vocal orthodox obsequy, the *panikhida*. At fig. 86 the imitation is so literal that you can almost hear the stringed instruments intone the *vechnaya pamyat'* (Eternal Remembrance), the concluding requiem hymn (Ex. 2.1). This near-citation comes in the second half of the movement, in the midst of a process that could be described thus: 'the solo instruments of the orchestra file past . . . in succession, each laying down its . . . melody . . . against a . . . background of tremolo murmurings'. That is Stravinsky's description, from his *Chroniques de ma vie*, of his *Pogrebal'naya pesn'*, the funerary chant he composed in memory of Rimsky-Korsakov.[41] Performed once only, in 1909, it is now lost and obviously can have had no influence on Shostakovich. But it was a representative of a distinct genre of Russian orchestral pieces that Shostakovich surely did know: in memory of Rimsky-Korsakov there were also compositions of this type by Glazunov and Steinberg, Shostakovich's teachers, and there were also well-known 'symphonic

---

or to the author's reputation) was put out by Khubov's interpretation of the Largo, though many ambiguities in the wording of the relevant passage defeat evaluation of the claim:

> One day Dmitriy Dmitriyevich thrust towards me a magazine that had fallen into his hands and pointed to a page on which I read that the trouble with the Largo was its colouration of 'deathly despondency'. Dmitriy Dmitriyevich said nothing about this 'revelation' by the famous critic, but his face very graphically reflected a bewildered question ('. . . Ya vsyo ravno budu pisat' muzïku', *Sovetskaya Muzïka* (9/1989), 48).

On the same page Glikman records that at the first performance 'I was shaken to see that during the Largo . . . many, very many were weeping: both women and men' (cf. note 26).

[40] For explication of these actually quite useful terms, which go back to Asaf'yev, and whose meanings are actually disguised by their English cognates, see Malcolm H. Brown, 'The Soviet Russian concepts of "intonazia" and "musical imagery"', *Musical Quarterly*, 60 (1974), 557–67. (Shostakovich's Seventh Symphony furnishes the practical illustrations.)

[41] Igor Stravinsky, *An Autobiography* (New York, 1962), 24.

Ex. 2.1(a) Shostakovich, Symphony No. 5, third movement, fig. 86

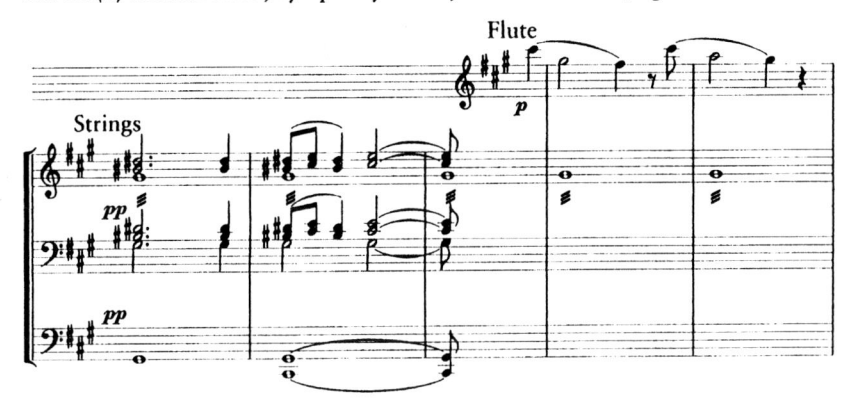

Ex. 2.1(b) *Obikhod notnogo tserkovnogo peniya*, ed. N. I. Bakhmetev (St Petersburg: Pridvornaya pevcheskaya Kapella, 1869), ii, p. 330, transposed up a semitone to facilitate comparison

Ex. 2.1(c) Mahler, *Das Lied von der Erde*, II 'Der Einsame im Herbst', fig. 3 + 1; IV 'Der Abschied', fig. 41 + 2

preludes', as the genre was called, in memory of the publisher Mitrofan Belyayev, the arts publicist Vladimir Stasov and others. They all quoted from the *panikhida*; it was a defining attribute of the genre.

In the Largo of Shostakovich's Fifth, the evocation of the *panikhida* comes amid a sequence of woodwind solos – first the oboe, then the clarinet (accompanied by flutes), then the flute, all accompanied by a steady violin tremolo. The melody these instruments play resonates neither with the orthodox liturgy nor with Russian folk song (as some Soviet writers have maintained), but with Mahler – specifically, with two movements from *Das Lied von der Erde*: 'Der Einsame im Herbst' (The Lonely One in Autumn), and, of course, 'Der Abschied' (The Farewell) (See Ex. 2.1 (c)). That Shostakovich's movement was a mourning piece cannot be doubted – and surely was not doubted, though it could not be affirmed openly. It has been suggested that the movement was a memorial to Mikhail Nikolayevich Tukhachevsky, Marshal of the Soviet Union and Shostakovich's protector, whose infamous execution – now the very emblem of the Yezhovshchina and perhaps its single most terrifying event – had taken place during the symphony's gestation. But why limit its significance? Every member of the symphony's early audiences had lost friends and family members during the black year 1937, loved ones whose deaths they had had to endure in numb horror.

The agony of suppressed grief comes to the fore in a searing *fortissimo* at fig. 90, when the farewell melody is transferred to the cellos, the clarinets reinforcing the liturgical tremolo, and the double basses emitting violent barks of pain (to which only Leonard Bernstein's, among recorded performances, have done justice).[42] One would think no one could miss the significance of this passage, but someone did. Prokofiev, a composer of prodigious invention and facility but a man of small feeling, sent Shostakovich a grudging note of congratulations on the Fifth, reproaching him however for one detail: 'Why so much tremolo in the strings? Just like *Aida*.'[43]

As for the finale, the quality of intrusion from without, which Khubov found 'severe and threatening' and therefore unconvincing as optimistic life-affirmation, applies not only to the beginning, in which the brass section, silent throughout the Largo, bursts in upon and destroys its elegiac mood. It is explicitly confirmed within the movement. The long, quiet stretch from fig. 112 to fig. 121 (and could it be a coincidence that it is cast

---

[42] Particularly worthy of recommendation is Columbia MS 6115 (1959), with the New York Philharmonic, recorded immediately after returning from a Soviet tour in which the orchestra had performed the symphony in the composer's presence.

[43] M. G. Kozlova (ed.), *Vstrechi s proshlïm*, iii (Moscow, 1978), 255.

Interpreting Shostakovich's Fifth Symphony 43

Ex. 2.2(a) Shostakovich, Symphony No. 5, fourth movement, fig. 120

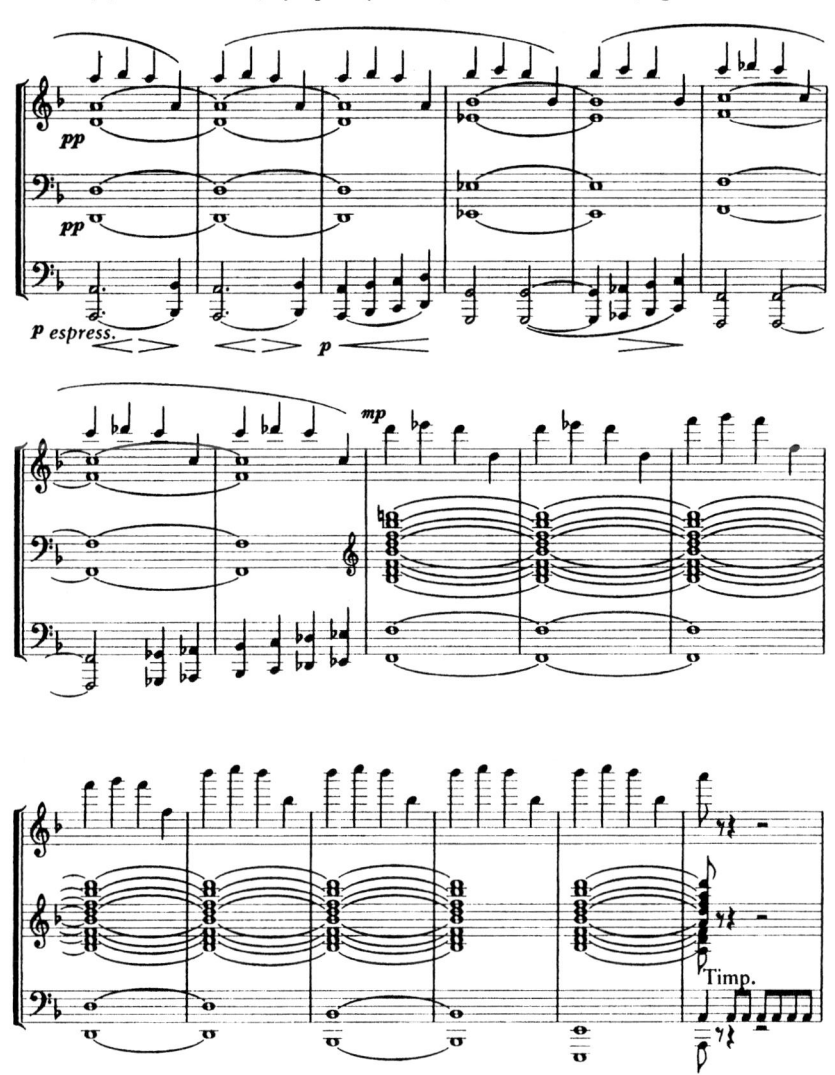

in the key of B♭ major, the alternative tonality of Beethoven's Ninth and the key of its visionary slow movement?) culminates, at fig. 120, in self-quotation, the violins, and later the harp, alluding to the accompaniment to the final quatrain in Shostakovich's setting of Pushkin's poem, 'Rebirth' (*Vozrozhdeniye*, Op. 46/1), composed immediately before the Fifth Symphony, Op. 47 (Ex. 2.2).

Ex. 2.2(b) Shostakovich, *Vozrozhdeniye*, Op. 46/1, bb. 18–29 (end)

In this poem a painting that had been defaced but is restored by time is compared to a spiritual regeneration: 'So', the final quatrain runs, 'do delusions vanish from my wearied soul, and visions arise within it of pure primeval days' (*Tak ischezayut zabluzhden'ya / s izmuchennoy dushi moyey, / i voznikayut v ney viden'ya / pervonachal'nïkh, chistïkh dney*). The image suggests not the promise of a bright future but an escape into the past.[44] When the local tonic chord is resolved as a submediant to the dominant of the main key in the restless six-four position; when that dominant, A, is hammered out by the timpani as a tattoo, reinforced by the military side drum, over a span of fifteen bars; and when the woodwinds bring back the main theme to the accompaniment of a pedal on all four horns (the whole manoeuvre replaying the approach to the coda in the finale of Tchaikovsky's Fourth Symphony), the effect is that of puncture, of sudden encroachment (of the present, of unsettling objective reality) on that subjective escape into the past. The resulting affect of grim passivity mounts into ostensible resolution as the coda is approached.

That coda, emulating a whole genre of triumphant 'Fifth Symphony' finales from Beethoven's to Tchaikovsky's to Mahler's, has been a special bone of interpretative contention from the very beginning. Many musicians have found it – like Tchaikovsky's and Mahler's! – simply inadequate or perfunctory: Myaskovsky, writing to Prokofiev (on the basis of rehearsals he had attended) shortly before the Moscow première, pronounced it 'altogether flat'.[45] Yevgeniy Mravinsky, the conductor of the première, offended the author of *Testimony* when, comparing the finale of the Fifth with that of the masterly Tenth (where 'there is a full synthesis of the objective and the subjective'), he wrote that in the earlier work:

> Shostakovich makes a great effort to make the finale the authentic confirmation of an objectively affirmative conclusion. But in my view this confirmation is achieved to a large extent by external devices: somewhere in the middle of the movement the quick tempo spends itself and the music seemingly leans against some sort of obstacle, following which the composer leads it out of the cul-de-sac, subjecting it to a big dynamic build-up, applying an 'induction coil'.[46]

[44] The point is worth insisting on, since the English-language literature on Shostakovich, however it has construed the passage, has consistently relied on the inaccurate rendering of Pushkin's quatrain in George Hanna's translation of David Rabinovich's *Shostakovich* (Moscow, 1959), 49: 'And the waverings pass away / From my tormented soul / As a new and brighter day / Brings visions of pure gold'. See, *inter alia*, Ian MacDonald, *The New Shostakovich* (Boston, 1990), 132.

[45] S. S. Prokofiev and N. Ya. Myaskovsky, *Perepiska* (Moscow, 1977), 455.

[46] 'Tridtsat' let s muzïkoy Shostakovicha'. Of course the Tenth has an equally famous 'finale problem' (see Fanning, *The Breath of the Symphonist*, chapters 5 and 6).

UNTOUCHED BY THE FORCES OF EVIL?

The question, of course, is whether the coda fails on purpose, as, in the wake of *Testimony*, many writers now contend. Is the ultimate meaning of the symphony, or its method, one of mockery? Behind that question lurks a much bigger one; for if we claim to find defiant ridicule in the Fifth Symphony, we necessarily adjudge its composer, at this point in his career, to have been a 'dissident'. That characterisation, popular as it has become, and attractive as it will always be to many, has got to be rejected as a self-gratifying anachronism.

There were no dissidents in Stalin's Russia. There were old opponents, to be sure, but by late 1937 they were all dead or behind bars. There were the forlorn and the malcontented, but they were silent. Public dissent or even principled criticism were simply unknown. 'People's minds were benumbed by official propaganda or fear', Adam B. Ulam has written, continuing, 'How could there be any public protest against the inhuman regime when even a casual critical remark to an old acquaintance would often lead to dire consequences, not only for the incautious critic but for his family and friends?'[47]

Precisely with the collapse of Soviet power and the opening up of the past has come (or should come) the painful realisation that the repressive Stalinist apparatus left few of its hostages uncoopted. It is all too convenient to forget that pervasiveness now. 'Anyone who did not wish to take part' in the evil of those days, as honest late- and post-Soviet writers admit, 'either left this world or went to the Gulag'.[48] The warning is most often addressed to those who would accuse their fathers, but it applies with equal pertinence to would-be romanticisers.

Dissidence resulted from the loosening of controls, not the other way around. It began very mildly, under Khrushchov, with circumspect critiques of the bureaucracy like Vladimir Dudintsev's novel *Not By Bread Alone* (1956); it gained momentum with samizdat (clandestine self-publication in typescript) and tamizdat (publication abroad), and only flared into open conflict when the Brezhnevite regime tried to reinstitute Stalinist controls (most visibly in the 1966 trial of Andrey Sinyavsky and Yuliy Daniel for

---

[47] Review of Yuri Orlov, *Dangerous Thoughts: Memoirs of a Russian Life*, *New York Times Book Review* (7 July 1991), p. 6.

[48] Andrey Ustinov, 'Pravda i lozh' odnoy istorii' ('The truth and falsehood of a certain story' – concerning the authorship of 'Muddle instead of music'), *Muzïkal'noye obozreniye* (July–August 1991), 3; trans. David Fanning.

tamizdat) but lacked the will or the wherewithal to reinstitute full Stalinist repressions. Even so, outspoken anti-Communism – as against specific policy critique, vindication of victims or defence of the historical record – did not make its real début until the Gorbachov years. Even Solzhenitsïn only preached explicit anti-Communism from abroad. And yet Shostakovich is now portrayed, both in Russia and in the West, as if he had done so at the height of the Terror.

It is natural that latter-day dissidents would like him for an ancestor. It is also understandable, should it ever turn out that Shostakovich was in fact the author of *Testimony*, that he, who though mercilessly threatened never suffered a dissident's trials but ended his career a multiple Hero of Socialist Labour, should have wished, late in life, to portray himself in another light. The self-loathing of the formerly silent and the formerly deluded has long been a salient feature of Soviet intellectual life. But genuine dissidents like Sakharov and Solzhenitsïn, having paid for their dissent with reprisals, have not been ashamed to admit that they had once been silent or deluded. Lev Kopelev, the exiled scholar, confessed to having as an idealistic young Communist participated enthusiastically in forced collectivisation, starvation tactics and denunciations during the winter of 1932–3. In a chilling passage from his memoirs, he even admitted to having collaborated – precisely out of misguided idealism – with the secret police.[49]

Yet now that the dissidents have won, it seems nobody ever really believed in the Soviet way of life. Commonplace now are media interviews in which comfortably situated post-Soviet intellectuals and celebrities like Tatyana Tolstaya or Vasiliy Korotich, to say nothing of the egregious Yevtushenko, blandly assure their interlocutors that everyone had always seen through everything.

---

[49] Lev Kopelev, *To Be Preserved Forever*, trans. Anthony Austin (Philadelphia and New York, 1977), 111:

> The GPU representative at the factory, a stern but good-natured veteran of the Cheka, would often visit us in the evenings, asking us to take note of the workers' attitudes, keep an eye out for kulak propaganda and expose any remnants of Trotskyist and Bukharinist thoughts. I wrote several reports on conditions at the plant, although there was little I told him that I had not already said at meetings or written in our paper. My editorial colleagues did the same. The GPU man would chide us for our frankness in public. 'Don't you see, now they'll hide things from you – they'll give you a wide berth. No, fellows, you've got to learn Chekist tactics.' These words didn't jar us. To be a Chekist in those days seemed worthy of the highest respect, and to co-operate secretly with the Cheka was only doing what had to be done in the struggle against a crafty foe.

It is to that pharisaical pretence, so forgetful of the way things were in the Soviet Union until so very recently, that Shostakovich is now being eagerly assimilated. How pleasant and comforting it is to portray him as we would like to imagine ourselves acting in his shoes. For a vivid illustration of the process, we need only survey chronologically a few readings of one of the most striking pages in the Fifth Symphony – the march episode in the first movement's development section (figs. 27 to 29) – beginning with Alexey Tolstoy, who like General Grant evidently knew only two tunes (one the International, the other not). For him, a march was a march. 'It is like a short discharge of the whole orchestra's breath', he wrote, 'foreshadowing the symphony's finale, a finale of grandiose optimistic exaltation'.[50]

For those who could actually hear music, and could appreciate the march's discordance and its harsh timbre, there could be no question of optimism. The interpretations grow progressively more negative. Alexander Ostretsov saw frustration: 'In this passage all human willpower and fortitude are concentrated, but they can find no outlet'.[51] For Georgiy Khubov, committed to an autobiographical reading, the march epitomised 'the sharply dynamic, troubled, anxious character of the development (and of the whole first movement), some kind of strained craving to find *within oneself* the positive, life-affirming strength of creative victory'.[52] Ivan Martïnov, comparing Shostakovich's methods to Tchaikovsky's (in the *Symphonie pathétique*) or Skryabin's (in the Ninth Sonata), calls the march a 'tragic grotesque. . . . In this transformation of the main theme there is something incongruous. It is like a monstrous mask, a deformed grimace frozen on one's face.'[53]

By the Khrushchov period, as we have seen, the symphony's meaning had been divorced from autobiography. Genrikh Orlov interprets the march as 'the source of tormenting premonitions', a generalised, disembodied 'image of aggression and annihilation', suggesting that, in contradistinction to the Seventh Symphony, which treats of actual military conflict, the Fifth concerns the struggles 'of daily life, and within the human soul, the struggle that defines the essence of life'. He, too, sees Shostakovich's march in terms of a tradition – the tradition of Berlioz's 'Marche au supplice' from the *Symphonie fantastique,* or the menacing fanfares in Tchaikovsky's Fourth

[50] 'Pyataya simfoniya Shostakovicha', *Izvestiya* (28 December 1937), p. 6.
[51] 'Pyataya simfoniya Shostakovicha', *Sovetskoye Iskusstvo* (2 February 1938).
[52] *Sovetskaya Muzïka* (3/1938), 21–2.
[53] *Dmitriy Shostakovich*, 46.

Symphony. In all of these symphonies, 'the moment of the decisive onslaught of the forces of evil is given a martial, bellicose character'.[54] By the time of Khentova's biography, of which the relevant volume was published in 1980, the march has been effectively pigeonholed. She calls it, simply, 'the march of the forces of evil', and, contradicting Orlov, equates its purpose and effect with those of the invasion episode in the Seventh Symphony.[55]

It remained for the post-*Testimony* literature to define those forces. The definition is altogether predictable, but the assertive self-assurance with which it is advanced is nevertheless extraordinary. Ian MacDonald, whose colourfully written recent book *The New Shostakovich* puts him at the forefront of this latest revisionism, has brought the Emperor's-new-clothes rhetoric of *Testimony* to a supreme pitch. His commentary on the Fifth Symphony is riddled with intimidating echoes of Volkov's Shostakovich ('You have to be a complete oaf . . . 'etc.). Here is how he paraphrases the lengthy passage that proceeds from the march episode on into the recapitulation:

A startling cinematic cut sends us tumbling out of the world of abstraction and into representation of the most coarsely literal kind. We are at a political rally, the leader making his entrance through the audience like a boxer flanked by a phalanx of thugs. This passage (the menace theme dissonantly harmonised on grotesquely smirking low brass to the two-note goosestep of timpani and basses) is a shocking intrusion of cartoon satire. Given the time and place in which it was written, the target can only be Stalin – an amazingly bold stroke.

The appearance of the Vozhd [Leader] evokes an extraordinary musical image of obeisance, the orchestra thrumming the one-note motto in excited unison before bowing down to the symphony's keynote D. . . . At the peak of a wildly struggling crescendo, [the main theme's] basic two-note component abruptly, and with vertiginous ambiguity, turns into a flourish of colossal might on drums and brass, punctuating a frenzied unison declamation of the motto rhythm. . . . There can be absolutely no doubt that introspection plays no part in this, that it is objective description – Shostakovichian, as opposed to Socialist, realism.

As this declamatory passage ends, the brass and drums de-crescendo in triumph on the three-note pattern from bar 4, as if grimly satisfied with their brutalisation of the rest of the orchestra and of the symphony's earnestly questing opening bars, all elements of which have been deformed during this convulsion. Over the thrumming rhythm, flute and horn now converse in a major-key transposition of the second subject: two dazed delegates agreeing that the rally had been splendid and the leader marvellous. (A typical stroke of black comedy here has the

[54] *Simfonii Shostakovicha*, 80–2.
[55] *Molodïye godï Shostakovicha*, ii, 181.

horn doggedly copying everything the flute says, to the point of reaching for a B clearly too high for it.)[56]

Perhaps needless to say, this apodeictic paraphrase cannot be refuted on its own terms. Every one of MacDonald's points has its referent in the score; with one exception, the musical events he describes are undeniably there. It does no good to point out that his characterisation of the melody first heard quietly at fig. 1 as the 'menace theme' is arbitrary, and that the reading of the march passage is therefore tautological. That will not dislodge the interpretation from its internal consistency, and internal consistency is what always 'proves' a verificationist thesis (or a conspiracy theory). One cannot empirically determine that a snatch of music does not represent Stalin. But all of this is as true of Tolstoy's reading of the symphony (or even of Stravinsky's version of Tolstoy's) as it is of MacDonald's. They are all internally consistent, and all therefore tautologically true, impervious to empirical refutation.

The exception, the one point in the cited passage that can be empirically 'falsified', is the last point, about the horn's high 'B'. It is based on a footnote in the score: 'If the hornist cannot play the top "B" *piano*, then [the] lower octave should be played, as indicated'.[57] But what the footnote shows is that Shostakovich wished to avoid the very effect to which MacDonald calls attention. The only performance he sanctions is one in which the horn's high B does not sound 'clearly too high for it'.

So there is no black comedy at that point. What about the rest? One could easily and, I think, rightly object on grounds of anachronism, as outlined earlier with respect to 'dissidence' in general: if it is indeed true that 'there can be absolutely no doubt that . . . it is objective' mockery of Stalin Shostakovich meant to perpetrate, then it would have been more than 'an amazingly bold stroke' to have had the Fifth Symphony performed. It would have been suicide. The considerations that caused Shostakovich to withdraw his Fourth Symphony under duress on the eve of its première were no less relevant a year later, when the political atmosphere had grown incomparably more stringent. If any oaf could hear the 'shocking intrusion of cartoon satire', so could any informer.

But even this is not the really decisive argument against MacDonald's interpretation. The question was raised earlier as to what in principle can

---

[56] *The New Shostakovich*, 129–30.
[57] Edition Eulenburg, no. 579, p. 58. The high horn note, as those who can read an orchestral score do not have to be told, is an E.

validate or refute an interpretation of music. It seems to me that the standards one applies to musical interpretations of this kind should be no different from those one applies to any theory. That theory is better which better organises the available information, or organises the most information. MacDonald's reading pays attention only to the most local extroversive referents. Every one of the events that make up the caricature of Stalin entering the hall (and, by the way, were grand entrances his style?) and delivering a thunderous Hitlerian oration (and, by the way, was not his a tremulous high-pitched Georgian-accented voice, and were not his public speeches few?) is a transformation of previously presented material, as is the purported exchange between the two delegates that follows. Any convincing exegesis, therefore, should account for the introversive semiotic along with the extroversive; it should relate the various thematic or motivic appearances to one another, not merely take note of the immediate musical environment – the local dynamic level, the local instrumentation or the locally characteristic harmonies – surrounding a single one.

Leaving aside the motifs that carry loaded labels in MacDonald's analysis (the 'menace theme', the 'two-note groups' which for MacDonald invariably spell 'STA-LIN' even when they are iambic), there is the theme that constitutes the actual content of Stalin's purported 'declamation'. It had been heard only once before, between fig. 3 and fig. 5, a quiet passage in the violins that links up with others (such as the one that comes four bars before 12) that have the characteristics of recitative, musical 'speech'. When recitative appears in an instrumental context (e.g., in Beethoven's late quartets, or Shostakovich's) it is well understood to be an iconic convention, one that creates a sense, as Kerman puts it, of 'direct communication' from the author, a special 'immediacy of address'.[58] There is an inescapably subjective, self-referential component to the expression; the melody MacDonald associates with Stalin's farcical harangue had already been marked for us as the composer's own voice. Failure to note the thematic relationship here – the introversive semiotic – has led, I believe, to a fatal misconstrual of the extroversive. I am convinced that those critics – Khubov for one – are right who have seen the climactic unison passages as representing the efforts of the brutalised subject – the hostage, if you will – to regain a sense of control at any cost.

The same point, writ much larger, applies to the much-debated coda. Leo Mazel' has recently contributed a convincing, and very moving,

[58] Joseph Kerman, *The Beethoven Quartets* (New York, 1979), 199–200.

intonatsionnïy analiz of the very last gesture in the symphony, in which the stereotyped manifestations of rejoicing give way to a sudden modal mixture that introduces not only dissonances but also a melodic progression Shostakovich frequently employed in other works, including texted ones, to evoke 'a sorrowful, gloomy, or angrily plaintive character'.[59] This may be viewed as irony, perhaps; but it is not mockery. Like the funereal third movement, it is an act of witness that gives voice to the wounded. And it does so not by 'objective description' but by the purposeful intrusion of subjective feeling, the composer having learned that this subjectivity alone is what gives art – his art – its enduring value.

This is what sensitive Soviet listeners perceived from the very beginning. It is what Georgiy Khubov sensed and signalled to his readers even in 1938, though he had to do so under cover of ostensible censure. It is what Alexander Ostretsov sensed and signalled when, also under cover of complaint, he informed his readers that 'the pathos of suffering in a whole series of places is driven to the point of naturalistic wails and howls; in some episodes the music seems almost capable of evoking physical pain'.[60] It is what Leo (then Lev) Mazel' recorded in 1960, though he had to do so under cover of ostensible reference to the Patriotic War, trusting that his readers would remember the Fifth Symphony's actual date:

A sense of responsibility, consciousness that 'the struggle of progressive humanity with reaction is not over', that one must remember fallen heroes and think of future generations, that into our thoughts of victory our former grievous anxiety and the tormenting pain of former misfortunes must flow like a living current – all this permeates the work of this composer. And it is important for understanding him – for understanding, for example, why there is a mournful episode in the finale of the Seventh Symphony, and why even the dazzlingly bright major-mode conclusions to the finales of the Fifth and Seventh symphonies are interspersed with intimations of the minor and sharp dissonances.[61]

And it is what has kept Shostakovich's Fifth Symphony, alone among the products of Soviet music from the time of the Terror, alive not only in repertory but in critical discourse and debate.

AN UNHAPPY CONVERGENCE

So Ian MacDonald's reading is no honourable error. It is vile trivialisation. After all, what level of criticism is it that seeks to anthropomorphise every

---

[59] Leo Mazel', 'K sporam o Shostakoviche', *Sovetskaya Muzïka* (5/1991), 35.
[60] 'Pyataya simfoniya Shostakovicha', *Sovetskoye Iskusstvo* (2 February 1938); quoted in Khentova, *Molodïye godï Shostakovicha*, ii, 190.
[61] Lev Mazel', *Simfonii D. D. Shostakovicha* (Moscow, 1960), 8–9.

fugitive instrumental colour and every dynamic shade, and from these analogies assemble a literalistic narrative paraphrase of the unfolding music? Shostakovich himself gave the answer. In a forum that appeared in *Sovetskaya Muzïka* during its first year of publication, three years before he was attacked in *Pravda* (indeed, before *Lady Macbeth* was even performed), at a time when he was still a brash and confidently outspoken young man and the musical *perestroyka* still new and ostensively benign, Shostakovich took a swipe at the backwardness of Soviet music criticism. 'When a critic, in *Rabochiy i Teatr* or *Vechernyaya krasnaya gazeta*, writes that in such-and-such a symphony Soviet civil servants are represented by the oboe and the clarinet, and Red Army men by the brass section, you want to scream!'[62] I don't imagine he would have felt any differently were the civil servants represented by the flute and the horn.

And what kind of investigator builds sweeping forensic cases on such selectively marshalled evidence? To that question the answer is obvious, and sinister. MacDonald's description of the Fifth Symphony reads exactly like a confession State Procurator Vïshinsky might have given Shostakovich to sign, had things not gone quite so well on the night of 21 November 1937. The critic's method is precisely what is known in the West as McCarthyism.

Sometimes the McCarthyite stratagems are even more overtly deployed. When challenged to defend his thesis that Shostakovich was a committed anti-Communist dissident from his twenty-fifth year, MacDonald has resorted to the rank tactic of guilt by association. Naming a few anti-Utopian writers of the 1920s – Zamyatin, Olesha, Bulgakov, Zoshchenko – he has written:

> Shostakovich knew these writers personally, collaborating with one . . . and exploring a major project with another. . . . There is nothing to suggest that the composer . . . opposed the non-Party writers; on the contrary, the evidence is that he sympathised with them – which is presumably why he read their books, watched their plays and socialised with them.[63]

Ian MacDonald, it thus transpires, is the very model of a Stalinist critic. This would be merely comical to relate, were it not that the same reversed stereotype is now being applied to the composer in his homeland, too, in the spirit of *glasnost'*. The politically correct late- or post-Soviet position on Shostakovich has become a facile inversion of the old official view. Black

[62] 'Sovetskaya muzïkal'naya kritika otstayot' [Soviet music criticism is lagging], *Sovetskaya Muzïka* (3/1933), 121.
[63] Letter to the editor, *Times Literary Supplement* (28 September–4 October 1990), 1031.

and white have been conveniently reversed, all grey still resolutely expunged. This new, inverted or negative portrait came strikingly into view in the September 1989 issue of *Sovetskaya Muzïka*, which contained a quintet of revisionist pieces on the composer. He is portrayed now as a martyr to his beliefs, as a romantically heroic resister from the start. 'He was not afraid of Stalin', proclaims the title of one of these articles, by Rudolf Barshai, the now-emigrated conductor who gave the first performance of the Fourteenth Symphony. Another, by the Leningrad theatre historian Isaak Glikman, takes its title from a remark the composer is said to have made in response to the martyrdom of *Lady Macbeth* in 1936: 'Even if they cut off both my hands, I'll go on writing music just the same, holding the pen between my teeth'. A third, entitled 'His greatness and his mission', places the world-renowned and decorated Shostakovich in the same category as Roslavets and Mosolov, silenced composers, and compares them all with repressed literary figures such as Bulgakov, Zamyatin, Pasternak and Pilnyak.

An essay by a self-styled 'kulturolog' named Georgiy Gachev practises a familiar form of ventriloquism on the music. For him, as for Ian MacDonald, the Fifth Symphony is an objective narrative, wholly reducible to paraphrase:

And now, 1937 – to the howl of mass demonstrations, marching, demanding the execution of the 'enemies of the people', the guillotine machinery of the State goes resoundingly into action – and there it is in the finale of the Fifth: the USSR is building – only it is unclear what it is building, a bright future or a Gulag.[64]

The height of impertinence is reached when Gachev begins playing compulsively, irresponsibly and untranslatably, with words: '*Ne prosto muzïkoVED – Shostakovich, no muzïkoVOD, vozhd' Muzïki*': 'No simple musicologist was Shostakovich but a music-leader, the Führer of music'.[65] *Vozhd'* – Führer – was Stalin's sobriquet. Gachev makes Shostakovich the anti-Stalin – Stalin's equal, Stalin's match, the musical Stalin – but, needless to say, a good Stalin.

One understands the motives – or rather, the compulsion. The author's father, Dmitriy Gachev, a Bulgarian-born Communist and an old RAPMist who crusaded for *partiynost'* in musical criticism in the early days of the Composers' Union,[66] had fallen victim to that roaring guillotine the Fifth

---

[64] 'V zhanre filosofskikh variatsiy', *Sovetskaya Muzïka* (9/1989), 36.
[65] *Ibid.*, 39.
[66] See D. Gachev, 'Za partiynost' khudozhestvenno-muzïkal'noy kritiki', *Sovetskaya Muzïka* (5/1933), 152–8.

Symphony is supposed to illustrate. Romanticising Shostakovich as an avenging angel is for members of Georgiy Gachev's generation a cathartic. But now that anything can be said in Russia, the inevitable inflation of rhetoric has produced correspondingly diminished returns. The hedged, risky, guarded statements of the past were so much more powerful, so much richer. Viewing Shostakovich through them brought understanding and exhilaration. The discourse of *glasnost'* produces a sense of futility. It is not, after all, by egoistically trivialising the agonies of the Stalin years that whatever replaces Soviet music will find its way to the twenty-first century.

For what is true of discourse about music is true of music itself. The age of heroic classicism is over – or should be. Shostakovich remained committed to it after the Fifth Symphony. That was his personal *perestroyka*; it was real, it was permanent, it was necessary – and it was tragic. The changes wrought in him by his ordeals lent his voice a moral authority perhaps unmatched in all of twentieth-century music. But the impulse to communicate urgently in an atmosphere of threat did lead, at times, to an overreliance on extroversive reference as bearer of essential meaning, and a correspondingly debased level of musical discourse.

There are works of Shostakovich – the much-admired Eighth Quartet is one – that sound as though they were written to be paraphrased. And the paraphrase, especially when informed by ready-made assumptions, all too easily replaces the music as primary experience. The tendency to paraphrase Shostakovich's works rather than listen to them was an old Soviet vice, to be sure, but in the spirit of revisionism it has infected and debased the reception of his music in the West as well. Ian MacDonald is, once again, the most extreme manifestation of an unfortunate tendency when, after paraphrasing yet again the anti-Stalinist programme he finds in each and every Shostakovich composition, he writes of the Ninth and Tenth Quartets, 'one can be forgiven for thinking that we have been over this ground once too often'.[67] Having ears only for the paraphrase, he is finally unable to distinguish his own boring voice from Shostakovich's.

To me, the most heartening bit of writing on Shostakovich in quite some time was a piece by Liana Genina, the deputy editor of *Sovetskaya Muzïka*, writing this time in a rival journal, *Muzïkal'naya Zhizn'*. It is called 'Hoping for justice', and it calls for a halt to a cheap inversionism: to the insistence on reading formulaic ideological programmes in every Shostakovich composition – only the reverse of what was read before –

---

[67] *The New Shostakovich*, 235.

and especially to the easy presumption that Shostakovich, 'in the grip of horror, said, signed and did one thing, but always thought another'.[68]

So far, most commentators, both in and out of Russia, have followed the line of least resistance to a specious, falsely comforting sense of purification. But, as Caryl Emerson has written, 'the genuine de-Stalinisation of Shostakovich, like the de-Stalinisation of the [former] Soviet Union in every other area, will require a much more critical look at the ethical dimension, and a much more painful catharsis'.[69]

We can learn a great deal from the cultural artefacts of the Stalinist period, but only if we are prepared to receive them in their full spectrum of greys. The lessons may be discomforting, unpalatable, even repellent, but all the more necessary and valuable for their being so. The chief ones may well be the moral ambiguity of idealism, the inescapable ethical responsibilities of artists, and the need to resist the blandishments of Utopia. Stalinism was a double thing, as Irving Howe, an impeccable anti-Stalinist, had the courage to remind us shortly before he died. I want to end by quoting, in tribute, some eloquent words of his:

If humanity cannot live without a measure of idealism, idealism can turn upon humanity. Prompted by impatience with the laggard pace of history, idealism generated a counterforce from within itself, an involuntary poisonous secretion. Dostoyevsky understood this brilliantly when he wrote in *A Raw Youth* about man's 'faculty of cherishing in his soul the loftiest ideal side by side with the greatest baseness, and all quite sincerely'.[70]

The last four words are the words that count.

[68] 'S nadezhdoy na spravedlivost", *Muzikal'naya Zhizn'* (5/1991), 3.
[69] Caryl Emerson, 'Grotesque modernism in opera: Shostakovich's *Nose* and *Lady Macbeth*', paper read at a panel, 'Russian Modernism: Art and Literature', at the annual convention of the American Association of Teachers of Slavic and East European Languages, Washington, DC, 1989. My thanks to Prof. Emerson for allowing me to quote from the typescript (p. 13).
[70] Irving Howe, 'The great seduction', *The New Republic* (15 October 1990), 47.

3

Form in Shostakovich's instrumental works

YURIY KHOLOPOV

Dmitri Shostakovich is among those who represent a clearly defined and necessary line in the evolutionary flow of twentieth-century music. The idea of this artistic trend is fused with its embodiment in the musical forms of the classical tradition, which externally has something in common with neoclassicism. The influence of neoclassicism on Shostakovich manifests itself in his quotations of some of the idioms of the musical language of the baroque or the Viennese classics, especially their melodies and stylistic forms – for example in the First Piano Concerto and the first movement of the Sixth Symphony; and the second movement of the Second String Quartet ends with a quotation of the standard formula for a cadence of baroque recitative. The influence also shows in his addressing typical polyphonic forms of the pre-classical style, in particular the fugue and passacaglia.[1]

Strictly speaking this is not a neoclassical but a neobaroque attitude; but these are frequently not differentiated. And the influence of neoclassicism is not contradicted by the fact that Shostakovich's thinking is firmly based on forms which had grown up among the great Viennese classics such as Haydn, Mozart and Beethoven, which in the context of the twentieth century is not so much neoclassicism as 'classicity' or (classical) tradition. Many composers of the twentieth century set out on their creative path in this channel of tradition.[2] The direction in which they headed after that was

---

[1] It follows from some of Shostakovich's statements that he understood polyphonic forms as simply the tradition of the past. For instance, talking of 'fugues and canons' he was referring to Tchaikovsky – see Sof'ya Khentova, *Shostakovich: Tridtsatiletiye 1945–1975* (Leningrad, 1982), 159.

[2] The problem of 'classicity' was posed by Klaus Niemöller in the keynote lecture at the international symposium in honour of Shostakovich in *Internationales Dmitri-Schostakowitsch-Symposion Köln 1985*, ed. Klaus Niemöller and Vsevolod Zaderatsky (Regensburg, 1986), 1–15.

a matter of fate. Shostakovich, having tasted the temptations of New Music in the twenties, deliberately turned thereafter towards the world of traditional forms. The point of this path was 'to be old in a new way'. Many of Shostakovich's compositions are *chefs d'œuvre* of modern music in classical-type forms.

FORMAL TYPES

The musical classics are held sacred. But at the crossroads of the twentieth century an adequate idea of the language of classical form had been largely lost, particularly in respect of the form-building role of the harmonic process. There is therefore some point in reminding ourselves of the common origins of these forms.

The universal classical autonomously musical forms, secular in spirit, are based on the rhythm of folk song and folk dance, strongly permeating them with the symphonism of the idea of dialectic development, deriving secondary ideas from the main one. Hence the basic structural opposition within the form: song and passage (in German, *Gang*). They are to form what the consonance–dissonance opposition is to harmony. Song (or song form, ABA, *Lied* form) is a type of stable (in German, *fest*) structure based upon a metric eight-bar cell in strict single tonality without modulation. Passage is the opposite of song in its loose and flowing character, the absence of periods and larger song structures;[3] modulations belong to the category of passage (both terms are derived from the theories of Adolf Bernhard Marx – see below).

On this basis are built three main types of form: song forms, rondo (or type of rondo) and sonata allegro.

Song forms have no passages or modulations. Sub-categories are the simple song form (on a single theme), the compound song (for example, a minuet and trio, or two trios; later the form of the Viennese waltz), the couplet song, and the theme and variations which is similar to it. The song form (period 4+4, large sentence 2+2+1+1+2, three-part or two-part single-theme form) is also characteristic of the principal themes of large forms such as rondos, sonata form.

[3] [Periods are conventional balanced phrase-patternings based on immediate contrast followed by varied restatement, whereas sentences proceed by immediate restatement followed by varied extension – see Arnold Schoenberg, *Fundamentals of Musical Composition* (London, 1967), chapters 5 to 8 (ed.).]

Form in Shostakovich's instrumental works

The classical *rondo*[4] presupposes modulatory transitions from the principal theme to others. There are three types: small rondo (e.g. the second movement of Beethoven's Sonata Op. 31 No. 2), i.e. with only one secondary theme; large rondo, with two or more secondary themes (the finales of Beethoven's Sonatas Op. 2 Nos. 2 and 3); and sonata rondo, if instead of the second secondary theme there is a development (Beethoven, finale of Sonata Op. 90).

Sonata form is based on the development of a single musical idea, whence the predominance of passages in it and of the modulation structure; the most characteristic part of sonata form is the development.

For the most concise and accurate designation of the parts of a classical type form it is necessary to adopt abbreviations:

MT = main theme, Tr = transition, ST = secondary theme, Retr = retransition, T = the tonic tonality, Mod = modulation, D = the dominant tonality, Int = introduction, Con = conclusion or coda, Dev = development.

And within the theme (or song):

Sen = sentence, Per = period, Mid = middle of the theme (harmonically unstable), Int = introduction.

These abbreviations are as necessary for operating with the concepts of classical form as function signs are for harmony, and they will be used extensively in the tables and examples below (see also note 8 *infra*).

GENERAL PRINCIPLES

The general principles of Shostakovich's form (in his main, central period of creative work) can be presented as classical forms by means of modern harmony in an individual stylistic treatment. The opposition of song and passage acquires a new aspect in harmony remote from the classics; however, the principles of the relationships are fully preserved. In the finale of the Fifth Symphony, for instance, the principal theme is a tonic expanse with complete supremacy of the key of D minor in a firm song form of three strophic units. In sharp contrast is the modulatory passage, from fig. 102, in which there are neither sentences nor other song forms; the main core is a two-bar structure.

---

[4] Historically three completely different forms are known by a single name: the poetic *rondeau* of the fourteenth century, the couplet *rondeau* of the French harpsichordists and the classical *rondo* (Mozart, Beethoven). Here I am referring to the third meaning.

The form scheme and the original modulation to D♭ major (the beginning of Ex. 3.1)[5] are as follows (in addition to the abbreviations noted above, upper- and lower-case letters have their conventional meaning of major and minor tonality, respectively):

MT	Tr	ST1
Per; Mid; Sen	Pas	Sen
9 8 11	2 2 1 1	1+4
d	Mod	D♭

Ex. 3.1 Shostakovich, Symphony No. 5, fourth movement

[d] SUBM.

D♭ Lydian: T $\frac{5}{3}$ ♭3 ♭2 1 Tparallel

The functionally strong harmony enables the beauty of the proportions to be revealed: a fleeting first secondary theme in a remote shared-third key (*odnotertsovïy*, in German *Terzgleiche* – the note F is shared by D minor and D♭ major) is in opposition to an expansive main theme with a strongly emphasised tonic. And statements of the themes in song form rise above the modulation streams around them. The song forms are structurally stable (*fest*), the passages are unstable or loose (*locker*).

SONG FORMS

Song forms possess the clamping-force of high symmetries, based on eight metrical bars (= 1 stanza); moreover, they are frequently composed of a number of such stanzas: 8+8+8 and so on. The energy of the metric extrapolation which gives rise to the cadences also gives strength to the

---

[5] The originality is already evident in the harmony which first contradicts D minor at fig. 102: why B♭ minor? The logic is obvious: within the main theme there have already been A–D–G–C–F minors; the next, not yet used, must be precisely B♭ minor. And following along this same chain, E♭ minor will begin the restatement of the theme at fig. 104.

tonal gravitation. Digressions, in Shostakovich's harmony right to extremes of remoteness (e.g. to the tritonal pole, 'Tri'), in song form only strengthen the sense of monotonality (e.g. the main theme of the third movement of Symphony No. 5, 12+12 bars).[6] Song form is formed in accordance with the iambic law 'unaccented–accented' at several levels of metric pulsation. Hence the functions of the metrical bars of song form:[7] 1 2 3 4, 5 6 7 8 (with various transformations). The peculiarity of Shostakovich's metre is in his tendency to complicate the system of repeats (of the symmetry), see the opening of the last movement of the Second Piano Sonata, Example 3.2.

Ex. 3.2 Shostakovich, Piano Sonata No. 2, finale

Here the theme has not yet started, yet its metre is overturned by the introductory motif, in effect in 3/2. Syncopation displaces all the motifs by a half-beat (see brackets below the staff); only the reprise, from b. 22, puts them all in their right places. The three-part song is strictly in a single key, without modulation, however, with extremely remote intratonal digressions as far as F major and B♭ major. The reprise starts with this latter chord (after its introduction).[8] The entire three-stanza song, written analytically in metrical bars, is as Example 3.3.

[6] Igor' V. Sposobin named such digressions 'subsystems'.
[7] Regarding metrical bars (as distinct from notated ones) see Ebenezer Prout, *Musical Form* (London, 1893), chapter 8; also his *Applied Forms*, 3rd edn (London, 1895). In the fourth movement of Shostakovich's Eighth String Quartet, where among the quotations there is the popular Soviet Revolutionary song 'Zamuchon tyazholoy nevoley' (Tormented by heavy captivity), one metrical bar equals four notated ones – figs. 58–60.
[8] Signs used henceforth for modern chromatic tonality: upper and lower mediants – MED, med; upper and lower submediants – SUBM, subm; tritonal pole – Tri; °N = minor Neapolitan harmony; upper and lower leading-note-chords (*Atakta*) – At (tends to be a semitone lower) and AT (tends to be a semitone higher). *Atakta* is a special term introduced by the Polish theorist Tadeusz Zieliński – see his *Problemy harmoniki nowoszesnej* (Kraków, 1983), 116.

Ex. 3.3

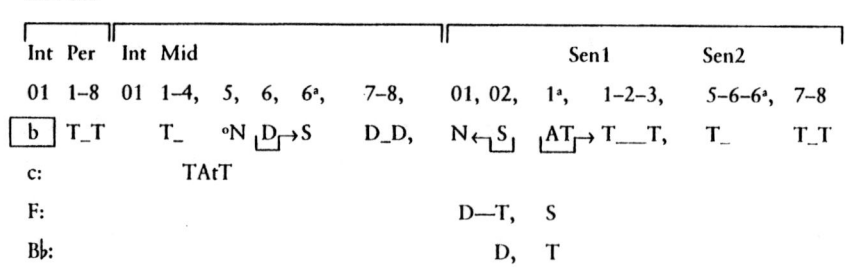

	Int Per	Int Mid					Sen1		Sen2	
	01 1–8	01 1–4,	5,	6,	6ª,	7–8,	01, 02,	1ª, 1–2–3,	5–6–6ª,	7–8
b	T_T	T_	ºN	D→S		D_D,	N←S,	AT→T__T,	T_	T_T
c:		TAtT								
F:							D—T,	S		
B♭:							D,	T		

For brilliant specimens of Shostakovich's song form see also, for example, the themes of the second movement of Symphony No. 7 (32 bars), or the fourth movement of Symphony No. 8. Shostakovich writes simple song forms in the majority of his piano preludes (the melodic piece in C♯ minor from Op. 34, the witty F♯ major and A♭ major).[9] Among his sets of variations I would cite the second movement of the String Quartet No. 1; some variations of the *non-modulating* theme sound *as though in other keys*.

An extremely original combination of song forms makes up the form of the Scherzo of the Fifth Symphony. Instead of a single main theme Shostakovich uses a block of two themes (see Ex. 3.4).[10]

Ex. 3.4

	MT	ST1	ST2	MT	ST1	Con
Number of bars:	44	42	70	44	42	8
	a	c	C	a	c♯–c	a

RONDO

A new principle of form (in comparison with song forms) appears under the general term 'rondo'. This form is based on the links of the themes and on modulation and presupposes the development of musical thought,

---

[9] Nikolay Zhilyayev suggested a humorous programme for the A♭ major Prelude: it is a declaration of love of which you cannot believe a single word.

[10] A similar concentration of form leads to an unusual result in the second movement of the Seventh Symphony; each of the three main sections is itself executed in song form with a trio (large blocks in B minor, C♯ minor, B minor). The rarely encountered tonal relation of a major second may be due to the circumscribing of the symphony's tonic C. The same idea is found in the tonal architecture of the symphony as a whole.

Form in Shostakovich's instrumental works 63

not only its exposition or comparison, as in the compound song form of the last example. Hence the transitions from one thought to another are in the form of passages with their own inherent modulations. A typical feature of rondo forms is recurrence of the sections. The basic term 'rondo' ('a round') is taken from the names of the finales of classical sonatas and concerti. The 'round' effect actually occurs in the exposition of the classical rondo (see Ex. 3.5).

Ex. 3.5

```
   ⌒
MT  ST        or:     MT    Tr    ST    Retr    MT
   ⌣                  |_T_|  Mod  |_D_|  Mod   |_T_|
```

(Alternatively the secondary theme may be restated in the tonic; or both the secondary and the main theme may reappear.) With one secondary theme there is one modulation: from the tonic to the dominant and back again. In Shostakovich the problem of contrast of a single tonality in the themes and the modulatory quality of the passages is even more acute. The themes are more or less definitely built on the basis of the metric cells with their metrical functions (see previous section) and motivic structure.

An example of the compositional problems of the Shostakovich rondo is the Largo of the Second Piano Sonata. In this particular case both passages are illustrated: towards the secondary theme and from the secondary theme. Furthermore, in the latter case the first passage is repeated and the main theme is abbreviated (the same as the lyrical part in the first movement of the Sixth Symphony). The form as a whole is given in Example 3.6.

Ex. 3.6

MT			Tr	ST	Retr	MT			Con	(mt)
a	b	b				a	b	b	mod	Sen
12,	9,	12	11	8+8	8+9	17,	9,	12	8,	9
A♭			Mod	C	Mod	A♭			A♭	

In the main theme is a rare form of period with a trochaic metre, where the odd bars are strong bars. As a result it is not the fourth or eighth bars which are the cadence bars, as in an ordinary iambic period, but the third (see Ex. 3.7) and seventh; but with expansion (bb. 5ᵃ, 8ᵃ) this anomaly is corrected.

64   Yuriy Kholopov

Ex. 3.7 Shostakovich, Piano Sonata No. 2, second movement

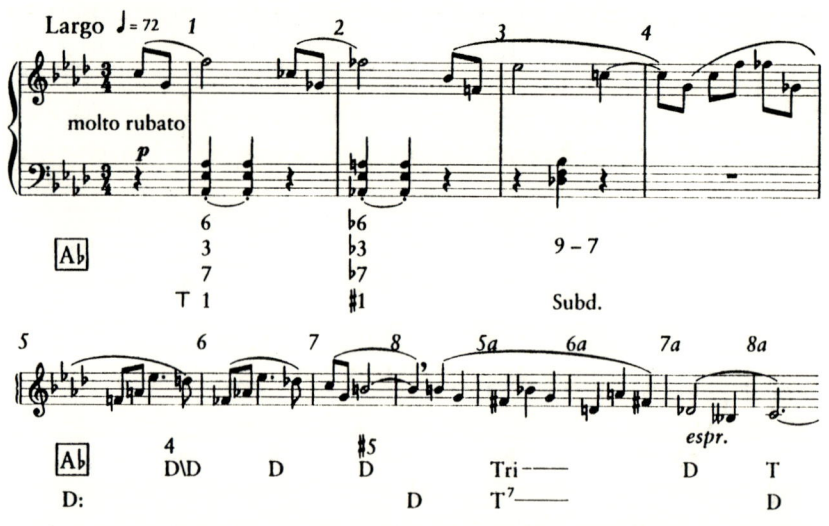

The altered dominant A♭ major also easily resolves to D major (deviation to tritonal pole without changing the overall tonality). Such a strong tonality also fixes the form of the theme for its entire length.

The strength of the tonal mass in the main key also enables its destruction to be very effective in the connecting passage. The thinking of Shostakovich the symphonist shows in the intensity of the thematic development, as intense as in sonata form. The motifs F–F♭–E♭ and A♭–A–B♭ from the main theme, by transforming, prepare the secondary theme (see Ex. 3.8).

Ex. 3.8

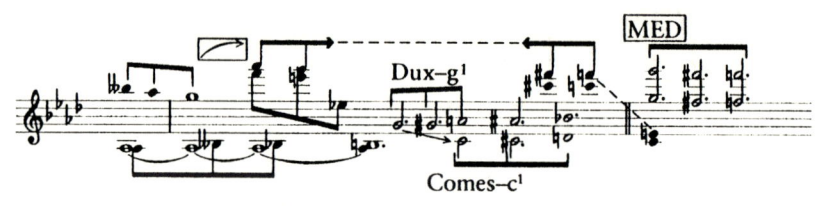

Song forms do not have such a force of development. Here modulation expresses the delightful effect of an elevation of the musical feeling which cannot be expressed in words. This is the *structural dissonance*. Moreover, the particular subtlety of this form consists in the opposite feeling when moving from the tonic to the secondary tonality and moving back again.

Typical of such forms in Shostakovich is his invention of an individual and brilliant new solution in each case. Here Shostakovich uses a principle which one has to resort to the terminology of physics to describe: the 'black box' principle – not a passing through such and such a key, as in the Viennese classics, but the gradual obscuring of the feeling of any tonality whatsoever, after which any key, even at times a fantastical new tonic (for example a dissonant one), would seem to be convincing.

In the movement in question, after repeating a phrase from the theme a passage of sixths comes into force, bringing us by b. 41 to complete uncertainty. And suddenly the tonal fog disperses and the light of the 'white' key of C major arises (see Ex. 3.9).

Ex. 3.9

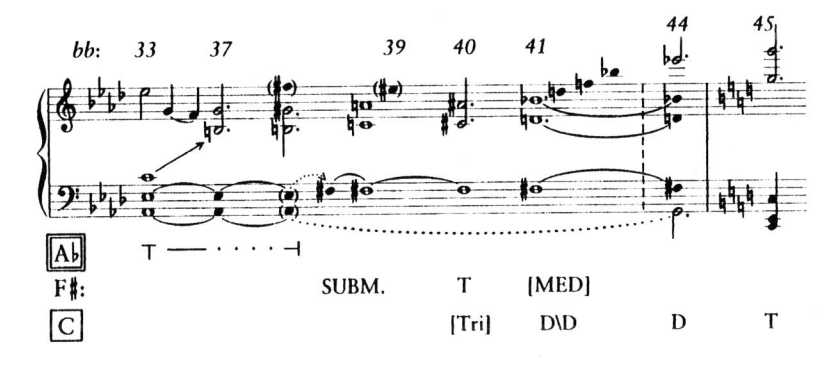

The example quoted refers to the 'small rondo', that is, with a single 'rotation' (and a single secondary theme) regardless of whether one counts the repetitions of the sections or not.

The problems of the 'large rondo' include a new issue for the master: the interrelationship of two (or more) secondary themes with one another, their contrast with one another and their different relationships to the main theme and its tonic. Shostakovich follows the classical prototype extremely accurately, but only thinks in categories of modern harmony. Thus, in the Largo of the Fifth Symphony the main theme (twenty-four bars) in a stable F♯ minor has two themes subordinate and in opposition to it. The first secondary theme (from fig. 79) together with its return to the main theme occupies 4+8 bars; its tonality is fragilely unstable, fluctuating between B minor and G minor. The second secondary theme is similar to a large trio section, in the developed form of a three-part (thirty-three bar) song. However, it yields to the main theme in tonal firmness – it has different keys (C minor, C♯ minor) and, moreover, its exposition part fluctuates between F minor and C minor. The beauty of the Largo form as a whole is revealed in these aesthetic proportions of the relationships between the themes.

In the Shostakovich sonata rondo the development is usually not large. In the section between the exposition and the recapitulation he often introduces, apart from the development, either another episodic theme (the finale of the Sixth Symphony) or a reminiscence of the theme from one of his previous movements (the finales of the Third, Fifth and Sixth String Quartets).

It would not be an exaggeration to assert that Shostakovich created a special combination of the properties of the rondo and sonata form based on the principle of the sonata rondo. A generalised diagram (transitions are not shown; the key functions are approximate) would be as below (see Ex. 3.10).

Ex. 3.10

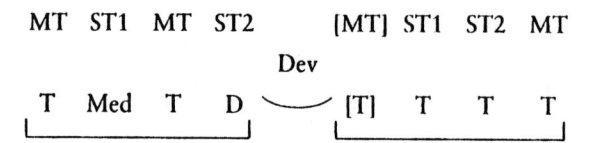

```
MT  ST1  MT  ST2        [MT]  ST1  ST2  MT
              Dev
   T   Med   T    D  ⌒  [T]   T    T    T
   |_____|    |_____|
```

None of the handbooks on musical form describes a rondo-sonata of this type.[11] In Shostakovich one encounters this variety in the finales of several important compositions of the forties and fifties: in Symphonies 8, 9 and 10, and in the Second Piano Trio. By analogy with the special 'Shostakovich modes' (minor with lowered degrees) discovered by Alexander Dolzhansky (see the chapter by Ellon Carpenter in the present volume) this form could be called a 'Shostakovich rondo'.

[11] If we take MT ST1 MT as a three-part main theme, the form coincides with sonata form. Against this suggestion is the fact that both the secondary themes are highly independent (this is particularly striking in the recapitulation) and highly contrasted with the main theme. It is also significant how Shostakovich himself treats the first secondary theme of the Second Piano Trio when he quotes it in the Eighth Quartet: it is the secondary theme that he takes and not the main theme (it is thus evident that it is not the 'middle') and it is to this secondary theme that he imparts conceptual importance, just as if it were an independent piece (figs. 21, 33). Both times he even retains its key of C minor, sharply contradicting the key of the finale of the trio – E major. Of the finale of the Tenth Symphony David Fanning observes: 'This is a sonata exposition with pronounced rondo characteristics' – *The Breath of the Symphonist: Shostakovich's Tenth*, Royal Musical Association Monographs 4 (London, 1989), 64.

A model is the finale of the Eighth Symphony (a simplified diagram without transitional parts is given as Ex. 3.11; Rem = Reminiscence).

Ex. 3.11

	B	C¹⁰	D	F	H	I	K	L⁹	M	¹⁵N	O
	124	129²	132	136	141	151	154	159	162	166	167¹⁰	172
	MT	ST1	MT	ST2	Dev	MT	Dev	Rem	ST2	ST1	MT	Con
	C	a	C	E	Mod [C]	Mod		e	A	C	C

For a better understanding of the logic of Shostakovich's forms one must bear in mind that when he was being taught in Russia it was the classical system of forms according to Adolf Bernhard Marx which was accepted.[12] This system was well known by Shostakovich's elder colleagues Prokofiev and Myaskovsky. Shostakovich, although he regarded himself as a non-theoretician,[13] undoubtedly knew the theory well and orientated himself according to this particular system, in particular the so-called 'five rondo forms'.[14] Evidently the composer adhered to his orientation within the system in some difficult situations. Thus, it is obvious that the large rondo in the finale of the Seventh Symphony belongs to the 'fifth form of rondo'. Its exposition contains a return to the main theme after the first secondary theme, which is typical of a rondo; then there is another large episode and at the end a conclusion based on the material of the main theme in counterpoint with the material of the introduction. (The replacement of the main theme by a concluding part was regarded as a characteristic of the fifth rondo form, see note 14.)

A short diagram of the exposition is given as Example 3.12.

Ex. 3.12

147	152	155	157	159	166²		175–7
Int	MT	Tr	ST1	MT	ST2	Tr	Con
cV	c	c mod	A	c	f♯	mod	E♭

followed by the central sarabande episode, figs. 179–89

After this follows the developed theme of the central episode in a rondo reminiscent of a type of trio.

---

[12] For example, his *Die Lehre von der musikalischen Komposition*, 1st edn (Leipzig, 1837–47).
[13] In reply to the present author in 1975 he said that he did not 'understand anything about theory'.

68   Yuriy Kholopov

SONATA FORM

In his handling of sonata form Shostakovich proceeds from the classical prototype via the experience of the dramatic symphonism of the Romantic era. Among typologically related phenomena of the past one can point to Tchaikovsky's Sixth Symphony (with which Shostakovich's symphonism has a lot in common) and Alexander Skryabin's Ninth Piano Sonata (as a composer Skryabin is completely alien to Shostakovich, but his late sonatas contain similar harmonic problems). Unlike the youthful sonata writing of the Viennese classics, which had a rich enough fund of dialectic contrasts of functional tonality, the modern composer feels the lack of harmonic 'fuel' for the 'engines' of such large-scale forms. In this situation a great help is the coupling-up of powerful means of emotional pressure offered by contrasts of tempo, texture (including instrumentation) and dynamics.

Shostakovich, following the traditions of Tchaikovsky and Mahler, presents sonata form as a powerful drama. Its contours in a number of characteristic cases are defined by restrained fluctuation in the exposition and concluding phases and a steady accumulation through the development section, carried over into the beginning of the recapitulation – cf. the first movements of Symphonies 5, 7, 8 and 10.

Within the exposition Shostakovich makes full use of the resources of tonally defined harmony, distributing them over the five sections typical of a sonata exposition of the Beethoven tradition. He observes the hierarchy of harmonic contrasts in these sections: a firm and strong tonic in the principal theme, a softened but definite tonality in the secondary theme, a short and well-directed modulation in the first passage (sometimes very laconic in the connecting part), a free fantasia in the second passage (between the secondary theme and the conclusion of the exposition); the concluding part is constructed variously, demonstrating the tonal definiteness of the end of the exposition and at the same time allowing the musical unfolding to flow over into the development section with no delays on cadence formulae. Diagrammatically this can be expressed as Example 3.13.

[14]   The five rondo forms may be presented in condensed diagrams:
    (1)   MT Pas MT (and repetitions)
    (2)   MT Pas ST Pas MT (and repetitions)
    (3)   MT ST1 MT ST2 – MT
    (4)   ⌊MT ST1 MT⌋ ST2 – ⌊MT ST1⌋
    (5)   ⌊MT ST1 Con⌋ ST2 – ⌊MT ST1 Con⌋

Form in Shostakovich's instrumental works

Ex. 3.13

1	2	3	4	5
MT	Tr	ST	Pas	Con
T	Mod	D	Pas	D

A typical example is the sonata moderato in the first movement of the Fifth Symphony. The expanse of the main part, which is extremely complex and detailed, is cemented with a strong D minor (see Ex. 3.14; IT = introductory theme).

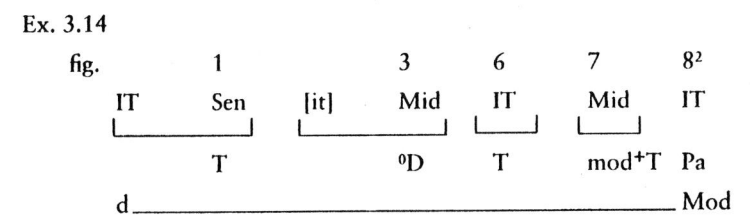

Ex. 3.14

fig.	1		3	6	7	8²
IT	Sen	[it]	Mid	IT	Mid	IT
	T		ºD	T	mod⁺T	Pa
d						Mod

The secondary theme, on the other hand, is stated in a loose (*rikhlï*) tonality (E♭ minor = ºN; this 'E♭ minor' is 'pulled out of the rib of' the principal theme, see fig. 1, bb. 2–4). Only the initial period of the secondary theme starts in the very clear key of E♭ minor (fig. 9), and it finishes on its Neapolitan harmony (fig. 11); the restatement begins in a Phrygian G and ends in a completely weak tonic E♭ major (fig. ³⁻²13).

The transition turns steeply away from a definite D major (fig. 8) to the clear E♭ minor (fig. 9). The second transitional passage (figs. 13–15) meditatively touches on remote (from any key centre) tonalities: B♭ minor – F♯ minor – B♭ minor – E major – E♭ major.

In the absence of a strong key centre even the main key of the secondary part (fig. 14) does not sound like its basis. Instead of the concluding part there is a restatement of the secondary theme returning to the tonic E♭ major (minor).

The fine structural differentiation of each of the sections of the exposition testifies to the composer's clarity of thought and his great craftsmanship.

Everything that has been described makes up only a sonata exposition with one powerful modulation D minor to E♭ minor. And so now begins the most important thing in sonata form, the development. But if all the strongest resources have already been exhausted, on what basis can the development exist when, according to the rules of the form, it should be an order of magnitude higher than the exposition? Let us remember that in the classics in the first instance a mass of new tonal material whose level of tension greatly exceeds everything displayed in the exposition is introduced into the development. In Shostakovich's movement if one considers all the harmonies prominently demonstrated in the exposition they will give an almost complete twelve-note chain, and moreover the main props are harmonies which are five steps away on the circle of fifths. Thus there is nothing left for the development.

Shostakovich's new solution as a twentieth-century composer consists of finding new effective means of contrast, an even higher order of dissonance. In the development section he now starts to place contrasted sound-layers one on top of another. The unity of the harmony in the vertical dimension is broken. The layers of *polyharmony* dissonantly contradict one another, as if the voices somehow are not listening to one another; in some places they even try to out-shout one another to see who can make the most noise. In places it becomes impossible to sense any tonality whatsoever. Supercharging the discordant mass of sound leads to a huge 'proclamation' at the beginning of the recapitulation, where uncoordinated shouting lines suddenly merge into a mighty unison.

This type of solution imparts new life to sonata form and other symphonised forms by means of development. The highest examples of this, perhaps, are again in the first movements of the Eighth and Tenth Symphonies.

In addition to such general sonata principles individual conceptions are also important, particularly in this strict and predetermined form. We shall mention one example: the recapitulation in the first movement of the Tenth Symphony. Somewhat unusually for Shostakovich's sonata forms the recapitulation of this E minor symphony begins in the Phrygian F minor; that is, a semitone higher, but on the bass of the dominant of E minor (see Ex. 3.15*a* and *b*). This profound idea consists of a unique design of achieving the highest link in the sonata recapitulation. The point is that the composer's original notion was the harmonic opposition of the themes in the exposition: the mass of the firm key of the main theme and the unusual *ambiguity* of the key of the secondary theme – simultaneously G♯ minor and G major. This means that in the secondary theme the two tonics are competing against one another all the time. The composer retains the key signature of G major, but ends the exposition with an A♭ major chord, which is the same as the tonic of G♯ minor ('like Bach'; fig. ⁴29).[15] Now Shostakovich transfers the

---

[15] For a detailed analysis of the phenomenon see David Fanning's remarkable book (*The*

Form in Shostakovich's instrumental works

relation of common-third tonics to the key of E major which is synonymous with the home key. And what you get with the main theme of the recapitulation in F minor and the E major of the secondary theme is: F – A♭ – C (over B)

E – G♯ – B.

Making this connection gives rise to yet another point of real genius in the first-movement form: in introducing the recapitulation of the secondary theme two 'lost' clarinets pensively converge on a melodious third in the harmony of some darkly remote key (Ex. 3.15c). And suddenly there is an instantaneous change! A soft but bright colour of unexpected generous, benedictory E major flashes out (Ex. 3.15d).

Ex. 3.15 Shostakovich, Symphony No. 10, first movement

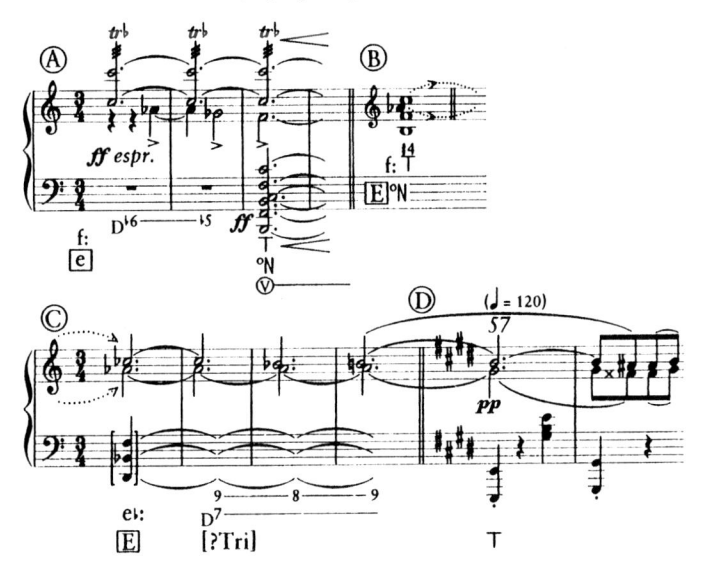

Musical creativity is always akin to investigating and discovering some artistic treasures or other. The peak of the form of the first movement of the Tenth Symphony, its recapitulation, is undoubtedly one of the revelations of a true artist.[16]

Breath of the Symphonist, 7, 9, 14–15, 26–8). He refers to the initial harmony of the recapitulation as 'the crisis-chord' (*ibid.*, 26).

[16] A small curiosity: in a short introduction during the first discussions of the just completed Tenth Symphony (1953) Shostakovich said: 'Again I have been unable to write a real sonata allegro'. Of course the first movement is not an allegro, but it is one of the master's finest sonata forms.

SONATA CYCLES

Shostakovich's sonata cycles reflect the stylistic evolution of his works. In his mature period the typical artistic genres of the classical Beethoven sonata cycle – the Sonata movement, Largo, Scherzo, Finale – comprise the basis of the overall form. But Shostakovich does not write to a fixed pattern. He writes as if he were inventing a new set of movements every time, but mainly selecting them from this traditional range. He also tries to vary slightly the mix of the performers. It is as if he set himself his own First Symphony as his basic model; this is the symphony which shot him immediately into the circle of significant composers of the century. Later, in the period of search for the avant-garde, he composed individualised cycles – the Second and Third Symphonies. Not even the Fourth Symphony was modelled on the Viennese classics.[17]

EXAMPLES OF SHOSTAKOVICH MOVEMENT-CYCLES

Fifth Symphony: I Sonata movement; II Scherzo; III Largo; IV Finale (a large rondo with dramatic development and a concluding apotheosis).
Sixth Symphony: I Sonata largo (typical small rondo); II Witty Scherzo; III Rondo finale.
Seventh Symphony: I Sonata allegro (with a unique idea, the representation of 'war'); II Moderato (original slow Scherzo); III Adagio (compound song form of the ABACABA type); IV Dramatic rondo finale with a concluding apotheosis of 'victory'.
Eighth Symphony: I Tragic sonata adagio; II Sarcastic scherzo; III Toccata (with a trio almost for wind band alone); IV Passacaglia (reaction to the severe pressure of the previous two movements); V Cathartically lucid pastoral rondo finale.

Most of the string quartets (whose value is not inferior to that of the famous symphonies) and the chamber-instrument sonatas are analogous. In Shostakovich the instrumental concerto also echoes the traditional type.

In the polyphonic finales of the Seventh and Eighth Quartets Shostakovich's invention is highly original. The composer's neoclassical orientation shows in the revival of certain baroque forms. Thus, some of his variations on a basso ostinato are remarkable: in the First Violin Concerto, the Sixth Quartet, the Second Piano Trio, in the *entr'acte* before

---

[17] From talking to people close to Shostakovich I know what he said at home about his Fourth Symphony: he wanted to write it without following any known models, writing freely, obeying only the thought which attracted him (report from the second half of the 1960s).

scene 5 of his opera *Katerina Izmaylova* and other compositions. In the Piano Quintet (1940) Shostakovich paid tribute to the baroque tradition with the Prelude and Fugue subcycle in the first two movements. But twenty years later in the Seventh and Eighth Quartets he made an inversion of the sense of this pair: he placed the pair at the end of the cycle and furthermore in reverse order. Thus he got a 'fugue and postlude' subcycle, and both times these are embodied in one finale – the third movement in the Seventh Quartet (with concluding reminiscences) and the fifth movement in the Eighth Quartet (also with a recapitulation-reminiscence of the first movement; as we know, the whole of this quartet consists to a large extent of reminiscences of Shostakovich's other compositions). It is true that in both quartets the movements are played without a break.[18]

EVOLUTION OF FORMS

An examination of the evolution of Shostakovich's musical forms reveals a number of other interesting and sometimes unexpected features. Shostakovich's early period is an era of daring quests, in particular in the instrumental forms of the 1920s and early 1930s.

The composer used avant-garde composition techniques in the Second Symphony (*Dedication to October*, 1927, composed for the tenth anniversary of the Bolshevik revolution), which in form is made up of a symphonic piece and a choral cantata. The symphony consists of a number of descriptive episodes. The first of these, with the rotating sonorous mass of the strings, growing like a snowball, sounds like an image of a huge, disorderly crowd moving on the square. In one of the following episodes (figs. 30–48), in an 'endless' fugato with various themes, the woodwinds and strings, each with their own melody, play as if they were not listening to one another, until finally with the entry of the brass they merge into streams of sonorous masses all overtaking one another (figs. 48–53). Such places anticipate the sonorities of the avant-garde at the Warsaw Autumn.

---

[18] Shostakovich once said that he intended to write twenty-four quartets and that is why there is no key repetition in them. Indications that the quartets are part of a cycle are evident:
(1) Six majors descending by thirds: 1 2 3 4 5 6
  C A F D B♭ G
(2) One minor by itself (tritone to the initial C): f♯ No. 7
(3) Four pairs of 'parallels': 8–9, c–E♭; 10–11, A♭–f; 12–13, D♭–b♭; 14–15, F♯(G♭)–e♭.

One of the daring *chefs d'œuvre* of this sort is the sonorous fugue for just nine untuned percussion alone in the *entr'acte* of the opera *The Nose* (1928, see Ex. 3.16).

Ex. 3.16 Shostakovich, *The Nose*, entr'acte to scene 4

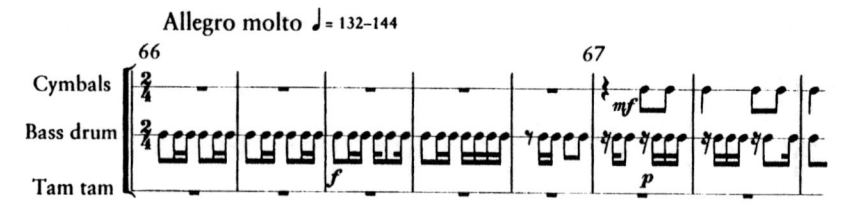

It would seem that to change the scenery in 'absolute darkness' (as in Stravinsky's *Petrushka*) all that is required is the black rattle of the percussion. But in this opera even absurdities are presented with deliberate seriousness.[19] And Shostakovich with complete seriousness, with the utmost tension of artistic fantasy and with great skill, writes his fantastic nine-part fugue. After four entries of the subject there is an intermezzo (just 'as in Bach'). In some intermezzos the five-part stretto-ostinatos form a sharply witty polymetric texture – 5/8 against 3/4. In others 3/4 and 4/4 metres struggle with stretto progressions 13/16, 21/16, 26/16, 31/16, whilst the eight-part polymetric canon-ostinato becomes a solid thunderous screen through whose cadential noise the burning cymbals cut with the subject of the fugue in quadruple augmentation (fig. 93).

Not so provocative, but just as innovatively written, is the 'atonal' linear fugue in No. 10 in this opera, the *entr'acte* to the sixth scene.

The master who created such bold modern fugues completely devoid of neoclassical 'syrup' and schoolboy clichés nevertheless rejected radicalism thereafter and went over to a more balanced and 'respectable' style, although also to a more ordinary polyphony and to a more academic form of fugue.

Some properties of the style of the early Shostakovich which took shape in the avant-garde compositions of the twenties (elements of the technique of twelve-note rows, pointillism) were left to one side, but received a second life in the later period. From 1967 twelve-note rows

---

[19] 'Gogol states all comic events in a serious tone.' D. Shostakovich, 'Pochemu Nos' [Why *The Nose*?], *Rabochiy i teatr* (3/1930), 11.

gradually became a noticeable feature of Shostakovich's technique. However, their role was melodic rather than form-building.[20] Typical examples of twelve-note rows in Shostakovich are in the first movement of the Violin Sonata (1968), in String Quartets No. 12 and No. 13 (1968, 1970) and in Symphony No. 15 (1971). Shostakovich sometimes constructs a polyphonic texture using twelve-note rows (but not on the basis of a series of the dodecaphonic type), for example in the canon from the seventh movement of Symphony No. 14, fig. 91ff. Paradoxically, because of the non-repeatability of twelve-note rows, the aggregation of semitones here seems to be greater than in serial polyphony.

In spite of the remarkable renewal of the expressiveness of his melodic and harmonic language thanks to twelve-note rows, the general principles of Shostakovich's form-conception remained unchanged.

CONCLUSION

'Any musical work is a form of the personal expression of its composer.'[21] The strength of Shostakovich's artistic individuality is extremely great; in the majority of cases we hear the voice of his artistic individuality, or his *intonation*, simply in the way his work sounds. This also applies to the relationship between the structural types of musical forms that he borrowed from the classical/baroque eras and the actual works that he created. The aesthetic principle of 'being old in a new way' gave Shostakovich the opportunity to create non-transient artistic values, investing musical forms of general significance with his 'personal expression'.

---

[20] From Shostakovich's words spoken in a conversation with his former pupil Boris Tishchenko one can deduce that during his own evolutionary process he was moving towards the twelve-note serial method of composition during his last years, but, not reckoning on his having many more years of life left, he presumed that he was not destined to get there.
[21] Shostakovich, cited in Khentova, *Shostakovich: Tridtsatiletiye 1945–1975*, 317.

4

Russian theorists on modality in Shostakovich's music

ELLON D. CARPENTER

Russian music theorists have been focusing on the question of modality in Shostakovich's music since at least the years 1944–5, when the two earliest articles on this topic were written.[1] However, the majority of works on mode in Shostakovich were written between the years 1966 and 1980.[2] The study of mode itself, though, has a much longer history in the development of Russian music theory; mode in fact constitutes one of the most important subjects within that discipline. Thus a brief definition of mode, a history of its development and an introduction to some of the issues in Russian modal theory pertinent to the analysis of Shostakovich's modal language are herein presented as a form of prolegomenon to the discussion of mode in Shostakovich's music.

DEFINITION

In Russian music theory, the concept of mode forms one of the major and most important tenets upon which that theory is based. In its broadest interpretation, the Russian concept of mode has no exact equivalent in

[1] Lev Abramovich Mazel', 'Zametki o muzïkal'nom yazïke Shostakovicha' [Notes on the musical language of Shostakovich], *Dmitriy Shostakovich*, ed. L. V. Danilevich, D. V. Zhitomirsky and G. Sh. Ordzhonikidze (Moscow, 1967), 303–59; rpt. *Etyudï o Shostakoviche* (Moscow, 1986), 33–82.
   Alexander Naumovich Dolzhansky, 'O ladovoy osnove sochineniy Shostakovicha' (About the modal basis of the compositions of Shostakovich), *Sovetskaya Muzïka* (4/1947), 65–74; rpt. *Chertï stilya Shostakovicha* [Traits of the Style of Shostakovich] (Moscow, 1962); and Dolzhansky, *Izbrannïye stat'i* [Selected Articles] (Leningrad, 1973), 37–51.

[2] This group includes works exclusively devoted to mode in Shostakovich's music. Not included in the general discussion here is Dolzhansky's article, 'Aleksandriyskiy pentakhord v muzïke D. Shostakovicha' [The Alexandrian pentachord in the music of D. Shostakovich], in *Dmitriy Shostakovich*, 397–439 (rpt. *Izbrannïye stat'i*, 86–120). This was Dolzhansky's last article before he died in 1966.

western music theory. The western idea of mode – the Greek modes, medieval or church modes, or folk modes, i.e., melodic scale patterns outside the major–minor tonal system – corresponds to just one of the separate elements making up the complex theoretical system that is mode in Russian music theory. According to theorist Yuriy Kholopov, in its widest application mode embraces the idea of the organic coherence of the musical material employed:

> As a whole, mode is revealed in the completeness of the structure enveloping the entire complex making it up – from the sound material through the logical regulating of the separate elements to the crystallisation of the specifically aesthetic systemic relationships of measure, of proportion, of interconformity (in a wide sense – symmetry). Always important also is the individual concretisation of a definite mode in a given work, revealing the richness of its possibilities and regularly expanding into a vast modal construction.[3]

Kholopov identifies three main elements, or subsystems, of mode: (1) scale, or the melodic motif, the primary form of the embodiment of mode (the western idea); (2) function, revealed through the stable and unstable notes in the mode, their relationships and interconnections, resulting in a hierarchy of pitch connections; and (3) intonation (*intonatsiya*), a complex Soviet musico-theoretical idea that represents the manifestation in mode of its emotional, social and historical connections.

HISTORY

This concept of mode developed in Russia over the course of nearly three centuries, paralleling the development of the discipline of non-chant Russian music theory.[4] Sometime in the first half of the seventeenth century, the theorist Ivan Shaydur worked out a system of church modes.[5] In the 1770s collections of folk music began to be published; in the

---

[3] Yuriy Nikolayevich Kholopov, 'Lad' [Mode], *Sovetskaya muzïkal'naya entsiklopediya* [Soviet Music Encyclopedia], iii (Moscow, 1976), col. 131.

[4] The history of non-chant Russian music theory begins with Nikolay Diletsky, *Ideya grammatiki musikiyskoy* [The Idea of Musical Grammar] ([Moscow], 1679). This work exists in manuscript form; it was recently translated (into Russian from Church Slavonic) and published as vol. 7 of *Pamyatniki russkogo muzïkal'nogo iskusstva* [Monuments of Russian Musical Art], trans. and ed. V. Protopopov (Moscow, 1979).

[5] Ivan Shaydur was a Russian singer and music theorist of the first half of the seventeenth century. See Maxim Viktorovich Brazhnikov, *Drevnerusskaya teoriya muzïki. Po rukopisnïm materialam XV–XVIII vv.* [The Old-Russian Theory of Music. From Manuscript Materials of 15th–18th cc.] (Leningrad, 1972).

preface to his 1790 collection, Nikolay L'vov pointed out the differences of folk modes from the European tonal system.[6] In the 1830s, the significance of folk music and its modal system began to be more widely recognised. In 1830, for example, the Russian term for mode (*lad*) was introduced.[7] In 1836, Glinka successfully merged the modal flavour of folk music with the forms of serious art music in *A Life for the Tsar*. Prince Vladimir Odoyevsky, the 'founder of Russian musicology' who first recognised Glinka's importance for Russian music, acknowledged the significance of Glinka's use of folk-inspired melodies and harmonies, and promoted both indigenous folk music and chant as serious subjects for research.[8] His own lengthy theoretical study of this music revealed to him its unique diatonic modal foundation, unrelated to contemporary western tonal music and its theory, on which so many transcribers of folk music relied.[9] Others followed Odoyevsky's lead, including the critic Alexander Serov and Pyotr Sokal'sky, both of whom developed theories based on the quartal-quintal foundation – i.e., supported by the notes making up those intervals within the octave – of folk music, as well as Alexander Famintsïn and Yuliy Mel'gunov.[10]

Yet by the turn of the century, although mode in its scalar embodiment had become an important component of the developing theory of

[6] Nikolay Alexandrovich L'vov, *Sobraniye russkikh narodnïkh pesen s ikh golosami. Na muzïku polozhi Ivan Prach* [A Collection of Russian Folk Songs with their Voices. Put to Music by Ivan Prach] (Moscow, 1790). Recent translation: *A Collection of Russian Folk Songs by Nikolai Lvov and Ivan Prach*, ed. Malcolm Hamrick Brown (Ann Arbor, 1987). Based on the 1806 edition, this translation contains an introductory essay and detailed descriptive commentary by Margarita Mazo.

Vasiliy Fedorovich Trutovsky, *Sobraniye russkikh prostïkh pesen s notami* (Collection of Russian Simple Songs with Notes), 4 vols. (St Petersburg, 1776–95). All four volumes were reissued in a new edition, edited by V. Belyayev, in Moscow, 1953.

[7] Johann Leopold Fuchs, *Prakticheskoye rukovodstvo k sochineniyu muzïki* [A Practical Guide to the Composition of Music], trans. M. D. Rezvoy (St Petersburg, 1830).

[8] Prince Vladimir Fedorovich Odoyevsky, 'Pis'mo k lyubitelyu muzïki ob opere g. Glinki: Ivan Susanin' [A letter to lovers of music about the opera of Mr. Glinka: Ivan Susanin], *Severnaya pchela* [Northern Bee], no. 280 (7 December 1836), and nos. 287 and 288 (15 and 16 December 1836); rpt. *Muzïkal'no-literaturnoye naslediye* (Musical-Literary Legacy), ed. G. Bernandt (Moscow, 1956), 118–26.

[9] Prince Vladimir Fedorovich Odoyevsky, *Muzïkal'naya gramota* [Musical Grammar] (Moscow, 1868); rpt. *Muzïkal'no-literaturnoye naslediye*, 346–69.

[10] Alexander Nikolayevich Serov, 'Russkaya narodnaya pesnya kak predmet nauki' [Russian folk song as a subject of science], *Muzïkal'nïy sezon* [The Musical Season], no. 18 (1868), no. 6 (1870) and no. 13 (1871); rpt. *Izbrannïye stat'i* (Selected Articles), i (Moscow, 1952), 81–108.

Pyotr Petrovich Sokal'sky, *Russkaya narodnaya muzïka, velikorusskaya i malorusskaya v eyo stroyenii melodicheskom i ritmicheskom i otlichiya eyo ot osnov sovremennoy*

folk song, an independent theory of mode still did not exist, either in the study of folk music or in the general sphere of music theory, which was still mired in western-style pedagogical theory.[11] However, the early years of the twentieth century witnessed changes in both directions. In 1908, the theorist Boleslav Yavorsky, in his major work *The Structure of Musical Speech*, established mode as an independent and important theoretical topic, and, along with his teacher Sergey Taneyev, the great contrapuntist, pointed the way to the eventual coming-of-age of Russian music theory in the 1920s.[12] To Yavorsky are traced numerous contemporary Russian ideas about mode: (1) recognition of the concepts of stability and instability and their distinction from the twin concepts of consonance and dissonance, which may be understood mathematically, acoustically or aesthetically; (2) the resulting gravitational tendency of an unstable note or interval to resolve to a stable note or interval (a notion akin to the modern western understanding of consonance and dissonance but with far greater implications); (3) the recognition of pitch systems outside the bounds of major and minor as special modes; (4) the separation of the idea of mode from that of tonality, the latter identified with a specific pitch level ('modaltonality' (*ladotonal'nost*) designates the

    garmonicheskoy muziki [Russian Folk Music, Great Russian and Little Russian in its Melodic and Rhythmic Construction and Distinctions of it from the Bases of Contemporary Harmonic Music] (Kharkov, 1888).
    Alexander Sergeyevich Famintsïn, *Drevnyaya indo-kitayskaya gamma v Azii i Evrope s osobennïm ukazaniyem na eyo proyavlenniya v russkikh narodnïkh napevakh. Muzk.-etnograficheskiy etyud* [The Ancient Indo-Chinese Scale in Asia and Europe with Particular Directions on its Manifestation in Russian Folk Songs. A Musical Ethnographic Work] (St Petersburg, 1889).
    Yuliy Nikolayevich Mel'gunov, *Russkiye narodnïye pesni neposredstvenno s golosov naroda zapisannïye i s ob'yasneniyami izdannïye* [Russian Folk Songs, with Voices of the Folk Directly Written down and Published with Explanations], 2 vols. (Moscow, 1879–85).

[11] Music theory in nineteenth-century Russia was primarily based on western pedagogical theory. Foreign pedagogues living in Russia and translations of foreign theory texts dominated the field until the founding of the conservatories began in 1861. Most of the native Russian theory books from the nineteenth century are textbooks based on western traditions, such as those by Tchaikovsky (1871) and Rimsky-Korsakov (1886). See Ellon D. Carpenter, 'Russian music theory: a conspectus', in *Russian Theoretical Thought in Music*, ed. Gordon D. McQuere (Ann Arbor, 1983), 1–81; and Carpenter, 'The theory of music in Russia and the Soviet Union, ca. 1650–1950' (diss., University of Pennsylvania, 1988).

[12] Boleslav Leopol'dovich Yavorsky, *Stroyeniye muzïkal'noy rechi* [The Structure of Musical Speech] (Moscow, 1908); Sergey Ivanovich Taneyev, *Podvizhnïy kontrapunkt strogogo stilya* [Movable Counterpoint in the Strict Style] (Moscow, 1909).

placement of a mode on a specific pitch level); and (5) the concept of intonation as referring to significant modal-melodic unfoldings.[13]

The Soviet theorists Yuriy Tyulin and Boris Asaf'yev developed several of Yavorsky's key concepts. Asaf'yev broadened Yavorsky's idea of intonation to embrace a wide range of musical meanings, such as those associated with aesthetics, sociology and history.[14] Mode reflects these meanings through their embodiment in the organisational characteristics of music – a system of intervals and scales – of a given epoch. Asaf'yev viewed mode as a system, always and consistently being found in a state of formation, of renewal. Mode becomes not just a general element of music, but a specific principle of artistic thought.

Tyulin based his important *Doctrine of Harmony* on two ideas derived from Yavorsky: mode as the primary foundation of musical thought, and the generation of basic melodic and harmonic connections by their respective modal functions.[15] Tyulin demonstrated melodic gravitation and function through the secundal connection of notes, and harmonic gravitation and function through the quartal-quintal connection of notes.[16] Central to his contribution to the theory of mode remains his theory of variable functions, or the opposition of a modal function to the basic modal direction within a mode (such as a dominant taking over the function of tonic within a given mode).

Due to emphasis by Tyulin and others during the 1920s and 1930s in both art and folk music, by the 1940s the theory of mode held an important place in Soviet music theory.[17] In the post-Stalin era, interest in mode and its theory developed further owing to the continuing enrichment and transformation of modal language by contemporary

---

[13] See Gordon D. McQuere, 'The theories of Boleslav Yavorsky', in *Russian Theoretical Thought in Music*, 109–64.

[14] Boris Vladimirovich Asaf'yev, *Muzïkal'naya forma kak protsess* [Musical Form as a Process], 2 vols. (Moscow, 1930–47).

[15] Yuriy Nikolayevich Tyulin, *Ucheniye o garmonii* [The Doctrine of Harmony] (Moscow, 1937).

[16] Function in its harmonic aspect had already entered Soviet music theory through the work of Georgiy L'vovich Catoire, *Teoreticheskiy kurs garmonii* [A Theoretical Course of Harmony], 2 vols. (Moscow, 1924–5).

[17] Alexander Dmitriyevich Kastal'sky, *Osobennosti narodnorusskoy muzïkal'noy sistemï* [Characteristics of the Russian Folk Musical System] (Moscow-Petrograd, 1923); Viktor Mikhailovich Belyayev and Viktor Alexandrovich Uspensky, *Turkmenskaya muzïka* [Turkmen Music] (Moscow, 1928); Nikolay Alexandrovich Garbuzov, *Teoriya mnogoosnovnosti ladov i sozvuchiy* [The Theory of Multi-based Modes and Chords], 2 vols. (Moscow, 1928–32).

composers and the attendant question of the analysis of their music, the expansion of knowledge in the sphere of folk music, and composers' attention to polyphony and its melodic-modal connections.[18] Khristofor Stepanovich Kushnaryov's interpretation of melodic modal function, in his significant work from this era, *Questions of the History and Theory of Armenian Monodic Music*, has served as a model for theorists investigating mode in the music of Shostakovich and others.[19]

THE CONCEPT OF DIATONICISM

Using the modal subsystems of scale and function, theorists have developed diverse approaches to the classification and analysis of mode. Acknowledging the complexities of modal classification, Kholopov limits his grouping to a basic five-tiered hierarchy based on the intervallic, scalar structure of mode: (1) extramelodicism (indefinite pitch); (2) anhemitonicism (no half steps); (3) diatonicism (no successive half steps); (4) chromaticism (successive half steps); and (5) microchromaticism (microtones).[20] But because so much music – particularly of the twentieth century – falls somewhere between the categories of strict diatonicism and chromaticism – that is, its seemingly chromatic musical language often is better explained in terms of functional diatonicism – theorists have sought to expand the definition of diatonicism, through either less strict intervallic criteria or greater emphasis on functional considerations.

This expansion of the concept of diatonicism has led to the development of a hierarchy of diatonic modes, which in its broadest interpretation encompasses at least six categories: (1) natural diatonicism; (2) altered diatonicism; (3) artificial diatonicism; (4) hemitonicism; (5) polydiatonicism; and (6) twelve-degree diatonicism. (See Table 4.1. These categories have been culled from the various sources mentioned in the following discussion; unfortunately, space does not permit full explanations of all the concepts introduced.) Theorists have recognised to some extent aspects of each of these modal categories in Shostakovich's music. This hierarchy of diatonic modes, for most Russian theorists, is based on a

---

[18] A conference on mode was held in 1965, with the proceedings published as *Problemï lada* [Problems of Mode], ed. K. Yuzhak (Moscow, 1972).
[19] Khristofor Stepanovich Kushnaryov, *Voprosï istorii i teorii Armyanskoy monodicheskoy muzïki* [Questions of the History and Theory of Armenian Monodic Music] (Leningrad, 1958).
[20] Kholopov, 'Lad', cols. 137–8.

Table 4.1 Modal categories of expanded diatonicism

1 Natural (Pure) diatonicism	2 Altered diatonicism	3 Artificial diatonicism
Tyulin: Terrian foundation no divided M2; P4 correlations; seven notes in octave; one of each interval from basic note (seven-degree limit), M3/m3, P5. Sokhor: Possible non-tertian foundation Heptatonic; M2/m2; no split M2.	Tyulin: Terrian foundation divided/split M2; P4 correlations; seven-nine notes in octave; one of each interval from basic note (seven-degree limit), M3/m3, P5. Sokhor: Possible non-tertian foundation (1) Heptatonic; combinations or variants of pure modes. (2) 'Hyper-diatonic' or 'Augmented' modes; 1–2 intervals of A2. Dolzhansky: 'Lowered' modes. Burda, Adam, Skrebkov: Displaced tonic. Sereda: Conditional/altered diatonicism = 'multifaceted'.	no hierarchy of degrees; often symmetrical or periodic; no tertian foundation.

4 Hemitonicism (Sokhor)	5 Polydiatonicism (Kon)	6 Dodecatonicism (Sokhor)
basic modal quality; seven–twelve degrees; hierarchy of degrees.	Polymodes (Kholopov)* Bimode (Burda)* Diachromaticism (Karklin) Heterotonicism (Sokhor) combined pure or altered modes with same tonic.	Twelve-degree Diatonicism each degree carries own function; no set hierarchy of degrees.

Note: *classified outside diatonicism. *Key to interval designations:* M: major; m: minor; P: perfect; A: augmented. 2: second, etc.

Pythagorean-derived quartal-quintal foundation, which is justified both acoustically and ethnomusicologically. Such a view assumes a hierarchy of note function, in which all notes in the mode may be related to this foundation. Yet additional intervallic or functional considerations, particularly at the highest hierarchical levels, may alter this view.

Tyulin, although he considers a modal hierarchy to be 'one of the basic characteristics of our musical thought', conservatively limits diatonicism to only the first two categories.[21] The 'natural' ('pure') modes form the basis from which the 'altered' modes are derived. In his view, these categories share not only a quartal-quintal foundation, but a tertian one as well (major or minor triad), made up of the stable, unalterable degrees of the modes. Altering the other, unstable degrees creates an altered mode with either different whole- and half-step patterns, often forming augmented intervals, or consecutive half steps between the stable degrees.

Tyulin classifies altered modes first by size. Eight-note modes form the largest group (78), followed by seven-note (48) and nine-note (22) modes, 148 in all. Diatonic modes with more than nine notes cannot be formed using his methods. He then classifies modes by the means of their formation, or, if only one means is used for a particular group, by the number of alterations. Of the five different methods of modal formation (or derivation) identified by Russian theorists either generally or specifically for Shostakovich's music and defined in Table 4.2, Tyulin recognises three but develops only two. Eight- and nine-note modes are formed from either modal (voice-leading) alterations (method Ib) or modal modulation (method II); seven-note modes are formed only from modal (harmonic) alterations (method Ia).

For Tyulin, these natural and altered modes signify the 'universality of diatonicism in folk music', which is opposed to 'artificial constructions of any sort'.[22] Although he places such 'artificial constructions' as the octatonic scale – which lacks both a pure diatonic foundation and all the requirements of chromaticism – in a separate category between altered diatonicism and chromaticism, other theorists include them under expanded diatonicism (category 3 in Table 4.1).[23] Many theorists also view

---

[21] Yuriy Nikolayevich Tyulin, *Natural'nïye i alteratsionnïye ladi* [The Natural and Altered Modes] (Moscow, 1971), 10.
[22] Tyulin, *Ucheniye o garmonii*, 81.
[23] One Soviet theorist attempted to trace the historical evolution of this scale using portions of variants and mixtures of major and minor modes, and thus give to this scale

Table 4.2 *Methods of modal formation or derivation*

(I) Modal alterations (inner-modal): Tyulin
   (a) Harmonic (bidirectional gravitation forming split degrees, i.e., functional bifurcation of one degree into two).
   (b) Voice-leading (filling-in of augmented second).

(II) Modal modulation (extra-modal):
   Tyulin: From nearly related tonalities outside the mode (combining parallel modes (modes with the same tonic, i.e., A major and A minor), which creates chromatic variants of degrees).
   Mazel': Attracting other lowered degrees to the original ones.
   Adam: 'Attraction' of a new mode to the old tonal centre; or combined with tonal modulation.
   Skrebkov: Interpenetration of parallel modes (including not only modes with shared tonic, but also those with either shared third or fifth); combined with degree alterations.
   Bobrovsky: Overlaps with tonal modulation.
   Burda: Bimode.

(III) Melodic alterations (extra-modal):
   Tyulin: Melodic ornaments or non-functional chord progressions or sequences.
   Mazel': Absorption of complex harmonic progressions.

(IV) Degree alteration:
   Dolzhansky: Lowered degrees.
   Mazel': Lowered degrees.
   Skrebkov: Combined with modal modulation.

(V) Tonal modulation (inner-modal) (theory of variable function):
   Adam: Tonic displaced to dominant ('Dominant' mode), mediant, or lowered submediant; or combined with modal modulation.
   Skrebkov: Same.
   Bobrovsky: Modal variability (simultaneous): two tonalities using the same scale.
   Passing variability (consecutive): tonality of lower order.
   Burda: Tonic displaced to seventh degree.

---

a semblance of a diatonic and historical foundation, but his argument is unconvincing. See I. A. Tyut'manov, 'Predposïlki obrazovaniya umen'shennogo minoro-mazhora v muzïkal'noy literature i ego teoreticheskaya kharakteristika' [Preconditions of the formation of the diminished major–minor in musical literature and its theoretical characteristics], in *Nauchno-metodicheskiye zapiski* [Scientific-Methodological Notes], ii (Saratov, 1959), 123–67. For a more realistic interpretation, see Yuzef Kon, 'Ob iskusstvennïkh ladakh' [About artificial modes], in *Problemï lada*, 99–112.

altered modes more liberally; Arnol'd Sokhor, for example, interprets 'heptatonic' diatonicism in a broader fashion than Tyulin, allowing tritones in place of perfect fifths (see Table 4.1).[24]

To accommodate still other types of modes and modal constructions, theorists have expanded the concept of diatonicism to the point where its intervallic aspect has been almost totally submerged by the property of function, the definite modal significance of each note.[25] Thus diatonicism may be understood not only according to its intervallic construction, but, as Sokhor put it, 'also as a system of musical sounds, each of which appears as an independent degree of the mode, independent from the intervallic structure of the scale formed by it'.[26] A. A. Drukt has labelled these two approaches to diatonicism the 'structural' approach, and the 'qualitative functional' approach.[27] Diatonicism in the latter sense has therefore been elevated from a mere category of intervallic structure to the level of a definite quality of mode, defining the principles of its functional organisation, which is determined by the significance of each note within the modal context.

[24] Arnol'd Naumovich Sokhor, 'O prirode i virazitel'nïkh vozmozhnostyakh diatoniki' [On the nature and expressive possibilities of diatonicism], in *Voprosï teorii i estetiki muziki*, iv (Leningrad-Moscow, 1965), 160–99. Sokhor constructs altered modes from a core of quintal links with some altered substitutions from non-adjacent links. His intervallic view of heptatonicism (seven-degree modes) includes pure diatonicism (whole and half steps, no split major seconds), 'hyperdiatonic' or 'augmented' diatonic modes (with one or two augmented second intervals) and non-octave modes (found in folk music). His three-tiered interpretation of pure diatonicism, less strict than Tyulin's, allows altered fifth degrees in the second and third tiers, which destroys Tyulin's diatonic triadic foundation. Sokhor interprets these modes as combinations or variants of natural modes; only six of them (out of fourteen) may be found in Tyulin's collection. In still another interpretation, A. Vyantskus divides his twelve modal categories, determined by size and intervallic content and all with a quartal-quintal foundation, into two large groups. Simple diatonic modes, with seven or fewer pitches, are essentially limited to the natural modes. Complex diatonic modes, with up to thirteen pitches, are interpreted as natural modes with altered variants, borrowing from Tyulin, or as polymodal, containing two simple modes, similar to Kholopov's polymodal chromaticism. See A. Vyantskus, 'Ladovïye formatsii. Poliladovost'' i politonal'nost''' [Modal formations. Polymodality and polytonality], in *Problemï muzïkal'noy nauki*, ii (Moscow, 1973), 30–47.

[25] Although formed from modal modulation, such modes as the ten-note mononomal major–minor mode (the combination of major and its parallel minor) and the eleven-note monotertian mode (the combination of one major and one minor mode, adjacent at the half step and sharing the same third degree) fall into a different category of expanded diatonicism, which is interpreted more according to function. The constituent notes in these modes each function as independent degrees, unlike Tyulin's altered modes in which the seven-degree diatonic limit is maintained.

[26] Sokhor, 'O prirode', 262.

[27] A. A. Drukt, 'Narodnaya diatonika i eyo otrazheniye v muzïke russkikh kompozitorov-

This qualitative functional approach to diatonicism, reflected in the categories 4 to 6 of Table 4.1, lies at the basis of numerous analyses by Russian theorists of the music of both Prokofiev and Shostakovich. They have coined a variety of terms to represent this quality of diatonicism within a twelve-note scale, such as these used for Prokofiev's modal language: 'expanded diatonicism', 'twelve-degree diatonic mode', 'synthetic diatonicism', 'natural chromatic scale with independent degrees', 'original chromatic scale having twelve sounds', 'chromatic tonal system', 'chromatic tonality', 'full chromatic system', etc. All these terms refer generally to the same basic phenomenon: a mode consisting of up to twelve different degrees, each independent in function. Thus twelve-degree diatonicism becomes a totality of basic degrees, any one of which could become tonic, that is, they are equal from the point of view of their potential modal function. Sokhor labelled this most complex type of expanded diatonicism 'dodecatonicism'; it constitutes category 6 in Table 4.1. The independent degrees of a mode from this category may enter into local systems or into a common system of stable and unstable notes connected by mutual gravities. To indicate such independence, Sokhor proposes changes in pitch nomenclature to avoid any hint of alteration or chromaticism.

Kholopov distinguishes this type of twelve-degree diatonicism from twelve-degree polymodalism, the scale for which may contain many different modes but is, in his view, neither diatonic nor chromatic.[28] Other theorists group this type under diatonicism – placed thus as category 5 in Table 4.1 – and have devised various terms for it: 'polydiatonicism' (Yuzef Kon) refers to the consecutive portrayal of normal seven-degree diatonicism in either expanded or chromatic systems; a 'diachromatic system' (Lyudvig Karklin) reflects both the merging of diatonicism and chromaticism and the system's polymodal nature; and 'heterotonicism' (Sokhor) indicates expanded modal understanding, characterised by the combination of various modal scales or their fragments, operating on local or temporary tonics.[29] Like Kholopov, V. V. Burda, who recognises

kuchkistov' [Folk diatonicism and its reflection in the music of the Russian composers-handful], in *Voprosï teorii i istorii muzïki* [Questions of the Theory and History of Music] (Minsk, 1976), 87.

[28] Kholopov, 'Lad', cols. 136–7.

[29] Yuzef Kon, 'K voprosu o variantnosti ladov' [On the question of the quality of variation of modes], in *Sovremennïye voprosï muzïkoznaniya* [Contemporary Questions of Musicology], ed. Yelena Orlova (Moscow, 1976), 259; Lyudvig Karklin, 'Ladogarmonicheskoye stroeniye proizvedeniy N. Ya. Myaskovskogo' [The modal-harmonic structure of the works of N. Y. Myaskovsky] (diss., Leningrad Conservatory, 1968). Within his somewhat limited application of his approach to the music of Myaskovsky,

polymodal constructions in Shostakovich's music, considers this category to be 'extradiatonic', outside the category of diatonicism. Category 4, 'hemitonicism' (Sokhor), consists of modes of up to twelve degrees that maintain a basic functional understanding or hierarchy among the degrees.

If function has replaced intervallic patterning as the main criterion for expanded diatonicism, how, then, do Russian theorists define modal function? Tatyana Bershadskaya has developed a broad approach to the classification and understanding of expanded diatonic modes incorporating a wide range of modal functional characteristics.[30] Similar approaches have been applied to Shostakovich's music (Sereda and Fedosova, see below).

Bershadskaya initially identifies modes according to their carriers of function – notes in melodic modes, chords in harmonic modes and a combination for mixed modes. Since Shostakovich's modes are primarily melodic, the discussion here concentrates on that category. In all modes, these carriers of function are organised into scales, which provide the basis for the unfolding of functional relationships, or differentiation. Since the variety of the functional carriers of melodic modes – their characteristic individual tonal functions – precludes classification, they are classified by the two modal subsystems of scale and functional relationships (Fig. 4.1). Their scales are defined by mood, scope and intervallic structure, which is either anhemitonic (no half steps) or hemitonic (with half steps), the latter further divided according to the presence or absence of diminished or augmented intervals from the tonic.[31]

The most general functional relationship between the notes of a mode is the correlation between stability and instability, 'the smallest cell serving as the constructive material of functionality in music'.[32] The stable note, which functions as the centre of gravity, is non-directional, monosignificant

Karklin does expand the traditional means of chordal designation and functional connections; Sokhor, 'O prirode', 174–5.

[30] Tatyana Bershadskaya, 'Printsipï ladovoy klassifikatsii' [Principles of modal classification], *Sovetskaya Muzïka* (8/1971), 126–30. Bershadskaya's diatonic modes are characterised by functional independence of modal degrees with no limitation on the number or type of notes or intervals.

[31] Under hemitonic scales, she originally had designated the categories of diatonicism and chromaticism, but, reflecting her functional approach to diatonicism, has since replaced them with categories representing the types of intervals formed with tonic: the presence or absence of diminished or augmented intervals. See Tatyana Bershadskaya, *Lektsii po garmonii* [Lectures on Harmony], 2nd edn (Leningrad, 1985), 87–8.

[32] A. Yusfin, 'O funktsional'noy organizatsii v narodnoy muzïke' [About functional organisation in folk music], *Sovetskaya Muzïka* (3/1973), 87.

Figure 4.1. Melodic modes: structure (derived from Bershadskaya, 'Printsipï ladovoy klassifikatsii' (1971) and *Lektsii po garmonii* (1985)).

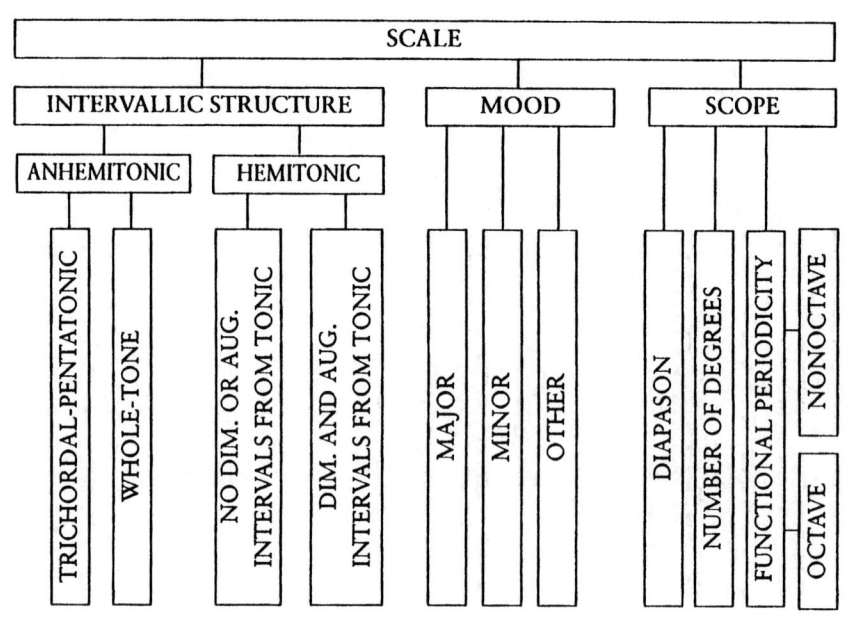

```
                                    SCALE
          ┌──────────────────────────┼──────────────────────┐
   INTERVALLIC STRUCTURE            MOOD                   SCOPE
    ┌───────────┴───────────┐   ┌────┼────┐      ┌──────────┼──────────┐
 ANHEMITONIC           HEMITONIC MAJOR MINOR OTHER DIAPASON  NUMBER   FUNCTIONAL  NONOCTAVE
 ┌─────┬─────┐        ┌────┬────┐                          OF DEGREES PERIODICITY
 TRICHORDAL- WHOLE-  NO DIM.  DIM. AND AUG.                                      OCTAVE
 PENTATONIC  TONE    OR AUG.  INTERVALS
                     INTERVALS FROM TONIC
                     FROM TONIC
```

and concentrated in only one point. In clear contrast, instability carries the function of motion, of dynamics. It is multi-significant, may appear in very different quality and number, and is directed towards the centre, the stable note, from different points. These unstable modal elements, unequal in their functional significance, require differentiation. Modes with strong functional differentiations are 'centralised', while those with less strong functional differentiations are 'weakly centralised' (Fig. 4.2).

The most centralised modes constitute a subcategory of modal type also called 'centralised', the most highly developed, organised and frequently occurring type.[33] This type exhibits a hierarchy of four differentiated functions. A central, basic support forms the stable centre of gravity. An 'opposing' or 'secondary support' carries the function of concentrated instabilities. These secondary supports, also called 'local'

---

[33] Four representative types of melodic organisation have been identified by A. A. Drukt in 'O tipakh ladomelodicheskoy funktsional'nosti v melodike kuchkistov' [On the types of modal melodic functionality in the melodies of the Handful], *Sovetskaya Muzïka* (1/1978), 43–7. I have added these types – 'centralised', 'balanced-stable', 'ostinato' and 'tonally changed' – to Bershadskaya's diagram as modal subcategories, thereby creating the composite shown in Figure 4.2.

Figure 4.2. Melodic modes: function (a combination and expansion of Bershadskaya, 'Printsipï ladovoy klassifikatsii' (1971), and Drukt, 'O tipakh ladomelodicheskoy funktsional'nosti' (1978)).

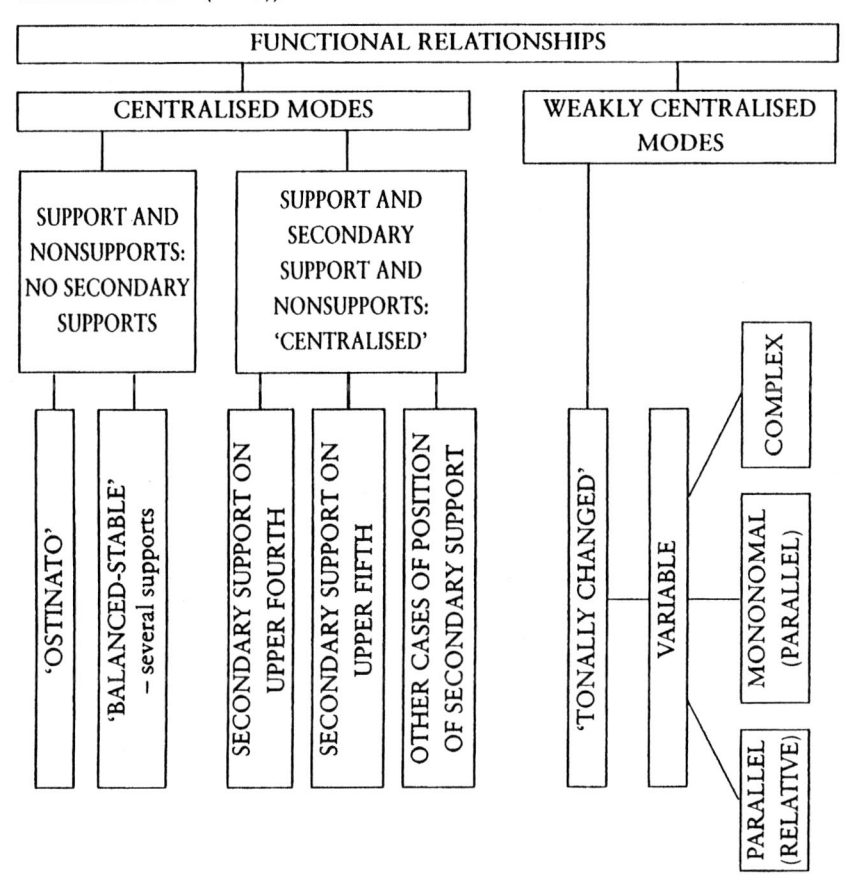

```
                        FUNCTIONAL RELATIONSHIPS
                    ┌──────────────────┴──────────────────┐
              CENTRALISED MODES                  WEAKLY CENTRALISED
                                                       MODES
        ┌──────────────┬──────────────┐
    SUPPORT AND      SUPPORT AND
    NONSUPPORTS:     SECONDARY
    NO SECONDARY     SUPPORT AND
    SUPPORTS         NONSUPPORTS:
                     'CENTRALISED'
```

- 'OSTINATO'
- 'BALANCED-STABLE' – several supports
- SECONDARY SUPPORT ON UPPER FOURTH
- SECONDARY SUPPORT ON UPPER FIFTH
- OTHER CASES OF POSITION OF SECONDARY SUPPORT
- 'TONALLY CHANGED'
- VARIABLE
  - COMPLEX
  - MONONOMAL (PARALLEL)
  - PARALLEL (RELATIVE)

or 'half' supports, while preserving their dynamic gravity towards and functional aspiration to move to the support note, are at the same time capable of concentrating around themselves the motion of other unstable notes, thus opposing the support note. Regarding the significance of these secondary supports, Bershadskaya states, 'Their intervallic position in relation to the stable note mainly defines the essence of mode no less significantly than mood'.[34] Further, 'the instability of these notes in the mode creates the dynamics of modal relationships'.[35] A. A. Drukt points

[34] Bershadskaya, 'Printsipï ladovoy klassifikatsii', 128–9.
[35] Tatyana Bershadskaya, 'K voprosu ob ustoychivosti i neustoychivosti v ladakh russkoy narodnoy pesni', in *Problemï lada*, 186.

out that these secondary supports, pulling to themselves adjoining non-supporting unstable notes, and the stable note together form the basic contour of the modal structure, its 'backbone'.[36] He expands upon Bershadskaya's approach, identifying the remaining unstable notes in a mode as either 'filling-in' (*zapolnyayushchiy*) notes, passive modal elements that fill in the distance between the main and opposing support, aspiring to either one of them ('dispersed instability') or 'expanding' (*rasshiryayushchiy*) notes, additions to the basic modal structure that reinforce or intensify the functional significance of the main or opposing support through their stepwise proximity to these notes ('supplementary activising instability').[37]

Other centralised modal types lack secondary supports. The 'ostinato' type contains one central support, with the remaining notes functionally non-differentiated; the 'balanced-stable' type contains several supports, each equal in functional significance to the others and constituting a sphere of stability balanced by a sphere of instability created by the non-differentiated non-supporting notes. The one type of weakly centralised mode, the 'tonally changeable' type, contains support notes that shift the supporting function from one note to another. Theorists have applied the specific melodic modal functions described – but not the specific type of modal construction, although that would be possible – to the analysis of Shostakovich's music, as we shall see.

MODALITY IN SHOSTAKOVICH'S MUSIC

Russian theorists investigating mode specifically in Shostakovich's music generally agree that his modes are linear and melodic, diatonically based, and varied, representing different diatonic categories and subcategories. And they accept Tyulin's notions of a modal hierarchy, diatonicism's quartal-quintal foundation (but not always the primacy of tertian chords) and variable function. They often disagree, however, on the relative significance of the scalar and functional aspects, the extent of diatonicism or chromaticism, the origin and formation of the 'new' modes, the expression of melodic function, and the existence and interpretation of bimodal, polymodal or polytonal structures. Their approaches may be broadly grouped into three categories: (1) an intervallic, scalar, 'structural' unimodal approach, in which all notes of a

---

[36] Drukt, 'O tipakh ladomelodicheskoy funktsional'nosti v melodike kuchkistov', 45.
[37] *Ibid.*

given melody are analysed as one mode, usually altered (the earliest approach: Dolzhansky and Mazel'); (2) an intervallic, pre-functional but still largely 'structural' approach that is either multi-tonal, in which all notes of a given melody are analysed as one mode with variable tonic functions, the change of which creates essentially a new mode, either consecutively or simultaneously (Adam, Skrebkov, Bobrovsky and Burda), or multi-modal, in which melodic notes are analysed as two simultaneous modes with one tonic (Burda); and (3) a 'qualitatively functional' approach in which melodic notes are analysed only according to modal function, going far beyond the earliest 'structural' approach (the most recent: Sereda and Fedosova).

All altered or derived modes produced from the first two approaches are shown in Example 4.1*a*. As with Tyulin, the modes contain seven to nine notes. Two-thirds of these modes correspond to an altered mode of Tyulin's,

Ex. 4.1(a) Various scalar systems and derivations

(b) Adam's method of modal derivation

and are so identified. Those that do not correspond lack either a perfect fifth, a leading note (in the eight- or nine-note modes), or a particular scale degree of the mode. In two cases the same mode (one seven-note and one nine-note mode) was derived independently by two or more theorists working separately with different methods. In several respects, all the modes are quite similar. If divided into tetrachords, either overlapping (seven-note), adjacent (eight-note) or separated by one note (nine-note), all modes contain at least one tetrachord – upper or lower – encompassing a diminished fourth. It most commonly occurs with the intervallic pattern 1 2 1 on the lower tetrachord, B–C–D–E♭ (six modes); its variant 2 1 1 (B–C♯–D–E♭) occurs almost as frequently (five modes). The same pattern 1 2 1 also occurs on the upper tetrachord, F♯–G–A–B♭ (four modes); a different variant 1 1 2 (F♯–G–A♭–B♭) occurs twice. The same pattern (1 2 1) in both tetrachords occurs only twice – Dolzhansky's double-lowered Phrygian and Adam's mediant-derived mode (shared by Burda and Dolzhansky). This tetrachord encompassing a diminished fourth is significant for Shostakovich's music, and both Sereda and Fedosova devote special attention to Shostakovich's use of it.

A. N. DOLZHANSKY AND L. A. MAZEL'

Alexander Naumovich Dolzhansky 'pioneered' the study of mode in Shostakovich's music, being the first to formulate and publish a definite theory of modal formation and relations for Shostakovich's music.[38] He discusses the modes – their formation, structure, distinctive features and component elements – and their application, including their inter-relationships and role in large forms. Concentrating on melodic modes formed from 'stepwise melodic gravitation' (i.e., medieval and folk modes) Dolzhansky illustrates Shostakovich's application not only of the medieval modes, in pieces in which single themes 'modulate' from one mode to another (Tyulin's theory of variable function), but also of 'new' modes derived from these 'old' modes and therefore based – although he does not express it as such – on a diatonic foundation.[39]

[38] Alexander Naumovich Dolzhansky (1908–66), a professor at the Leningrad Conservatory (1937–48; 1954–66), based this article on his study of then-recent works of Shostakovich from the years 1937–42 – the Fifth, Sixth and Seventh Symphonies, the Quintet and the Second Piano Sonata, as well as the opera *Ledi Makbet* (*Katerina Izmaylova*) from 1932. In a footnote to the republication of this article in *Izbrannïye stat'i* (p. 37), Dolzhansky later denied changing his opinion as expressed in this article on the basis of Shostakovich's subsequent works.

[39] Dolzhansky, 'O ladovoy osnove sochineniy Shostakovicha', *Izbrannïye stat'i*, 37. Other

Dolzhansky derives these new modes, because of their minor quality and altered, usually lowered, degrees, from two of the most 'lowered' minor diatonic modes, Phrygian and Aeolian: 'the lowered Phrygian mode' (lowered fourth degree), 'the double-lowered Phrygian mode' (lowered fourth and eighth degrees), and 'the double-lowered Aeolian mode' (lowered fourth and eighth degrees), with its variant, 'the Aeolian double-lowered melodic mode' (also with the lowered fifth degree, filling in the augmented second) (see Ex. 4.1 and also Ex. 4.6, the latter illustrating the lowered Phrygian mode). He explains this last mode as combining characteristics of several modal varieties, similar to the combined minor or the major–minor system; in this sense it could be classified as 'polymodal' (category 5 in Table 4.1).[40] Dolzhansky also reveals new chords created from these modes, and discusses their treatments and resolutions.[41]

A fifth 'maximally-lowered' mode, a compressed mode consisting of all diminished intervals in relation to the tonic, is theoretically possible (Ex. 4.1a).[42] Shostakovich never used this maximum mode, but occasionally came close to it: the passacaglia from *Ledi Makbet* contains four diminished intervals from the tonic, on the fourth, fifth, seventh and eighth degrees (see Ex. 4.2, discussed below).

modes, such as those in the major–minor modal system, are formed from 'chordal harmonic gravitation'.

[40] Yavorsky identified this mode, a symmetrical mode with the pattern 2 1 1 2 1 1 2 1 1 (related to the whole-tone scale), as 'augmented' (*Stroyeniye muzikal'noy rechi*, p. 18).

[41] For instance, in the lowered Phrygian mode, the seventh chord on the dominant becomes diminished; and the triad on the lowered fourth degree becomes augmented (replacing, Dolzhansky points out, the augmented triad on the third degree characteristic for the harmonic minor mode). The latter chord, IV+, resolves to tonic only through the dominant, and when incomplete (lacking its third) should not be mistaken for the parallel tonic major triad, to which it is enharmonically equal. The minor triad on the second degree is also unique to this mode (and the double-lowered Phrygian, but only among Dolzhansky's modes, that is); and Dolzhansky points out that the juxtaposition of two minor triads a minor second apart results in six of the seven notes of this mode, thus providing a harmonic means for generating this mode. As an example Dolzhansky provides the F♯ minor song of Katerina from *Ledi Makbet* (Act I scene 3, marked Adagio, fig. 144 in *Sobraniye sochineniy*, vol. 22 (Moscow, 1985), first seven bars), which contains the outline of the G minor triad.

[42] Dolzhansky, 'O ladovoy osnove sochineniy Shostakovicha', 45. Thus the tonic triad for this mode is a 'minor-diminished' triad (diminished third on the bottom, a minor third on top) with three possible 'parallel majors' – diminished, minor ('double major') and major ('triple major') triads. For this reason, Dolzhansky says, the major triad in Shostakovich's works sounds particularly bright.

94   Ellon D. Carpenter

Ex. 4.2(a) Shostakovich, *Ledi Makbet* (1932), Act II, *entr'acte* between scenes 4 and 5, theme from passacaglia

Modal interpretations: (b) Dolzhansky, near-maximum lowered mode; (c) Dolzhansky, Alexandrian pentachord; (d) Burda; (e) Sereda; (f) Fedosova

(b)

(c) AP V

(d) d minor

(e) Quartal and tertian coordinates   Basic and secondary harmonic supports

(f)

To explain modal relationships, Dolzhansky advocates 'the theory of harmonic opposition', in which a mode is harmonically opposed by the mode with triads of opposite structure on opposite degrees (Ionian–Aeolian, Mixolydian–Dorian, Lydian–Phrygian and Locrian–Locrian).[43]

[43] A mode is opposed melodically by its inversion (Phrygian–Ionian, for example). Dolzhansky uses the theory of harmonic opposition to explain the evolution of the

From the opposition of the lowered modes, Dolzhansky creates additional new 'raised' modes, such as the Lydian mode with raised second degree (harmonically opposed to the Phrygian mode with lowered fourth degree). The double-lowered Phrygian and Aeolian modes are opposed by modes with two varieties of the fifth degree, 'in opposition to the two varieties of the first degree in the minor modes. And in fact, such modes become representative of major modes of Shostakovich.'[44]

Dolzhansky also derives new interpretations of the relative and parallel relationships between harmonically opposed major and minor modes. Such modes are relative modes at the distance of a diminished fourth, the distance at which they share the most notes; for example, B 'minor' double-lowered Phrygian mode is relative to E♭ 'major' double-raised Lydian mode. Parallel modes share common notes but not a common tonic. Because the double-lowered modes have essentially two tonics, on the first and lowered eighth degrees, there may also be two tonalities. Parallel to B minor (double-lowered Aeolian), for example, is B♭ major, not B major (both double-raised Ionian), since B♭ major shares more common notes with B minor than does B major. The parallel relatedness of two keys that share a common third, usually a minor key and its major 'neighbour' a half step below, is an accepted phenomenon in Russian music theory.[45]

Dolzhansky uses the first movement of Shostakovich's Piano Sonata No. 2 in B minor, Op. 61, to illustrate these relationships. The primary idea in B minor is contrasted by the secondary idea in its relative major,

> major–minor modal system as well as Shostakovich's modes. Thus the Ionian mode was singled out because it contains the acoustically correct dominant-seventh chord and tonic triad. The Aeolian entered the major–minor modal system because it is harmonically opposed to the Ionian. This foundation provided symmetrical paths for modulation to closely related modes to these modes. The harmonic minor mode arose as a result of the aspiration towards an acoustically correct dominant-seventh chord and a leading note; the harmonic major mode (with a major third from tonic) arose later, as a stimulus from the harmonic minor. The melodic minor arose from the need to eliminate the augmented interval between VI and VII in the harmonic minor mode; the melodic major arose as an 'answer' to the melodic minor.

[44] Dolzhansky, 'O ladovoy osnove sochineniy Shostakovicha', 61.
[45] See S. D. Orfeyev, 'Odnovisotniye trezvuchiya i tonal'nosti' [Monopitch triads and tonalities], in *Voprosï teorii muziki* [Questions of the Theory of Music], ii (Moscow, 1970), 54–85; and N. F. Tiftikidi, 'Teoriya odnotertsovoy i tonal'noy khromaticheskoy sistem' [The theory of the monotertian and tonal chromatic system], in *Voprosï teorii muziki*, ii (Moscow, 1970), 22–53. Orfeyev interprets Dolzhansky's double-lowered Aeolian mode as having arisen from the use of monotertian tonics and subdominants (major and minor triads sharing the same third) (p. 84).

E♭ major. The recapitulation then juxtaposes B minor with its parallel major, B♭ major. Yet Dolzhansky is unclear with regard to which of the lowered or raised modes he is referring to. He illustrates the secondary idea as being in the raised Lydian mode (bb. 66–70), but the primary idea is clearly in double-lowered Aeolian, not lowered Phrygian, to which raised Lydian is properly harmonically opposed. Dolzhansky's intriguing premise, which in the instance he gives is insufficiently illustrated and explained, has not been explored by other theorists.

Although theorists have criticised Dolzhansky's concentration on the scalar aspects of mode, they have all recognised his contribution to the understanding of basic modal characteristics of Shostakovich's music, particularly its melodic basis and use of lowered intervals. Dolzhansky was the first to apply a strict methodology with which to analyse the modal and harmonic aspects of Shostakovich's music. In a subsequent work he reinterpreted Shostakovich's modal basis as a pentachordal portion of the octatonic scale, the 'Alexandrian pentachord', which when expanded or combined creates non-symmetrical intervallic patterns (see Ex. 4.1*a*).[46]

Lev Abramovich Mazel''s interpretations of mode in Shostakovich's music largely coincide with those of Dolzhansky regarding the most fundamental ideas – the melodic nature of Shostakovich's music and its diatonic foundation, the lowered degrees and modal variety.[47] Like

[46] Dolzhansky's other works on Shostakovich include: *Shostakovich: Kamernïye proizvedeniya* [Shostakovich: Chamber Works] (Moscow, 1955); *24 prelyudii i fugi D. Shostakovicha* [The 24 Preludes and Fugues of D. Shostakovich] (Moscow, 1963); *Kamernïye instrumental'nïye proizvedeniya D. Shostakovicha* [The Chamber Instrumental Works of D. Shostakovich] (Moscow, 1965); 'O kompozitsii pervoy chasti Sed'moy simfonii D. Shostakovicha' [On the composition of the first movement of the Seventh Symphony of D. Shostakovich], *Sovetskaya Muzïka* (4/1956), 88–98 (*Izbrannïye stat'i*, 52–66); 'Kratkiye zamechaniya ob odinnadtsatoy simfonii' [Short observations on the Eleventh Symphony], *Sovetskaya Muzïka* (3/1958), 29–36 (*Izbrannïye stat'i*, 66–76); and 'Iz nablyudeniy nad stilem Shostakovicha' [From observations on the style of Shostakovich], *Sovetskaya Muzïka* (10/1959), 95–102 (*Izbrannïye stat'i*, 76–86). See also his article on mode: 'Nekotorïye voprosï teorii lada' [Some questions on the theory of mode], in *Problemï lada*, 8–34. This article was compiled from lectures Dolzhansky gave at the conference 11 October 1965.

Yet during the 1940s Dolzhansky was criticised both directly for his 'formalist' views and indirectly, through the harsh comments levelled at Shostakovich in the late 1940s – 'guilt by association'. Thus he published nothing more about Shostakovich's music until 1956 in the article on the Seventh Symphony. Today in Russia, though, Dolzhansky is viewed as a founder of the field of theoretical research on Shostakovich's music.

[47] Mazel', an advocate and practitioner of 'integrated analysis', a Marxist-influenced approach that mandates the analysis of all possible factors attendant to a piece of music,

Dolzhansky, then, Mazel' recognises Shostakovich's use of old modes and major and minor enriched with new modes. In addition, he identifies three ways in which Shostakovich uses the medieval church modes as a modal foundation – fragmented, with their characteristic intervals enhancing the major–minor system; independently, as a whole; or independently, enriched by new intervals created predominantly by lowered degrees. This last method intensifies the mode's 'minor expressiveness', resulting in the 'intensified Phrygian' mode, with lowered second and fourth degrees (Dolzhansky's 'lowered' Phrygian mode), or just the lowered fourth degree (see Ex. 4.1).[48] Mazel' explains other lowered degrees as a form of modal modulation (Table 4.2, method II), the result of short modal deviations into the related modal spheres of the original lowered degrees, which act independently and attract their own functional counterparts – the lowered first or doubly lowered seventh degree for the lowered fourth or the lowered fifth for the lowered second degree (the finale of the Second Quartet and the second movement of the Ninth Symphony).[49]

applies this method to melody in Shostakovich, blending interpretations of intonation, mode, metre, rhythm, historical precedent, aesthetic significance, sociological connections and methods of thematic construction into a unified whole. Integrated analysis includes not only strictly musical factors but also sociological, aesthetic and historical ones. A model for this type of analysis is Mazel''s book on Chopin: *Fantaziya f-moll Shopena: Opït analiza* [The F minor Fantasy of Chopin: An Experiment in Analysis] (Moscow, 1937). Other works by Mazel' include *O melodii* [On Melody] (Moscow, 1952) and *Problemï klassicheskoy garmonii* [Problems of Classical Harmony] (Moscow, 1972).

Mazel', a professor at the Moscow Conservatory, had planned to publish this article on Shostakovich in a collection of articles from the Conservatory. Publishing delays initially postponed this work, but eventually the critical attacks on Shostakovich in the late 1940s caused Mazel' to withdraw his article. He was able to publish it in its original form only in 1967. He had used separate ideas from it in various later publications, and admitted from the later vantage point of twenty years he would approach certain aspects differently. However, as testimony to past events, he chose not to alter it.

In his study Mazel' concentrates on a small number of recent works by Shostakovich, primarily the Symphonies 5–9 (1937–45), and, in addition to the opera *Ledi Makbet* and the Piano Concerto No. 1, Op. 35 (1933), from the early 1930s, works for instrumental chamber groups or piano from the 1940s – the Piano Quintet in G minor, Op. 57 (1940), the Piano Sonata No. 2, Op. 61 (1943), the Piano Trio, Op. 67 (1944) and the Quartet No. 2 in A major, Op. 68 (1944).

[48] Mazel', 'Zametki', 321.
[49] For example, in the finale of the Second Quartet, in A major, Op. 68 (first statement of fugue theme, bb. 17–31), the lowered fifth 'accompanies' the lowered second in the capacity of its subdominant. However, this lowered fifth then becomes the focus, engendering the original lowered tonic (as its subdominant) and, in a chromatic descending line, the original lowered fourth and lowered sixth (of A minor), which rewritten enharmonically becomes the original dominant, before returning to the original tonic. Another example is the melody from the second movement of the Ninth Symphony,

He also invokes a method of modal formation similar to Tyulin's third method (Table 4.2, method III), the absorption into the mode of complex extramodal harmonic progressions. This may involve single notes or triads, as in the F♯ minor song of Katerina from *Ledi Makbet* (Act I scene 3) in which the minor triad on the lowered second degree, previously a harmonic phenomenon, becomes part of the melody (Dolzhansky used the same example for a similar interpretation), or a latent harmonic progression, as in the well-known opening theme of the Fifth Symphony, the progressive intervallic compression of which implies a harmonic progression in D minor (tonic–dominant–subdominant, the last preceded by its leading-note seventh chord).

L. ADAM, S. SKREBKOV, V. BOBROVSKY AND V. V. BURDA

This group of theorists applies primarily modal and tonal modulation (Table 4.2, methods II and V) to form new modes. L. Adam, using ideas from Tyulin, S. Skrebkov and I. Sposobin, developed a general approach that has been applied more specifically to Shostakovich's music.[50] In modal modulation, the new mode, the 'derived mode' (or 'daughter mode'), is 'attracted' to the old tonal centre of the 'original mode'. In tonal modulation, developed from Tyulin's theory of variable function, one of the less stable degrees 'takes over' the function of tonic, becoming the new tonal centre. The most common category of derived mode created in this way is the 'dominant mode', in which the fifth degree becomes the tonic.[51] The upper or lower major mediant may also assume the tonic function (Ex. 4.1*b*). With tonic transferred to the upper major mediant, this mode is identical to two other modes formed in different ways (see Ex. 4.1*a*). Adam illustrates a combined major–minor nine-note

---

Op. 70, E♭ major (bb. 1–21), in which the second, fourth, fifth and eighth notes are lowered. Unusual here is the direct juxtaposition of the F♮, the lowered fifth, with C♮, in B minor. Mazel' stresses this passage's clear support on major and major, which makes up 'one of the classical foundations of Shostakovich's style' (*ibid.*, 323).

[50] L. I. Adam, 'O nekotorïkh ladogarmonicheskikh osobennostyakh muzïki sovetskikh kompozitorov' (About some modal–harmonic characteristics of music of Soviet composers), in *Nauchno-metodicheskiye zapiski* [Scientific-Methodological Notes], ii (Novosibirsk, 1960), 133–46; Adam, 'O nekotorïkh ladoobrazovaniyakh v sovremennoy muzïke' [On some modal–harmonic formations in contemporary music], in *Teoreticheskiye problemï muzïki XX veka* [Theoretical Problems of Music of the 20th Century], ed. Y. Tyulin, i (Moscow, 1967), 69–90.

[51] Igor' Vladimirovich Sposobin, *Elementarnaya teoriya muzïki* (Moscow, 1954), 150. Sposobin originated the term 'dominant mode'.

mode (C–D–E♭–E–F–G–A♭–B♭–B–C), which becomes G–A♭–B♭–B–C–D–E♭–E–F–G with the dominant as tonal centre, or A♭–B♭–B–C–D–E♭–E–F–G–A♭ with the lower major mediant as tonal centre. Adam, expanding somewhat on Skrebkov's 1957 example, interprets the Più mosso section of the first movement of the Tenth Symphony as incorporating both the dominant and submediant tonal centres simultaneously.[52] Based on the original tonality of C major–minor, the derived tonal centre of the melody is G, which contrasts the A♭ derived tonal centre of the accompaniment, thus creating a bitonal mode. (See the top half of Ex. 4.3. The bottom portion, the analytical extracts, is explained in the section below on V. Sereda.)

In his 1965 essay on Shostakovich, Sergey Sergeyevich Skrebkov follows the same line of thought, recognising three of the methods of modal formation in Shostakovich's music already identified – alterations of existing modes (method IV), tonal modulations (method V, which Shostakovich frequently used in conjunction with an altered mode) and modal modulations (method II), which he explains, in a somewhat broadened interpretation, as the interpenetration of parallel modes not only with shared tonic, but also with either shared third or fifth.[53]

In his 1960 article on Shostakovich's String Quartet No. 7, Viktor Petrovich Bobrovsky also accepts the ideas of both altered modes and bitonal modes, or simultaneous modal variability, 'the sounding of separate fragments simultaneously in two tonalities', using the same scale.[54] The first theme of this quartet, for example, is in both F♯ minor and G minor, with the scale F♯–G–A–B♭–C–C♯–D–E♭–F♯.

In his 1972 article, Bobrovsky expands upon this approach in his analysis of the Largo from the Symphony No. 5, applying the concept of modal variability both horizontally and vertically.[55] However, in neither case does he grant the resulting tonality (Adam's 'derived mode') stature equal to that of the original; he thus stops short of interpreting such instances as a true modulation (horizontal) or as strict bitonality (vertical).

[52] Sergey Sergeyevich Skrebkov, 'O sovremennoy garmonii' [On contemporary harmony], *Sovetskaya Muzïka* (6/1957), 74–84. The Shostakovich example is discussed on pp. 81–2.
[53] Sergey Sergeyevich Skrebkov, *Garmoniya v sovremennoy muzïke* [Harmony in Contemporary Music] (Moscow, 1965). The chapter on Shostakovich, 'Garmoniya Shostakovicha' [The harmony of Shostakovich], is on pp. 87–103.
[54] Viktor Petrovich Bobrovsky, 'Sed'moy kvartet D. Shostakovicha' [The seventh quartet of D. Shostakovich], *Sovetskaya Muzïka* (8/1960), 68.
[55] Viktor Petrovich Bobrovsky, 'O nekotorïkh storonakh ladotonal'noy peremyonnosti v muzïke D. D. Shostakovicha' [On some sides of modal–tonal variability in the music of D. D. Shostakovich], in *Problemï lada*, 239–51.

Ex. 4.3 Shostakovich, Symphony No. 10, first movement: explanations of modal content: (a) Adam

(b) Dolzhansky (1967)

[musical notation: 2 AP V, W H W H H, (bb. 210–213)]

(c) Sereda

[musical notation]
Supports with superstructure

In a 'passing' or 'secondary' type of variability, a linear phenomenon, a temporary modulation is brought about by a transfer of tonic function to a new 'temporary' tonic. A tonality of a 'lower order' results, 'greater than a chord with its function and less than a tonality in its full view'.[56] In a 'modal–tonal division', a vertical phenomenon, 'one and the same melody may be heard in two tonalities', imparting to its sound a sort of 'modal iridescent quality'.[57] This gives rise to an intermediate level between tonic (stable) function and unstable functions; since both tonalities are 'mutually subsidiary, . . . an exact tonic becomes elusive'.[58]

V. V. Burda also uses alterations, and modal and tonal modulations, mostly simultaneous, resulting in bimodal and bitonal modes, to derive and explain Shostakovich's modes.[59] In general she advocates bimodality, explaining all the given notes of a melody or theme as the combination of two diatonic modes sharing a common tonic rather than one large mode. These diatonic modes consist of natural minor and one of the three lowered modes she identifies, the 'nine-note lowered' mode (the others being the 'eight-note lowered' mode and the 'nine-note melodic lowered' mode; see Ex. 4.1a). The resulting twelve-note 'bimode' creates a third category equal in her view to diatonicism and chromaticism (see Ex. 4.4).

Burda disagrees with Adam about the origin of the lowered modes. Although she accepts his theory of tonal-centre displacement, she prefers to displace the tonic to the raised seventh degree of minor (her 'eight-note lowered' mode). Adding the fifth degree from this new tonic provides the

[56] *Ibid.*, 249.   [57] *Ibid.*, 245–6.   [58] *Ibid.*, 251.
[59] V. V. Burda, 'O nekotorïkh osobennostyakh ladovogo mïshleniya D. D. Shostakovicha' [About some characteristics of modal thought of D. D. Shostakovich], in *Nauchno-metodicheskiye zapiski* [Scientific-Methodological Notes], vii (Sverdlovsk, 1972), 116–44.

102   Ellon D. Carpenter

Ex. 4.4(a) Shostakovich, Symphony No. 9, second movement, bb. 1–30

(b) Burda, bimode

'nine-note lowered' mode. Such a tonic displacement with the harmonic minor results in the 'nine-note melodic' mode, with lowered second, fourth, fifth and eighth degrees from the new tonic, which, however, is equivalent to Adam's mediant-derived mode.[60] She summarises the main characteristics of these lowered modes: they contain five lowered degrees, no octave limit and a second, 'upper', but 'weaker' tonic (the lowered eighth degree, which may also function as a leading note); they oppose both major and minor; and they constitute a 'new diatonicism' (from Dolzhansky).[61]

In addition, she has found in the Second Cello Concerto 'a twelve-note bitonal system', a lowered mode with different tonics, occurring, as in Bobrovsky's approach but with more independent results, either simultaneously (resulting in a bitonal structure) or consecutively (resulting in a 'permanent' modulation).[62] Tonalities are most often joined at the interval of a minor second, tritone or diminished octave. It would be possible to have as well a 'polytonic bimode', in which the principles of polytonality and bimodality are combined.[63] 'Twelve-note subsystems' – smaller entities within a larger bitonal system – may also occur. Such subsystems would include a lowered mode, a bimode, a major–minor mode or a whole-tone mode.

V. SEREDA, A. TEBOSYAN AND E. P. FEDOSOVA

Rejecting earlier theorists' concentration on the scalar aspects of Shostakovich's music, this group of theorists focuses on melodic modal function. V. Sereda's definition of mode relies on those of Kushnaryov and Asaf'yev: 'Mode as a totality of intonational connections is manifested in the logical relations of notes, which make up the most important basis of intoning'.[64] Her general application of mode is based on Tyulin, who first isolated both the melodic and harmonic modal

---

[60] Burda considers it 'unlikely' that Shostakovich's special modes arose 'by a natural path', through the lowering of degrees in the natural minor mode. She disagrees with Adam's displacement to the submediant of a mode that was already altered, calling his treatment 'somewhat artificial' (Burda, 'O nekotorïkh', pp. 121–2).
[61] *Ibid.*, 122.
[62] *Ibid.*, 132.
[63] *Ibid.*, 137.
[64] V. Sereda, 'O ladovoy strukture muzïki Shostakovicha' [On the modal structure of the music of Shostakovich], in *Voprosï teorii muzïki* [Questions of the Theory of Music], ed. S. Skrebkov, i (Moscow, 1968), 332.

functions, and her specific application is based on Kushnaryov, who demonstrated melodic function in folk music. Thus both the horizontal and vertical aspects of music are different manifestations of the intonational process. The harmonic basis consists of notes co-ordinated in definite relationships creating a relatively stable (and consonant) whole. As in Tyulin's approach, tertian and quartal co-ordinations are the most important and specific manifestations of this harmonic basis. The melodic basis consists of the 'energetic connection of notes', the gravitation of one degree towards another, either stepwise or at a distance.[65] Secundal co-ordinations characterise melodic function.

A modal system, best revealed in strongly thematic, stable statements, may exist only when its component elements are clearly differentiated yet joined on a common basis. These component elements consist of several varied aspects on different hierarchical levels. The melodic line itself is understood as a combination of melodic cells, clearly isolated from each other, called 'melodic subsystems'. These subsystems may be combined into 'melodic phrases', which are also inwardly closed and exhibit linear unity. In Shostakovich's music, the limitation of the diminished intervals, particularly the diminished fourth, most frequently provides this melodic isolation, leading to closed structures. Diatonic intervals – perfect fourth, perfect fifth, major or minor third – may also serve to isolate melodic subsystems.

These melodic subsystems may exist on the basis of both melodic and harmonic tonal relations. In melodic subsystems and phrases limited by diminished intervals, the harmonic basis functions as either the 'harmony-resonator' (for subsystems) or 'harmony-regulator' (for phrases).[66] Sereda refers to this harmonic basis in general as the 'support', and the melodic subsystems surrounding the support, which have their own harmonic co-ordinates, as the 'superstructure'. The resulting modal stratification, as well as the simultaneous combination of different levels of harmonic supports, contributes to the multi-faceted, multi-layered structure of mode. This modal structure is represented by the possible hierarchy shown in Figure 4.3.

The resulting modal structure is diatonic, not chromatic. Following Tyulin, Sereda distinguishes diatonicism (the full seven-note version) from chromaticism mainly through its quartal-quintal and tertian co-ordinates. But unlike diatonicism, chromaticism has no constructive

[65] Ibid., 328.   [66] Ibid., 336.

Figure 4.3. Sereda: Hierarchy of modal structure.

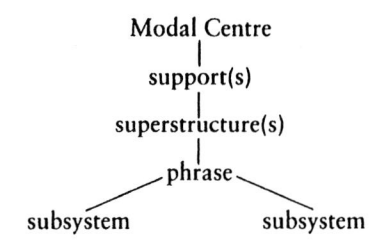

```
              Modal Centre
                   |
               support(s)
                   |
            superstructure(s)
                   |
                phrase
              /        \
        subsystem      subsystem
```

principles save the tritone, which may not be co-ordinated or combined with other intervals to create a single whole. She states, 'Modal chromaticism exists on the basis of diatonicism, and is manifested through the disruption of diatonic co-ordinates'.[67] Thus, she concludes, the scales and structure of the supports belong to basic, strict diatonicism; and the scales and structure of the superstructure belong to 'conditional, or altered' diatonicism, or 'diatonicism of the second order'.[68] The entire modal structure as a whole becomes, then, 'multi-faceted' diatonicism.

She also allows for the possibility of polymodality and polytonality, which represent the highest degree of inner-modal differentiation. For example, the beginning of the scherzo of the Symphony No. 10 combines the tonalities of B♭ minor and D♭ minor. However, she disagrees with Adam regarding the second theme of this symphony's first movement (Ex. 4.3). The harmony-regulator (the support for the phrase) is relatively simple, the tonic fifth G–D. In contrast the superstructure is more complex, consisting of two aspects: a 'common-third' triad on A♭ minor, and a melodic subsystem embracing a minor third, symmetrically arranged around the tonic G. Thus, first of all, the basic mode is not derived from C minor, nor is it an example of polytonality (Adam and Skrebkov), since the A♭ minor 'may not pretend to the right of tonality':

Thus, to speak in connection with this example about polytonality would be an exaggeration; (yet) to reduce the analysis to a seven-degree tonal scale would be too great an oversimplification. The expansion of the sphere of influence of the tonic occurs here mainly not through the chromatic alteration of the basic seven degrees of the tonality, but by the application of different forms of inner-modal differentiation and synthesis, through the formation of a multifaceted modal system.[69]

A. Tebosyan, in his article devoted to Shostakovich's Seventh Quartet, adopts Sereda's theory of melodic subsystems, and derives the thematic

---

[67] Ibid., 340.   [68] Ibid., 340–1.   [69] Ibid., 351.

structure of the quartet from a 'binary diminished fourth subsystem' from the tonic F♯ minor, also allowing F♯ major and G minor (F♯–G–A–B♭, dovetailed with A–B♭–C–C♯) (see below, Ex. 4.7).[70]

The culmination of the two paths of prominent thought on mode, diatonicism and melodic modal function, may be found in Eleonora Petrovna Fedosova's work.[71] Her approach, more than in previous studies of Shostakovich's music, is based on principles of melodic modal formation derived from folk music. She combines its diatonic intervallic quartal-quintal foundation and system of melodic functions into one unified whole, and interprets Shostakovich's modal language as having been developed

in the sphere of an organised special form of diatonicism. The leading principle of its organisation is a flexible, expanded modal structure, capable of very different modifications and including in its makeup several modal systems, based on a clear differentiation of the melodic functional role of notes.[72]

Her approach, therefore, may easily accommodate any of the six modal categories from Table 4.1, depending on the complexity of the melody.

In Fedosova's theory, the general diatonic basis of Shostakovich's music rests on a foundation of quartal supports, similar to Tyulin's concept of expanded diatonicism. The special form of diatonicism results from the logical functional differentiation of the components making up the mode. Mode therefore becomes a flexible system of logically differentiated groups of notes, joined around their support. These groups of interconnected notes, forming an initial modal cell or system, usually

[70] A. Tebosyan, 'Sed'moy kvartet D. Shostakovicha. K voprosu o svyazi strukturi lada i tematizma' [The seventh quartet of D. Shostakovich. To the question of the connection of the structure of mode and thematicism], in *Voprosï muzïkal'nogo analiza* [Questions of Music Analysis], xxviii, *Sbornik trudov* [A Collection of Works] (Moscow, 1976), 167–90. Tebosyan criticises Dolzhansky's 'static' pentachordal and scalar analysis of Shostakovich's music in which enharmonic changes are necessary to make his point (p. 189).

[71] Eleonora Petrovna Fedosova, 'O diatonicheskikh ladakh u D. Shostakovicha' [On diatonic modes in D. Shostakovich], in *Voprosï teorii muzïki* [Questions of the Theory of Music], ii (Moscow, 1970), 363–81; Fedosova, 'Diatonika kak osnova tematizma poemï D. D. Shostakovich "Kazn' Stepana Razina"' [Diatonicism as the basis of the thematicism of the poem of D. D. Shostakovich 'The Execution of Stepan Razin'], in *Problemï muzïkal'noy nauki* [Problems of Music Science], ed. G. Orlov *et al.*, i (Moscow, 1972), 138–68; Fedosova, 'Pyatnadtsatïy kvartet i al'tovaya sonata D. Shostakovicha' [The fifteenth quartet and the viola sonata of D. Shostakovich], in *Voprosï muzïkal'nogo formoobrazovaniya* [Questions of Musical Form], xlvi, *Sbornik trudov* [A Collection of Works] (Moscow, 1980), 71–89; Fedosova, *Diatonicheskiye ladï v tvorchestve D. Shostakovicha* [Diatonic Modes in the Musical Works of D. Shostakovich] (Moscow, 1980).

[72] Fedosova, *Diatonicheskiye ladï v tvorchestve D. Shostakovicha*, 128.

constitute tetrachords, sometimes pentachords. Similar initial systems are joined into and become units of systems of a higher order. The connection of these systems is made on the basis of the variable melodic functions of degrees, which results in a change of gravitational sphere, with a new stable foundation.

Within the initial modal cells, the hierarchy of melodic function equals essentially what Bershadskaya and Drukt formulated but with some changes and an addition. There is the stable foundation or support, the main centre or modal support; the half-foundation or half-support, which has the capability to become the main foundation, thus creating a new system in a different sphere of gravity; the filling-in notes, modal definers that Fedosova calls 'formants' (*formantï*); and the expanding notes, which form part of a group Fedosova refers to as 'ornamenting' or 'accessory' (*vspomogatel'nïy*). Fedosova identifies in Shostakovich's music a special type of expanding note, which she calls 'culminating' (*kul'minantïy*). With reference to the modal foundation, this note is the lowered eighth degree, which serves as the upper limit of the modal structure consisting of two tetrachords but which functions only as an upper neighbour note to the seventh degree, expanding its function.

Fedosova's interpretation of the main theme from the first movement of Shostakovich's Sonata for Violin and Piano, Op. 134, illustrates her approach (Ex. 4.5). Although outwardly chromatic, this theme in its unfolding exhibits an inner multi-linked diatonic structure that is consecutive and logical in its design. The first (bottom) system reveals the diatonic tetrachordal and pentachordal framework of the mode. Interesting here in the three inner systems is the preponderance of Shostakovich's characteristic interval of the diminished fourth. These inner systems function independently, as supporting points, but serve also as transfer degrees in their intermediate position between the two outer diatonic quartal-quintal systems. The supports of these 'framing' systems, which vary between the fourth and the fifth, are co-ordinated on the principle of the diminished octave – B–B♭, E–E♭ and F♯–F. The ornamenting note to the upper support in the top system, here the G♭, which usually exhibits this principle of the diminished octave, the culminator, therefore has, in Fedosova's view, a sort of 'silent partner' in the melody, the G, in the first system, which, however, does occur in the piano part.

108 Ellon D. Carpenter

Ex. 4.5 (a) Shostakovich, Sonata for Violin and Piano, first movement, bb. 9–24 (violin part)

(b) Fedosova, modal content

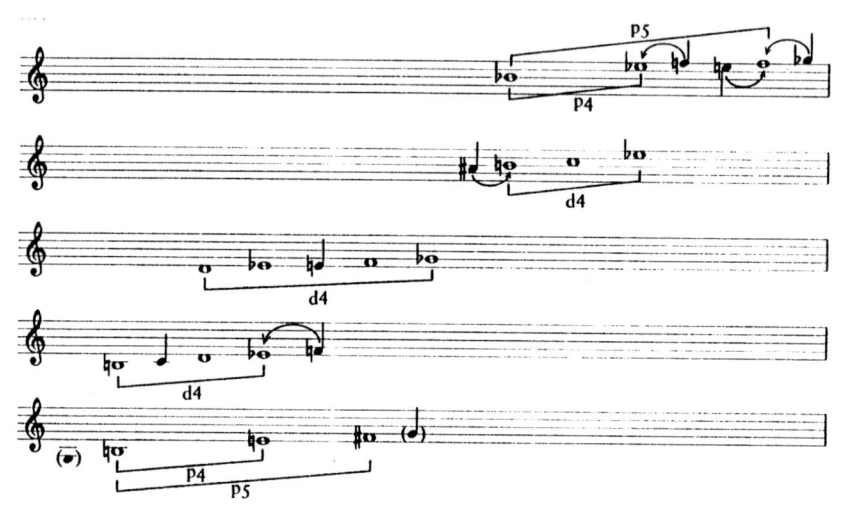

COMPARISONS

The varied approaches of the theorists discussed herein may best be illustrated by comparing analyses. The passacaglia theme from *Ledi Makbet* (Act II, the *entr'acte* between scenes 4 and 5) is shown in Example 4.2a. Initially Dolzhansky interpreted this theme as an example of Shostakovich's use of a near-maximum lowered mode (Ex. 4.2b). Later he used it to illustrate the 'Alexandrian pentachord V', in which the fifth degree is varied, calling this 'the first "fundamental" application by Shostakovich of the Alexandrian pentachord' (Ex. 4.2c).[73] In Burda's view, the 'Shostakovich mode' is produced from the minor mode lying a half step above the tonic, since all the notes (except the G♯) belong to D minor, with C♯ as the leading note (Ex. 4.2d). She points out Shostakovich's avoidance of G♯, while stating G twice. The 'added' fifth degree (G♯) is produced only at the end of the theme, 'as if with the goal "to avoid misunderstanding" and as the usual cadential perfect fifth leap clearly to define the tonality of C♯'.[74] Sereda initially analyses the theme according to its quartal and tertian co-ordinates, but extracts as its basic harmonic support the fifth C♯–G♯, with the diminished seventh C♯–E–G–B♭ serving as a 'secondary harmonic support' (Ex. 4.2e). She views this secondary support as a sign of the diminished (octatonic) mode, which in fact the theme partially outlines (lacking the A). Fedosova uses this theme to demonstrate modes that culminate in the lowered eighth degree (Ex. 4.2f). She sees the G, though, not as an altered or alternate fifth degree as in Dolzhansky and Burda, but as an upper neighbour to the F. The F and the G♯ thus outline with the C♯ both the diminished fourth and the perfect fifth, respectively, both important intervals in Shostakovich's modal language.

The flute theme from the first movement of the Sixth Symphony constitutes, for Dolzhansky, the 'lowered Phrygian mode' (Ex. 4.6). Sereda gives it two harmonic supports, a primary support, the perfect fifth B–F♯, and a secondary support, the diminished seventh C♯–E–G–B♭ (again, denoting the presence of the diminished (octatonic) mode, which here, though, appears only in part). Fedosova, in a discussion of the role of the diminished fourth in Shostakovich's modal system, stresses the role of the E♭ as the note culmination of the first phrase of the melody, but she subordinates it to the D. In effect, she says, the diminished fourth is not an autonomous system, but a derived one; and although it may provide melodic boundaries, it always functions as a subordinate note, usually to the note a half step below.[75]

[73] Dolzhansky, 'Aleksandriyskiy pentakhord v muzike D. Shostakovicha', *Izbrannïye stat'i*, 91.
[74] Burda, 'O nekotorïkh', 119.
[75] A similar comparison between Dolzhansky and Fedosova may be made with the bassoon solo from the recapitulation of the first movement of the Seventh Symphony. Whereas Dolzhansky sees it as an example of 'lowered Phrygian mode', leaving out the very prominent E♯ (Dolzhansky, 'O ladovoy osnove sochineniy Shostakovicha', 40), Fedosova interprets it as F♯ minor, with the diminished fourth B♭ moving to the minor third A. She points out the doubly diminished fifth between the E♯ and the B♭ as well (Fedosova, *Diatonicheskiye ladï v tvorchestve D. Shostakovicha*, 109).

110   Ellon D. Carpenter

The fugue theme from the finale of the Seventh Quartet also has several different interpretations (Ex. 4.7). Dolzhansky interprets the opening motif as an example of the Alexandrian pentachord V from F♯, Bobrovsky accepts this interpretation, but interprets the remainder of the

Ex. 4.6(a) Shostakovich, Symphony No. 6, first movement, flute solo, rehearsal no. 27

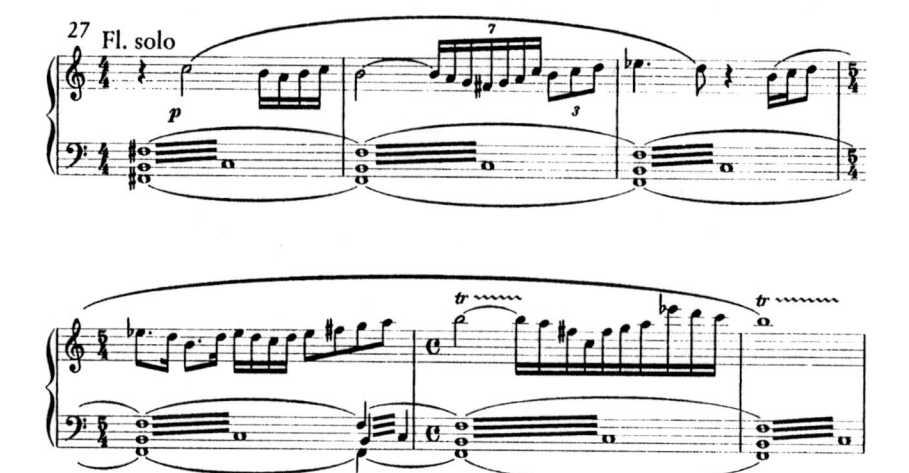

Modal interpretations:

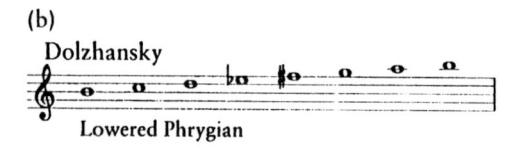

(b) Dolzhansky
Lowered Phrygian

(c) Sereda
Harmonic supports

(d) Fedosova
(1st 3bb.)

Ex. 4.7(a) Shostakovich, Quartet No. 7, third movement, fugue theme, bb. 13–19, viola

Modal interpretations:

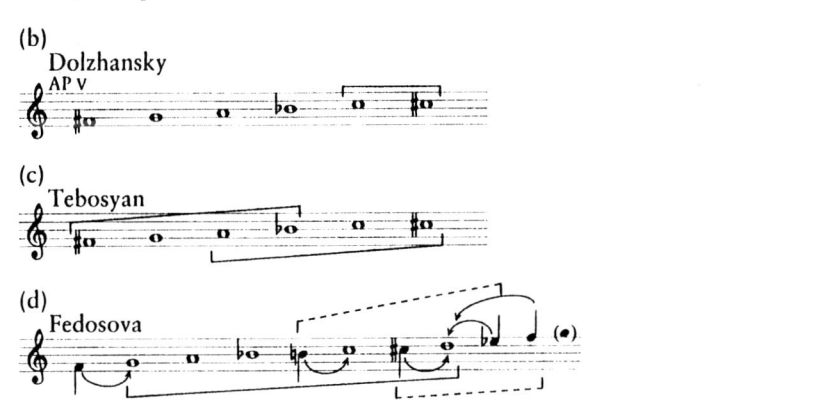

(b) Dolzhansky

(c) Tebosyan

(d) Fedosova

theme as modulating to G minor, the C♯ thus becoming the raised fourth degree. Tebosyan interprets the same fragment intervallically. The perfect fifth F♯–C♯ and the perfect fourth G–C within it are included 'in a scale of two coupled diminished fourth subsystems, lying at the foundation of the fugue theme'. (In order to interpret this statement correctly, one must enharmonically change the A to a G𝄪, a practice for which Tebosyan has criticised Dolzhansky.) Fedosova views the diatonic basis of the theme as the pentachord G–A–B♭–C–D, within the range of a diminished octave from F♯ to F. For some reason she ignores the final G of the theme.

CONCLUSION

Thus theorists' interpretations of mode in Shostakovich's music – and its diatonic underpinnings – have mirrored fairly closely the general trend in the overall study of mode, that is, towards focusing less on its structural components and more on its qualitative functional components. In essence, theorists have recognised the greater importance of the process of modal unfolding and of the revelation of modal function – which dates back to Yavorsky – over the scalar results of that unfolding. Dolzhansky's calculation of note content at the expense of melodic function has been superseded by the very aspect he ignored.

Yet the emphasis on melodic modal function and process in Sereda, Tebosyan and especially Fedosova, although informative, reveals only how the notes function as modal degrees. This general approach does not address the question of how these notes contribute to the melodic or thematic statement itself; the process of the unfolding of the melody, both within themes and throughout an entire movement, is not considered. Temporal process, the unfolding of the musical statement, concentrated in the melody, is overlooked.

Recalling Kholopov's expansive definition of mode from the beginning of this article, we see that the approaches presented herein fall short of comprehensiveness. In sum, they appear too reductive and not sufficiently explanatory. Modal language in Shostakovich's music has not been addressed in its totality, but only in part. Now that the unfolding of its diatonic basis has been examined, a more processive and all-inclusive approach needs to be applied, in order to reveal each piece's unique modal–tonal embodiment in and contribution to the thematic structure.

5

The cycle of structure and the cycle of meaning: the Piano Trio in E minor, Op. 67

PATRICK McCRELESS

Sometimes we encounter a work for which a standard critical interpretation seems so solidly secured by the tight fit of the circumstances of its composition and the music itself that we see little reason to engage the music more closely and seek for it a more careful and nuanced reading. Such a work is Shostakovich's Piano Trio in E minor, Op. 67. Wherever we look, it seems, whether in biographies of the composer, critical studies, programme notes or liner notes in recording, we read that the composition of the Trio was Shostakovich's anguished response to the sudden and unexpected death, in February 1944, of his closest friend, the musical writer and scholar Ivan Sollertinsky, to whom the work is dedicated; that it was during this same time that Shostakovich learned of the Nazi concentration camps at Treblinka and elsewhere, and that the grotesque, dance-like, *allegretto* finale, the first of his 'Jewish' works of the mid- to late 1940s and early 1950s, is a grim commentary on the camps; and finally, that the work as a whole, especially the last two movements, is permeated with images of death.[1]

[1] Shostakovich began composition of the Trio on 15 February 1944, four days after the death of Sollertinsky. He completed the second movement on 4 August and the entire work soon thereafter, on 13 August. See Derek Hulme, *Dmitri Shostakovich: A Catalogue, Bibliography, and Discography*, 2nd edn (Oxford, 1991), 169.

For representative critical discussions of the Trio, see David Rabinovich, *Dmitri Shostakovich: Composer*, trans. George H. Hanna (Moscow, 1959), 91–4; Eric Roseberry, *Shostakovich: His Life and Times* (New York, 1989), 111; Ian MacDonald, *The New Shostakovich* (Boston, 1990), 172–4; Rostislav Dubinsky, notes to the Borodin Trio's recording of Shostakovich's Piano Quintet in G minor and the E minor Piano Trio (Chandos CHAN 8342, 1983). Dubinsky, the first violinist of the Borodin Quartet, which was formed in Moscow in 1943, attended the Moscow première of the E minor Trio on 28 November 1944 (the world première was in Leningrad on 14 November), in which Shostakovich was the pianist. His account conveys a sense of the sort of impact the work has made from the beginning: 'The music left a devastating impression. People cried openly. The last, "Jewish Part" of the Trio, by popular demand had to be repeated.'

Now there is little reason to revise the main lines of this standard interpretation, which, given the biographical and musical evidence that supports it, seems wellnigh unassailable. But the ostensible transparency of the Trio masks an elegant and compelling musical argument that the conventional wisdom about the piece has discouraged us from hearing. The aspect of the work that most needs to be problematised is the very feature that seems most straightforward about it: the cyclic return of themes. Underlying the explicit and readily audible return, in the finale, of the first movement's introductory canon and the third movement's passacaglia theme is a complex of thematic and tonal integration that, once we are aware of it, deepens our appreciation of the work's structure and raises new and intriguing questions of interpretation. The purpose of the present essay is to interrelate what we might call the 'cycle of structure' (the network of thematic and tonal development and return across movements) with what we might call the 'cycle of meaning' (the way that the multi-movement work as a whole makes a coherent extra-musical statement). I will begin by re-examining briefly the notion of 'cyclic' organisation of multi-movement instrumental works, both in general and with respect to Shostakovich in particular, and then proceed to a detailed elaboration of cyclic aspects of structure and interpretation in the E minor Piano Trio.

CYCLIC STRUCTURE AND CYCLIC MEANING: A REINTERPRETATION

The adjective 'cyclic' is a standard musical term that arose from a correct intuition, but from the beginning incorporated contradictions that compromised its usefulness. It was coined to acknowledge the historical phenomenon that, from the early nineteenth century (or even the late eighteenth century) on, many composers tended more and more to conceive of multi-movement instrumental works not only in terms of conventional notions of balance and proportion and genre-determined successions of movement-types (e.g., fast–slow–fast for the concerto, or fast–slow–menuet–fast for the symphony), but also in terms of a technical and poetic unity that could transcend the individual movements. In so far as the term 'cyclic' articulates one technical aspect of this phenomenon – the recurrence of the same motifs or themes in different movements – its use is unexceptionable. But as a descriptive term in musical analysis it is far too crude, inasmuch as its usage rests upon a simple, if not simplistic, binary opposition: either a piece is 'cyclic' or it is not; either it brings back a theme in different movements, or it does not.

Such a simple opposition fails to capture important musical distinctions, both structural and interpretative. Structurally, the term 'cyclic' by itself tells nothing about how extensive the interconnectedness of movements is in a given piece. It fails, for example, to distinguish between pieces that bring back a central theme in all of its movements, as in Berlioz's *Symphonie fantastique* or *Harold in Italy*, and pieces in which a single theme from an earlier movement simply returns for a single appearance in the last, as in Brahms's Third Symphony. Nor does it address the issue of thematic transformation: the two Berlioz works mould their principal themes into different contexts in each movement, constantly reshaping them into new forms, while the cyclic recurrence of the opening gesture of the Brahms Symphony is an essentially literal restatement. And it completely ignores the many pieces that involve no thematic recurrence as such, but do methodically work out specific tonal and motivic problems over the course of their separate movements – for example, Beethoven's String Quartets in E minor, Op. 59 No. 2, and in F minor, Op. 95, both of which elaborate the tonal opposition established by the flattened second scale degree, or his Seventh Symphony, which turns on a similar opposition involving the flattened third and sixth scale degrees (C♮ and F♮ in A major.

On the interpretative, extramusical side there are problems as well. The impulse towards inter-movement thematic recurrence and transformation in the nineteenth century arose in close association with two related trends in Romantic literature: the tendency to portray subjectivity in action, and the inclination to structure works around tropes such as that of heroic triumph over adversity (as is so frequently read in, or read into, Beethoven's Fifth Symphony, and as Anthony Newcomb reads in Schumann's Second Symphony), or that of the journey, in which the Romantic subject ventures out into the world of experience, suffering and learning, eventually after many trials to return, transformed and redeemed, to the point of departure.[2] In nineteenth-century music, the

---

[2] Anthony Newcomb, 'Once more between absolute and program music: Schumann's Second Symphony', *19th Century Music*, 7 (1984), 233–50. On the notion of 'subjectivity in action', especially in the Romantic Lied, see Lawrence Kramer, 'The Schubert Lied: Romantic form and Romantic consciousness', in *Schubert: Critical and Analytical Studies*, ed. Walter Frisch (Lincoln, Nebr., 1986), 200–36. On the trope of the circular Romantic journey, the classic account is Morris H. Abrams, *Natural Supernaturalism* (New York, 1971).

adherence to a single theme, transformed across the changing contexts of different movements, constituted an apt metaphor for the self, or of the self's view of experience. Transformation of a theme or themes according to established musical figures (the funeral march, grotesquerie of various sorts, the pastoral, the heroic apotheosis and so forth) could project subjectivity across the action of an entire work and suggest one of these standard Romantic tropes, or others as well. The term 'cyclic' alone cannot tell us what, if any, trope is involved in a given piece; yet its root meaning, suggesting an ordered process which ultimately effects a return to an initial state of affairs, strongly implies the departure-and-return model, whether this is in fact relevant to a given piece or not. Thus the term is incapable of specifying any extramusical interpretation, any more than it can indicate, structurally speaking, the degree of thematic interrelatedness in a work, the presence or absence of thematic transformation, or the functioning of tonal and motivic issues across separate movements when thematic recurrence is not involved.

Shostakovich's symphonies and instrumental chamber music fall, in both time and place, outside the nineteenth-century central European tradition that spawned so many cyclic and programmatic works, and that developed a thriving critical tradition to analyse and interpret them as well. Yet Shostakovich, however strong his roots in Russian music, was also nourished by the tradition that produced the Beethoven quartets, Berlioz's *Symphonie fantastique* and *Harold in Italy*, and the Bruckner, Franck and Mahler symphonies; and his works raise many of the same analytical and interpretative questions concerning inter-movement relationships that those of his predecessors did. When weighed in the balance of the simple opposition 'cyclic or non-cyclic', a preponderance of his multi-movement instrumental works falls into the former category rather than the latter. But, as with his nineteenth-century forebears, the mere label tells us very little of what we want to know. How extensive is the return of themes? Does it involve primarily the return of a single theme at a single place, as a rudimentary knowledge of those works that bring back the theme of a slow-movement passacaglia at the end of the final movement – the Fourth and Sixth Quartets, and the First Violin Concerto, for example – might suggest? Or is thematic return more integral to the relationship of movements, involving perhaps more than one theme, or aspects of motivic and thematic development and transformation as well? Colin Mason, for example, shows an increasingly intricate thematic integration in the first eight string quartets, from a point of little or no interrelatedness in the First Quartet to a maximum in the Eighth.³ And does the interrelationship of movements involve tonal relations, as it so often does in the nineteenth-century German symphonic tradition? Finally, and most of all, what are we to make of Shostakovich's multi-movement cycles in terms of their poetic or extramusical import?

The critical traditions, both Russian and western, that have arisen around Shostakovich's music have tended more or less to take as a priori the notion that the movements of the symphonies and chamber works project coherent sequences of what Schumann called *Seelenzustände* – moods of the soul.⁴ Both Russian criticism, beginning with major studies published during Shostakovich's lifetime, such as those of Ivan Martïnov and David Rabinovich, and English-language criticism from that of Gerald Abraham to the more recent work of Hugh Ottaway, David Fanning and Ian MacDonald, interpret the multi-movement instrumental works in this way.⁵ That is, such critics see them as conveying across movements what Jean-Jacques Nattiez would call 'extrinsic meanings' (meanings that provide a link to 'socio-cultural, ideological, political, artistic and philosophical contexts'). Of course, if a particular work exhibits explicit cyclic thematic or tonal relationships, its inter-movement structure also involves what Nattiez calls 'immanent meanings' (meanings embodied in intrinsically musical relations) as well.⁶ Now some of these critics (Ottaway and Fanning, for example) give more attention to immanent, structural relations, while others (Abraham, Martïnov, Rabinovich and MacDonald) concentrate on poetic content. But none seems to question the power of the music to convey a comprehensible unfolding across movements of some sort of extramusical content, whether their view of that content involves explicit narrative, a succession of emotional states or political commentary, either pro-Soviet or anti-Soviet.

---

³ Colin Mason, 'Form in Shostakovich's quartets', *The Musical Times*, 103 (1962), 531–3.
⁴ Leon B. Plantinga, *Schumann as Critic* (New Haven and London, 1967), 120. See also Newcomb, 'Once more between absolute and program music', 233–4.
⁵ Ivan Martïnov, *Dmitri Shostakovich: The Man and His Work*, trans. T. Guralsky (New York, 1947; rpt. New York, 1969); Rabinovich, *Dmitri Shostakovich*; Gerald Abraham, *Eight Soviet Composers* (Oxford, 1943); Hugh Ottaway, *Shostakovich Symphonies* (London, 1978); David Fanning, *The Breath of the Symphonist: Shostakovich's Tenth*, Royal Musical Association Monographs 4 (London, 1988); MacDonald, *The New Shostakovich*.
⁶ Jean-Jacques Nattiez, '"Fidelity" to Wagner: reflections on the centenary Ring', in *Wagner in Performance*, ed. Barry Millington and Stewart Spencer (New Haven and London, 1992), 78.

That the tradition of Shostakovich criticism should have developed in such a manner is hardly surprising. The composer himself provided extensive extramusical commentary on his works. For example, whichever of his interpretations of the final movement of the Fifth Symphony one believes – that it hails the triumphant end of an artistic journey that led from creative poverty to the acceptance of the truth of socialist realism (as implied by the symphony's famous subtitle, 'A Soviet Artist's Practical Creative Reply to Just Criticism'), or that it involves the dissident 'false rejoicing' of the *yurodivïy* composer who mocks the system even as he submits to it (the account given in Solomon Volkov's *Testimony*)[7] – there can be no doubt of his own willingness to recognise extramusical content in the work. Furthermore, both of his interpretations imply a coherent projection of poetic meaning across movements; whether the rejoicing in the finale of the Fifth Symphony is true or false, it comes only as a response to what has preceded it.

Shostakovich's music – and the critical tradition that has grown up around it – has also, like the music of his contemporary, Prokofiev, been generally ignored by theorists of the Anglo-American positivist tradition. Whether this rejection stems from theorists' finding the music structurally uninteresting, from their taking offence at the notion of 'tonal' twentieth-century art music, from their being scared off by the language and cultural distance that separates us from the music of Shostakovich and other Soviet composers, from the overriding sense that one cannot deal with this music without coming to grips with its extramusical content, or from the fact that the currently dominant analytical theory of tonal music (Schenkerian theory) discounts the 'cyclic', cross-movement relations that are so prominent in Shostakovich's symphonies and chamber works, the fact remains that the music thus far has been resistant to any inroads by what is now rather derisively called the 'analytical formalism' of Anglo-American theory.

Yet the music itself clearly demands a marriage of analytical and interpretative approaches, a reckoning with both its immanent and its extrinsic meaning. For Shostakovich was, on the one hand, a sophisticated composer in a high-art tradition, a composer who, as a central part of his creative task, took it upon himself to master and imaginatively to extend the artistic traditions of formal structure, thematic development and tonal relations that he inherited from the nineteenth-century symphonic

[7] Solomon Volkov, *Testimony: The Memoirs of Dmitri Shostakovich as Related to and Edited by Solomon Volkov* (London, 1979), 140.

repertory and from his immediate Russian predecessors. But, on the other hand, he was also a composer who lived in a culture that passionately believed in the power of music to communicate extramusical meaning, and that relied on a well-established complex of critical conventions to gain access to and articulate that meaning.

What a more detailed and nuanced reading of the E minor Piano Trio requires is not just the *analysis* of immanent musical meanings, nor just the critical *interpretation* of extrinsic meanings, but rather a balanced approach that combines the insights of both. In attempting to provide such a reading, I will not invoke any single system, but will adopt analytical and critical techniques as they seem appropriate. On the analytical side, my reading will bear a clear debt to theorists such as Schoenberg, Rudolph Réti and Hans Keller, who are known for their sensitivity (or hypersensitivity, in the case of the latter two), to both intra-movement and cross-movement motivic relationships, and to Schenker's concept of structural levels. On the critical side, it will draw upon the work of such recent scholars as Leo Treitler, Anthony Newcomb and Lawrence Kramer, all of whom have offered provocative interpretations of symphonies in the nineteenth-century German tradition (Beethoven's Ninth, Schumann's Second and Liszt's *Faust Symphony*, respectively) through careful readings of the extrinsic significance of various aspects of the musical surface and structure across the individual movements, and through the synthesis of such readings into a global interpretation of the whole work.[8]

CYCLIC MEANING AND CYCLIC STRUCTURE: HOW THEY INTERACT

The manner in which the E minor Piano Trio is cyclic seems, on the face of it anyway, to be relatively straightforward. That is, it does not seem to be, and previous critical writing has not interpreted it as being, a work that develops a particular theme across different movements as an *idée fixe*, or one that generates a network of hidden motivic parallelisms, or one that works out a particular tonal issue in more than one movement.

---

[8] Leo Treitler, 'History, criticism, and Beethoven's Ninth Symphony', and '"To worship that celestial sound": motives for analysis', in *Music and the Historical Imagination* (Cambridge, 1989), 19–45 and 46–66, respectively; Newcomb, 'Once more between absolute and program music'; Kramer, *Music as Cultural Practice, 1800–1900* (Berkeley and Los Angeles, 1990).

Nor is there any evidence, musical or documentary, that the Trio unfolds an extramusical narrative over the course of its four movements. Rather, the cyclic aspect of the work seems to turn on, first, the conventional musical associations with death that lend to the entire work a certain topical unity (the minor mode, the dark tone, the doleful melodies of the first movement, the sombre passacaglia and so forth); and second, the return, at the end of the final movement, of both the opening canon from the first and the passacaglia theme from the third movement. From the point of view of immanent meaning, these returns serve to effect a re-establishment of tonal and thematic stability in a closing gesture that encompasses the whole work rather than just the finale itself. And from the point of view of extrinsic meaning, they serve to place the fourth movement's ghastly dance of death in the context of the more sombre reflections that were heard in the first and third movements.

But the shattering emotional power of the end of the Trio suggests that something more than structural thematic recall and conventional extramusical reminiscence must be involved here. To probe what that something is requires that we step back from the closing bars and take a broad analytical and hermeneutic look at the whole work: that we read the signs of its sequence of movements, its musical forms and its musical surface in the light of the convincing external, documentary evidence and internal, musical evidence that its 'topic' is death. Once we have developed a focused interpretative perspective, we will return to the explicitly cyclic closing section of the finale and show that what is involved here is more than the simple return of themes – that, with both telling musical logic and a witheringly accurate dramatic sense, this section in fact ties together into a devastating peroration elements of musical and extramusical meaning that have been developed throughout the Trio.

If the extramusical intent of the Trio is virtually indisputable, it is equally clear that Shostakovich (like Beethoven, Schumann and Liszt, in the nineteenth-century symphonies noted above) is content to work within the limitations of conventional musical forms and a standard sequence of movements. The Moderato opening movement is a sonata form, with exposition themes 1 (E minor) and 2 (G major) at fig. 6 and fig. 14 respectively, development at fig. 18, and recapitulation themes 1 (E minor) and 2 (E minor) at fig. 21 and fig. 25 respectively.[9] To this

[9] References to the score of the Trio will cite rehearsal numbers rather than bar numbers. References to bars not coinciding exactly with a rehearsal numbers will count bars from the first bar of a rehearsal number. Thus, for example, the first three bars of fig. 25 would be labelled: fig. 25; fig. 25, b. 2; fig. 25, b. 3.

sonata-form proper the *andante* three-part canon serves as an introduction. The brusque scherzo, in F♯ major, is a loose ABA' form, with a rowdy waltz (figs. 45–9) in G major assuming the role of the trio. The grim passacaglia, whose eight-chord ostinato progresses in each of six statements from a two-chord i–V in B♭ minor to a B diminished triad, leads without pause into the final E minor Allegretto, the most anomalous of the four movements from a formal point of view. Initially suggesting an unexceptional rondo (A at fig. 64, B at fig. 66, A' at fig. 68, C at fig. 71, A" at fig. 75), the movement begins to boil up at fig. 77 into an increasing developmental frenzy, juxtaposing, transforming, foreshortening and contrapuntally combining elements of the A and C themes, and culminating with the return of the tonic E (now in the major mode) at fig. 91. It is at this crucial point that the cyclic thematic returns begin, first with the piano twice arpeggiating the chord progression of the passacaglia, and then, at fig. 92, with the restatement of the entire three-part canon from the beginning of the opening movement, now with a florid piano accompaniment. The return of the initial A and B themes, now both in the tonic E, at figs. 99 and 101, respectively, is loosely interpretable in the rondo scheme, and the final invocation of the passacaglia theme at fig. 105 and an echo of the A theme round off the movement and the work as a whole.

Grounded as it is in the tradition of 'pure' instrumental music, the E minor Piano Trio – both its individual movements and its movements considered together as a cycle – yields readily to musical analysis, to explanation of its immanent musical relationships in musical terms. It would indeed be easy enough at this point to proceed from a general consideration of form to a progressively more detailed discussion of thematic and tonal relationships, all completely independent of extrinsic meaning. What is it that compels us to come to grips with this music in extramusical terms as well? Surely it is, at least in part, our knowledge of the circumstances under which the piece was composed. But there are musical signs as well – signs that compellingly suggest links to a world exterior to purely musical relations. For, even if musical signs bear the capability of functioning self-referentially, they also, as postmodernists are at pains to show us, necessarily function as cultural signs that connect them to social practice at large.

Such signs are evident from the very beginning of the Trio. It hardly requires explicit knowledge that Shostakovich composed the piece while coping with the shock of the death of a close friend to catch the import of the opening canon. That the instruments begin, not together as an ensemble, but separately, each with the same slow, halting, modal, pale, almost directionless line; that the cello begins, not with its natural voice, but with the disembodied shadow of its harmonics, and that both cello and violin are muted; that the piano begins in octaves, in the depths of its registral space; the fact – assured by the canon, of course, but significant (and 'signifying') none the less – that at first the instruments cannot speak independently, but can only trudge through the same plodding line: all suggest a hushed, dumb response – to what, we may not know, but something devastating that seems to have stunned the instruments and rendered them almost speechless.

The canonic introduction provides a frame of reference, a context, for the movement proper. It is indeed the frame of reference provided by the slow introduction that inclines us to hear the rest of the movement, and the rest of the work, as referring to something outside itself. We might say that, in the traditions of the genre (of the piano trio, of sonata form), the introduction is 'marked' with respect to the movement itself. For whereas the introduction virtually clamours for extramusical interpretation, the sonata form beginning with the Moderato presents itself as a more believable 'purely instrumental' piece, a piece that we can comprehend quite well just using formal, thematic and tonal logic. Yet even here there are gestures that we may read as topical musical signs – if not of death, at least of loss – especially when they are heard in the context of the introduction: the insistent, repeated quavers that relentlessly continue through most of the exposition and recapitulation, a throb that will not go away; the hollow, open fifth on which this quaver accompaniment begins; the haunting sound, equally hollow, of the languid main theme, played four octaves apart by the two hands of the pianist; and the general spareness of the texture throughout. We might similarly read the lack of energy of both principal themes: their tendency to cadence on the tonic before they really articulate a full thematic statement. The main theme cadences three times on a downbeat tonic E, and the second theme is really nothing but a matter-of-fact, canonically reiterated two-bar scalewise descent to the local tonic G, which again always arrives on the downbeat, thus hammering home (needlessly? excessively?) an inexorable sense of finality.

Nowhere is this sense of finality more pronounced than at the very end of the movement. When the second theme returns in the recapitulation (at fig. 25), it is not transposed literally from G major to E minor

(Ex. 5.1). Rather, the theme begins on the tonic of the key rather than the fifth, the initial leap of the ascending ninth is altered to an octave, and the reiterated figure is reduced to a single bar, so that what is first heard is simply the repeated figure shown in Example 5.2. But then at the fourth bar of fig. 25, the cello seems to pick up the incomplete line from the piano and to drive it home, A3–A3–G3–G3–F♯3–F♯3–E3.[10] At the end of the second bar of fig. 26, the violin latches on to this descending $\hat{4}$–$\hat{3}$–$\hat{2}$–$\hat{1}$ idea (Ex. 5.3). Together the violin and cello play this idea six successive times: beginning at five octaves apart and progressing to two octaves apart (the hollowness of these octaves being reminiscent of the first theme), with the violin stating each successive repetition more softly, and with the final statement in augmentation. In a movement whose themes seem obsessed with arriving on the tonic, the impression here – especially with the repetition of the third and second scale degrees, $\hat{3}$–$\hat{3}$–$\hat{2}$–$\hat{2}$–$\hat{1}$, and the downbeat emphasis on the first $\hat{3}$ and the cadential $\hat{1}$ – is that of forcing ourselves to believe something that seems obvious, but that we somehow cannot grasp or accept.

When considered in the light of the entire movement, these cadential reiterations begin to suggest a broader hermeneutic reading. The movement begins in stunned disbelief, one voice at a time, with the instruments unable to do anything but repeat the same material. Gathering themselves together for a 'real' movement, they do so with some success – a faster tempo, a legitimate formal structure with real themes and thematic development. But images of the grim reality haunt the movement, and the themes never really get out of their rut. At the end, the sense of finality that is submerged in the themes throughout the movement

Ex. 5.1 Exact transposition (hypothetical) of theme 2, first movement, to the tonic

Ex. 5.2 Reiterated second-theme figure in the recapitulation of the first movement

---

[10] Designation of specific octaves is given according to the scheme established by the Acoustical Society of America, whereby the lowest C of the piano is C1, and middle C thus C4.

Ex. 5.3 $\hat{4}$–$\hat{3}$–$\hat{2}$–$\hat{1}$ figures leading to the cadence of the first movement

ultimately rises to the surface when the second theme is placed in the tonic. The strings, once they lock into the cadential idea, can do nothing but repeat it. The piano ventures a reminiscence of the first theme at fig. 26, b. 3, over the E–B open fifth (now with a quaver neighbour note), but it soon cadences by winding its way quickly to a downbeat E. Trailing off through a descending scale, the piano then makes a final attempt to keep the movement going by introducing the ascending scalar figure that began the bridge at fig. 11, only to find that it, too, moves directly to E. What the movement seems to portray is, first, a sense of shock and loss, followed by a determined, if forced and eventually unsuccessful, attempt to proceed with life as usual, and finally the inevitable realisation of the truth, the reality of which must impress itself upon us repeatedly for us to believe it.

The second movement, of course, hardly suggests the topic of death. If anything, it must serve as a memory, of happier and more exuberant times. It does share certain features of the first movement, such as the frequent voicing of melodies in parallel two or more octaves apart, a generally, though not consistently, spare texture, and especially, cadential figures leading scalewise in equal note values to downbeats on the tonic or other melodic points of arrival. Here these figures tend not to be $\hat{3}-\hat{2}-\hat{1}$, or $\hat{4}-\hat{3}-\hat{2}-\hat{1}$ (although these occur – see fig. 38, bb. 7–8, in the strings, and leading into fig. 41 in the cello), as in the first movement, but rather $\hat{5}-\hat{6}-\hat{7}-\hat{8}$ (as in the strings at fig. 37, bb. 3–4 and 12–13, at fig. 55, bb. 7–8, and at fig. 56, bb. 3–4 and 7–8), or even a chromatic ascent or descent to the goal note (as in the piano at fig. 31, bb. 5–6, and leading into fig. 35), or in the strings at the final cadence of the movement. One might even hear the $\hat{5}-\hat{5}-\hat{3}-\hat{3}-\hat{1}$ cadence of the main theme of the trio (see fig. 45, bb. 9–11) as a variation of this idea.

After the swirling memories of the second movement, the passacaglia is a mournful elegy in which the stolid ostinato chord progression in the piano undergirds an impassioned lyrical duet in the violin and cello. The ostinato provides a twentieth-century variation on the baroque topic of the lament bass with the descending chromatic tetrachord. Here, the eight-bar bass turns not on one, but on two tetrachords: B♭–F–G–A and F♯–G–A–B. Each tetrachord suggests its own key – the first B♭ minor, the second a modal E minor, towards which the ostinato continually presses, but to which it never resolves, at least until the resolution provided by the beginning of the finale. Also, the disposition of the two tetrachords is such that neither is descending or chromatic, as was the case in the historical model. Rather, the tetrachords themselves are separate and diatonic, while the chromatic descent takes place not in the bass, but in the upper voice of the right hand, which chromatically connects F4 down to B3 (omitting only C♯4; see Ex. 5.4).

126 Patrick McCreless

Ex. 5.4 Passacaglia theme, third movement

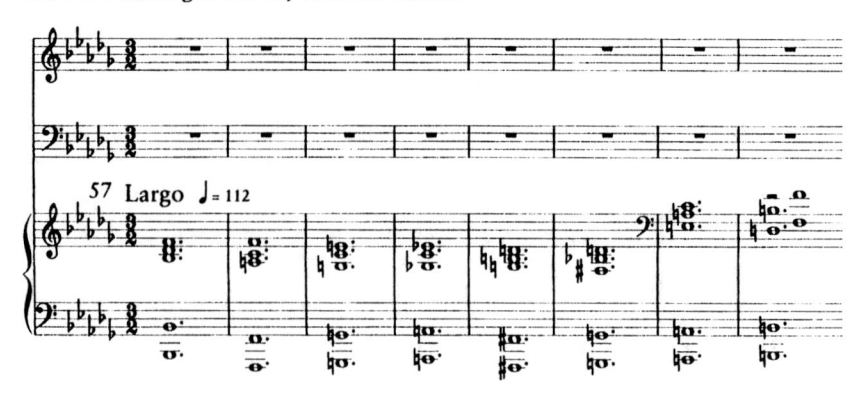

The main body of the final movement – that is, up to the cyclic recurrences at fig. 91 – seems to turn from private loss to public horror. Ian MacDonald articulates the external motivation for the movement:

> Written rapidly in late July and early August [of 1944], [the finale] is the first of Shostakovich's 'Jewish' pieces, in this case provoked by reports in the Soviet press of the Red Army's liberation of the Nazi death camps at Belzec, Sobibor, Majdanek, and Treblinka. Horrified by stories that SS guards had made their victims dance beside their own graves, Shostakovich created a directly programmatic image of it. This harshly realistic movement is meant to shock and, at its height, the impression of someone stumbling about in exhaustion is painfully vivid.[11]

In addition to musical topics already noted in the first two movements (the repeated staccato quaver figure, parallel thematic statements voiced two octaves apart), Shostakovich deliberately adopts in much of the movement a Jewish folk idiom: jaunty, highly accented, metrically regular dance rhythms; the pizzicati, strummed multiple-stop chords and soloistic effects of the Jewish fiddler; and the ubiquitous flattened-second scale degree and melodic augmented seconds.

CYCLIC RETURN IN THE FINALE: AN ANALYTIC AND HERMENEUTIC READING

What we have in the Trio as a whole, then, is, in MacDonald's words, a work 'begun in grief and concluded in anger'.[12] MacDonald's observation is surely correct, so far as it goes; there can be little doubt that the finale

[11] MacDonald, *The New Shostakovich*, 173–4.   [12] Ibid., 174.

The Piano Trio in E minor, Op. 67

carries us from a private world to a public one. But what about the conclusion of the finale, the cyclic return of themes from the first and third movements? Does the anger continue here? For MacDonald, apparently not. Describing this section, he suggests:

> ... death mercifully supervenes in pealing baroque arpeggios, leaving the ghost of the main theme dancing sepulchrally in the bass, like the murdered Petrushka at the end of Stravinsky's ballet. With a final memory of the passacaglia, the Trio twitches to a stop: a broken puppet.[13]

MacDonald's interpretation of the end of the Trio is plausible, but it leaves important questions unanswered. What evidence is there that 'death supervenes' in the arpeggios at fig. 91? Why do these arpeggios articulate the chord progression of the passacaglia (a point that MacDonald does not mention)? Why does the entire canon from the introduction to the first movement reappear (another point that MacDonald does not mention)? If death arrives with the arpeggios and there is little left but the 'ghost of the main theme' in the bass (at fig. 99 or at fig. 103?) and 'a final memory of the passacaglia', why is there an 'appassionato', *fortissimo* statement of the B theme of the finale at fig. 101? Rather than answering these questions directly, I propose another hypothesis, which in my view makes more sense critically, and which avoids the anomalies of MacDonald's interpretation. What MacDonald has failed to see is the centrality of the ending of the finale (from fig. 91 to the end) to the structure and meaning of the entire work. The section is not just a conclusion in which reminiscences of earlier musical ideas allow the wild energy of the movement to dissipate, but in fact the key to the cyclic aspects of the Trio as a whole.

The first clue as to what the section might mean involves what we might call the shift of *voice* that occurs at fig. 91. The quasi-rondo that constitutes the main body of the finale is a 'dance of death' – a dance that, if it shares affinities with Stravinsky's music, seems closer to the macabre fiddler of *L'Histoire* than to *Petrushka* – that towards its end whips itself more and more into a frenzy. But this frenzy is not allowed to consummate itself in a violent conclusion for the work, as might be the case, say, in a tarantella. As MacDonald intimates, *something* supervenes, or *intervenes*, at fig. 91. What it is that intervenes is not death itself, but rather a new tone, a new voice: a voice that we heard earlier in the passacaglia. And soon thereafter, after two statements of the arpeggiated

[13] *Ibid.*

passacaglia theme, another voice, similar in character, though not the same, reappears – that of the canon from the first movement.

What distinguishes both these voices is that they seem *subjective*, personal. Indeed, casting a broad view over the entire Trio, we might suggest that the Trio, as a work about death, turns precisely on an axis of two aspects of our experience of death: a subjective, inner-directed, reflective aspect that involves the subject's response to and coping with loss; and a more objective outer-directed aspect that, though still in essence an inner experience, peers out of the self towards the one or ones who have died, with a view to sharing a memory of them in a more public way. I would argue that the Trio presents both these aspects – the inner-directed one in the introduction to the first movement and in the passacaglia, and the outer-directed one in the dance-like scherzo movement and the ghostly finale. And we might also surmise that both Shostakovich's friend Sollertinsky, whose death provided the original impetus for the composition of the Trio in February 1944, and the victims of the Nazi death camps, about whom the composer learned in the summer of the same year, are memorialised in both the private and public ways. Thus, in the introduction to the first movement and in the second movement we might surmise that the object of the subject's (the composer's) memory is Sollertinsky (the private shock of the sudden loss of a friend in the introduction, and recollections of the public side of a close friendship in the second movement). Similarly, in the passacaglia and the finale the focus is on the Jewish victims of the Holocaust (private mourning in the passacaglia, public horror in the finale). The sonata form of the first movement combines elements of both the subjective and the objective, the themes suggesting a subjective attempt to come to grips with the finality of death, the masterful treatment of the standard (public) form suggesting a memorial to the departed. It is precisely the quality that I am calling *voice* that differentiates the inner- and outer-directed aspects of the experience of death musically. The inner-directed voice is individualised, alone; the outer-directed one is more conventional, more public. The distinction can be captured perfectly by comparing the lone, dolorous, individualised voice, taken up by each instrument in its turn, of the opening canon, to the foursquare, folk-like dance tunes of the second movement. Or compare the passacaglia's improvisational chord progression and the anguished, lyrical lines of the violin and cello duet above it to the grotesque dance of the finale. In the one case the individual looks inside, aggrieved with loss; in the other, the individual looks out and ponders his or her relationship with those who have died.

An awareness of the change of voice that takes place at fig. 91 makes possible, first, a general sketching out of an interpretation of the cyclic returns that occur here, and then a more detailed analytical corroboration of this interpretation. Leading into fig. 91, the dance of death whirls to a peak of intensity, and just before fig. 91 it seems as though it will continue for ever, or else accelerate to a frantic, cataclysmic cadence. But at the bar before fig. 91, the dance is suddenly interrupted – at first by a rest, and by the absence of the piano. What intervenes, what stops the dance – or, in the context of the whole Trio, what *returns* – is only the themes with the *inner-directed* voice, which is to say, the subject: the subject who pondered the death of an individual in the previous movement, and now must absorb death on a vaster, more horrifying scale. It as though the subject (composer? pianist?) abruptly stops while watching the dance at its height and forcefully asks, 'How can *I* (as a subject) absorb such terror?' Returning first to the contemplative progression of the passacaglia of the previous movement, now energised and made more desperate by the experience of wholesale rather than individual death, the subject finds that this thought leads back even further, to the sense of shock that initiated the whole Trio. But now the canonic theme that earlier embodied this numb sense of shock is radically transformed: transformed into private rage – against death itself (against the 'dying of the light', as it were) and against murder institutionalised by fascism (and perhaps also by Stalinism). The entire canon recurs, now accompanied by a piano filigree that continues to dissipate the energy of the dance.

The change of voice thus does not bring peace, and does not silence the voices of the victims. The main theme of the finale returns (at fig. 99), now in grisly parallel fifths in the low register of the piano, accompanied in its second statement by the strings *col legno* on the E–B open fifth. As if this reminder of the horror were not enough, suddenly the second theme of the finale cries out hoarsely in a high register in the strings (at fig. 101), and threatens, as it reaches the semiquavers of the sixth bar of fig. 101, to carry us precipitously back to the fury of the main body of the movement (as it was, say, at fig. 85 to fig. 86).

But, thankfully, this is not to be. The fury of the second theme of the finale subsides and gives way to a final statement of the first theme (now *pianissimo* and in octaves in the piano rather than fifths; see fig. 103). The rhythmic energy of the movement plods to a virtual halt, and just before what promises to be the end – at the bar before fig. 105, where we expect a cadential E in the piano – the strings hold on to their F, and the piano and strings join in one final statement of the subjective, contemplative passacaglia progression. Still, over the cadential E major chord, the ghost of the dance sounds one last time in the violin and once in the cello, and the two instruments exchange pizzicato chords before joining together in a final one. Hermeneutically, we might interpret this last sequence of events to suggest that, even though subjective reflection can finally bring a certain degree of acceptance and peace about death, as instantiated in the resolution of the last statement of the B♭ minor passacaglia theme to the global tonic of E, still one cannot avoid being haunted by the deaths of innocents, as symbolised by the incipit of the 'Jewish' finale theme and pizzicato chords at the end.

That such is the import of the final pages of the Trio is, I believe, justified by the way Shostakovich uses musical signs. A close reading of the musical surface in the light of conventional extramusical associations makes the interpretation at least plausible and, I hope, persuasive. But a reading of the musical surface can in no way demonstrate the sophistication that Shostakovich the musician has brought to bear upon the final section of the fourth movement. An analytical look below the musical surface – at thematic and tonal relationships – not only supports the extramusical interpretation put forth here, but also shows how integrally this central passage (beginning at fig. 91) is linked to the entire work, and how intimately bound up is 'the cycle of meaning' that I have identified thus far with 'the cycle of structure' that I have already outlined briefly in the discussion of form and a few tonal and thematic relations, and that I will flesh out now. Analysis will also illuminate certain extramusical aspects of the work that have not been touched upon yet.

We have seen how the final section of the fourth movement of the Trio emphasises the notion of *voice* in making its extramusical point. A closer look shows how surface can merge almost imperceptibly into structure, criticism into analysis. Consider, for example, the two principal examples of the 'inner-directed' voice – the opening canon of the first movement, and the passacaglia. Although these two themes share an inner directedness (the individual line in the canon, the contemplative progression in the passacaglia), they actually are binary opposites in one respect: the canonic melody is purely diatonic and modal, while the passacaglia's progression and its upper melodic line are densely chromatic. We might suggest that the modal–diatonic and the chromatic represent opposite sides of the inner response to death, the diatonic suggesting a kind of emotional numbness, the chromatic a more cognitive reflection. Such an interpretation seems supported by the following evidence: that in the Trio the shock comes first, long before cognitive consideration; that the thoughtful passacaglia theme, which begins in B♭ minor, seems continually to progress towards modal resolution in the global tonic of E minor, but is never able to do so with the passacaglia itself, just as it takes repeated re-experiencing of a loss to accept it; that when the passacaglia theme does achieve resolution directly into E minor for the first time, at fig. 92, it leads not to any sense of inner peace, but to the enraged statement of the canon – perhaps depicting the psychological truth that, after cognitive acknowledgment of bereavement, emotional denial and rage necessarily precede acceptance; but that, when the passacaglia theme resolves into E for the second time (now in the major mode, at the end, between figs. 105 and 106), the strings, significantly, take on the primary *surface feature* (that is, harmonics) of the opening cello line while playing the melodic *content* of the descending chromatic line of the passacaglia, thereby suggesting that the loss is somehow absorbed and accepted, both cognitively and emotionally, after reflection. (Of course, as noted above, the echo of the main theme suggests that the unjust deaths portrayed in the finale itself can never be accepted.)

But this diatonic–chromatic polarity is not just a surface signifier; it is also integral to the musical argument of the entire cyclic structure. For example, when the long canon of the introduction ends, around fig. 4, there appears an extended ascending line in the right hand of the piano, connecting C4 up to E4 diatonically, but E4 up to B4 chromatically. The idea of direct chromatic succession then becomes thematic for the whole work. In the sonata form of the first movement it makes a brief appearance, again in the right hand of the piano, after the initial statement of the opening theme (see fig. 8, b. 6, to fig. 9, b. 5); and it defines the transition theme, in both cello and piano, at fig. 11. In the second movement, as we have seen, the melodic cadential figures that approach the tonic through scalewise motion from above or below are frequently chromaticised. And having been reversed to a descending chromatic line in the passacaglia, the idea appears in another descending transformation as the C theme of the finale (fig. 71).

Another motivic element that functions both as an extramusical signifier and as an integral element of musical logic is the double neighbour figure of the opening theme of the finale: E–D♯–E–F–D♯. In the context of the fourth movement, this suggests a circling around the tonic, in a manner reminiscent of the tonic emphasis of the themes of the first movement, and its flattened second scale degree also connotes the Jewish folk idiom. But it is also clear that, simply as a melodic shape, the double neighbour or turn is a central idea of all the movements: it is present in the G–F♯–A–G at the beginning of the first theme of the Moderato in the first movement, the D♯–C♯–B♯–C♯ of the main theme of the second movement, and the C–B♭–A–B♭ of the lyrical violin and cello theme that is introduced above the passacaglia progression.

A musical element that effects a telling connection between extramusical signification and musical argument is the tonal polarity E–B♭. We have already noted this polarity in the two primary cyclic, subjective themes – the canonic theme in E minor, the passacaglia theme in B♭ minor. Of course, the two are directly juxtaposed when the subjective element suddenly asserts itself – into the rabid dance at fig. 91. I have also suggested that the fact that the passacaglia continually moves from B♭ towards a modal resolution on E, but that that resolution is never achieved until (1) the moment of cyclic return of the canon, and (2) the final cadence just before fig. 106, might signify a subjective working towards the ultimate acceptance of a painful reality that is initially resisted. But I have not shown how the E–B♭ polarity is elegantly interwoven into the musical fabric of the entire Trio. B♭ makes its first appearance in the middle of the principal sonata theme of the first movement (see Ex. 5.5). After the initial lyrical sequence that begins the theme moves (prematurely, it seems) to E5 at fig. 7, the theme progresses scalewise up from E5 to B♭5 (E–F–G–A–B♭), then up through a B♭ major triad to F6, down through an improbable $\hat{5}$–$\hat{4}$–$\hat{3}$–$\hat{2}$–$\hat{1}$ in B♭, and then down scalewise through the flattened second again to E5. Underlying this motion in the bass of the piano is, first, an E1–F1–B♭ motion at fig. 7 (a pattern a tritone removed from the A♯–B–E figure of the second theme of the finale), and then a figure that imitates the piano right hand of fig. 7, B♭. 3–7, almost note for note. B♭ is tonicised again towards the end of the closing section (at fig. 15: note the strong $\hat{4}$–$\hat{3}$–$\hat{2}$–$\hat{1}$ cadence in the right hand of the piano immediately before fig. 16 – obscured, however, by the simultaneous E♭ cadence in the strings and left hand), and it is the first key tonicised by the piano when it enters in the development (fig. 18, b. 9).

The Piano Trio in E minor, Op. 67

Ex. 5.5 First theme of the Moderato, first movement

Finally, perhaps the most far-reaching of all the motivic and tonal cross-movement relationships is one that involves the principal theme of the finale and the melodic cadence that occurs between fig. 104 and fig. 105. We have already seen how the beginning of this theme (fig. 64) shares a double neighbour figure with principal themes of other movements. But compare also the end of this theme (see Ex. 5.6a) to the cadence in B♭ major, noted immediately above, just before fig. 16 of the first movement (Ex. 5.6b). The close relationship between the themes is instantly apparent – note the ascending $\hat{1}$–$\hat{5}$–$\hat{8}$, the cadential $\hat{4}$–$\hat{3}$–$\hat{2}$–$\hat{1}$ and, of course, the repeated notes – the one significant difference being that, at x in the theme from the finale, the melody turns down so as to cadence on the second scale degree, whereas in the theme from the first movement, it leaps up to $\hat{4}$, so as to cadence on the tonic. Two points are noteworthy here. First, the cadential theme, as it appears in the first movement, is in fact generated from the descending scalewise motion that constitutes the second theme; an incomplete version of this cadence, which augments the second theme's descent by stretching it out with repeated quavers, is evident, in G, two bars before fig. 15. It is, of course, this same $\hat{4}$–$\hat{3}$–$\hat{3}$–$\hat{2}$–$\hat{2}$–$\hat{1}$ figure, transposed to the tonic, that forms the conclusion of the first movement. Second, Shostakovich treats the finale version of the tune as something of a compositional problem, inasmuch as it cadences a step higher than it begins. His standard solution is, in Schenkerian terms, to convert the second scale degree (F♯) to a large-scale passing note by inserting a G and proceeding to the next theme, as at figs. 64–5 (see Ex. 5.7).

To pursue most of his other solutions would take us to a level of detail beyond what is necessary here. But the tune is crucial to the final melodic cadence of the Trio, and only through an understanding of its history can we adequately appreciate the elegance of this cadence. At fig. 103, under the open fifths of the strings, the piano begins what seems to be a last, halting version of the main theme of the finale, with a bar of rest articulating each subphrase of the tune. Then at fig. 104, after omitting the fifth, sixth, and seventh bars, the tune continues, now in augmentation, with the repeated notes split between the piano in low register in octaves and the string harmonics. But since beginning this subphrase on E would again result in a cadence on F♯, Shostakovich allows the parallel string fifths of the bar before fig. 104 to carry the tune down to D, so that, using the same intervallic pattern, it will conclude on the goal tonic of E.

The Piano Trio in E minor, Op. 67

Ex. 5.6 Comparison of the opening theme, final movement, with passage from the first movement   (a) Opening theme, final movement

(b) Cadence in the piano leading to theme 2, first movement

Ex. 5.7 Linear analysis of the opening theme, final movement

The brilliance of the compositional stroke at two bars before fig. 105 thus becomes apparent. We expect a cadential E here. The subversion of the movement to E and substitution of an F instead – the 'molto vibrato' instruction here captures the sense of this subversion perfectly – marks for one last time the intrusion of the subject attempting to comprehend the dance of death going on about him. But now the 'subject' is not just the individual whose experience the Trio thus far seems to have portrayed. Now, because the rhetorically marked note is F, and because it is precisely this note that is the characteristic flattened-second scale degree that signifies the Jewish victims of the camps, the individual 'subject' of the Trio merges his identity with that of the victims. From a compositional point of view, this F not only dramatically problematises, in one brief moment, the characteristic flattened-second scale degree of the movement, but it also ushers in the B♭ minor of the passacaglia theme, and in addition beautifully dovetails the D–C♯–B–A–G♯–F♯–(E?) of the descent of the transposed main theme and the F–E–E♭–D–C–B of the top voice of the passacaglia theme. Yet this upper line of the passacaglia theme never attains full melodic resolution; it never achieves a descent to the tonic, but only to the dominant. From a critical point of view, its non-resolution then poses the real interpretative question of the piece: will not the subject's indelible consciousness of unjust deaths by political terror (as embodied in the 'Jewish' F) always throw that subject back to the searching and mourning of the passacaglia, which constantly attempts, but always fails, to gain peace? And thus, at the end of the work, do we not now realise that the finality of death, which the first movement's second theme so hammers home, and which the theme of the last movement seeks but never attains, is offered only to the dead? To us, the living, it is denied. Having at first fought to reject it, we eventually, having cast a cold eye on life and death and having learned, we thought, to accept it, find out that we cannot – and, if we are to believe Shostakovich, we must not.

6

Leitmotif in *Lady Macbeth*

DAVID FANNING

The Lady Macbeth of Mtsensk District contains one of the most notorious sex scenes in all opera. At the end of Act I, Katerina Izmaylova and Sergey, the new foreman on her family's estate, become lovers, to the accompaniment of a virtuosic orchestral galop complete with additional brass band and culminating, at least in the original 1932 version, in orgasmic trombone glissandi.[1] This musical setting was famously summed up by an American reviewer as 'pornophony'.[2]

Understandably, perhaps, less attention has been paid to what comes next, which is unfortunate, since the beginning of Act II throws fascinating light on the musical language of the opera. The scene is later the same night. Katerina's father-in-law, the insomniac Boris Timofeyevich, is on watch. He remembers when he was young. He got no sleep then either, but for different reasons . . . (Ex. 6.1).

Anathema though it may be to opera-lovers, to the Russian musical temperament in general and to the prevailing mode of Shostakovich commentary, I should like to consider this passage in the first instance (and so far as possible) as 'pure music'. In these terms the music of Example 6.1 is a rhapsodic slow introduction, disturbing and menacing in tone. Its musical language is highly chromatic and not at all easy to explain theoretically. Many harmonic directions are suggested, only for the music to divert away from them. But eventually, at the end of the extract, the opening G minor is reconfirmed as a tonic; and when that happens, the many ambiguities in the harmony resolve into a larger pattern, shown in the analytical sketch on pp. 142–3.

---

[1] For details of revisions to the score, including the suppression of these glissandi, see Laurel Fay's chapter in the present volume.
[2] Uncredited review of the New York production, 'The murders of Mtsensk', in *Time* magazine (11 February 1935), pp. 34–7.

138 David Fanning

Ex. 6.1

Cl.b.
202
It seems to me all the time that burglars try to
Cl.b.
Cl.b.
203
break in; I walk a - bout, watch - ing my house
Cl.b.
Fag.

204
Was young once, also couldn't sleep but for a different reason.

Leitmotif in *Lady Macbeth*   141

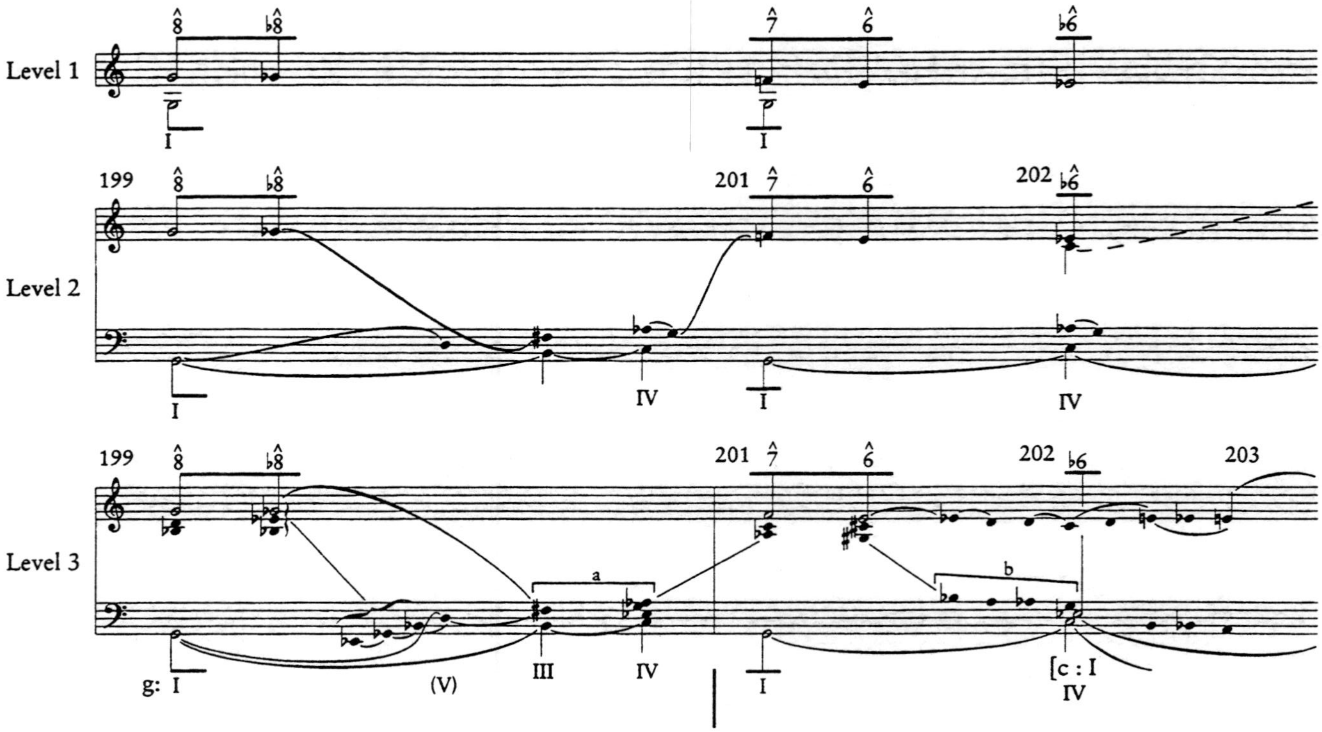
Level 1
Level 2
Level 3
199
201
202
203
g: I
(V)
III
IV
[c : I
a
b

Level 1

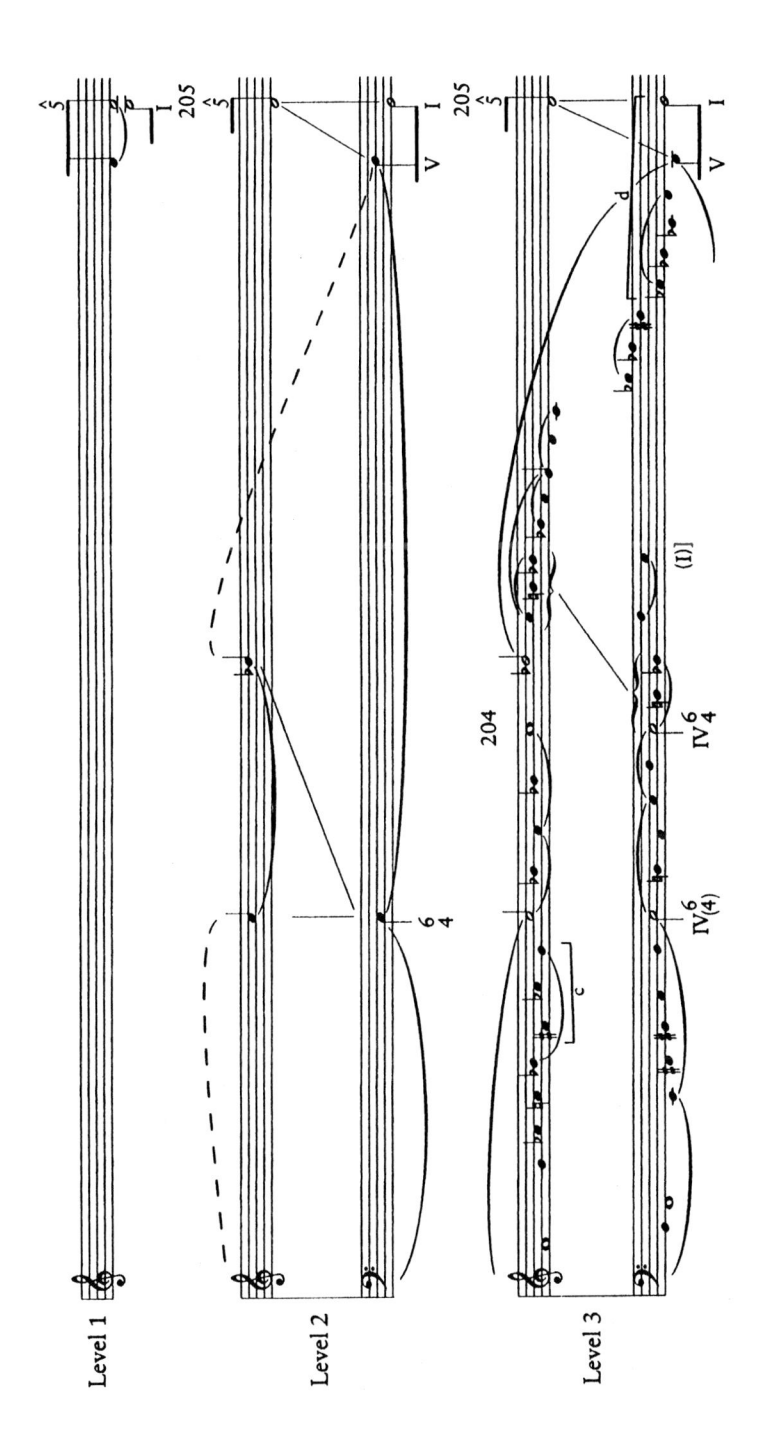

Level 2

Level 3

144   David Fanning

This reductive sketch is founded on Heinrich Schenker's hierarchical concept of tonal harmony. For the last thirty or forty years Schenker's theories have been central to Anglo-American analytical musicology, at least for the repertory of German music from Bach to Brahms. But even though their application has been extended to other eras and styles they have not, so far as I know, yet been tried out with Shostakovich.[3]

Example 6.1 shows three hierarchic levels, each progressively more detailed. Ideally it should be self-explanatory, at least to the reader well versed in this type of analysis. But a general explanation may not do any harm.

Level 1 seeks to show a relationship between the specific and the universal – between the piece of music in question and the universal coherence of tonal music, as Schenker understood it, based on a 'composing-out' of the tonic triad. It gives the skeleton of the harmony, which in this case is simply a prolongation of the G minor tonic through a chromatic linear descent in the top voice which is clearly defined by the phrase structure of the music.

Level 2 adds some vital organs and muscles to this skeleton. It shows how each stage of the melodic descent itself is elaborated by harmonic support and contrapuntal motion – in this instance the most significant factor is subdominant harmony. The first of the two structural subdominants is approached via the upper mediant and resolves in quasi-plagal fashion back to a pedal-point G; the second structural subdominant is more directly approached but then much more extensively prolonged, both by motion towards its own subdominant and by unfolding of an inner voice through octave transfers up and down. The overall aim of Level 2 is to show the pacing and interrelation of the main harmonic events – in other words, how the structure of the music 'breathes'.

Level 3 continues the process of elaboration, showing how at the beginning of the extract the harmonisation of the upper-voice G♭ influences the bass clarinet's melodic response, then how varied chromatic resolutions define structural harmonic changes throughout the extract (bracketed motifs *a* to *d*), and how the octave transfers of figs. 202 to 205 are effected by means mainly of scale progressions of a third. Here the aim is to show that Shostakovich's Linear Polyphony is rich, multi-layered and musically self-sufficient.[4]

[3] There is a short example in my 'Writing about Shostakovich – performing Shostakovich', paper read at the University of Michigan Shostakovich conference, *Shostakovich: the Man and his Age*, February 1994, publication forthcoming.

[4] The passage from fig. 203 to 204 in particular recalls the style of Shostakovich's

Leitmotif in *Lady Macbeth*   145

Now, putting 'pure music' on one side for a moment, I should like to consider this extract for what it is – part of an opera. What is happening here in stage terms? In effect, nothing. Boris is thinking, reminiscing, waiting – a state of mind which is obviously rather important in *Lady Macbeth*. This is how we observe Katerina herself at the beginning of the first scene, for instance, and a similar atmosphere of festering lethargy dominates the first interlude (at least in the 1930s versions of the opera).

The opposite pole to this oppressive inaction is oppressive action, notably in the notorious scenes of sexual harassment, seduction, flogging, murder and law enforcement. And the musical common factor between these dramatic poles is the language of Linear Polyphony (see note 4). Some of the action scenes, such as Aksinya's molestation in Act I scene 2, can be understood theoretically in much the same way as Boris's reminiscences examined above.[5] But there is an important distinction to be drawn.

The action scenes in *Lady Macbeth* are violent, manic and satirical in tone, and their musical language is a sadistic intensification of the intonations of such genres as waltz, polka, galop and cancan. But whereas these scenes are carried along by the characteristic rhythms of their respective genre-models, the slow, contemplative scenes employ a fluid Musorgskian *recitativo accompagnato* or arioso style. In part the texture here is responsive to the intonations of the voice line. But in part also, it is built around motifs which recur throughout the opera and which have a semantic dimension. (Such motifs may also be found in the 'action' scenes, but to a far lesser extent.) And it is the significance of these motifs that will be the focus of the rest of this chapter.

A nine-bar extract from Example 6.1 offers particularly rich pickings. On Example 6.2 I have bracketed three motifs, which I should like to consider in turn.[6]

Motif *a*, instances of which are shown in Example 6.3, is widely recognised as the motif of Force.[7] I am happy to accept that label, and to agree that the semantic quality of the motif is established in the second

Aphorisms, Op. 13 (see the opening of No. 4, 'Elegy'). For a discussion of Linear Polyphony in Soviet music see, for example, Detlef Gojowy, *Neue sowjetische Musik der 20er Jahre* (Laaber, 1980), 122–32, 258–96.

[5] See Fanning, 'Writing about Shostakovich'.
[6] Rehearsal numbers in the musical examples which follow are from the 'original' score (published in 1979 by Sikorski Musikverlag, Hamburg).
[7] See, for instance, Ekhart Kröplin, *Frühe sowjetische Oper* (Berlin, 1985), 220–1, 235, 472–90.

Ex. 6.2

scene, where it appears in conjunction with Aksinya's molestation. Its identity is primarily rhythmic (although many instances are formed from a scalic minor-third descent, thus overlapping with another important motif – see Example 6.8 below), and in its most forceful appearances it concludes with two accented repeated notes, this being the form of its most extended treatment, in the police music of scenes 7 and 8. The fact that this motif starts with such a strongly accented downbeat as well as finishing with those two accented notes enables it to function equally well as a beginning of a phrase or a conclusion. In fact it appears in the opera as much for reasons of structural emphasis as for the dramatic representation of force, and this joint structural and dramatic function of motifs is an important general issue to bear in mind. (An example of the same rhythmic motif liberated from close semantic ties is the passacaglia theme of the slow movement of the First Violin Concerto.)

Motif *b* (Ex. 6.4) is associated with Katerina, Boris and the prisoners. (Incidentally, it is also the motif Shostakovich quotes in the last movement of his autobiographical Eighth String Quartet.) In the first scene this motif undergoes a process of evolution, shown in Example 6.4, from its first appearance as an accompaniment to Katerina's opening words – 'Akh, ne spit'sya bol'she' (Ah, I can't sleep any more) – through three clear steps to become Boris's main theme, as if to confirm the influence he has on her life. Other appearances of this motif suggest a more specific connotation, which is to do with sleeplessness. Consider the textual contexts where the motif appears: in scene 1 Katerina cannot sleep because she has already

Leitmotif in *Lady Macbeth* 147

Ex. 6.3

[Boris: And I am always on watch]

Katerina: You're a rat   Aksinya: What a shameless man   Chorus: Ha-ha-ha...

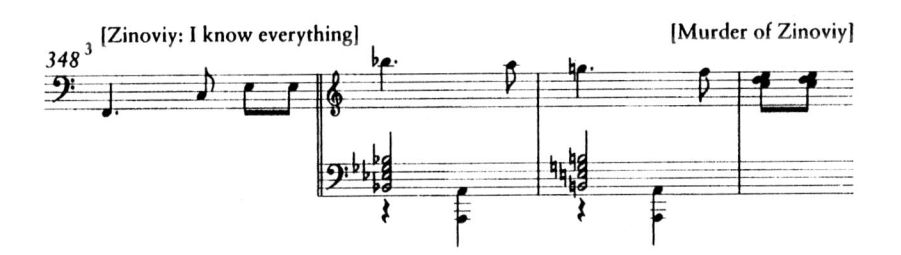

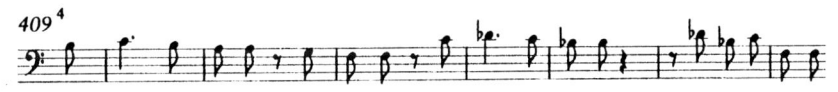

[Zinoviy: I know everything]   [Murder of Zinoviy]

Sergeant: If only we had a pretext.   Although a pretext can always be found

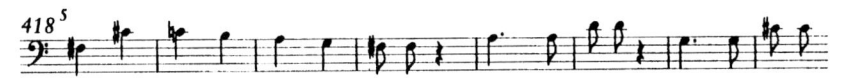

Sergeant: So that no one will accuse us of being slack or inattentive

[*Entr'acte* scenes 7 – 8]

148   David Fanning

Ex. 6.4

[Katerina: Ah, I can't sleep any more]   [Katerina: I lay down again]

[Katerina ponders]

Katerina: The ant drags along its straw

[Entrance of Boris]

Boris: And why did we take
[the likes of you into our house]

[Scene 9, introduction]

Katerina: Ah, Boris Timofeyevich, [Why have you left us?]

Boris Godunov, Prologue

Chorus: Why are you forsaking us?

Symphony No. 7, first movement

b.10 Symphony No. 8, first movement

slept too much; in scene 4 Boris cannot sleep because he is on watch and because he is old; once upon a time he could not sleep because he was *young* . . . ; and in the final scene the prisoners crave sleep at the end of a day's marching. As with the Force motif, there seem to be two distinct versions – one with repeated notes, which is more closely tied to Boris, and one without, which is more associated with Katerina.

Noteworthy too is the inversion of the Boris version of this motif, which appears in scene 4 when Katerina sings her crocodile-tears lament after Boris's death – 'Akh, Boris Timofeyevich'. Its derivation from the insincere crowd pleas in the Prologue to *Boris Godunov* and its echoes in themes from Shostakovich's Seventh and Eighth Symphonies are clear enough, but it needs to be said that it is only the 1930s versions of the vocal line which have the motif at all. As Laurel Fay also points out in her chapter, in the 1963 revision it disappears because of Shostakovich's adjustments to the extremely high tessitura of Katerina's lines. In general many of the associations between text and motif in *Lady Macbeth* are lost in the 1963 revisions, which of course affected the text as much as the music.

Motif *c* (Ex. 6.5) is simply a descending triad, which seems rather too innocuous to qualify as a leitmotif. Nevertheless, it figures prominently through the opera, and consistently with reference to worthless males. This may not be entirely surprising, since all the males in the opera, with the exception of the old convict, are indeed thoroughly worthless. But it is particularly their worthlessness as sexual beings that is being commented on in places where the motif is used. The first appearance in scene 1 introduces us to Katerina's sexually dysfunctional husband Zinoviy Borisovich; further instances include Katerina's scene 3 aria, 'The foal runs after the filly' (*zherebyonok k kobïlke toropitsya*), and references to Sergey's comeuppance in scenes 4 and 6. As for its appearance in the nine-bar passage of Example 6.2, Boris's reference to his own promiscuous past falls neatly into the same overall category of male worthlessness. Once again there are two rhythmically distinct manifestations of the motif, the dactylic version being associated with impotence, especially Zinoviy's, and the anapaestic with potency, both Boris's, and from time to time Sergey's.

I have already managed to smuggle in the word 'leitmotif'. But what *is* a leitmotif? Clearly there are relatively formal and informal ways of using the term. Certainly, all operas have a semantic dimension more or less determined by the text; and many operas have recurring musical themes. But not

150 David Fanning

Ex. 6.5

35^3

[Entrance of Zinoviy]

140

Katerina: The foal runs after the filly

206^4

Boris: I've had a good life

222^{-3}

[Parting of Katerina and Sergey]

251

[Porter: We've locked Sergey in the storeroom]

269

[Second foreman: It means he's really bad]

297^3

[Katerina: Seryozha]

361^{-2}

[Scene 6, introduction]

375^{-2}

Shabby peasant: Sergey too was poor and low

380

Shabby peasant: Oh, what a stink

506^2

Sergey: Unbearable pain

all operas with recurring themes have leitmotifs, unless we take an extremely permissive view of the term. And we have to bear in mind the composer's own statement that 'In the music of "Lady Macbeth" there are no so-called leitmotifs'.[8] Certainly, Shostakovich does not attach motifs exclusively or even predominantly to one character, in the manner of many of the undisputed leitmotifs in Wagner's *Ring* cycle or Berg's *Wozzeck*.[9] And he may allow a theme to metamorphose as it transfers from one character to another, as we saw with motif *b*, which I labelled 'Sleeplessness'.

Essentially the motifs in *Lady Macbeth* are attached not to individuals but to states of being. Even then, however subtly and sensitively one labels that state of being and the motif that goes with it, the motif in question sometimes appears in other textual contexts; and occasionally there are explicit references to the state of being in question which are *not* accompanied by the corresponding motif. That all suggests a less conscious and systematic approach on the composer's part than a strict usage of 'leitmotif' would seem to allow. Also we have to remember that the term was coined partly to stress the *leading* function of such motifs in Wagner's musical argument. When earlier composers, such as Méhul, Cherubini, Marschner and Spohr, used motifs with character or situation associations but without Wagner's degree of thoroughness, those motifs have become generally known as 'Erinnerungsmotive' – reminiscence motifs.[10] So maybe it would be prudent to suggest that Shostakovich's network of motifs falls somewhere between reminiscence motif and leitmotif.

On the other hand it is worth remembering that studies of leitmotif in Wagner, especially in *Tristan und Isolde* and *Parsifal*, have disagreed quite markedly over the labelling of leitmotifs, without worrying about the appropriateness of the term itself. So the various important caveats in respect of leitmotif in *Lady Macbeth* are not necessarily an argument for avoiding the term altogether. Given the relative compactness and flexibility of the motifs in question, maybe 'sub-' or 'quasi-leitmotifs' would be the most accurate designation (though 'micro-leitmotif' also has a certain charm).

---

[8] 'Novaya opera Shostakovicha' [Shostakovich's new opera], *Vechernyaya Moskva* (21 December 1932).

[9] The classic study of leitmotif in *Wozzeck* is by Peter Petersen, *Alban Berg, Wozzeck: Eine semantische Analyse unter Einbeziehung der Skizzen und Dokumente aus dem Nachlass Bergs* (Munich, 1985).

[10] See Arnold Whittall, 'Leitmotif', in *The New Grove Dictionary of Opera*, ed. Stanley Sadie (London, 1992), ii, 1137.

152 David Fanning

For the time being it is worth re-emphasising the point that once the semantic association of the motif is well established, Shostakovich feels free to use it as much for structural as for representational purposes. A good example is another widely acknowledged motif (Ex. 6.6), which the East German scholar Eckart Kröplin simply calls Katerina's theme,[11] which Marina Sabinina associates with 'violence' and 'cynicism',[12] and which Alla Bogdanova sees as the 'other' Katerina – 'rebellious, savage and blind'.[13] I propose to call this simply 'Katerina's self-assertion'.

Ex. 6.6

Katerina: Let the woman go [*Entr'acte* scenes 2/3]

Katerina: What is it? I'm sleeping

Katerina: We didn't go to the theatre or to dances

[Shabby peasant: What a stink]

[*Entr'acte* scenes 6/7]   [Katerina: Ah, Sergey, forgive me]

Sergey: Do you know, Sonyetka, who we are like?

---

[11] Kröplin, *Frühe sowjetische Oper*, 220–9, 480–2.
[12] 'Zametki ob opera "Katerina Izmaylova"', in *Shostakovich*, ed. Givi Ordzhonikidze (Moscow, 1967), 159.
[13] *Operï i baletï D. Shostakovicha* (Moscow, 1979), 176.

The first appearance of this motif is in the second scene where Katerina instructs the workmen to cease taunting Aksinya. Self-assertion is clear enough here and again in scene 5, where Katerina tells her suspicious husband insolently but truthfully that she 'never went to the theatre' (*po teatram ne khodim*), and it is clear in the last scene where the motif's meaning is mocked in Katerina's pleas for forgiveness and Sergey's taunts of her. The reduction of the motif to a near monotone in the early part of scene 3 is an effective way of suggesting self-assertion simmering away beneath the surface. But the most extensive use of the motif comes in the two polka interludes – between scenes 2 and 3, just after Boris has discovered Katerina and Sergey wrestling, and between scenes 6 and 7 where the shabby peasant rushes off to tell the police he has discovered Zinoviy's body, and the melodic shape of the motif bends appropriately into the opening of the 'Dies Irae'. Here the semantic and structural dimensions of the motif are as one.

These interludes are symphonic developments of, respectively, Katerina's self-assertion, and the impending self-destruction which that self-assertion has brought about. Although self-assertion provides the dramatic context here, what we perceive in this interlude, provided the producer can resist the temptation to add a visual gloss,[14] is essentially music running riot, symphonic music.

Another example of a motif whose semantic and structural roles are well balanced is the setting of Katerina's opening words (Ex. 6.7). As already suggested, this is not the motif that carries the connotation of sleeplessness, despite the fact that it accompanies the words 'Akh, ne spit'sya bol'she'. What it does acquire in the course of the opera, however, is associations with sexuality, especially frustrated sexuality (see the accompanying texts to Ex. 6.7).

With the exception of Boris's music in scene 1 the variants of the motif hardly go beyond the range of a rising minor third; and they hardly ever vary the semitone first step. At times frustration gives way to action in the more explicitly sexual scenes, such as the molestation of Aksinya and the seduction of Katerina, and here the minor-third scale is

[14] As, for instance, David Pountney did in his highly effective but provocative mimed allegory of denunciation and political imprisonment, which accompanied the scene 6/7 interlude in his production for English National Opera, first staged 22 May 1987 at London's Coliseum. Against this it may be said that Shostakovich seems to have sanctioned such *mise-en-scènes* in Boris Pokrovsky's production of *The Nose* – see Wilson, *Shostakovich: A Life Remembered* (London, 1994), 386–7.

154 David Fanning

Ex. 6.7

[Musical notation with the following labels:]

b. 2 — Katerina: Ah, I can't sleep any more [Katerina: What boredom] [Boris: I told my son not to marry Katerina]

29 — [Boris: And I am always on watch]

50 — [Boris: Make her swear an oath to be faithful to you] Aksinya: He will seduce any woman

72³ — [Aksinya: Where are you touching me?] [Aksinya: Ah!]

138 — [Katerina undresses] Sergey: Don't be afraid Katerina: What is it, Sergey?

193⁻³ — Katerina: I am a married woman Boris: Is there anything left from supper?

274 — Boris: It's her, it's her [Shabby peasant: What a stink] [Entr'acte 6/7]

435⁻² — [Scene 8, introduction] Katerina: Ah, Seryozha, please forgive me

476⁻² — [Katerina: Stepanich! Let me pass] [Katerina: Seryozha]

481 — Katerina: I forgot everything when you were with me [Sergey: And who was it who made me a convict?]

486⁻¹ — [Katerina: It's not easy after joys]

Leitmotif in *Lady Macbeth* 155

emancipated from its anchor-note and becomes allied to its inversion and a chromatic variant (Ex. 6.8). Repeated incessantly this motif then assumes the structural *and* representational function of climax-building.

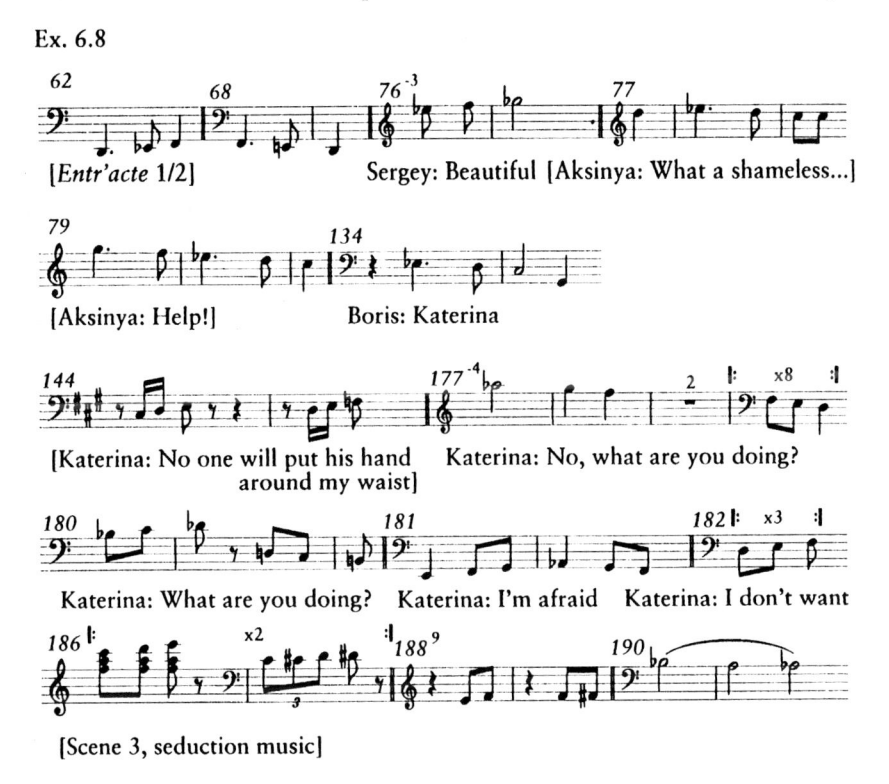

Ex. 6.8

[Entr'acte 1/2]   Sergey: Beautiful [Aksinya: What a shameless...]

[Aksinya: Help!]   Boris: Katerina

[Katerina: No one will put his hand around my waist]   Katerina: No, what are you doing?

Katerina: What are you doing?   Katerina: I'm afraid   Katerina: I don't want

[Scene 3, seduction music]

The only remaining motifs to which I want to draw attention derive from the opening bar of the work (Ex. 6.9). The motif in the treble, whether melodically or harmonically expressed, seems to be associated with Katerina and Zinoviy's sexless relationship, and in particular with Boris's comments on it. Derived from this is a group of motifs associated with Katerina's imprecations to Sergey to kiss her (*potseluy menya*).[15]

The inventory of motifs could be extended, but only at the risk of forcing a point, and the above examples cover the main ground.[16] Of

---

[15] See Bogdanova, *Operï i baletï*, 173. She notes the recurring motif, but misses the textual correlation because at the time of writing she did not have access to the original text in the 1932 version.

[16] Kröplin offers further examples in his discussion of formal and motivic construction in *Lady Macbeth – Frühe sowjetische Oper*, 472–90.

156   David Fanning

Ex. 6.9

[Scene 1 introduction]   Boris: This is the fifth year of her marriage

[Boris's exit]   [Katerina: I swear!]

Katerina: Kiss me! Not like that, not like that

Katerina: [Your business is] to kiss me   Katerina: Kiss, kiss, kiss me

Katerina: Kiss, kiss, kiss me

course motifs are not the only musical element with semantic force in the opera. There is some non-systematic tonal symbolism – G minor is Boris's key (though it also underpins the teacher's music in scene 7), F♯ is the love key (though also that of the policemen's fast-forward march to the Izmaylovs), and F minor serves as Peripeteia in Act I and Catharsis in Act IV. Instrumental tone-colour is a factor, too, although writers do not always agree precisely in what way, except that in general exotic woodwinds, such as the bass clarinet and alto flute in Example 6.1, are used to suggest the degeneracy of the male characters.

It should also be said that there is another side to the question of thematic representation of dramatic states. So far I have been considering the use of motifs to highlight and differentiate between states of being. But Shostakovich also uses thematic techniques to relate states of being he might otherwise have been expected to keep separate, more especially in the 'action' scenes. Principally that entails using the characteristics of the operetta galop to forge an association between Aksinya's molestation,

Katerina's seduction, Sergey's flogging and the policemen's march to the Izmaylovs. This stresses the common elements of power and victimisation; and the exaggeration of tempo and gesture adds an element of silent-film comedy which makes for an uncomfortable ambivalence.

But those are side-issues to my main purpose, which is to supplement Russian accounts of the music and to challenge western scholars such as Erik Fischer, who assert that whatever recurring ideas there are in the opera they carry no semantic association.[17] I hope that the examples above are in themselves effective enough. I am not unduly worried about Shostakovich's reluctance to use the word 'leitmotif', except in so far as I believe it has thrown commentators off an important scent. 'Reminiscence motif' or 'sub-leitmotif' or 'quasi-leitmotif' will do just as well. Even Wagner himself preferred circumlocutions such as 'thematisches Motiv', 'Ahnungsmotiv', 'Grundthema' and 'Hauptmotiv', and what most seemed to bother him about Hans von Wolzogen's famous guide to *The Ring* was precisely that it highlighted the representational rather than the structural role of the motifs (what he would have made of structural analysis of the Schenkerian kind is of course another matter . . .), and that it was in danger of trivialising the drama for the sake of public accessibility. Apart from probably sharing that fear, I suspect that Shostakovich was also aware how the too-obvious presence of leitmotifs always seems to invite hostile polemic – witness Hanslick and Stravinsky against Wagner. Nor, given the generally 'negative' nature (in socialist-realist terms) of the leitmotivic associations, is it surprising that he had no qualms about losing them when the text of the opera was (repeatedly) overhauled.

Does any of this conflict with Shostakovich's insistence on the symphonic continuity of the score?[18] In Russia that may not be an issue, because the designation 'symphonic' is most often used in a rather general sense to mean large-scale, orchestrally reinforced continuity.[19] Of course we

[17] See his *Zur Problematik der Opernstruktur, Beihefte zum Archiv für Musikwissenschaft*, Band 20 (Wiesbaden, 1982), 132.
[18] 'Its music develops symphonically from the first to the last note' (*simfonicheskoye razvitiye ot pervoy do posledney noti*); 'The music flows in an uninterrupted current until the end of an act, after which it continues in [the] next act, progressing [not] by small bits but developing as a big symphonic whole' (*Muzykal'noye techeniye idyot nepreri̇vno, obri̇vayas' lish' po okonchanii kazhdogo akta, i vozobnovlyaetsya v sleduyushchem, idya ne malen'kimi kusochkami, no razri̇vayas' v bol'shom simfonicheskom plane*). Cited in D. Shostakovich, *Sobraniye sochineniy, tom dvadtsatïy* [Collected Works, vol. 20 (1985)], fourth page of editorial introduction.
[19] See, for example, Bogdanova, *Operï i baletï*, 184, 205.

have that meaning in the West too, just as we make more or less informal use of 'leitmotif'. But there is a distinct difference of emphasis, in that many more western musicians and writers are inclined to understand 'symphonic' as something more specific – not only large-scale continuity but also movement, a sense of 'travelling', of processes such as growth and decay, or conflict and resolution, strongly contrasted and yet integrated in one over-arching, purely musical experience.[20] This is an understanding of 'symphonic' which might seem difficult to reconcile with the presence in such number of such powerful extramusical signs as leitmotifs, and indeed with the whole concept of opera.

There is surely some virtue in retaining something of this western understanding. Certainly to call *Lady Macbeth* 'symphonic' should mean more than just identifying a kind of crypto-sonata form with Katerina and Sergey as the two main themes and their drama as a development section and so on.[21] 'Symphonic' should mean at least a rich, many-layered and large-scale musical coherence. I hope I have managed to show how one might begin to analyse such coherence in the passage presented at the beginning of this chapter. Obviously a study that did full justice to the symphonic aspect of the entire opera in that amount of detail would be extremely complex, but I believe that in principle it should be possible and certainly worth doing.

As to the possible incompatibility between leitmotifs and symphonism, Wagner certainly would not have seen any. No one could say that a passage such as the Prelude to Act III of *Siegfried*, which is saturated with leitmotifs, does not work symphonically too, whatever one's definition of the terms. Moreover, recent western Wagner scholarship has challenged the common understanding of the whole concept of leitmotif and thus challenged the apparent dichotomy. For instance, Carolyn Abbate has written that: 'Wagner's motifs have no referential meaning'.[22] She means, I think, that the way leitmotifs are *used* emancipates them from whatever semantic associations they may have acquired and returns them to their natural state, which is to say, music.

---

[20] See Robert Simpson, editor's introduction to *The Symphony*, i (London, 1967), and Robert Layton, editor's introduction to *A Companion to the Symphony* (London, 1993).

[21] See, for example, Viktor Bobrovsky, 'Simfonicheskaya opera', *Sovetskaya Muzika* (4/1964), 45–9.

[22] Carolyn Abbate, 'Wagner "On Modulation" and "Tristan"', *Cambridge Opera Journal*, 1 (1989), 45.

In conclusion, then, there is no necessary contradiction between leitmotivic and symphonic construction in *Lady Macbeth*; nor need we feel any inhibitions about investigating these aspects in tandem and using both terms. But to gain a true understanding of the symphonic aspect requires going into a lot more detail than existing studies do; and neo-Schenkerian methods are one effective means of embarking on that. And a true understanding of the leitmotivic dimension requires far more systematic work than has been carried out hitherto, with careful reference to the original version of the libretto.

Perhaps the title of this chapter should really have had a question mark at the end: 'Leitmotif in *Lady Macbeth*?' The answer has to be: yes and no; but surely more yes than no. And not only. . . .

7

From *Lady Macbeth* to *Katerina*
Shostakovich's versions and revisions[1]

LAUREL E. FAY

It is well known that Shostakovich's *Lady Macbeth* exists in two different versions. The first, designated Op. 29 in the composer's catalogue, was completed late in 1932 and staged almost simultaneously in Leningrad and Moscow, both rival productions having their premières in January 1934. Despite the initial popular success of these productions, the opera effectively disappeared from view soon after it and its composer came under official attack in 1936. Almost thirty years later, when it was finally revived in Moscow in January 1963, the libretto had been thoroughly reworked, the music somewhat less so. To underscore the differences, the composer gave this new version the opera's alternative title, *Katerina Izmaylova*, and assigned it a new opus number, Op. 114. It was in this revised form that the work quickly regained its place in the repertory both at home and abroad.

It is often assumed that Shostakovich's new version resulted *solely* as a response to the public censure of the opera in 1936. Previous comparisons of the two versions of *Lady Macbeth* have frequently been used to demonstrate how effectively the Soviet regime's aesthetic criteria were applied: the opera 'before' and 'after' socialist realism; the opera as a showcase for the benefits (or abuses) of political intervention; and so forth.

In fact, interest in the alternative versions all but evaporated after 1979, when the 1932 score of *Lady Macbeth* surfaced again in the West, inaugurating a spate of new productions based on this rediscovered 'original' version. By now the earlier text, presumed to represent not simply Shostakovich's first but also his best intentions – before any

---

[1] Research for this article was supported in part by a grant from the International Research & Exchanges Board (IREX), with funds provided by the National Endowment for the Humanities and the United States Information Agency. None of these organisations is responsible for the views expressed.

external political tampering took place – has completely supplanted the later revision (*Katerina Izmaylova*, Op. 114) in the repertory of European and American companies.[2] The fact that Shostakovich himself repeatedly expressed a preference for his own revised score is usually discounted; for how could the composer have been in a position, even after Stalin's death, to tell the 'real' truth? But this supposition grants the composer no room for second thoughts, no independent capacity for initiating changes or improvements.

In Russia, even after the demise of Communism, the status of Shostakovich's opera has remained equivocal. In the arts, as in other spheres of life, the energies of scholars and professionals have been directed towards the revival and rehabilitation of everything suppressed during the Soviet period. No one now questions the devastating impact that the 1936 *Pravda* editorial and the campaign that followed had on Shostakovich himself. But scholars there, as well as family members and friends of the composer, seem more inclined to take Shostakovich at his word when it comes to the work which precipitated that campaign. The revised *Katerina Izmaylova* is still accepted at face value as the standard version, the one bearing the composer's own stamp of approval. Indeed, most discussions of the opera in Russian sources, while recognising it as a product of the 1930s, still follow the text of the 1963 version without reference to revisions. While it is true that Russian scholars have had very limited access to productions of the 'original' version or to the rediscovered score, they have so far been surprisingly reluctant to take advantage of their country's unique holdings of archival documents, letters and other manuscript and print materials in order to give us the kind of full and objective account of the opera's composition, production and revision that it so clearly deserves.

Even from a cursory examination of archival sources in Moscow and Leningrad, the preliminary picture that emerges about Shostakovich's work on the opera is far more complex and intriguing than the two-version confrontation would suggest. Opera is, after all, a collaborative, synergistic enterprise; it is common for the operatic composer to have to accommodate the visions of other artists (singers, directors, etc.) in the process of bringing a new work to the stage. From the beginning, Shostakovich showed an open-minded, creative approach to the staging of

[2] According to promotional literature, more than thirty new productions of the 'original' *Lady Macbeth* had been mounted in the West from the première in Wuppertal in 1980 to June 1994.

his new work. An active collaborator in all three of the Russian productions mounted in 1934 and 1935,[3] he willingly made minor musical changes, offered alternative texts, sanctioned cuts and other modifications when problems arose during rehearsal. This was, of course, well before there was any reason to anticipate the coming catastrophe – that is to say, before specifically political motives could have preoccupied him. There are also indications that Shostakovich's renewed attention to the score in the 1950s may have been motivated, at least initially, by a private inner impulse rather than by any outside pressure to compromise his creative integrity.

The publication history of Shostakovich's opera is complicated. While the 'original' version of the opera, as completed by the composer in December 1932, was not published during his lifetime, Shostakovich did supervise the preparation by Muzgiz in Moscow of a piano-vocal score, issued in late 1935,[4] that already contained significant changes from the 1932 version. For the revised *Katerina Izmaylova*, Op. 114, on the other hand, both full and vocal scores were published in Moscow in 1965.[5] The 'original' 1932 version finally saw publication in 1979, by Hans Sikorski in Hamburg.[6] To avoid confusion in the discussion which follows, the published editions will be identified by their date of attribution: 1932, 1935 and 1963.

Sending both orchestral and vocal scores to Grigoriy Stolyarov on 23 February 1933, Shostakovich cautioned the conductor that he would

---

[3] See below pp. 169 ff. for others involved in these productions.
[4] Dmitry Shostakovich, *Lady Macbeth of Mzensk*, '*Katerina Izmailova*', Op. 29, opera in 4 acts and 9 scenes, libretto according to N. Leskov by A. Preis and D. Shostakovich, English version by L. Soudakova (Moscow, 1935). The same piano-vocal score, with German translation, was issued simultaneously in Vienna by Universal Edition (Ed. No. 10740).
[5] D. Shostakovich, *Katerina Izmaylova*, Op. 29/114, opera in 4 Acts, 9 Scenes (Revised Edition, 1963), Libretto by A. Preis and D. Shostakovich, English translation by E. Downes. Full score in two volumes, also piano-vocal score in one volume. Moscow: Muzïka, 1965. This was the version of the opera included in the forty-two-volume Collected Works of the composer; see *D. Shostakovich: Sobraniye sochineniy*, tom 20–2 (Moscow, 1985).
[6] Dmitri Schostakowitsch, *Lady Macbeth von Mzensk, Oper in 4 Akten (9 Bildern), Urfassung 1932 (Erstausgabe)*, libretto von A. Preis und D. Schostakowitsch nach der gleichnamigen Erzählung von N. Ljeskow, Deutsch von Jörg Morgener und Siegfried Schoenbohm. Klavierauszug. Hamburg: Sikorski, 1979 (Ed. No. 2313). I wish to express my gratitude to G. Schirmer, Inc., for the loan of the full score of this version, otherwise available only on rental.

need the vocal score back by 1 March when it was due at the engravers.[7] On 16 November 1933, Shostakovich reported to Ivan Sollertinsky from Moscow, 'I have been busy from morning to night. In the morning there are rehearsals of "Lady Macbeth", in the afternoon and evening I am correcting the Muzgiz proofs of same.'[8] Publication of the Muzgiz piano-vocal score dragged out for almost two more years: it was submitted for production on 16 June 1934 and, once passed by the censor, sent to press on 7 August 1935, appearing in print before the year was out.[9] It is not known whether Shostakovich made further changes in the piano-vocal score between the time he had been correcting proofs in 1933, before the opera had even been produced, and the date of publication in late 1935. But the 1935 score does differ in subtle and significant respects from the 'Version 1932 (First Edition)' resurrected and published for the first time in 1979.[10]

The uncredited 'Notes on the History of the Opera' which preface this publication outline the most significant modifications from the 'original' version of 1932 to the first publication of 1935, including changes in text chiefly intended to moderate vulgar language and erotic allusions, alterations in tessitura, dynamics, orchestration, etc. Unfortunately, while claiming to present the opera 'as the author had it in view',[11] the source for the publication, autograph or other, is not identified. If Act IV was only finished on 17 December 1932, then the description of this publication as 'Version 1932 (First Edition)', with its implied claim of authoritativeness, would appear to refer to Shostakovich's opera at the stage while the ink was still wet on the page, before any practical creative collaboration with directors, conductors and singers, before any second thoughts by composer or librettist, let alone before input from censors and critics. Even if this version of the opera is the earliest extant one, it is simplistic to assume that that automatically makes it the definitive one. In fact, there is some reason to doubt that this score is indeed the earliest. A two-volume conductor's

[7] D. D. Shostakovich letter to G. Stolyarov, 23 February 1933, Glinka Museum of Musical Culture (GTsMMK) fond 291, edinitsa khraneniya 90 [archive 291, bit of storage 90].
[8] L. Mikheyeva, 'Istoriya odnoy druzhbï' [Story of a friendship], *Sovetskaya Muzïka* (9/1986), 33. Muzgiz is the abbreviation for Gosudarstvennïy muzïkal'nïy izdatel'stvo (State Music Publishers). The opera was actually produced in Moscow under an alternative title, *Katerina Izmaylova*.   [9] See note 4.
[10] See note 6. That the alterations were not all *that* extreme, however, is evidenced by the fact that the 1979 Sikorski vocal score appears to have used the modified plates of the 1935 Muzgiz vocal score as the basis for its edition.
[11] *Lady Macbeth von Mzensk*, 5.

164   Laurel E. Fay

full score (hereafter referred to as GLINKA-271) is preserved in the Glinka Museum in Moscow. Especially with respect to the libretto, it appears to pre-date the 1932 edition.[12]

A key passage in establishing the chronology is Katerina's famous aria from Act I scene 3, which conveys the full force of her misery and longing with unaffected lyrical warmth. The text of this aria underwent substantial revision in the successive published editions, tempering the explicit, naturalistic language with a more abstract, poetic expression of longing.[13] In GLINKA-271, the text originally underlaid for this aria has been crossed out, but a substitute text, penned above it in blue ink, corresponds closely to what is published in the 1932 edition of the score. The deleted text for the aria, while it begins like its better-known replacement ('The foal runs after the filly, the tom-cat seeks the female'), has a mosquito rather than a dove hastening to its mate in the next phrase, and prolongs its mundane catalogue of mating pairs (cows, dogs, snakes) before finally shifting focus to the heroine's loveless plight.[14] The replacement, with its

[12] GTsMMK f. 32, ed. khr. 271. The card-file entry for the opera lists it as 'Katerina Izmaylova [Ledi Makbet], Op. 29'. This conductor's score (in the hand of a copyist) bears no title page or other identifying markings or dates and some pages are missing from the beginning of volume 2 (Act III). Nevertheless, the version of the opera is clearly that of the 1930s. What has been widely billed as the autograph manuscript of the first version of the full score is preserved in the Russian State Archives of Literature and Art (RGALI fond 2048, opis' 2, edinitsa khraneniya 32–5 [archive 2048, schedule 2, bit of storage 32–5]). Although this manuscript is indeed an autograph, much of it has been taped over, razored and otherwise mutilated in the process of revision so that, ironically, it no longer provides a satisfactory source for the original version of the opera. It does, however, record the dates of composition: Act I was begun in Leningrad on 14 October 1930 and completed on 5 November 1931 in Tiflis; Act II was begun on 19 November 1931 in Leningrad and completed on 8 March 1932 in Moscow; the beginning of Act III is dated 5 April 1932 and its completion dated 15 August 1932 in Gaspra; the beginning of Act IV is not dated, but it was completed on 17 December 1932 in Leningrad.

[13] The 'Notes on the History of the Opera' in Sikorski Ed. 2313, p. 5, for instance, juxtapose translations (German and English) of the texts of 1932 and 1935 editions to demonstrate the severe differences. See also Royal S. Brown, 'The three faces of Lady Macbeth', *Russian and Soviet Music: Essays for Boris Schwarz*, ed. Malcolm Hamrick Brown (Ann Arbor, 1984), 247–50.

[14] GTsMMK f. 32, ed. khr. 271:
Zherebyonok k kobïlke toropitsya,
Kotik prositsya k koshechke,
Komar k komarike stremitsya,
I tol'ko ko mne nikto ne speshit.
Bïchen s korovkoy laskayutsya,
Kobelek za suchkami begayet,
Zmey so zmeyey oblivayutsya.
Tol'ko menya k grudi ne prizhmut,
etc.

1932 Edition (Sikorski Ed. 2313):
Zherebyonok k kobïlke toropitsya,
Kotik prositsya k koshechke,
A golub' k golubke stremitsya,
I tol'ko ko mne nikto ne speshit.
Beryozku veter laskayutsya,
I teplom svoyim greyet solnishko
Vsem chto-nibud' ulïbayetsya,
Tol'ko ko mne nikto ne pridyot,
etc.

more varied poetic imagery and style, is clearly a substantial improvement. GLINKA-271 is a copyist's score, not an autograph; it incorporates other modifications relative to the 1932 edition, suggesting that the 1932 edition is already a revision of some earlier version of the opera.[15] Another discrepancy between the two scores helps to explain one of the more curious incidents in the same scene. Both scores still contain the full, 123-bar instrumental 'rape' interlude (figs. 183–92), including the notorious pre- and post-tumescent trombone glissandi (the latter subsequently excised in a twenty-one-bar cut made to the passage in the 1935 piano-vocal score). It is in the immediate aftermath of the interlude that the textual differences are found:

1932 edition (Sikorski Ed. 2313):[16]

192	KATERINA: Now go away for God's sake. I am a married woman.
193	SERGEY: Ho, ho. Seems I have never seen married women give themselves to me so quickly. Ho, ho. Zinoviy heh Borisovich. Ho, ho, ho, ho, ho . . . ho, ho . . . ho, ho . . . ho, ho, ho, ho, ho, ho, ho.
194	Let's not speak of that.
	KATERINA: I have no husband, only you alone.

Katerina's entreaty to Sergey to leave and respect her marriage vows is greeted by a fourteen-bar unaccompanied recitative (figs. 193–4) in which Sergey cynically mocks her and her husband. When the orchestra re-enters at fig. 194, Sergey abruptly curtails his sport, for no apparent

The foal runs after the filly,	The foal runs after the filly,
The tom-cat seeks the female,	The tom-cat seeks the female,
The mosquito hastens to its mate,	The dove hastens to its mate,
But no one hurries to me.	But no one hurries to me.
The bull snuggles up to the cow,	The wind caresses the birch-tree
The dog runs after the bitches,	And the sun warms it with its heat
The snake entwines with its consort,	Something smiles upon everyone,
But nobody presses me to their breast,	Only no one will come for me,
etc.	etc.

[15] Unfortunately, virtually nothing is known about the contribution of Shostakovich's co-librettist, Alexander Preys (1906–42), or how active a role he may have played in the revisions discussed here.

[16]
192 KATERINA: Uidi ti radi boga. Ya muzhnyaya zhena.
193 SERGEY: kho, kho. Chto to ne videl ya, chtob muzhniye zhyony tak bïstro mne otdavalis', kho, kho, Zinoviy to Borisovich. Kho, kho, kho, kho, kho . . . kho, kho . . . kho, kho . . . kho, kho, kho, kho, kho, kho, kho.
194 Ne nado ob etom.
    KATERINA: Net u menya muzha. Tol'ko tï odin.

166   Laurel E. Fay

reason, singing 'Let's not speak of that'. The explanation for this strange twist can be seen in the corrections to the passage in GLINKA-271:[17]

192 KATERINA: ~~Why did you do that?~~ Now go away for God's sake. I am a married woman.
193 [SERGEY: Ho, ho. Seems I have never seen married women give themselves to me so quickly. Ho, ho. Zinoviy heh Borisovich. Ho-ho-ho-ho . . . he couldn't [****] his wife . . . ho-ho-ho-ho-ho-ho-ho.] [*fourteen bars deleted*]
194 ~~KATERINA: Let's not speak of that.~~ [*original underlay*]
     ~~KATERINA: My own darling.~~ [*1st revision*]
     SERGEY: [illegible] of that. [*final revision*]
     KATERINA: I have no husband, only you alone.

In the initial underlay for Sergey's recitative, he makes unambiguous reference to the impotence of Katerina's husband and it is she who responds 'Let's not speak of that'. However, once Sergey's fourteen-bar recitative had been cut (crossed out in blue pencil), and the score skipped directly from fig. 192 to fig. 194, Katerina's original response ceased to make sense in its new context. After first altering her line to read 'My own darling', the passage 'Let's not speak of that' was reassigned to Sergey, in response now to Katerina's 'I am a married woman'. It seems likely that, in restoring the excised recitative, the editors of the 1932 edition failed to take into account the alteration its removal had necessitated; they kept the phrase at fig. 194 as Sergey's.[18] Incidentally, Katerina's 'Why did you do that?' at fig. 192 in GLINKA-271 leaves less room for doubt about what has just happened to her than later versions would.[19]

Another contemporary score of *Lady Macbeth* in the Glinka Museum archive (hereafter referred to as GLINKA-284) also reflects interim modifications, particularly in the libretto of the opera.[20] In this score, the

[17] 192 EKATERINA: ~~Zachem tï sdelal eto?~~ Uidi tï radi boga. Ya muzhnyaya zhena.
      193 [SERGEY: Kho, kho. Chto to ne videl ya chto-b muzhniye zhyony tak bïstro mne otdavalis'. Kho, kho. Zinoviy to Borisovich. Kho-kho-kho-kho. Zhenu ne smog. Kho-kho-kho-kho-kho-kho-kho.][*fourteen bars deleted*]
      194 ~~EKATERINA: Ne nado ob etom.~~ [original underlay]
           ~~EKATERINA: golubka rodnaya~~ [1st revision]
           SERGEY: [illegible] pro eto. [*final revision*]
           EKATERINA: Net u menya muzha tol'ko tï odin.
[18] This is the case in both vocal and full scores.
[19] In the 1935 piano-vocal score, this line was changed to 'Why, why, Seryozha' (*Zachem, zachem, Seryozha*).
[20] GTsMMK f. 32, ed. khr. 284. This is a conductor's full score, in a copyist's hand, bound in three volumes. The card-file entry lists it as 'Katerina Izmaylova [Ledi Makbet], op. 29'. There is no title page or other identifying markings.

words to Katerina's Act I scene 3 aria correspond almost exactly to those in the 1932 edition (and the revised GLINKA-271), up to fig. 146, when the underlaid text breaks off until fig. 149. Above the original text, however, the words subsequently found in the 1935 edition have been pencilled in. GLINKA-284 also contains the complete 123-bar 'rape' interlude. Sergey's fourteen-bar unaccompanied recitative (figs. 193–4), with only part of the text written in, has been crossed out in pencil. At fig. 194, the designation of Katerina to sing 'Let's not speak of that' has been crossed out and Sergey has been substituted.[21]

Following in the spirit of these corrections to the Glinka Museum copies, the 1935 published piano-vocal score also omitted Sergey's mocking recitative (fig. 193 is missing).[22] Katerina's declaration 'I am a married woman' elicits, after one bar's rest, Sergey's comment 'Let's not speak of that'. As brief as it is, the recitative in question proved a troublesome spot in the opera. Sergey's callous gloating in front of Katerina right after their lovemaking is shocking and crude; it makes it hard to justify her blossoming love for him. It posed problems of dramatic credibility even for the early producers of the opera, and was apparently excised from both original productions in Leningrad and Moscow,[23] as well as from the published libretti of the period and all other contemporary materials examined for this study. Ironically, in the 1979 recording of the 1932 version by Galina Vishnevskaya and Mstislav Rostropovich – where a letter is reproduced in the notes boasting that 'We are happy that we were able to realise the recording of the *complete* [emphasis added] original version of the opera. . . .' – this passage is also cut.[24] All available evidence points to the conclusion that, at some early stage in the process of theatrical collaboration, Shostakovich accepted the elimination of this passage from the opera as a genuine improvement.

According to the 'Notes' in the Sikorski edition, significant musical alterations, too, were made between the 1932 and 1935 editions. For

---

[21] The placement of rehearsal numbers is analogous in all period materials, including the 1935 piano-vocal score, where cuts resulted in the deletion of some of the numbers. The location of rehearsal numbers was revised in the 1963 edition of the opera.

[22] Due to a case of mistaken identity, Royal S. Brown is incorrect in his claim that the 1935 piano-vocal score does, in fact, contain this recitative (Brown, 'Three faces', 250). His confusion may derive perhaps from the patently inaccurate description of the 'risqué character' of the recitative in the 'Notes' to the Sikorski edition.

[23] See below, notes 32 and 49.

[24] Angel SCLX-3366 (LP); EMI CDS 7 49955 2 (CD). The passage *is* retained in the more recently released CD version by Myung-Whun Chung and the forces of the Bastille Opera (Deutsche Grammophon 437 511-2).

instance: 'The stirring passacaglia between the fourth and fifth scenes was replaced by a moderated version played by the organ'. In fact, the music which appears in the 1932 piano-vocal score (Sikorski Ed. 2313) and in the 1935 piano-vocal score – scored on three staves as for organ, but with intermittent indications of instrumentation – is identical.[25] In GLINKA-271, both versions are bound into the score. The organ passacaglia (figs. 284–94) appears first and the orchestrated version (figs. 284–94 repeated) has been interpolated between the last page of the organ solo and the continuation of the opera, i.e. it has been added later. In the second volume of GLINKA-284, organ and orchestral versions were bound successively with rehearsal numbers repeated and the organ solo was later crossed out in pencil. In his review of the first production of the opera, Ivan Sollertinsky stated explicitly that this instrumental interlude was originally written for organ.[26]

On 17 January 1933, less than a month after the completion of Act IV of *Lady Macbeth*, the organ passacaglia was performed in an all-Shostakovich concert at the Philharmonic Bolshoy Hall in Leningrad.[27] When he sent the full and vocal scores of the opera to Stolyarov on 23 February 1933, Shostakovich reminded him to be sure to give the organ *entr'acte* to Mikhail Starokadomsky, a professionally active organist, composer and long-time friend.[28] Presumably Shostakovich envisaged the organ passacaglia as a self-contained excerpt that might thrive independently of the opera. It seems incontestable that the organ version of the passacaglia pre-dated the orchestral version. But there is no indication that Shostakovich ever intended the organ version of the passacaglia to replace the orchestral in a staged production of the opera. Writing in late 1933, shortly before the premières in Leningrad and Moscow, A. Ostretsov singles out this 'monumental symphonic *entr'acte*' as a pivotal episode in the composer's conception of the tragedy of Katerina's fate, but makes no reference to the version for organ.[29]

Ostretsov's critical appreciation, the first detailed study of the music and drama of Shostakovich's opera to appear in print, yields another

[25] The full score of the 1932 edition, needless to say, contains the orchestrated variant.
[26] I. Sollertinsky, 'Ledi Makbet Mtsenskogo uyezda', *Vechernyaya krasnaya gazeta*, no. 20 (25 January 1934), p. 3.
[27] *Pis'ma k drugu* (Moscow and St Petersburg, 1993), 7.
[28] D. D. Shostakovich letter to G. Stolyarov, 23 February 1933, GTsMMK f. 291, ed. khr. 90.
[29] A. Ostretsov, 'Ledi Makbet Mtsenskogo uyezda; opera Dmitriya Shostakovicha', *Sovetskaya Muzika* (6/1933), 9–32.

From *Lady Macbeth* to *Katerina* 169

unexpected insight into the chronology of revisions to Shostakovich's opera. One of the most distinctive modifications in the 1935 piano-vocal score was the less coarse, more figurative substitute text for Katerina's Act I scene 3 aria ('Once I saw from my window a little nest, a little nest under the roof . . .'). It has long been assumed that this change resulted from the pressure of theatrical or editorial censors.[30] Ostretsov devotes considerable space to this important aria, and his two accompanying musical examples (Exx. 5 and 6; totalling thirty-seven bars) reproduce the text exactly as it subsequently appeared in the 1935 edition. It is still possible, of course, that the editors of Muzgiz or *Sovetskaya Muzïka* were responsible for pressuring the creators to modify the sexual explicitness of the aria. What is clear, however, is that the modified version of the aria existed already in 1933, before anyone had seen the opera on stage. Nevertheless, despite the availability of the modified version, both the Moscow and Leningrad productions opted – and were permitted by the censors – to include the more explicit version of the aria when they opened in January 1934.[31]

As mentioned above, Shostakovich took an active part in preparing all three Russian productions of his opera. *Lady Macbeth of the Mtsensk*

---

[30] See, for instance, Sikorski Ed. 2313, p. 5. Further evidence of the author's endorsement of the revisions published in the 1935 piano-vocal edition can be found in a letter from March 1955 when, in anticipation of a proposed revival of the opera by the Malïy Opera Theatre Shostakovich reminded Isaak Glikman to phone the conductor 'and tell him to copy the text from the published vocal score into the full score. Before publication I somehow managed to correct a lot.' *Pis'ma k drugu*, 109.

[31] See below, notes 32 and 38. In conjunction with the first American production (in Russian) of the opera in Cleveland on 31 January and 2 February 1935, an English translation of the libretto by Sonia Benderoff was published (Cleveland, 1935). A competing translation by Wladimir Lakond, billed as the 'Authorized English Synchronized Translation', was published simultaneously (New York, 1935). Above and beyond natural differences in the language, it is clear that the two translators were working from different texts of the opera; Benderoff translated the version of the libretto used in the Nemirovich-Danchenko production, whereas Lakond's translation corresponds to the text in the 1935 piano-vocal score, including the more 'poetic' version of Katerina's Act I scene 3 aria. The competition between libretti can perhaps be explained by the battle for the American première, adroitly swiped in the autumn of 1934 by Artur Rodzinski and the Cleveland Orchestra away from the officially sponsored Philadelphia Orchestra. At the time, Wladimir Lakond was director of the music division of the Amkniga Corporation in New York, the American representative for the State Music Publishers in Moscow. The 'authority' for his translation presumably means that it was the version officially sanctioned by the Soviet publisher. Which version of the opera was actually performed in Cleveland, and subsequently by the same forces in New York, has not yet been established.

District – directed by Nikolay Smolich and conducted by Samuil Samosud at the Malïy Opera Theatre (MALEGOT) in Leningrad – received its première on 22 January 1934. Two days later, on 24 January, Moscow's rival production of the opera – supervised by Vladimir Nemirovich-Danchenko, conducted by Grigoriy Stolyarov and employing the contrasting title *Katerina Izmaylova* – was unveiled at Nemirovich-Danchenko's Musical Theatre. The third production was also in Moscow, again directed by Smolich, and believed to be closely modelled on MALEGOT's earlier production whose title it used. It opened at the Bolshoy Theatre's Filial (a smaller affiliate house) on 26 December 1935 with Alexander Melik-Pashayev conducting. For each of the three, a different programme booklet was issued, containing informative articles, cast-lists, etc.; fortunately, the booklet for the Nemirovich-Danchenko production also includes a complete libretto.[32]

In his staging, Nemirovich-Danchenko emphasised the tragic elements of the story and soft-pedalled the satire.[33] He took issue with what he considered Shostakovich's gratuitous whimsy, for instance the episode in scene 7 when a village teacher is apprehended by the police as he attempts through dissection to ascertain whether frogs have souls.[34] To strengthen the dramatic realism – the gap between Zinoviy's disappearance and Katerina's nuptials with Sergey is suspiciously short, after all – Nemirovich-Danchenko substituted for the teacher the arrival of an ecclesiastical messenger with a dispensation for the wedding.[35] Among other minor refinements to the text, Katerina's confession of yearning desire for a baby in Act I scene 3, and Sergey's cynical riposte that babies are the result of an action and do not spring from nowhere, was replaced in the Nemirovich-Danchenko production by Katerina's expression of regret that she cannot read and Sergey's more neutral response that even reading two books at once does not always drive away boredom.[36] Katerina's aria in the same

---

[32] L. Kaltat (ed.), *Katerina Izmaylova, opera v 4-kh deystviyakh i 9 kartinakh; libretto* (Moscow, 1934). The libretto printed in the programme booklet for the Nemirovich-Danchenko production reproduced the version used in that production (*ibid.*, 25).

[33] For an appreciation of Nemirovich-Danchenko's distinctive approach to Shostakovich's opera, see P. A. Markov, *Rezhissyura V. I. Nemirovich-Danchenko v muzikal'nom teatre* (Moscow, 1960), 214–24.

[34] In the 1932 score the teacher is described by his captor as a 'socialist'. In the 1935 score, the teacher is described as a 'nihilist', and in the 1963 score the character has become simply a 'local nihilist' and is no longer identified as a teacher.

[35] Kaltat (ed.), *Katerina Izmaylova, libretto*, 36.

[36] Although provided with a revised text, an exchange about reading was also substituted for that about babies in the 1963 version of the opera. The vocal and full scores of the

scene, however, retained the more sexually explicit variant found in the 1932 score.[37]

Smolich's staging of Shostakovich's opera at MALEGOT was meticulously documented by N. Shul'gin in a four-volume director's blocking 'score' and thirty-two pages of schematic graphs co-ordinated with the rehearsal numbers of the vocal score.[38] The title page indicates the beginning of work on the staging, 10 October 1933, and the première date, 22 January 1934. A third date, 28 November 1933, listed with the city (Leningrad) at the bottom of the page presumably pinpoints the completion of the blocking. Smolich's certification also appears on the title page: 'The work done by N. Shul'gin is an authentic and complete director's score, allowing full possibility to revive and restore the given spectacle'.[39] A transcript of Smolich's exposition of the opera in front of his company on 10 October 1933 is included in the documentation.

Neither blocking scores nor printed libretti can indicate what cuts, if any, may have been taken by the producers in the purely musical sections of the opera, specifically in the controversial 'rape' music of Act I scene 3. That the two productions did, in fact, pursue different approaches to this scene is underlined in a letter from Sergey Radamsky to *The New York Times* in February 1935. Radamsky, who claimed to have seen the Leningrad and Moscow productions a total of thirteen times in the first year of their runs, was distressed by the deliberate sensationalism of the Cleveland production as seen at the Metropolitan Opera House: 'You might also be interested to know that the several low notes which the trombone utters at the end of the love scene of the first act have been, with

---

1932 edition published by Sikorski in 1979 are in conflict on this passage. The vocal score contains the 'baby' talk, which is also reflected in the English translation provided in the full score. However, the hand-written Russian in the latter actually reproduces the text about reading, exactly as found in the libretto for the Nemirovich-Danchenko production. Presumably, the passage in the full score has simply been miscopied.

[37] It is noteworthy in this connection, that when a preliminary orchestral run-through of Shostakovich's opera was organised by the Nemirovich-Danchenko Theatre in May 1933 for the purpose of vetting by commissar Bubnov, the latter 'approved the musical composition and moved that the libretto (Preys and Shostakovich) be carefully worked over to clean up the language'. See '"Katerina Izmaylova" v teatre imeni V. I. Nemirovich- Danchenko; beseda s rezhissyorom B. Mordvinovim', *Literaturnaya Gazeta* (24 January 1934).

[38] *Ledi Makbet Mtsenskogo Uyezda 'yedinaya-graficheskaya-dokumental'naya rezhissyorskaya partitura'* [Unified Graphical-Documentary Director's Score], preserved at the St Petersburg State Museum of Theatre and Music (SPgGMTMI), 16256/149 oru 16997 a-i. A carbon copy of the typed material, in addition to copies of the graphs, is preserved at the Maliy Theatre. Despite its description as a 'score', it contains no musical notation.

[39] *Ibid.*

the consent of the composer, very much subdued in the Leningrad performances and entirely eliminated in the Moscow production'.[40] Judging by this report, the 'rape' interlude in the Nemirovich-Danchenko production may well have employed the abbreviated, 102-bar version published in the 1935 piano-vocal score.

After the tenth performance of MALEGOT's production on 27 February 1934, Shostakovich expressed his satisfaction with it in a letter to Smolich: 'The show is going fine. The public listens very attentively and begins to run for its galoshes only after the final curtain. There is very little coughing. In general there are quite a number of pleasant things that make my author's heart rejoice. . . .' Shostakovich was pleased too that all ten performances had sold out and that the audience was enthusiastic in its demand for curtain calls. He was extremely grateful to Smolich for his contribution to the success: 'As a whole it must be said that in your production, *Lady Macbeth* has "reached" the spectator. There is tension, there is interest and there is sympathy for Ekaterina Lvovna.' But Shostakovich also drew the director's attention to what he considered a couple of defects in the production.[41]

One of the flaws he pinpointed concerned the interpretation of the character of Sonyetka in the last act. During rehearsals, mezzo-soprano Nadezhda Vel'ter had confessed to the composer that she was reluctant to play Sonyetka as vulgar and crude. While Shostakovich did not want to circumscribe Vel'ter's portrayal, he offered her the following advice: 'In my conception Sonyetka is not so much vulgar, as reckless and unbridled. Her behaviour is governed not by cruelty, but by the bitterness brought about by unfairness and endless degradation.'[42] Vel'ter subsequently tried to alter her characterisation of Sonyetka from a 'mischievous tart' to a 'neglected street wench'.[43] After Smolich's departure, by the tenth per-

---

[40] Sergei Radamsky, 'About "Lady Macbeth"', *The New York Times* (17 February 1935), section 8, p. 8.

[41] G. Yudin, '. . . Vasha rabota dlya menya sobïtiye na vsyu zhizn"', *Sovetskaya Muzïka* (6/1983), 92.

[42] N. Vel'ter, *Ob opernom teatre i o sebe; stranitsï vospominaniy* (Leningrad, 1984), 82. In her reminiscences, Vel'ter also confesses that originally she had been desperate to sing the role of Katerina and tried unsuccessfully to convince Shostakovich, through Samosud, to make modifications to the heroine's music to accommodate her own range. Samosud warned her that the tessitura of the part would ruin her voice and Sollertinsky was adamant in his opposition to any changes in the score. Eventually Vel'ter became convinced that they had indeed been right and that the tessitura of Katerina's part is high even for a soprano (*ibid.*, 79–80).

[43] *Ibid.*, 83.

formance of the opera the portrayal of Sonyetka – not only by Vel'ter but also by the other two singers (Golovina and Leliva) who sang the role – had degenerated into presenting her as a 'female vampire, a vicontesse-coquette or a fashionable courtesan . . .'. Shostakovich reflected, 'In my vision, Sonyetka should be a simple, coquettish wench, without a touch of "demonism"'.[44]

The other, perhaps more critical, flaw in the production Shostakovich identified in his letter occurred at the end of scene 5, after the murder of Zinoviy Borisovich: 'Every time when Sergey begins to drag away the "corpse" there is loud laughter in the hall. Something must be done, undone or redone.'[45] Clearly, levity was not the mood the composer had intended to produce here.

Fine-tuning the characterisation of Sonyetka is not something that would have involved major alterations in the staging, but there is evidence that Shostakovich's complaints, and perhaps those of others, might have resulted in at least a few mid-course staging adjustments in the two-year run of the MALEGOT production. Two alternative graphs with two corresponding pages of blocking instructions were appended to the material preserved at the St Petersburg State Museum of Theatre and Music.[46] One of these graphs corresponds precisely to the section of scene 5 – identified by Shostakovich in his letter to Smolich – after the murder of Zinoviy; it offers an alternative staging for the ending of the act, beginning at fig. 350. Katerina's exclamation 'he's gasping!' (*khripit!*; four bars after fig. 351), becomes the final word sung in the scene, eliminating the brief exchanges between the lovers as Katerina lights the way for Sergey to remove the corpse of Zinoviy to the cellar, as well as the awkward stage business with the corpse that audiences found so hilarious.[47] The new instructions indicate that instead, the remainder of the scene is to be mimed against the orchestral background up to rehearsal fig. 359, as follows:

After Ekaterina Lvovna's 'he's gasping', she raises the candle in her outstretched hand and slowly approaches Sergey, glancing at and listening to her dead husband

[44] Yudin, '. . . Vasha rabota', 92.
[45] Ibid.
[46] These extra, unbound, sheets are found only with the copy at SPgGMTMI, *not* in the copy at the Maliy Theatre. The graphs appear to have been drawn by the same hand as the originals and the explications are typed. No dates are given.
[47] Katerina's repeated entreaties to Sergey to kiss her (five bars before fig. 357 in the 1932 vocal score) had already been cut from the original staging, leaving her intoned 'Teper' tï moy muzh' (Now you are my husband) at fig. 358 as the final words in the original production.

fearfully. She stops after several steps. Sergey, poised frightened and motionless on one knee over the corpse of Z. B. with his eyes opened wide, looks at the corpse in silence. Mute scene. The curtain [harlequin/black velvet] is lowered slowly during the last bars of fig. 359 of the vocal score.[48]

One assumes that the final thirteen bars of the scene after fig. 359, forming an instrumental coda, were to be performed with curtain lowered.

Perhaps the substitute blocking did not, in the event, supplant the original. Apparently Shostakovich did not regard it as a permanent compositional solution to the problem, for in this section the 1935 vocal score still duplicates the 1932 piano-vocal score, as well as the full scores GLINKA-271 and GLINKA-284, in all essentials. Despite some minor textual alterations, the 1963 revision too retains Sergey's removal of the corpse to the cellar.[49]

The second variant blocking for the MALEGOT production corresponds to the last section of Act I scene 3, the notorious sexual encounter between Katerina and Sergey, which reaches its climax in the instrumental 'rape' interlude (figs. 183–94). The substitute marks a radical departure in the dramatic concept of the scene, as a comparison will show:

Original Staging [Act I scene 3; vocal score: 160–96]

183–94   [mute struggle] Sergey draws Katerina behind the curtain, she escapes from his grasp and runs to the door but Sergey does not let her go – renewed struggle – Katerina runs into a dead end at the window. Sergey drags her away from the window. She escapes and runs to the toilet but does not reach it, falling to her knees at the chair. Sergey lifts Katerina from her knees, grasps her tightly and carries her again behind the curtain.

195   *Boris Timofeyevich* [behind the door] KATERINA
Katerina [frightened] FATHER-IN-LAW.
(continues as in 1932 vocal score to end of scene).[50]

---

[48] SPgGMTMI chpo 16256/149 oru 16997 a-i.

[49] The 1935 vocal score even retains Katerina's passionate entreaties for Sergey to kiss her that were evidently cut altogether from the MALEGOT production. In the 1963 edition, corresponding to the widespread sanitisation of naturalistic elements in the libretto, especially as they reflect on the character of Katerina, her thrice-repeated appeal for a kiss was reset to the text 'I am trembling all over . . . how terrified I am' (*Ya vsyo drozhu . . . kak strashno mne!*).

[50] Judging by this description, the MALEGOT production may well have dispensed not only with Sergey's cruel gloating (figs. 193–4), but also the brief exchange between the lovers at fig. 194 before the appearance of Boris Timofeyevich. See above, pp. 165–7.

Alternative Version [Act I scene 3; vocal score: 160–96 and 152–3]
From 160 to 182 of the vocal score, all *mises-en-scène* remain unchanged.
From 183 of the vocal score: mute struggle, then Sergey grasps Katerina tightly and carries her in his arms behind the curtain.
From 183 to 194 of the vocal score, the stage is empty. Sergey and Katerina are behind the curtain. Musical scene.
From 195 to 196 of the vocal score, Katerina alone comes out frightened from behind the curtain. After 196 of the vocal score there is a cut to figs. 152–3 of the vocal score. Accompanied by this music, Sergey exits from behind the curtain, embraces Katerina and slowly they move to the window under the roof. Sergey, getting ready to leave, stretches one leg out the window and, sitting on the sill, embraces Katerina – a long kiss.
The curtain lowers slowly on the final two bars of the vocal score.

In the original staging, the physical violence of Sergey's attack and Katerina's futile attempts to resist his overpowering will are acted out during the instrumental interlude in full view of the spectator. In the alternative version, the struggle and seduction are played out only in the listener's imagination. But *both* versions specify that Katerina is dragged behind a curtain, which is clearly indicated in the diagram of the stage set screening the bed from audience view. None of the action of this scene takes place on the bed.[51] Even more critical, however, is what happens after the lovemaking. In the original, after the brief interruption by the prowling Boris Timofeyevich, Sergey refuses to leave Katerina; her yielding cry 'Darling!' leads to a thirteen-bar reprise of the spirited interlude that preceded the scene. In the revised staging, Boris Timofeyevich's intervention proves decisive. Replacing the exchange between the lovers and the boisterous music of the original ending is a seamless transition back to the somnolent C major–minor syncopations and languorous flute melody that accompanied Katerina's preparations for bed just before Sergey's arrival (fig. 152). Against this more discreet musical background, Sergey is seen to embrace Katerina and make his departure through the window as the curtain lowers slowly.

The alternative version of the ending for scene 3 was obviously designed to counterbalance the more uninhibited naturalism of the original, perhaps in response, or in anticipated response, to censors or prudish critics. We do not know when it was blocked, when or even if it was actually interpolated into the production. Given the close working

---

[51] Radamsky emphasised this point about the MALEGOT production: 'For instance, the "bed chamber scene" in the first act is done in the Leningrad Opera House without seeing the lovers getting in or out of bed . . .'. Radamsky, 'About "Lady Macbeth"'.

relationship and mutual trust between Shostakovich and Smolich, however, it is inconceivable that this version would have been devised or substituted for the original without the composer's consent. The printed libretto for the Nemirovich-Danchenko production corresponds to the original ending, as do the GLINKA-271 and GLINKA-284 scores and the 1935 piano-vocal edition. Using the intervention of Boris Timofeyevich as the excuse to defuse the tension in this scene was, in fact, the approach eventually pursued in the final, 1963 version of the opera; there, however, the 'rape' interlude was eliminated altogether and the sexual resolution was postponed safely beyond the end of the act. While, at best, the substitute blocking represented a temporary expedient, it draws attention to this scene as the 'lightning conductor' for apprehensions about the opera's sexual explicitness.

Little has been uncovered about the third Russian (second Moscow) production of the opera that opened on 26 December 1935; this is the staging that Stalin went to see a month later. Directed by Smolich and designed by Vladimir Dmitriyev, who had also collaborated on the production at MALEGOT, it has customarily been assumed that this production hewed closely to the Leningrad model, though – with the conspicuous exception of the performances of conductor Melik-Pashayev and the orchestra – scoring considerably less critical or popular success.[52] In one of the few reviews that managed to appear before the opera was attacked, however, the observations of critic Matias Sokol'sky suggest that this production was not a carbon copy of MALEGOT's staging.[53] Sokol'sky complained about the poor direction, citing as questionable, for instance, the decision to locate all the action of six scenes of the opera in the Izmaylovs' courtyard under an apple tree: 'In this courtyard they sleep, they make love, they eat, they commit murder'.[54] Despite his own

[52] This view was advanced by the reviewer for *Vechernyaya Moskva*, who reported that the set for Act IV, the scene in the convicts' camp, reproduced the MALEGOT model down to the smallest details. See E. Kann, '*Ledi Makbet Mtsenskogo uyezda* v filiale Bol'shogo teatra', *Vechernyaya Moskva* (27 December 1935), p. 3; also E. Kann, 'Ledi Makbet Mtsenskogo uyezda', *Vechernyaya Moskva* (9 January 1936), p. 3.

[53] M. Sokol'sky [pseud. for M. Grinberg], '"Ledi Makbet Mtsenskogo uyezda", prem'yera v filiale Bol'shogo teatra', *Sovetskoye Iskusstvo* (29 December 1935), p. 3.

[54] *Ibid.* This information might help to illuminate one of the more puzzling allegations contained in the *Pravda* editorial – something that characterised neither the MALEGOT nor the Nemirovich-Danchenko productions of the opera – that 'The merchant's double bed occupies a central place in the staging. On it all problems are solved.' ('Sumbur vmesto muzïki', *Pravda* (28 January 1936) p. 3). The first three acts of the MALEGOT production also employed a single set, but the different scenes were staged in different

reservations about the production, especially about the lack of an underlying concept and weak dramatic characterisations, Sokol'sky reported that 'The première of *Lady Macbeth* was a great success'.[55] Shostakovich, who was an enthusiastic admirer of the artistry of Melik-Pashayev, had been present at the final rehearsals and expressed his satisfaction. A few other conclusions about the production can be drawn on the basis of the plot synopsis provided in the programme booklet: (a) the total number of scenes was reduced to eight by the conflation of scenes 1 and 2, (b) the text quoted for Katerina's famous Act I scene 3 (here scene 2) aria is drawn from the 'poetic' version as published in the 1935 piano-vocal score and (c) the scene with the teacher, in scene 7 (here 6), was retained.[56]

*

In the aftermath of the *Pravda* attack on *Lady Macbeth*, Shostakovich was forced to shelve his opera although he did not participate in denouncing it. That it remained a creation dear to his heart was no secret to his closest friends. In April 1936 he confessed wistfully to composer Andrey Balanchivadze that

> I have suffered and done a great deal of thinking in the recent past. So far I have come to the following conclusion: *Lady Macbeth*, for all her enormous flaws, is for me the kind of work that I could never stab in the back. I could be wrong and it could be that my courage is insufficient, but it seems to me that one needs courage not only to murder one's things but also to defend them. Since the latter is currently impossible and useless, I am not undertaking anything in that direction. . . . If you find out sometime that I have 'dissociated myself' from *Lady Macbeth*, then know that I did it 100 per cent honestly. But I think that this won't happen very soon. Not at least for five–six years; after all, I am slow-witted and very honest in my work. . . .[57]

In response to the suggestion, as early as 1940, that it might be feasible to revive *Lady Macbeth*, Shostakovich after evident deliberation concluded

---

sections of its modular, multi-level design. As pictures of the production attest, the bed did not occupy a central position, nor was there any apple tree in evidence. One of the participants in Nemirovich-Danchenko's production subsequently speculated, unquestionably naively, that if the unknown people who decided the fate of the opera had gone to see their more 'realistic' production of the opera, instead of the production at the Bolshoy, the criticism would not have been as harsh. See I. Kazenin, *Vladimir Kandelaki* (Moscow, 1987), 53–4.

[55] Sokol'sky, '"Ledi Makbet"', p. 3.
[56] *Ledi Makbet Mtsenskogo Uyezda; Opera v 8 kartinakh* (Moscow, 1935), 28, 30, 38.
[57] *Andrey Balanchivadze: sbornik statey i materialov* (Tbilisi, 1979), 16.

that it was not yet worth expending the effort.[58] But *Lady Macbeth* was one of only four scores – the others being the manuscript of the as-yet-incomplete Seventh ('Leningrad') Symphony, and his four-hand arrangement and the score of Stravinsky's *Symphony of Psalms* – that he opted to take with him when evacuated from besieged Leningrad to Kuibïshev in October 1941.[59]

In his hour of grief after the untimely death in December 1954 of his wife, Nina Vasil'yevna, to whom he had dedicated *Lady Macbeth*, Shostakovich took out the score and began to make corrections to the part of Boris Timofeyevich. Isaak Glikman recorded the composer's comments:

> I noticed many errors there. Besides which, the part is very inconvenient for the singer. The second and third acts I am leaving untouched. I want to talk with you about the finale of the opera. However, I am not doing this for the theatre. The question of whether the opera will be staged again or not is of little concern to me.[60]

By March 1955, hopes for restaging the opera had become more concrete; Shostakovich was invited to Leningrad on 19 March to demonstrate his new version of *Lady Macbeth* at MALEGOT. Glikman recalled that the composer was extremely nervous before going to the theatre, where he played not only the two new *entr'actes* but the entire opera. The audition went well and the decision was made to mount the opera in the 1955–6 season. Galvanised by the prospect, the next day Shostakovich handed Glikman the vocal score of *Lady Macbeth* and asked him to look over the entire libretto: 'The words are inseparable from the music, you can't tear them apart, but when you look with your eyes and not your ears at the text of the score, then a lot of it seems tasteless. Please review the whole vocal score and correct everything you deem necessary.'[61] In a letter dated

---

[58] D. D. Shostakovich letter to L. T. Atovm'yan, 15 January 1940, GTsMMK f. 32, ed. khr. 1764.

[59] L. Mikheyeva, *I. I. Sollertinsky: zhizn' i naslediye* (Leningrad, 1988), 149.

[60] *Pis'ma k drugu*, 110. V. A. Kandelaki, who created the role of Boris Timofeyevich in Nemirovich-Danchenko's production, had griped at the time: 'The only thing I might complain about is the vocal tessitura of the part, and not only of mine but of the others as well. I consider that the author was not entirely in control of his vocal material here, but undoubtedly he will overcome these difficulties soon.' ('Koloritnïy nasïshchennïy spektakl'', *Katerina Izmaylova* [collection of articles published by the Nemirovich-Danchenko Theatre] (Moscow, 1934), 21–2). Criticisms of the high tessitura of the vocal writing in the opera were not uncommon.

[61] *Pis'ma k drugu*, 111.

21 March Shostakovich enumerated a number of specific problems for Glikman's attention.[62]

Examining the passages that Shostakovich identified for Glikman, we can see that in the 1963 edition the composer did indeed effect significant musical alterations to the part of Boris Timofeyevich from the versions of 1932 and 1935, particularly in the first act. The low limit of his range has been raised a tritone from low F♯ to C, and the typically disjunct and angular melodic writing has been levelled into a smoother, conjunct line. Once begun, the composer did not stop at the first act. In his letter to Glikman, he specifically asked the latter to find a substitute for Boris's repeated exclamations of 'no man, no man' (*a muzhika, a muzhika*) as he steels his resolve to visit Katerina in her bedroom early in Act II, explaining that 'puritanically minded listeners don't like such coarse naturalism'.[63] (In the 1963 edition, Boris's exclamations are divided between 'what a beauty!' and 'just to look'.) The composer made fewer alterations to the character of Boris's melodic line in this scene, although he relieved the strain of Boris's shouting when he captures Sergey by transposing an extended section of the scene (figs. 218 to 226) down a semitone.

Other textual infelicities Shostakovich identified to Glikman at this early stage of revision also deal with vulgar language and sexual innuendo. The composer expressed his dissatisfaction with the beginning of the second scene, the molestation of Aksinya by the workers. While acknowledging the difficulty of separating the words from music in the complex texture, he suggested that Glikman concentrate on the part of Aksinya, which stands out as the only female voice as well as the highest register.[64] Already in the 1930s the verbiage here had been toned down; in the libretto for Nemirovich-Danchenko's production and in the 1935 piano-vocal score, for instance, the Shabby Peasant had shifted his fondling from Aksinya's 'boobs' (lit. udders; *vïmya*) to her chubby arms. But in the final version the verbal coarseness has been neutralised considerably further; new words, presumably provided by Glikman, have been grafted to the

[62] Ibid., 109–10. Shostakovich's page references in the letter are to the 1935 piano-vocal score.
[63] Ibid., 109.
[64] Shostakovich's argument about the inseparability of the words from the music loses much of its persuasiveness in view of the fact that a significant portion of this very scene between Aksinya and the workers (rehearsal nos. 79 to 89 in both 1932 and 1935 versions) almost certainly was transferred into the opera, with the vocal parts grafted on, from the purely instrumental number, 'Bacchanalia of John of Kronstadt and Paraskeva Pyatnitsa' written for the ill-fated 1931 music hall spectacle *Declared Dead* (*Uslovno ubitïy*). See Laurel E. Fay, 'Mitya v myuzik-kholle: eshchyo odin vzglyad na *Uslovno ubitïy*', *Muzïka Rossii*, vyp. 10 (Moscow, forthcoming).

existing music. Instead of their blunt calls to 'grope' and 'feel up' her plump arms and legs, Aksinya's attackers make do with less explicit encouragements. Her hysterical screams of 'Oh, you swine' (*Akh, tï svoloch'*)[65] were replaced by 'Shameless devil' (*Chort besstïzhiy*). And after paying lascivious tribute to her charms, Sergey's derisive slur 'but her mug is pimply' was transformed into 'she's not a woman but a fire'.

In Act II scene 5, the second of the two bedroom scenes in the opera, Shostakovich asked Glikman to shift Katerina's focus from the slaking of her sensual appetites to her concern for Sergey's recovery after his beating. Accordingly, in the final version, Katerina does not wake Sergey with the entreaty to 'kiss me so that my lips ache, so that the blood rushes to my head, so that the icons fall from their case'. Instead, to the identical melodic line she tells Sergey 'when the old man beat you unconscious, the blood rushed to my head, my heart ached so badly'. Throughout this scene, Katerina's demands for kisses were deleted.

If one can characterise the single, most significant difference between the 1932 and 1963 versions of the opera it is in the efficient elimination of the traces of Katerina's voracious carnal appetite – as Shostakovich termed it, the 'motif of the insatiable female'[66] – ironically rendering her both a more conventional operatic heroine and one more in keeping with Shostakovich's original ideal. With this dimension removed, the raw, shocking sexual component of the opera is relegated to the euphemistic; Katerina appears relatively guileless and more obviously deserving of our compassion. The motives for her crimes seem to derive more from her rebellion against an oppressive family and social situation than from sheer, unadulterated physical lust.

Glikman's brief had been to work with the text only, fitting new words, where necessary, to existing music. On 15 April 1955, Shostakovich examined the corrections Glikman had proposed, which spanned all four acts, and approved them, expressing his gratitude in a letter of 21 April: 'Thank you so much for your work. I am now adapting [*prisobachivayu*] it into my vocal score and really regret that you have produced this only now and not twenty-two years ago.'[67] Undoubtedly there was a certain element of hyperbole here in Shostakovich's disparagement of the original libretto, particularly in view of his earlier statement that words and music were

---

[65] Shostakovich also asked Glikman to eliminate Sergey's use of this term of abuse towards Katerina in the final scene of the opera. As replacement, at the appropriate spot in the final version, Sergey brands her a 'murderess'.

[66] *Pis'ma k drugu*, 109.   [67] Ibid., 113.

inseparable. But the whole process of textual revision at this stage, with Shostakovich taking the initiative and singling out offending expressions with speed and sureness, suggests a predisposition more voluntary than capitulation to some hypothetical 'puritanically minded listeners' or an exercise of political self-censorship. By the mid-1950s, Shostakovich, middle-aged widower and protective father of two teenagers, was a much more self-conscious and discreet person than he had been in his twenties when he wrote *Lady Macbeth*. It is certainly conceivable that he himself may have been a trifle embarrassed by some of its grosser youthful excesses.[68]

In replacing two of the instrumental *entr'actes* – those linking scenes 1 and 2, as well as scenes 7 and 8 – Shostakovich may or may not have been motivated by something beyond aesthetic concerns, but the changes have little impact on one's interpretation of the opera. The replacement *entr'actes*, however, are arguably musical improvements over their predecessors; both serve to tighten the symphonic drama within the respective acts, one of the composer's stated goals from the outset.[69] The original fifty-one-bar interlude between scenes 1 and 2 had prolonged the low, ominous tones from the end of the previous scene into a relatively static, lethargic mood piece (Largo ♩ = 80) that backs unexpectedly into the erupting chaos of scene 2. Shostakovich replaced this with a more structured and rhythmically dynamic 140-bar *entr'acte* (Allegretto ♩ = 104). The grotesque little ditty that provides the main theme, with its accompaniment figures in the bass, accelerates directly into the related material at the beginning of scene 2. While the original *entr'acte* provides a psychological coda to the first scene, the new *entr'acte* serves to propel the listener forward into the second scene.

Both the original and replacement interludes after scene 7 begin with the frenzied timpani strokes and rallying trumpet calls clearly portraying the police as they rush off to intervene at Katerina's wedding to Sergey.

---

[68] While as author of most of the textual revisions he is not an entirely unbiased commentator, Glikman takes issue with the notion that it was outside pressure that caused Shostakovich to undertake the textual revision of his opera. He cites the composer's dissatisfaction with the audience's sniggering reaction, in the MALEGOT production, to some of the vulgarity and naturalistic language, the display of an 'unhealthy interest' that undermined his own perception of the drama (*ibid.*, 111–12).

[69] The description – in the 'Notes' for the 1932 edition (Sikorski Ed. 2313) – of the original *entr'actes*, particularly the first, as 'aggressive' seems singularly inappropriate. The same can be said about the evaluation there of the two replacement *entr'actes* as 'novel compositions in rather pathetic style'.

Whereas the revised version (168 bars; Presto $\jmath$ = 126) sustains the pace and tension tautly from beginning to end, foreshadowing along the way the fugue theme from the next scene into which it segues smoothly, the original version (134 bars; Presto $\jmath$ = 120, Allegro $\jmath$ = 152) lets the momentum flag by digressing into unrelated episodes. An awkward reprise of trumpets and drums at the end leads to a full stop and scene 8 starts from scratch.

Glikman makes no mention of other additions or revisions to the music of the opera at this early stage in the 1950s. That such revisions were undertaken, however, can be deduced from Shostakovich's public announcement, in a September 1955 conference in Moscow, that the revised version of *Lady Macbeth* would probably be performed in Leningrad the next year: 'Mr. Shostakovich disclosed that one-third of the first act and one-fourth of the second act score would be new, while the third and fourth act scores would be practically unchanged'.[70]

Shostakovich's announcement was premature. By January 1956, the Maliy Theatre had not yet procured official permission to stage *Lady Macbeth*, with or without revisions. At the insistent request of Boris Zagursky, Director of the Maliy Theatre, Shostakovich broached the topic to Vyacheslav Molotov, First Deputy Chairman of the USSR Soviet of Ministers, who apparently directed that an 'authoritative' commission of the Ministry of Culture should audition and consider the new version of *Lady Macbeth*. The requisite commission, chaired by Dmitriy Kabalevsky, was finally assembled and the audition took place at Shostakovich's Moscow apartment in March 1956. After Shostakovich played the opera, the members of the commission subjected *Lady Macbeth* to a vicious verbal lashing, reminiscent of the attacks of twenty years earlier. Much of the harshest invective was drawn directly from the notorious *Pravda* editorial.[71] The commission voted unanimously to recommend against production of the opera in view of its serious ideological-artistic defects.[72] The time when *Lady Macbeth* could be restaged, even in a sanitised

---

[70] Harry Schwartz, 'Opera is revised by Shostakovich', *The New York Times* (28 September 1955), p. 70. Shostakovich's announcement was made to Carleton Smith, Director of the National Arts Foundation, a private American cultural organisation. The conference was also attended by the composers Reinhold Glière, Tikhon Khrennikov and Dmitriy Kabalevsky.

[71] A detailed account of the 1956 débâcle can be found in Glikman, 'Kazn' Ledi Makbet', *Sovetskaya Kul'tura* (23 September 1989), p. 9; see also *Pis'ma k drugu*, 120–1.

[72] *Pis'ma k drugu*, 120–1.

From *Lady Macbeth* to *Katerina* 183

version, had not yet arrived. That this second rejection came as a humiliating blow to Shostakovich there can be little doubt.

In the next several years there were other attempts to revive *Lady Macbeth* in Russia. In June 1957, Shostakovich's *Ekaterina Izmaylova* was one of two new productions included in the repertory plan of the Kirov Theatre for its 1958 season; on its postponement until the 1959–60 season, the artistic management recorded its opinion that 'Attracting D. Shostakovich to our theatre is extremely important, since he has given agreement in principle to write new works for the theatre'.[73] The Kirov's scheduled production was repeatedly postponed.[74] By 1960 it had disappeared entirely from the Kirov's repertory plans, apparently because the opera had not been approved by the Leningrad authorities for presentation on the city's pre-eminent operatic stage.[75]

Shostakovich deflected an approach from La Scala in June 1958 to stage the new version of his opera; his claim that he was currently completing the second edition and hoped to have it done in two or three months, if not longer, was probably a convenient fabrication.[76] There is no other indication that he was actively engaged on work on the opera at that time. In any event, he would have been in no position to export it before it had been officially sanctioned for performance in the USSR. In

[73] Iosif Rayskin, 'Kak teatr Kirova ne stal teatrom Shostakovicha; dokumental'noye povestvovaniye', *Ars Peterburg: Mariinsky – vchera, segodnya, vsegda*' (St Petersburg, 1993), 99.

[74] During a meeting of the artistic council of the Kirov Theatre, on 31 March 1959, to discuss repertory plans, the baritone Laptev declared that 'Prokofiev's [*sic*] *Lady Macbeth* also needs to be staged', while another baritone, Shashkov, voiced his scepticism, 'There has been talk here about Shostakovich's *Lady Macbeth*. But who guarantees that spectators will go to see this show?' (RGALI, St Petersburg, fond 337, op. 1, d. 781, 75, 76). I am grateful to Iosif Rayskin for supplying this information.

[75] *Pis'ma k drugu*, 126. Glikman reports that the attempt to mount the opera in 1960 at the Kirov Theatre was scuttled by a certain Bogdanov, Secretary of the Regional Party Committee in Leningrad, who decreed categorically that Shostakovich's opera should not be staged at the Kirov but at the Maliy Theatre (*ibid.*, 155).

[76] D. D. Shostakovich letter to Francesco Siciliani, 16 June 1958, RGALI f. 2048, op. 2, ed. khr. 107. The Deutsche Oper am Rhein (Düsseldorf) traded on the prospect of the imminent revision to present the German stage première of 'Lady Macbeth auf dem Lande' in the composer's original version – the first production of the opera in over twenty years – on 14 November 1959. Announcing the upcoming première the theatre's management described it as 'the last time the work will be shown in its original version; according to the composer's wish it will be replaced in the future by a new version Shostakovich is now preparing'. See *Musik und Szene: Theaterzeitschrift der Deutschen Oper am Rhein*, supplement (Düsseldorf, 1959/60). It seems unlikely Shostakovich had any association with this project.

1961, *Lady Macbeth* finally obtained a satisfactory verdict, this time at the Union of Composers in Moscow, which led to the successful production of the revised version of the opera, under the title *Katerina Izmaylova*, at the Stanislavsky-Nemirovich-Danchenko Theatre in Moscow in late 1962.[77]

Available sources do not reveal whether any further changes were made between 1955 and 1963, the date given for the definitive revision of *Katerina Izmaylova*, Op. 114. In the autograph of the 1963 score, Shostakovich dated the end of each act: Act I, 5 October (*sic*, see note 12 above) 1931 – 24 December 1962; Act II, 8 March 1932 – 9 January 1963; Act III, 15 August 1932 – 24 January 1963; Act IV, 17 December 1932 – 31 January 1963.[78] Although the date 1963 has been commonly accepted for this version, it is highly improbable that Shostakovich was still effecting any but the most insignificant revisions to the final three acts of his opera after its première.[79] In a letter dated 28 January 1963 – that is, between dating the revisions of the third and fourth acts – Shostakovich informed Glikman that he was almost done with putting the score of *Lady Macbeth* in complete order.[80] Presumably, having savaged the autograph of the original version while revising the opera, he made a fair copy of the new version once he could be sure that no further revisions would be necessary, transposing dates from the original score as well as commemorating the completed revision.[81] Once he had signed off on the score, however, he recognised it as definitive and would sanction no deviations. He was distressed to learn, in 1964, that La Scala was contemplating staging the

---

[77] The 'unofficial' première of the production was held on 26 December 1962 and the 'public' première on 8 January 1963. See the reminiscences of M. Vaynberg and I. Glikman in L. D. Mikhaylov, *Sem' glav o teatre: razmïshleniya, vospominaniya, dialogi* (Moscow, 1985), 66–7, 80–3. Glikman's contention – that the renaming of the opera was suggested by Yuriy Shaporin at a discussion after one of the final rehearsals in late December 1962 and accepted only passively by Shostakovich, who continued to refer to the opera as *Lady Macbeth* – is questionable. In a *Pravda* interview published on 21 October 1962, for instance, the composer already referred to the revised opera as *Katerina Izmaylova*.

[78] RGALI f. 2048, op. 3, ed. khr. 17–20.

[79] 'Editor's note', D. Shostakovich, *Sobraniye sochineniy*, tom 20 (Moscow, 1985).

[80] *Pis'ma k drugu*, 186.

[81] In his letter to Glikman, Shostakovich asked whether he thought he should change the Russian designation 'kvartal'nïy' for the Police Chief in scene 7 to 'uryadnik' (village constable) as a more appropriate indication of the character's provincial status. We can assume that Glikman suggested another alternative because in the published score the designation of the character was changed instead to 'ispravnik' (superintendent), the period classification for the head of a district constabulary. Although there were no changes in range and overall tessitura, the vocal designation of the role was also changed from baritone to bass. *Ibid*.

From *Lady Macbeth* to *Katerina*

original version of the opera and wrote to intermediary Nicolas Benois: 'I have been able to make many corrections and improvements in the new version and I beg you to tell them to produce my opera in the new version by *all means*, or to leave it alone. . . . And one more thing: I *categorically object* to any cuts or rearrangement of episodes.'[82] The 'Composer's note' to the published score contains a similarly unequivocal proscription against cuts.[83]

In her memoirs, Galina Vishnevskaya, whom Shostakovich invited to sing the title role in the 1966 film of *Katerina*,[84] perpetuates the exclusively political rationale for Shostakovich's revisions to the opera: 'The people in the Central Committee's Department of Agitation and Propaganda . . . told him that if he agreed to reword the opera and change the title, they would allow it to be produced at the Stanislavsky-Nemirovich-Danchenko Musical Theatre in Moscow. But if not, well. . . .'[85] As we have seen, much if not all of the textual revision had taken place long before either the Central Committee or the Stanislavsky Theatre became involved.

Vishnevskaya also confuses revisions accomplished already before 1936 with those undertaken for the 1963 edition, specifically the textual variants of Katerina's Act I scene 3 aria. But she does point out the most significant of Shostakovich's changes to the tessitura of Katerina's part in the 1963 version. Treacherous octave leaps on B♭ from middle to upper register, to be spanned seamlessly *piano* to *pianissimo*, in the 'boredom' aria of scene 1 were eliminated from the 1963 version. Also eliminated were the repeated high B♭s of Katerina's lament after the death of Boris Timofeyevich.[86] These revisions can hardly have been founded on political grounds. Vishnevskaya herself underscores the technical difficulty: 'True, when I

---

[82] Letter from Zagreb dated 5 January 1964; facsimile of p. 1 in *Dmitri Schostakowitsch 1984/85: Wissenschaftliche Beiträge. Dokumente. Interpretationen. Programme* (Duisburg, 1984), 172; translated in 'Editor's note', *Sobraniye Sochineniy*, tom 20 (The date is given here incorrectly as 5 May 1964).

[83] D. Shostakovich, *Katerina Izmaylova*, Op. 29/114, vol. 1 (Moscow, 1965), 4.

[84] *Katerina Izmaylova*, directed by Mikhail Shapiro (Lenfilm, released 1967).

[85] Galina Vishnevskaya, *Galina* (San Diego, 1984), 352.

[86] In eliminating the high B♭s here, Shostakovich also disarmed a transparent instance of operatic parody: that of the chorus of coerced supplication to Boris Godunov in the first scene of the prologue of Musorgsky's opera. On the other hand, Shostakovich inserted at least one richly evocative new spoof, if only textual, of another operatic classic in the 1963 version of his opera: in Act I scene 3, when Katerina complains that she is unable to read, Sergey echoes Yevgeniy Onegin's condescending rejoinder to Tatyana, '[Knigi inogda] dayut nam bezdnu pishchi dlya uma i serdtsa' ([Books sometimes] give us abundant food for the mind and heart) from Act I of Tchaikovsky's opera.

first saw the very high phrases that Dmitri Dmitriyevich had written into my copy, both in the dramatically tense scene of Sergey's flogging and in the scene of the old man's poisoning, I confess that my head swam, it frightened me so'.[87] Shostakovich's assertion, reported by Vishnevskaya, that she was the first soprano able to perform his original intentions – when he wrote it, ostensibly, all the sopranos had refused to sing it and he had been obliged to rewrite the vocal part[88] – needs further documentation. None of this 'rewriting' is evident in the 1935 vocal score. In the 1963 edition, a number of the most strenuous of Katerina's passages in the scene of Sergey's beating are coupled with easier alternatives, leaving the choice to the discretion of the performer. Similar options are offered for certain of Boris Timofeyevich's passages in the opera.

Cuts aside, the revisions in orchestration from the 1932 to the 1963 versions of *Lady Macbeth* were much less drastic than has been widely assumed; the opera retained its characteristic colour and texture. With a couple of very minor modifications, the orchestra used in both versions is identical. The claim that the additional brass band used in certain scenes of the original version was cancelled in the revised edition is false.[89] Although it consists of fourteen, rather than the original fifteen, performers, the brass band performs in the 1963 version in exactly the same contexts as in the 1932 version, with the exception of the 'rape' interlude of Act I scene 3, which, as we have seen, was eliminated from this version altogether. The 1932 score has no indication for placement of the band, whereas in the 1963 version it is specifically designated as 'off stage' in scene 8, when the police gate-crash Katerina's wedding to make their arrests. The source for the notion that, in his original conception, Shostakovich wanted the band placed on stage[90] is unclear. There is no indication of an on-stage band in the schematic set diagrams or detailed descriptions for the original MALEGOT production.[91] Nor do contemporary photos of the Leningrad or Moscow productions reveal the presence of an on-stage band.

The most conspicuous change affecting both drama and music in the 1963 version of the opera is also the one most readily explainable as a concession to prudishness or 'political correctness'. It occurs, not surprisingly, in Act I scene 3. The 'rape' interlude which, in one form or another in

---

[87] Vishnevskaya, *Galina*, 353. [88] Ibid., 356–7. See also note 42.
[89] 'Notes' (Sikorski Ed. 2313), 5. In the 1932 full score – published in 1979 – the Banda is incorrectly listed as 'ad lib. (solamente in versione 1932)'.
[90] N[icholas] J[ohn], 'The versions of *Lady Macbeth*', *Lady Macbeth of Mtsensk* (English National Opera at the London Coliseum, 1986/7), unpaged.
[91] SPgGMTMI 16256/149 oru 16997 a-i.

all earlier versions had ignited as the tension of Katerina's struggle with Sergey reached its climax, has been entirely eliminated in the final version of the opera. Instead, the mounting musical and dramatic tension is rudely 'interrupted' at its peak by the threatening reappearance of Boris Timofeyevich prowling with his lantern in the courtyard. Katerina pleads once more with Sergey not to ruin her, but he is unmoved. In the 1963 version, the inevitable consummation of the sexual tension is left entirely to the listener's imagination, suggested only by the boisterous thirteen-bar coda.

Shostakovich made one musical addition to the final version of his opera that bears an unmistakably personal imprint. After the drowning of Katerina and Sonyetka in the final scene – a scene that came through the various revisions relatively unscathed – he superimposed a new line for the Old Convict above the final reprise of the convicts' chorus as they trudge onwards to Siberia: 'Akh, why is this life of ours so dark, so fearful? Is man really born for such a life?' The drama has already ended; the reflection – though appropriate to the context – contributes little to our perception of the tragedy that has taken place on stage. That it appears only in the final version of the opera, however, is significant, particularly since its presence would likely be overlooked by anyone not intimately familiar with the original versions of the opera.[92] What it suggests strongly is that Shostakovich is explicitly identifying here with the Old Convict, appropriating his voice to convey his own misgivings about the all-too-real adversity and tragedy that exists outside the confines of the theatre. Personal 'signatures', communications and subtexts were by no means uncommon in the composer's works, particularly after the 'autobiographical' Eighth String Quartet (1960). In view of the trials and tribulation of his own career, epitomised in the ordeal that his opera *Lady Macbeth of the Mtsensk District* endured, it is hardly surprising that, in his final revision of the opera, Shostakovich would take one more opportunity to attest subtly but personally to the universality of suffering.

Shostakovich was not a composer who routinely reconsidered and revised his earlier works. The facile explanation for his return to *Lady Macbeth of the Mtsensk District* is that, after the authoritative official denunciation of the opera in the 1930s, he was obliged to do so in order to have any hope

---

[92] In recalling his sensations on attending the one, final performance of *Lady Macbeth* at MALEGOT in Leningrad after the appearance of the *Pravda* editorial 'Sumbur vmesto muzïki' in 1936, Isaak Glikman remembered comprehending the final chorus as a funeral rite for the great opera. See *Pis'ma k drugu*, 315.

of seeing his opera on the stage again.[93] There is undoubtedly some truth to this. But, as we have seen, even in the 1930s *Lady Macbeth* was still evolving. In conjunction with the various early productions, the composer tinkered, or permitted others to tinker, with both text and music. Some of the refinements found their way into the published 1935 piano-vocal score. It now appears that, at least initially, Shostakovich's return to the opera in the 1950s was sparked by personal considerations, not by outside influence. Though we may regard it with informed scepticism, Shostakovich's endorsement of the revised *Katerina Izmaylova* should not be dismissed offhand. And once political preconceptions are set aside, careful comparison of the variants and versions of Shostakovich's opera will no doubt yield much further insight into his developing mastery as a theatrical composer.

[93] Inspired by the première of the revised version of the opera, Yevgeniy Yevtushenko quickly penned a poem about it, 'Second Birth', which he dedicated to the composer. While touched by both the thought and the verse, Shostakovich did not approve of the title: 'My music never died and therefore it did not need to be reborn a second time'. (From a letter dated 7 January 1963; see *Pis'ma k drugu*, 184.)

8

The Golden Age: the true story of the première

MANASHIR YAKUBOV

Shostakovich's three ballets – *The Golden Age*, Op. 22 (1929–30), *The Bolt*, Op. 27 (1931) and *The Limpid Stream*, Op. 39 (1935) – remain today, sixty years after their first appearance and twenty years after the death of the composer, among the least known works in his musical legacy.[1]

These huge ballet scores flowed from the pen of the young genius at the time of his rapid and dazzling rise to fame. It is sufficient to recall that they appeared at the same time as *The Nose* and *The Lady Macbeth of Mtsensk District*, the First Piano Concerto and the Twenty-Four Preludes, the Cello Sonata, the early film scores (*New Babylon*, *Alone*, *Golden Hills* and *The Passer-By* (sometimes known as *Counterplan*)) and numerous works for the theatre. Just a single year separates *The Limpid Stream* from the Fourth Symphony and two years from the Fifth. This alone should be sufficient to arouse our interest in the ballets.

I shall examine here the history of the première of the first of them – *The Golden Age*. In doing so, the main and almost the only object of attention will be the première itself and the subsequent fate of the performance in the 1930–1 season. Not that other issues surrounding *The Golden Age* are unimportant. But the success or failure of a première plays no small part in the fate of a work and in the life of the composer. History knows many cases of the sensational success of a theatre première being followed by rapid and complete oblivion, as well as the fiasco of a first performance being followed by prolonged and steady fame (*The Barber of Seville*, *Carmen* and *The Rite of Spring*). The fate of *The Golden Age* is, however, a singular event completely different from the standard case, an

---

[1] In 1994, after completion of this article, the first complete recording of *The Golden Age* appeared, conducted by Gennadiy Rozhdestvensky (Chandos, CHAN 9251/2). *The Bolt* followed in March 1995 and publication of all three scores has been mooted, in Irina Antonovna Shostakovich's *DSCH* edition.

example not only of specific historical interest, but also of some general methodological value.

The fate of *The Golden Age*, like the other two ballets, is inseparable from the fate of Shostakovich's oeuvre as a whole. After the notorious editorials in Stalin's *Pravda* attacking *Lady Macbeth* ('Muddle instead of music', on 28 January 1936) and the ballet *Limpid Stream* ('Balletic falsity', on 6 February 1936) the label of 'formalism' was for a long time attached to Shostakovich's music as a whole, and of course to his music-theatre works in particular.

In the course of the critical campaign of 1936 one of the articles stated, 'Our ballet . . . in its time . . . has suffered from the measles of formalism. Typically formalistic . . . have been . . . performances to the music of D. Shostakovich's *The Golden Age* and *The Bolt*.'[2] Among the famous artists of the Leningrad opera and ballet to sign this article was, unfortunately, Galina Ulanova. The unfavourable evaluation of *The Golden Age* stuck for decades. The scathing formulae were not just repeated in a stereotyped manner but became progressively more severe, achieving the limit of their harshness at the end of the 1940s and the beginning of the 1950s, after the well-known Central Committee resolution condemning Muradeli's opera *The Great Friendship* (1948).

'The growth of the Soviet ballet has been hampered by the formalist trend', states one of the generalising works on Russian music:

This trend, hostile to Soviet musical art, can be seen at its clearest and most extensive in the works of Shostakovich, who wrote several ballets at the beginning of the thirties – *The Golden Age, The Bolt, The Limpid Stream* – which grossly distorted the Soviet theme. These works were deeply alien to Soviet art; formalism stood out here in its consummate and most blatant form. Complete contempt for melody, for folk song and dance; musical cacophony; piling up alien orchestral stunts – these are the distinguishing features of these ballets. Just a small handful of gourmet musicians who have broken away from the artistic needs of the people have been giving as much publicity as possible to these 'highly eccentric works' of Shostakovich, which have had an extremely negative effect on the development of the genuinely Soviet realistic ballet.[3]

[2] N. Pechkovsky, P. Zhuravlenko, G. Ulanova and A. Lopukhov, 'Kirovskiy teatr', *Leningradskaya Pravda* (4 April 1936).
[3] T. Tsïtovich, 'Sovetskiy balet na novom etape' [Soviet ballet at a new stage], in *Sovetskaya muzïka na pod'yome* [Soviet Music on the Ascent] (Moscow, 1950), 181–2. See also, for example, M. S. Kiselyov, 'Balet', in *Ocherki sovetskogo muzikal'nogo tvorchestva* [Studies of Soviet Musical Works], i (Moscow and Leningrad, 1947), 42–3; M. Rittikh, 'Balet', in *Istoriya russkoy sovetskoy muzïki* [History of Soviet Russian Music], i, 1917–34 (Moscow, 1956), 215–17; V. V. Bogdanov-Berezovsky, *Leningradskiy*

This review is not an exception, although it does stand out as having its full complement of abusive features. But for us what is more important is what it says about the stage history of Shostakovich's ballets: that they had no success with the spectators.

Another author of those years stated it even more distinctly: 'The aesthetic taste of the Soviet audience proved to be better than that of Shostakovich, and his ballets flopped one after the other'.[4]

The 1970s and 1980s saw the first attempts to make an objective evaluation of Shostakovich's ballet music.[5] Unfortunately, frankly politicised negative descriptions of *The Golden Age* are encountered even in the most recent literature. Thus, S. Sapozhnikov in an article published in 1983 again confirms that Shostakovich's ballet 'distorted the ideals of the new life'.[6] However, although such statements are today more the exception than the rule, the version that the première of *The Golden Age* was unsuccessful is persistently repeated, even in the works of responsible researchers. Thus, in her book of 1979 Alla Bogdanova, plainly and completely without reservation, refers to *The Golden Age* as a flop.[7]

Let us turn to the facts.

The score of *The Golden Age* was completed by the composer in October 1929 and handed over to the State Academic Theatre for Opera and Ballet not later than 1 November.[8] In 1930 during the process of rehearsing the performance Shostakovich, at the request of the producers and the conductor, added several numbers to the score; in particular he introduced his transcription of Vincent Youmans's 'Tea for Two' (renamed *Tahiti Trot* in the Soviet Union) as an *entr'acte* to the third act. In addition, during the orchestral rehearsals he made corrections to the instrumentation brought about by the peculiarities of the sound of the ballet orchestra in the pit.

gosudartsvenniy akademicheskiy ordena Lenina Teatr operï i baleta [The Leningrad State Academic Order-of-Lenin Kirov Opera and Ballet Theatre] (Leningrad and Moscow, 1959), 61–3 and 106–8.
[4] M. Koval', 'Tvorcheskiy put' Shostakovicha (prodolzheniye)' [Shostakovich's career as a composer (continuation)], *Sovetskaya Muzïka* (3/1948), 33.
[5] See first and foremost A. Bogdanova, *Operï i baletï Shostakovicha* (Moscow, 1979), 109–44, also S. Katonova, *Muzïka sovetskogo baleta* (Leningrad, 1980), 53–61.
[6] 'Snova zvuchit muzïka Shostakovicha: Balet Dmitriya Shostakovicha "Zolotoy Vek" v Bol'shom teatre SSSR' [Shostakovich's music is heard again: Dmitri Shostakovich's ballet *The Golden Age* at the Bolshoy Theatre], *Sovetskiy Balet* (1/1983), 6.
[7] *Operï i baletï*, 111 and 113.
[8] This is proved by the inscription of the musical director of the production, the conductor A. V. Gauk, on the first page of the autograph score: 'Sent for copying I/XI. 29 A. Gauk'. The autograph is preserved in the Shostakovich family archive.

The production team for *The Golden Age* were the talented young choreographers Vasiliy Vaynonen and Leonid Yakobson, acknowledged later as outstanding masters of Soviet choreography, and a whole galaxy of ballet dancers, whose names speak for themselves (at least to Russians and to balletomanes): Yelena Lyukom, Ol'ga Yordan, Galina Ulanova, Ol'ga Mungalova, Leonid Lavrovsky, Vakhtang Chabukiani, Konstantin Sergeyev.

Their task was to create a Soviet choreographic performance, modern in both subject matter and the expressiveness of the dance, which was to include new forms of pantomime and depictions of sports events. This point was specially emphasised, even in the conditions of a competition for the libretto of a Soviet ballet:

It is desirable that the scenario of the ballet should give the choreographer material for pantomime and choreographic experiment; that is, in order for it to be staged it must contain not only the old pantomime and the classics, but new forms of dance as well, such as acrobatics, gymnastics *et al.* and the new pantomime gesture.[9]

As a result of the competition A. V. Ivanovsky's libretto *Dinamiada*, on which Shostakovich's ballet was based, was judged to be the best and was awarded the first prize.

Dinamiada is a story of the adventures of a Soviet soccer team (Dynamo) during a visit to a capitalist country (called Faschland (= fascist) in the original version). According to the generally accepted view, Ivanovsky's libretto itself was 'sketchy and involved'[10] – the first cause and the source of all the future misfortunes of *The Golden Age*. Meanwhile, the subject of the ballet, which unfolds against a background of an industrial exhibition, games and sports competitions in a stadium, and finally in a music hall on a public holiday, gave ample opportunities for creating a many-levelled and brilliant show, just like that foreseen in the competition conditions. The details of the detective story (the shadowing of the heroes by plain-clothes detectives, provocation, arrest, the escape, pursuit, changing clothes, the exposure) and the ironically presented elements of the romantic love plot (the passion of the stage dancer Diva for the Soviet footballer, the jealousy of her partner Fascist, the hysterics of Diva and her

[9] 'Usloviya konkursa na libretto sovetskogo baleta' [Rules of a competition for a libretto of a Soviet ballet], *Zhizn' Iskusstva* (2/1929, 6 January), 2.

[10] R. Kosachova, 'Baletï Shostakovicha v svete mirovogo baletnogo teatra 20-x – 30-x godov' [The ballets of Shostakovich in the light of the world ballet theatre of the 1920s and 1930s], in *Internationales Dmitri-Schostakowitsch-Symposion Köln 1985*, ed. Klaus Niemöller and Vsevolod Zaderatsky (Regensburg, 1986), 598.

The Golden Age: the true story of the première

vengeance) – all this gave the plot a certain dramatic logic and undoubted entertainment value.

The synopsis of the ballet is as follows. A group of Soviet sportsmen comes to an industrial exhibition The Golden Age in a large capitalist city. A local celebrity, the variety dancer Diva, has become interested in the captain of the Soviet football team and in order to attract his attention dances a passionate, seductive dance (Adagio). Her behaviour provokes the jealousy of her partner (Fascist), and the city authorities, the organisers of the exhibition (Director, Chief of Police), want to use the situation which has arisen for their own purposes: if the Diva manages to entice the Soviet sportsman, their joint number during the festivities in honour of the exhibition could be presented as an example of 'class peace'. The captain of the Soviet football team politely refuses to dance with the Diva, giving rise to noisy indignation among her admirers – the fascist 'golden' youth. Meanwhile, the dance of 'class unity' has already been announced in the festival programme. In order to implement their plan the organisers decide to organise a provocation and arrest the Soviet footballer. At the festival concert the Diva dances with the Fascist, who has dressed up in Soviet sports strip to the delight of those visiting the music hall. However, at the last moment there is an unexpected denouement: the western working-class sportsmen release their Soviet colleague and appear with him at the music hall. The fake is exposed, the 'Dance of Solidarity' between the Soviet and western workers ends the act.

On the whole, Ivanovsky's libretto loses nothing at all by comparison with other libretti of Soviet ballets of the twenties, including, for example, *The Red Poppy* by Glière (libretto by M. Kurilko) which was recognised as the top Soviet ballet and then as a model of the classical ballet of socialist realism. However, the box-office attractions of the State Opera and Ballet Theatre's repertory of those years were such pearls by Léon Minkus and Cesare Pugni as *Esmeralda*, *La Bayadère*, *Don Quixote* and *Le Corsaire* with their completely traditional plots and choreographic vocabulary of the nineteenth and even the eighteenth centuries. It was these that determined the tastes of the ballet fans and to a great extent the creative direction of the artistic ballet medium.

Alongside such works as these the subject matter of *The Golden Age* was simply not balletic. Ivanovsky has related how, at one of the rehearsals, the famous singer Ivan Yershov accosted him indignantly: 'What on earth are you doing? Surely you know that ballet is a fairy tale, a fiction?'[11]

[11] A. V. Ivanovsky, *Vospominaniya kinorezhissyora* [Memoirs of a Film Director] (Moscow, 1967), 215.

Scenes from the life of a large modern city; the urbanistic 'non-poetic' and 'inelegant' environment of an industrial exhibition; the idle crowd at the stadium, the *habitués* of the card-playing club, waiters, sportsmen, policemen, secretaries, detectives; the 'golden' young people dancing the tango, the cancan and the foxtrot, and finally the heroine from the music hall – everything was absolutely alien and unusual (and from the point of view of the purist critics also indecent and provocatively erotic), demonstratively not traditional and, in the ballet sense, anti-classical, and thus extremely difficult to choreograph and perform adequately.

Work on the performance dragged on for almost a year and the young choreographers, for whom *The Golden Age* was their first independent production, invested it with maximum invention and talent. Recently published memoirs and letters, and archival documents and the press of those early years, provide a fairly clear idea of the results of their enthusiastic endeavours.

Despite the inevitable mixture of choreographic styles resulting from the individual peculiarities of the four (!) producers (in addition to Vaynonen and Yakobson, the director E. I. Kaplan and the choreographer V. P. Chesnakov), *The Golden Age* appeared before the audience as a striking and impressive spectacle, captivating in the novelty of its choreographic efforts and achievements, the dynamism of the action, the brilliance of its divertissements (the stadium in the second act and the music hall in the third) and the talent of the outstanding young dancers. The work of the remarkable young designer Valentina Khodasevich was also outstanding in its originality, and the advertising poster for the performance which she made was one of the best works of that genre in Russia of the time. Even before the première it caused a scandal.

The spectacle reflected various tendencies of world ballet of the 1920s and absorbed a great deal not only from the modern concert-theatre and artistic life of Leningrad but also from the new phenomena of mass urban life: multitudinous processions, demonstrations, festivities, parades of gymnasts and olympiads. Seized with enthusiasm for renewing their art, the young choreographers boldly transferred on to the academic stage tricks borrowed from a wide variety of sources: from the classics to the music hall, the circus, sport, the *café chantant*.

Vaynonen made wide use of his experience of variety shows and turned to the vocabulary of Russian folk dance (in 'Soviet Dance'). Yakobson's imagination fed on complex acrobatic exercises more than anything else (in the 'Sports Quintet') and put an original construction on the experience of the cinema. The device of illusion, the skill of the quick-change artist, which was very popular in the variety theatre at that time, was used three times during the performance: in 'The Dance of the Indian' in the first act, in 'The Dance of the Pioneers' in the second act and in the 'Touching Class Unity with Slight Falsification' scene in the third. There were dancing puppets as well, which were a novelty known to those who visited the Leningrad music hall and those who watched the experimental version of *The Nutcracker* in F. Lopukhov's production (1929); there was also an operetta cancan and fashionable dances (the tango, foxtrot and a kind of tap-dance (*chechotka*)), as well as football, boxing and card-playing. In addition, fully in the spirit of the political review which grew out of the *Blue Blouse* and *Living Newspaper,* there was response to topical international news items: the polka 'Once upon a time in Geneva (Angel of Peace)' allegorically ridiculing the Geneva disarmament talks.

'This was an experimental performance', Galina Ulanova recalled half a century later. It was she who brilliantly played the part of the western Komsomol Girl. 'The youthful and impatient atmosphere of the rehearsal was also preserved in the performance itself which seethed with festive sports fervour.'[12]

A memorable type-image was created by Leonid Lavrovsky (the Fascist).[13] Into the colourful role of the Diva the ballerina Ol'ga Yordan introduced traits of the then popular negro singer and dancer Josephine Baker. Among the solo numbers her first Adagio stood out in particular. In this Vaynonen ironically united the virtuosic intelligent 'seductive' steps of the tango and foxtrot with elements of classical ballet.[14] Encores of Yordan's appearances were demanded.

Incidentally, the orchestral *entr'acte* to the third act was also encored. As Gauk recalled, when this number was performed 'the audience always reacted enthusiastically and demanded an encore'.[15]

Vaynonen's other choreographic successes were 'Soviet Dance', in which the traditional movements of Russian dancing were combined with

[12] Galina Ulanova, 'Khochu, chtobï bïlo chisto, blagorodno i muzïkal'no. . . .' [I want it to be pure, noble and musical. . . .], *Sovetskaya Muzïka* (1/1980), 64.
[13] See the memoirs of M. M. Mikhaylov in Leonid Mikhaylovich Lavrovsky, *Dokumentï, Stat'i, Vospominaniya* [Documents, Articles, Memoirs] (Moscow, 1983), 241.
[14] See the chapter on *The Golden Age* in K. Armashevskaya and N. Vaynonen, *Baletmeyster Vaynonen* [The Choreographer Vaynonen] (Moscow, 1971), 63–9, esp. 66.
[15] A. V. Gauk, 'Tvorcheskiye vstrechi: D. D. Shostakovich' [Artistic encounters: D. D. Shostakovich], in *Alexander Vasil'yevich Gauk: Memuarï, izbrannïye stat'i, vospominaniya sovremennikov* [Memoirs, Selected Articles, Recollections of My Contemporaries] (Moscow, 1975), 125.

acrobatics; 'Football' in the second act; the mass hysterics scene at the end of Act I; the comic scene with the policemen, which completes the episode of the flight of the Negro and the Soviet Komsomolka ('Pantomime of the Shadowing, Provocation and Arrest'); and the tap-dance 'Gutalin' in the third act, 'which is rhythmic and fast, syncopated, with a witty and broken pattern of movements'.[16]

A new 'plastic language in keeping with the present time and based on springy, strong, athletic movements'[17] was created by the choreographer Leonid Yakobson in his work on *The Golden Age*. The numbers that he introduced were among the most interesting episodes in the ballet. Particularly distinguished were the so-called Quintet ('The Dance of the Western Komsomolka and the Four Soviet Footballers') in which the soloists were (in turn) Ulanova and Mungalova, and the extremely effective 'The Magnifying Glass of Time' which Shostakovich recalled with delight. In general it was of the scenes introduced by Yakobson that the composer subsequently spoke with particular warmth:

What stuck in the memory was the dance of the komsomolka and the four sportsmen as performed by Ulanova, Mungalova, Chabukiani, Sergeyev, Yakobson himself and others. This composition was surprising because of its originality. The Pioneers' dance was very memorable. The students of the famous Leningrad choreographic school who participated in this ballet portrayed a game in which one of them represented a capitalist. He was dressed in tails and a top hat and suddenly dissolved into the crowd because his costume was suddenly torn off, unnoticed, and underneath he was dressed as a Pioneer. The laughter of the audience was the reward for this idea. But what particularly remained in the memory was the mass sports scene with Khodasevich's yellow scenery and costumes, just like patches of sunlight. There were all types of sports, which Yakobson transformed choreographically. Everything that was presented was so harmoniously reduced to a single entity that, when, after an unusually dynamic action, the entire crowd suddenly stopped and slowly floated as in slow-motion filming, I stopped hearing the music because of the audience's ovations for the choreographic device [it was this device of suddenly slowing down the motion which was called 'the magnifying glass of time', M. Y.] . . . It was an unforgettable evening! . . . It seemed to me that Yakobson and I were born for the first time in art, and my music sounded quite new in the choreographic interpretation.[18]

[16] Armashevskaya and Vaynonen, *Baletmeyster Vaynonen*, 66.
[17] B. L'vov-Anokhin, 'O Leonide Yakobsone' [On Leonid Yakobson], in *Leonid Yakobson: Tvorcheskiy put' baletmeystera, ego baletï, miniatyurï, ispolniteli* [Leonid Yakobson: The Career of a Choreographer, his Ballets, Miniatures, Performers] (Leningrad and Moscow, 1965), 6.
[18] D. Shostakovich, 'Nashi tvorcheskiye vstrechi s Leonidom Yakobsonom' [My artistic encounters with Leonid Yakobson], in *Leonid Yakobson*, 11.

The Golden Age: the true story of the première

The première of *The Golden Age* took place on 26 October 1930. In spite of the many allegations by later researchers it was a great and noisy success. 'The congratulations and prolonged noisy ovations which greeted the producers speak for themselves', commented one newspaper.[19] On 28 October Shostakovich wrote to the director of the Leningrad State Theatres, Z. I. Lyubinsky, who was not in the city at the time:

Dear Zakhar Isaakovich, the première of *The Golden Age* took place the day before yesterday. . . . In short, the performance went well. All of us who were responsible for writing it were very successful. There have not yet been any notices, but that is of little importance. What is important is that yesterday and the day before the audience judged our work. . . . The performance was so successful that on 6 November it will be performed . . . at a gala session of the Leningrad City Soviet.[20] It was the second and third acts which were the most successful. For some reason the first act left the audience unmoved. I put this down to the dance numbers being somewhat refined. So come along and see for yourself.[21]

In the 1930/1 session *The Golden Age* was given nineteen performances,[22] or two a month between October and June, which is rather a lot to be able to talk about the production being a flop; and it is simply ridiculous to say that the audience was hostile to the ballet.[23] Soon after the Leningrad première *The Golden Age* was performed in Kiev[24] and then in

---

[19] 'The Golden Age', *Spartak* (Leningrad) (7 November 1930). Cited in Armashevskaya and Vaynonen, *Baletmeyster Vaynonen*, 67.

[20] This circumstance was indisputable and important evidence of official recognition, in that the gala session of the Leningrad City Soviet on 6 November was to mark the anniversary of the October revolution, and the 'artistic part' of such an evening had to be in accordance with State (i.e. Party) directives in the field of culture.

[21] Letter from Shostakovich to Lyubinsky of 28 October 1930 in the Z. I. Lyubinsky archive held by the A. A. Bakhruskin State Central Theatre Museum. The composer himself, unlike the audience, did not rate the production that highly, and was sometimes extremely harsh on it, but the difficult problem of artistic self-assessment is another subject.

[22] For a list of ballets staged at the music theatres of Petrograd/Leningrad between 1917 and 1987 see A. Degen and I. Stupnikov, *Leningradskiy Balet: 1917–1987* (Leningrad, 1988), 246. To the eighteen performances stated in this publication must be added the tickets-paid performance of the morning of 25 October which preceded the official première. See 'Za 10 dney: teatr operï i baleta' [In ten days: the opera and ballet theatre], *Rabochiy i Teatr* (56–7/1930), 14.

[23] It is interesting to compare these data with the figures for a number of other ballets, for example those of Boris Asaf'yev in Leningrad between the 1920s and 1940s: *Solveg* (based on Grieg's music, 1922) – six performances; *Lost Illusions* (1936) – eleven; *Militsa* (1947) – five. However, there is no mention in the literature of any of these productions being unsuccessful, let alone a flop.

[24] Librettist V. Smirnov, choreographer E. Vigilyev, designer A. Petritsky, conductor N. Radziyevsky.

Odessa.²⁵ There are reasons for believing that in Leningrad the box-office returns were not at all bad, right up to the end of the season: in April 1931, six months after the première, the composer Arseniy Gladkovsky publicly invited Shostakovich to donate his honorarium to the construction of an aircraft.²⁶ In spite of this success *The Golden Age* was taken off.

Removing a performance on a topical modern theme from the repertory (and after all, *The Golden Age* was, in effect, almost the first anti-fascist ballet in Soviet theatre, if not in world theatre), a performance which had some success, could not be chance.

The theatrical life of Shostakovich's first ballet coincided with what proved to be a watershed in the history of the country as a whole and Soviet artistic culture in particular. 'The Great Break' (*velikiy perelom*) proclaimed by Stalin (1929) meant reorientation in all walks of life. Changes in policy and ideology inevitably also had to be felt in the arts. The so-called 'shake-up' (*peretryaska*) in the leadership in the state system of culture management began.²⁷ In 1929 Lunacharsky was relieved of his duties as People's Commissar for Education. The People's Commissar for Education was now headed by A. S. Bubnov, who had no previous experience of culture. Among the facts and events which were clearly characteristic of the processes taking place in Soviet art and literature at this time were the suicide of Vladimir Mayakovsky and Mikhail Bulgakov's letter to the government of the USSR requesting exile abroad, the liquidation of the Association of Contemporary Music which was orientated towards world culture, and the publication abroad of Boris Pilnyak's novel *Krasnoye derevo* [Mahogany] which was dubbed by the official literary critics 'a libel on Soviet reality'.

As early as 1928 Stalin had 'given a reminder' that 'our class enemies exist. And not only exist, but are increasing in numbers and are attempting to speak out against the Soviet regime.'²⁸ The thesis of intensification of the

---

[25] Here it was called *The Dynamiada or European Days*; choreographer M. Moyseyev, designer I. Nagarov, conductor N. Pokrovsky.

[26] Such requisitions were quite common at the time and were testimony to the loyalty of workers in the arts. See 'Na postroyku samolyota' [For the construction of an aeroplane], *Rabochiy i Teatr* (10/1931, 11 April), 21.

[27] There is a vast literature devoted to questions of cultural policy in the USSR. Among recent works, see M. P. Kim (ed.), *Sovetskaya kul'tura v rekonstruktivnïy period: 1928–1941* [Soviet Culture in the Period of Reconstruction: 1928–1941] (Moscow, 1988), 21, and T. E. O'Connor, *Anatoliy Lunacharsky i sovetskaya politika v oblasti kul'turï* [Anatoliy Lunacharsky and Soviet Policy in the Cultural Field] (Moscow, 1992), 123.

[28] Cited in N. Vert, *Istoriya sovetskogo gosudarstva: 1900–1991* [History of the Soviet State: 1900–1991] (Moscow, 1992), 196.

class struggle 'along the whole front' and the growing resistance of hostile elements was spread to the arts as well very quickly.

The class struggle which is being openly waged in all sections of socialist construction, which in the area of construction has led and is leading to organised attempts at sabotage, which in rural areas is expressed in the struggle of the kulaks against collectivisation – this struggle in other, undoubtedly veiled, forms exists in the area of ideology as well.[29]

In fact, in the guise of a discussion, cultural phenomena 'harmful to the proletariat' were dealt a crushing blow.

In December 1930 A. V. Mosolov's opera *The Dam*, which was almost ready for its première, was removed from the State Opera and Ballet Theatre's repertory as not 'corresponding to today's needs and incorrectly reflecting Kolkhoz construction'.[30] Regarding Shostakovich's opera *The Nose* RAPM (Russian Association of Proletarian Musicians) critics wrote that it was a 'nonsensical anecdote' and 'an ugly grimace'.[31] The opera was removed from the repertory at the Maliy Opera Theatre in Leningrad and from the forthcoming-performances list at the Bolshoy Theatre in Moscow. A performance of Prokofiev's *Pas d'Acier* at the Bolshoy in Moscow was also cancelled. The magazine *Proletarskiy Muzikant* described Rakhmaninov's cantata *The Bells* as 'fascism in a priest's cassock', and a noisy persecution campaign was unleashed against the composer. Not only the works of modern composers were declared to be alien to the proletariat, but Haydn's *The Creation* and the works of Tchaikovsky as well. We must not forget that the trials of 'enemies of the people' had already begun in Russia. Alongside information about rehearsal for Shostakovich's ballet, the magazine *The Worker and the Theatre* published announcements about meetings of artistic workers, calling upon the Supreme Court of the USSR 'to give no quarter to warmongers, wreckers or counter revolutionaries'. 'We demand that wreckers should be shot', declared the workers of the Leningrad Bolshoy Drama Theatre.[32]

The time of the alliance between the new art and the Soviet regime, to

---

[29] 'Tvorcheskuyu diskussiyu – v povestku dnya' [Artistic discussion on the agenda], *Rabochiy i Teatr* (6/1931), 1.

[30] 'Teatr operï i baleta' [Opera and ballet theatre], *Rabochiy i Teatr* (70–2/1930), 17.

[31] See L. Lebedinsky, *Novïye zadachi muzïkantov* [New Tasks for Musicians] (Moscow, 1930), 18; D. Zhitomirsky, '"Nos" – opera D. Shostakovicha' [D. Shostakovich's Opera *The Nose*], *Proletarskiy Muzïkant* (7/1929), 47.

[32] 'Otvet vreditelyam' [Reply to the wreckers], *Rabochiy i Teatr* (64–5/1930), 15.

whom this art only a very short time before seemed to have been in keeping with the revolutionary ideology of the new state, had now gone for ever. For the next decades the future of Soviet art was to belong to successful academicism. In these conditions Shostakovich's innovative ballet – which according to Sollertinsky's exact definition was the next stage in the development of Russian ballet music after Tchaikovsky and Stravinsky – was doomed.

On 6 November 1930, just ten days after the première and on the very day that the Deputies of the Leningrad Soviet were due to watch and listen to *The Golden Age*, *Rabochiy i Teatr* carried a long article by the influential theatre critic Yuriy Brodersen entitled 'Legalisation of time-serving'. The work of all the creators of the performance, apart from the composer (i.e. the librettist, the producer, the choreographers, the artist), were all subjected to scathing criticism in this article. In Brodersen's opinion *The Golden Age* had absorbed all the shortcomings of the previous new works for the theatre: 'Here one can find both blatant time-serving and vulgarisation of a responsible theme and an inordinate passion for formalism', and, most of all, the influence of music hall.

How could it happen that the ideology of the bourgeois music hall, that urbanist mongrel, *that ideology so hostile to the Soviet theatre* – how could it penetrate to the stage of the state ballet theatre, and what is more, in such an excessive dose? . . . Instead of using every means to prevent elements of bourgeois art from penetrating to the Soviet stage; instead of *completely exposing the producers who insinuated the ideology of the western pigsty on to the stage* under the guise of satirical interpretation, the Arts Political Council did everything it could to justify the staging of this unfortunate performance.

According to the critic, Vaynonen had been unable to surmount the 'faulty arrangement' of the libretto and on the whole was 'highly susceptible to formalist deviations'. Yakobson 'displayed undoubted talents as a choreographer', but 'individual formalist successes[?!] cannot justify the cultivation of a subjectless dance'. The article contained unfavourable evaluations of the libretto, the production and the work of the designer 'who had staged the performance in her usual aesthetic plan'. Even the name of the ballet seemed to Brodersen to be inexplicable and ridiculous.[33] An editorial note to the article stated that the magazine would 'return to an evaluation of Shostakovich's music in the next issue'.

Meanwhile the ballet music, which was performed before the première

[33] Yuriy Brodersen, 'Legalizatsiya prisposoblenchestva' [The legalisation of time-serving], *Rabochiy i Teatr* (60–1/1930), 8–9 (emphases added).

of the ballet itself in the form of an orchestral suite and a piano arrangement, had been extremely well reviewed in the press by a number of professional critics. As early as September 1929, after Shostakovich had performed the whole of the first act from the full score at a meeting of the theatre's Arts Political Council, Ivan Sollertinsky wrote: 'As always, witty, lively and at the same time fascinating in its real theatricality and dramatic character, this music has every reason to be ranked among Shostakovich's best works'. He emphasised that the score was 'a brilliant example of a combination of the greatest technical culture of writing and complete accessibility', and asserted that

in the history of Russian ballet music as a particular musical form, Shostakovich's score is a new step after Tchaikovsky . . . and Stravinsky. The best places in the first act are the beautiful and profound large-scale symphonic Adagio, the waltz constructed on a splendid build-up, the grandiose foxtrot and fugue in the finale, the rollicking dance of the Soviet [football] team.[34]

Furthermore, Sollertinsky noted that the music gave rise to 'universal delight'; that is, it was approved not only by the theatre specialists, but by the members of the Council as well; according to the customs of that time, by those 'actively engaged in public life – both workers and party members'.

It should also be emphasised that the positive, favourable opinions of the reviewers gave rise to concert performances of a number of fragments from *The Golden Age*. In the opinion of S. Gres, who not long before had criticised Shostakovich for his opera *The Nose*, *The Golden Age* revealed an important new facet in the composer: 'The young composer takes a significant step forward here and away from the musically formalistic excesses and exaggerations of *The Nose*. The healthy line of development triumphs.'[35] Another critic, the composer Klimentiy Korchmaryov, called the polka 'a *chef d'œuvre* of satirical music'. In Korchmaryov's opinion the most successful 'ironic episodes', which are strongly influenced by Stravinsky, do 'mimic' him, but 'technically Shostakovich makes it much more interesting and varied'.[36]

It was now, after Brodersen's article, that *The Worker and The Theatre* published the programme article of the Leningrad Section of the Russian Association of Proletarian Music (RAPM) entitled 'Bourgeois ideology in

[34] I. S. (Ivan Ivanovich Sollertinsky), 'Noviy balet "Dinamiada"' [The new ballet *Dinamiada*], *Zhizn' Iskusstva* (38/1929), 14.
[35] S. Gres, 'Simfonicheskiye novinki' [Symphonic novelties], *Rabochiy i Teatr* (17/1930), 9.
[36] Klimentiy Korchmaryov, 'Shostakovich i Pashchenko', *RABIS* (16/1930), 9. See also A. Startsev's review of the concert of the Nikolayev School, *Rabochiy i Teatr* (19/1930), 16.

music will be exposed to the end'. This article established that 'the class enemy is trying to penetrate deeper and deeper into working life'. Among the facts 'which point to the ideology harmful to the proletariat being extremely widespread in Leningrad' the authors of the article named the *entr'acte* (*The Tahiti Trot*) from *The Golden Age*.[37]

It is not difficult to understand that this had absolutely nothing to do with Vincent Youmans's music, which Shostakovich had arranged. After all, the *entr'acte* could have been replaced by another item, or it could simply have been withdrawn from the ballet. It was to do with Shostakovich's music. Clearly the reception of a new and essentially innovative artistic phenomenon, and that is what Shostakovich's *The Golden Age* was, could not be absolutely favourable. Not only negative opinions but direct opposition were encountered on the ballet's way to the stage and its audience. The singer Ivan Yershov, who has been mentioned already, an extremely authoritative person in the Leningrad theatre world, asked, 'Can one actually dance to such music?!' But it was not just the old tenor Yershov who did not understand the music of *The Golden Age*. Others who were actually taking part in the production did not appreciate it either.

To begin with there was much that I had difficulty in understanding. . . . For me music never becomes a fluent language immediately because one has to understand it, and it is impossible to understand it immediately. That is what happened at the time of the première of *The Golden Age* as well. The rhythms and intonations were unusual. And remember that a ballet artiste always has to beat time when learning a new part.[38]

That confession of the great Ulanova was made exactly fifty years after the première. And she was not the only one: 'they could not understand the music, which was strange to their ears',[39] according to Gauk, who was referring to the balletomanes, who at best were able to find their bearings in the works of Tchaikovsky and Glazunov. The success of this ballet

---

[37] Sekretariat LOVAPM [The Secretariat of the Leningrad Section of RAPM], 'Burzhuaznuyu ideologiyu v muzïke razoblachim do kontsa' [The bourgeois ideology in music will be exposed to the end], *Rabochiy i Teatr* (62–3/1930), 7. As early as March 1930 during the campaign against 'vulgar, light music', Shostakovich was obliged to acknowledge that the orchestral version of his arrangement *Tahiti Trot* had been 'a political mistake . . . being without the appropriate surroundings indicating the composer's relationship to the material': Dmitriy Shostakovich, 'Na fronte bor'bï s NEPmanskoy muzïkoy' [At the front of the struggle with NEPman (New Economic Plan-man) music], *Proletarskiy muzïkant* (3/1930), 25.
[38] Galina Ulanova, 'Khochu chtobï bïlo chisto', 64–5.
[39] Alexander Gauk, 'Tvorcheskiye vstrechi', 124.

The Golden Age: the true story of the première 203

forced the opposition, both in and outside the theatre, to be silent. But the appearance of these articles reflecting the official ideological stance (and at that time RAPM had enormous influence and spoke on behalf of the Bolshevik party) enabled them to lift up their heads. Soon after the publication of the statement of the Secretariat of the Leningrad Branch of RAPM quoted above, changes began to be made in the performance, or more accurately certain scenes were cut out. On 10 December a report appeared in the press to the effect that 'in accordance with the requirements of measures for safety at work(!) the management intend to remove a number of acrobatic dances from the ballet *The Golden Age*'.[40] At the end of December it was decided (of course, at the demand of the same safety at work organisation) to cut one of the most striking dances – the *chechotka* tap-dance at the beginning of the third act.[41] And even so, the ballet still remained in the current repertory until the end of the season.

However, the accusations brought in the course of 'the free creative discussion' were neither withdrawn nor disputed. The ballet was taken off. Shostakovich's remarkable score disappeared into the depths of the archives for several decades, inaccessible to either researchers or performers, and the history of its première and its subsequent fate were crudely falsified.

As we know, Yuriy Grigorovich staged *The Golden Age* at the Bolshoy Theatre at the beginning of the 1980s. The performance was highly and steadily successful and was staged during the company's tours of the most important musical capitals of the world. Grigorovich's work was an important factor in the rehabilitation of this forgotten and slandered production. Unfortunately, this production was put on using an edition far removed from the original; in fact it included music from a number of Shostakovich's other works. Furthermore, the libretto was absolutely new and contained nothing from the original libretto except the name. Giving the creators of this new version their dues for their talent and expertise and also for their services in attempting to revive this work, it is interesting to quote here a fragment from an unpublished letter from Shostakovich, which has a direct bearing on the matter under discussion:

A ballet, just like an opera, should be staged using the actual score and not an 'imaginary one'. Furthermore, in the choreographic world the approach to ballet music is still rather like the approach to a 'semi-finished' product at a factory, that is not deserving of any particular respect. . . . Respect for the composer's work should be the first commandment for interpreters, be they choreographer,

[40] 'Teatr operï i baleta' [The opera and ballet theatre], *Rabochiy i Teatr* (66–7/1930), 20.
[41] 'Teatr operï i baleta' [The opera and ballet theatre], *Rabochiy i Teatr* (70–2/1930), 17.

producer, conductor or designer. No distortions of the composer's text must be allowed; that is a rigid rule. And, of course, the ballet cannot be an exception in this instance.[42] In saying that, it is difficult to suppose that Shostakovich was not thinking of his own ballets as well.

The distortion of the historical truth revealed whilst studying the première of *The Golden Age* and which has been preserved for many decades in our music history forces one to wonder about the trustworthiness of Soviet history of music, not only regarding the interpretation of the artistic process but regarding the facts themselves. The history of Soviet music will be rewritten sooner or later, first and foremost its factual content.

[42] Letter from D. D. Shostakovich to Candidate member of the Politburo of the Central Committee of the Communist Party of the Soviet Union (CC of CPSU), Secretary of the CC of CPSU P. M. Ilemichev. Enclosure: a letter to the editorial office of the magazine *Sovetskaya Muzika* concerning a debate regarding the fate of Prokofiev's ballet *Romeo and Juliet* (1974). Cited from a typed copy in the archives of the author of the present article.

9

'And art made tongue-tied by authority'
Shostakovich's song-cycles

DOROTHEA REDEPENNING

Songs and chamber music in general had a much lower ranking in Soviet musical life than imposing works such as operas or symphonies. That also meant that works with small forces figured less in the routine musico-political discussions and were less harshly judged. Shostakovich took advantage of this state of affairs, at the latest following the catastrophe precipitated by his opera *The Lady Macbeth of Mtsensk District*. Until then he had considered himself primarily as a symphonist and opera composer; now in the more intimate genres of songs and string quartets he discovered the possibility of a non-coded means of artistic expression, as it were.

A few months before the Fifth Symphony – the 'answer' to the unfortunate *Pravda* article, 'Muddle instead of music' – he produced a modest, very private song-cycle on Poems by Pushkin (Op. 46, 1936–7). The first of the poems, 'Vozrozhdeniye' (Rebirth), deals with the moral superiority of the artist over his narrow-minded censor and describes Shostakovich's situation at that time very precisely.

> An artist-barbarian, with a casual brush
> Blackens a genius's picture,
> And his lawless drawing
> Scrawls meaninglessly over it.
>
> But with the years the alien markings
> Fall off like old scales;
> The work of genius appears before us
> In all its former beauty.
>
> Just so do delusions fall away
> From my exhausted soul,
> And within it there return visions
> Of original, pure days.

Shostakovich quotes the concluding part of this romance, the hopeful notion that the work of art outlives its detractors, in the finale of his Fifth Symphony, knowing well that this connection would remain unnoticed.[1] The thought that this Pushkin setting might relate to the damning critique of *Lady Macbeth* is voiced by Sof'ya Khentova in her Shostakovich biography,[2] but apart from David Rabinovich no author until recent years has pointed to the connection with the Fifth Symphony (see Richard Taruskin's chapter in the present volume, pp. 42–5).

How much Shostakovich may have related the Pushkin cycle not only to his own personal situation but also to the whole gruesome atmosphere which prevailed in the Soviet Union in the 1930s, is made clear by the fourth song, Pushkin's vision of death, with the title 'Verses' added by Shostakovich. Here the framework and foundation are provided by suggestions of the liturgical sequence 'Dies irae'. In the first contrasting section Shostakovich sets the text, 'I say: the years fly by, / And however much we do not see here, / We will all meet in eternity, / And anyone's hour is nigh' (bb. 21–9) to an acceleration of the basic tempo, with march rhythms and a dashing melody in the style of Soviet military music.[3]

Before the damning critique of *Lady Macbeth* there are only two song-cycles: the two Krïlov Fables (Op. 4, 1922), a youthful work which was only performed posthumously, and the Six Romances on Words by Japanese Poets (Op. 21, 1928–32), a declaration of love to Nina Vasil'yevna Varzar, Shostakovich's first wife. From 1936 on songs (excepting the Dolmatovsky settings, which were for public consumption)[4] occupied

---

[1] Both Sof'ya Khentova, *Shostakovich: zhizn' i tvorchestvo* [Shostakovich: Life and Works] (Leningrad, 1986), i, 441–2, and Vera Vasina-Grossman, *Kamerno-vokal'noye tvorchestvo D. Shostakovicha* [Shostakovich's Chamber-Vocal Works], cited in *Sovetskaya muzïkal'naya kul'tura* [Soviet Musical Culture], ed. D. Daragan (Moscow, 1980), 17, link the Pushkin cycle with the celebrations of the centenary of the poet's death in 1937. Nevertheless, the first performance took place only on 8 December 1940. The songs first appeared in print in 1943, a second edition followed in 1945, a third in 1960 from the state publishing house Sovetskiy kompozitor.

[2] Khentova, *Shostakovich*, i, 444. In the first edition (Leningrad, 1975) this indication is missing.

[3] In his instrumentation of the cycle Gennadiy Rozhdestvensky clearly underlines this military character. Tamara Levaya rightly comments that this same verse points forward to Shostakovich's Fourteenth Symphony – 'Tayna velikogo iskusstva: o pozdnikh kamerno-vokal'nïkh tsiklakh D. D. Shostakovicha' [The mystery of great art: on Shostakovich's late chamber-vocal cycles], in *Muzïka Rossiy*, ed. Alla Grigor'yeva (Moscow, 1978), ii, 279.

[4] The oratorio *The Song of the Forests* (Op. 81, 1949), 'Four Songs' (Op. 86, 1950–1) – the first, 'Rodina shlïshit' (The Homeland listens) gained popularity as the signature tune

a special place in Shostakovich's output. They differ from all other genres in their markedly simplified musical language and in their declamatory character – the poet's words are more important than the music which accompanies them. Also noticeable is the fact that Shostakovich only turns to songs in situations of special strain. It almost seems that with song composition he wanted, after the model of the Four Pushkin Romances, to free himself from particular psychic pressures. During the war there appeared the Six Romances on Verses by English Poets (Op. 62, 1942);[5] in 1948, after the decree on music in which Shostakovich and other prominent composers were publicly humiliated, came the cycle From Jewish Folk Poetry (Op. 79); during work on the cantata *The Sun Shines Over Our Motherland* we find the Four Pushkin Monologues (Op. 91, 1952). In addition there are the two Lermontov settings (Op. 84, 1950), apparently an occasional work.

The cycle From Jewish Folk Poetry could only be premièred publicly in 1955;[6] when the Pushkin Monologues were first performed in public is not known.[7] Shostakovich patently broke off work on his cantata on Dolmatovsky's state-glorifying text in order to re-establish his artistic values with the help of Pushkin's poetry. He deliberately named the four songs 'Monologues', not, as in the normal Russian idiom, 'Romances', in order to clarify their declamatory rather than song-like nature.[8] Here confessions are made, a philosophy is expressed in notes and this monologue-character sets the tone for Shostakovich's late song-cycles. The first song, 'Otrïvok' (Fragment), with its picture of a poor Jewish family hit by fate, links directly to the cycle From Jewish Folk Poetry. Its basis is a simple

for the news on Soviet radio; Yuriy Gagarin sang it in space and thereby underlined the patriotic meaning of the song – the cantata *The Sun Shines Over Our Motherland* (Op. 90, 1952), 'Five Songs' (Op. 98, 1954) – obviously produced as a token of thanks for the five poems Dolmatovsky dedicated to Shostakovich; and other music for stage and screen, as well as patriotic choruses.

[5] Soviet authors link the choice of English and Scottish poems with the political situation, the alliance between the USSR, Great Britain and the USA. Similarly inspired by the alliance are the Eight British and American Folk Songs (1953).

[6] The cycle was first published in 1958 in a German Edition by Edition Peters; in the Soviet Union it appeared in 1961 from Sovetskiy kompozitor. Shostakovich had orchestrated the songs in 1948; but since the première of the orchestral version only took place in 1964 this version has been erroneously dated to 1962/3, cf. Derek Hulme, *Dmitri Shostakovich: A Catalogue, Bibliography and Discography* (Oxford, 1991), 193–4.

[7] First publication 1960, Sovetskiy kompozitor.

[8] Vera Vasina-Grossman also emphasises the connection between the unusual genre-label and the declamatory character (*Kamerno-vokal'noye tvorchestvo*, 27).

minor-third motif repeated almost without alteration. Shostakovich interrupts it only at two points. When the poem speaks of the young Jewess crying over the empty cradle we hear a lamenting figure and the so-called 'Force motif'[9] – both motifs are topoi in Shostakovich's output from *Lady Macbeth* on; the unexpected knock on the door (in this context as a positive sign) is introduced by a chromatic figure which will later serve as the principal motif in the first movement of the Thirteenth Symphony, 'Babiy Yar' (Ex. 9.1).

The choice of Pushkin's poem 'Vo glubine sibirskikh rud . . .' (In the depths of the Siberian mines), the third Monologue, also depends on moral-ethical considerations. Pushkin's hope-dispensing greeting to the Decembrists condemned to forced labour corresponded to the Soviet reality of the early post-war years far more than Dolmatovsky's shallow paeans which Shostakovich felt he had to set at the time.

1960 – A TURNING POINT

Recent Russian publications have shown that the year 1960 evidently signified a second great turning point in Shostakovich's career, comparable to the *Lady Macbeth* affair of 1936. In 1990 Lev Lebedinsky wrote apropos the Eighth String Quartet (Op. 110, 1960):

Why did the composer introduce a musical overview of his works into this quartet? Because he believed that the Eighth Quartet would *round off* everything that he had created. . . . The Quartet was composed immediately after the acceptance of the composer into the ranks of the Communist Party. And this very outrage – entrance into the Party – was in Shostakovich's view synonymous with his death.

What forced the composer to accept his admission? Was pressure perhaps put on the composer in this instance? The following publicly revealed fact illuminates this circumstance. The widely advertised public Party meeting in which Shostakovich was to be 'admitted to the ranks', failed miserably, because the composer himself did not put in an appearance. They had to resort to an obvious lie and announce Shostakovich's unexpected illness, which had come over him so suddenly that there was no time to inform the invited guests of the cancellation of the meeting. But since vast numbers of people had turned up, the cancellation took on the

---

[9] In free imitation of the Soviet Shostakovich literature Bernd Feuchtner has given the label 'Force motif' (*Gewalt-Motiv*) to that striking figure that ends with two sharply accented notes or chords (*'Und Kunst geknebelt von der groben Macht': Schostakowitsch, künstlerische Identität und staatliche Repression* (Frankfurt, 1986)). See David Fanning, 'Leitmotif in *Lady Macbeth*', in the present volume, pp. 145–7.

Ex. 9.1 Op. 91, 'Otrïvok', bb. 17–22

character of a social scandal. The firm conviction sprang up that Shostakovich had been forced to join the Party. And although a few months later the composer was nevertheless admitted to the Party, the scandalous situation of the first meeting left traces in the Eighth Quartet, which is contemporaneous with this event. Only a few people close to the composer knew that he thought of suicide after the completion of the Eighth Quartet; friends were able to prevent the attempt.

There is no doubt that the Eighth Quartet was conceived as an autobiographical and *final* work.[10]

Lebedinsky's comments have recently been confirmed by Shostakovich's letters to Isaak Glikman. In a letter of 19 July 1960 he writes:

I have been considering that when I die, scarcely anyone will write a work in my memory. Therefore I have decided to write one myself. Then on the cover they can print: 'Dedicated to the author of this Quartet'. The main theme of the Quartet is the notes D–S–C–H, my initials. The Quartet contains themes from my works and the revolutionary song 'Zamuchon tyazholoy nevoley' [Tormented by heavy captivity]. My themes are the following: from the First Symphony, the Eighth Symphony, the [Second Piano] Trio, the [First] Cello Concerto and from *Lady Macbeth*. I have made allusions to Wagner (Funeral March from *Götterdämmerung*) and Tchaikovsky (second theme from the first movement of the Sixth Symphony). Oh, yes, I forgot my Tenth Symphony. A nice mish-mash.

With ironic self-distance, which only makes clearer his despairing situation, Shostakovich continues:

The pseudo-tragedy of this Quartet is such that I wept as many tears during its composition as you pass water after half a dozen beers. Back home I twice tried to play it through, and wept again. This time not only because of the pseudo-tragedy but also from astonishment at the wonderful wholeness of the form.[11]

In his commentary to this letter Glikman informs us in what a desolate psychic condition Shostakovich was at the time, and he makes clear, quoting Shostakovich, how despairingly the composer defended himself to the last against his entry into the Party, to the point of pleading religiosity as an argument.[12] Whether Shostakovich really could not have withstood

---

[10] Lev Lebedinsky, 'O nekotorïkh muzïkal'nïkh tsitatakh v proizvedeniyakh D. Shostakovicha' [On some musical quotations in Shostakovich's works], *Novïy mir* (3/1990), 264. See also Elizabeth Wilson, *Shostakovich: A Life Remembered* (London, 1994), 340–1.

[11] *Pis'ma k drugu* [Letters to a Friend] (St Petersburg, 1993), 159.

[12] 'Pospelov [a member of the Office of the Central Committee of the RSFSR] tried to persuade me with all possible means to enter the Party, in which under Nikita Sergeyevich [Khrushchov] it was now possible to breathe freely and easily. Pospelov was enthusiastic about Khrushchov, his youth (that's what he said, 'Youth'), his grandiose plans, and that

Shostakovich's song-cycles

the pressure, whether he perhaps nevertheless gave way out of opportunism and suffered frightful inner torment as a result, no one is entitled to pass judgement.

From 1960 until Shostakovich's death the relationship between vocal and instrumental works in his output is virtually in balance. Beside the large autobiographical song-cycles – the Seven Romances on Poems of Alexander Blok (Op. 127, 1967), the Six Poems of Marina Tsvetayeva (Op. 143, 1973), the Suite on Verses of Michelangelo Buonarroti (Op. 145, 1974) – appeared vocal-symphonic works – the cantata *The Execution of Stepan Razin* (Op. 119, 1964), the Thirteenth and Fourteenth Symphonies (Op. 113, 1962, and Op. 135, 1969), the revision of *Lady Macbeth* as *Katerina Izmaylova* (Op. 114, 1963) and an orchestral version of Musorgsky's *Songs and Dances of Death* (1962). A new genre of social-critical songs without especially artistic pretensions now appeared – the *Satires* to words by Sasha Chorny (Op. 109, 1960), the Five Romances on Texts from the Magazine *Krokodil* (Op. 121, 1965), the Preface to the Complete Edition of My Works (Op. 123, 1966) and the Four Poems of Captain Lebyadkin (Op. 146, 1974).

On the whole from 1960 text-based works take on such central importance that we may assume that the composer used words in order unequivocally to express his moral-ethical position, perhaps also, by the harnessing of word and music, to give a key to the understanding of his instrumental works.

SATIRES

The musical satires draw on the example of Modest Musorgsky. In songs such as 'Klassik' (The classicist), 'Seminarist' (The scholar), 'Kozel' (The he-goat), 'Ozornik' (The joker) and 'Rayok' (The picture gallery),

> I absolutely had to join the ranks of a Party headed not by Stalin but by Nikita Sergeyevich. Completely beside myself I tried as hard as I could to refuse this honour. I clutched at a straw by saying that I had never succeeded in mastering Marxism, that they should wait until I had studied him. Then I fell back on my religiosity. Then I said that it was possible to be Chairman of the Composers' Union without Party membership, after the example of Konstantin Fedin and Leonid Sobolov, who as non-Party members had leading posts in the Writers' Union. Pospelov rejected all my arguments and several times named Khrushchov, who was concerned about the fate of music and that I should take a part in it. I was completely broken down by the conversation. At the second meeting with Pospelov he again had me up against the wall. My nerves couldn't stand it, and I gave up.' Then follows the report of the celebratory Party meeting from which Shostakovich absented himself. *Ibid.*, 160–1.

Musorgsky created a genre comparable to literary models such as the pamphlet, the caricature and the satire, a genre which consciously ignores purely musical aesthetic criteria. Shostakovich went back to Musorgsky's example for the first time in his *Rayok*, composed between 1948 and 1958,[13] an angry persiflage on Zhdanov's speeches at the 1948 tribunal and on the realism–formalism discussion of the following years.[14] We must bear in mind that the satires published in Shostakovich's lifetime are also not just musical jokes but have concrete political relevance and may possibly also contain autobiographical aspects. These songs, following Musorgsky's example, make no claims to being 'high art'; their aesthetic value arises rather through the combination of semantic and stylistic levels which by received criteria would be mutually exclusive.

The Pictures from the Past ('Kartinki proshlogo') – thus the subtitle to the Satires on Texts by Sasha Chorny – appeared in June 1960,[15] at a time when Shostakovich had to come to terms with the question of his entry into the Communist Party. We also have to consider that after Stalin's death a phase of cautious cultural opening-up had begun and that the end of this so-called 'Thaw' (after Il'ya Erenburg's novel *Ottepel'*) was marked as early as 1958, when Boris Pasternak was awarded the Nobel Prize but was forced to refuse it.

Shostakovich's first Satire, with the title 'Kritiku' (To a critic), is a virtually *a cappella* scene directed at narrow-minded judges of art. In the second, 'Probuzhdeniye vesnï' (Spring's awakening), Shostakovich answers Chorny's quotes from sentimental nineteenth-century lyric poetry[16] with a quotation from Rakhmaninov's Romance 'Vesenniye vodï' (Spring waters).[17]

[13] When *Rayok* was composed has not been precisely established. Hulme's indication that Shostakovich composed the cycle in 1948 (*Dmitri Shostakovich: A Catalogue*, 320) is, as Sof'ya Khentova told me, most improbable, since some of the characters were still schoolboys or students at this time.

[14] For details see Manashir Yakubov, 'Dmitri Schostakowitschs "Antiformalistischer Rajok"', in *Sowjetische Musik im Licht der Perestroika*, ed. Hermann Danuser, Hannelore Gerlach and Jürgen Köchel (Laaber, 1990), 171–91.

[15] Hulme (*Dmitri Shostakovich: A Catalogue*, 268) gives 19 June, Khentova (*Shostakovich*, ii, 356) 18 June as the day of completion. The songs are dedicated to Galina Vishnevskaya and were first performed on 22 February 1961 by her and Mstislav Rostropovich. Vishnevskaya herself explains the subtitle as a ploy to ease the work's passage to official acceptance – *Galina: A Russian Story* (London, 1986), 282.

[16] For example, the phrase 'Kak mnogo dum navodit on' (How many thoughts he engenders) comes from the poem 'Vechernïy zvon' (Evening bells) by Ivan Kozlov (1779–1840) which has often been set to music.

[17] On quotations of popular motifs and in general on the genre of satire see E. Dobrïkin, 'Muzïkal'naya satira v vokalnïkh proizvedeniyakh D. Shostakovicha', in *Problemï muzïkal'noy nauki* [Problems of Musicology] (Moscow, 1975), 17ff.

Shostakovich may have been relating Chorny's parody of Spring feelings to the atmosphere of the time of the 'Thaw', an atmosphere of breakthrough which was nevertheless increasingly beset by contradictions. In 'Potomki' (Descendants) the picture of a joyless life and unfulfillable hope for a distant better future becomes grotesque by the combination of swung waltz rhythms and melancholy psalmodising melody. The 'Nedorazumeniye' (Misunderstanding) arises because a good-for-nothing takes literally the inflated love poetry of a bourgeoise poetess. In its content this parody refers back to the first Satire on literary ignorance. Musically the song is a homage to Alexander Dargomïzhsky's 'Titular Councillor', a little scene in which a worthy official is led astray by the daughter of a general. Sof'ya Khentova draws attention to an aspect which gives pause for thought. In the manuscript of the first movement of the Twelfth Symphony – 'The Year 1917', dedicated to the memory of Lenin – after twenty bars or so a nearly complete draft of 'Misunderstanding' appears out of the blue.[18] Whether this was intended as a private underground commentary on the great theme of the Twelfth Symphony must remain an open question.

In the last song, 'Kreytserova sonata' (Kreutzer sonata), the superimposition of incompatible semantic levels gains an extra dimension. Tolstoy's well-known tale of an empty marriage based only on transient infatuation and ending in jealousy, revenge and murder, is a plea for the maintenance of Christian virtues. Chorny transforms the subject matter into a parody on presumed marital happiness,[19] founded on the desire for coarse eroticism and on that same empty infatuation, moreover between partners who are mutually estranged and remain estranged: 'You are of the people, I am of the intelligentsia'. Of course Shostakovich does not avoid a quotation from Beethoven's Kreutzer Sonata. The sphere of the man, the representative of the intelligentsia, is indicated by a slow waltz, the sphere of the woman, the representative of the people, by a cancan. A short quotation from Lensky's Aria which precedes the duel scene in *Yevgeniy Onegin* serves as an introduction to the entry of the voice part and may be taken as an indication of the danger of such a misalliance.

The Five Romances on Texts from the Magazine *Krokodil*, a work of bitter irony, were composed on 4 September 1965. On the same day Shostakovich wrote to Glikman:

[18] Khentova, *Shostakovich*, ii, 263.
[19] The fact that Chorny calls the woman in his poetry Fekla may be intended as a homage to Gogol's comedy *The Marriage*.

In the magazine *Krokodil* No. 24 (1782) of 30 August 1965 there are some comic trifles. I have chosen five of them and set them for bass with piano accompaniment. Possibly you're not a subscriber to *Krokodil*, so I've cut out the texts and am sending them to you. I've thought up a title for each one. . . . In the musical language of this opus I have made use of folk output (the Russian folk song 'Vo sadu li, v ogorode' (In the garden, in the vegetable garden)) and the classical heritage (Tchaikovsky's opera *The Queen of Spades*). Apart from that I have used the 'Dies irae'. When I was composing the Romances I made use of the method of socialist realism.[20]

Similarly filled with bitter irony is Shostakovich's *Preface to the Complete Edition of My Works and Brief Reflections apropos this Preface*.[21] The basis is a paraphrase of a Pushkin epigram (to A. Khvostov, *Istoriya stikhotvortsa* (History of a versifier)) and a text by Shostakovich, in which he enumerates his honorary titles, prizes etc. Malcolm MacDonald proposes a plausible interpretation of this piece by making a connection with the finale of the Thirteenth Symphony, entitled 'A Career', specifically with the passage about Lev Tolstoy.[22] MacDonald gives no bar numbers; he has in mind the bars from the Foreword which frame Shostakovich's text and which correspond in their intervals, though not in their rhythm, to the Tolstoy passage in the finale of the Thirteenth Symphony (Ex. 9.2).

The allusion to Lev Tolstoy and Alexey Tolstoy, the opportunist and careerist of noble origins, is according to MacDonald:

not at all comical: it is a reminder of the fact that such honours are often a reward for compromises, if not worse. The question is posed (and it is to Shostakovich's eternal credit that he felt able to pose it): if Shostakovich is like Tolstoy, is he more of a Lev or a Count Tolstoy?[23]

ART AND THE ARTIST

The question of the morality of art and the artist comes increasingly to the fore in Shostakovich's late songs. The Seven Romances on Poems of Alexander Blok, completed in 1967 in hospital, are chosen according to

---

[20] *Pis'ma k drugu*, 205–6. Apart from the unmistakable 'Dies irae' theme in the third Romance I have been unable to trace the quotations.
[21] Composed on 2 March 1966; the Preface and the *Krokodil* Romances were first performed by Yevgeniy Nesterenko and Shostakovich on 28 May 1966 in Leningrad.
[22] Malcolm MacDonald, 'Word and music in late Shostakovich', in *Shostakovich: The Man and his Music*, ed. Christopher Norris (London, 1982), 125–47.
[23] *Ibid.*, 136.

Ex. 9.2 Preface to the Complete Edition of My Works, bb. 29–33

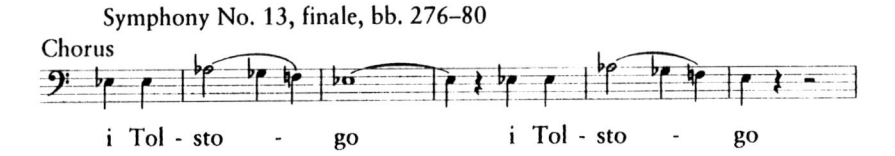

Symphony No. 13, finale, bb. 276–80
Chorus
i Tol - sto - go   i Tol - sto - go

these criteria: values such as faithfulness ('The song of Ophelia'), truth ('Gamayun, the prophet bird'), love ('We were together'), are sought in the face of loneliness ('The town sleeps'), threat ('The storm') and anxiety ('Secret signs'); these values alone count in view of God in Nature and in view of Death ('Music'). This last is Shostakovich's title for the last song; 'Storm' and 'Secret signs' are also his titles.[24]

With the rigorous reduction of all artistic means and with the elements of serial technique (in the sixth song) this cycle shows for the first time clear features of Shostakovich's late work. Melodic characteristics such as falling thirds, scale-segments of a third, and fourth-calls, also a penchant for extended unison writing and simple two-part writing, point towards the late compositions but also refer back to earlier works. The 'Song of Ophelia' links straight to the lament of the abandoned Katerina Izmaylova accompanied only by cor anglais (Act IV scene 9, in the 1963 version fig. 460). In the second song, 'Gamayun, the prophet bird', the bass motion always through a minor third corresponds to the opening of the Tenth Symphony. The march rhythms in the middle section at the words about a tartar attack 'and cowardice and hunger and fire' (bb. 31ff.) are generally a topos in Shostakovich's output, in this concrete meaning beginning with the Pushkin song 'Verses' and the Fifth Symphony (first movement development section, and finale). The form and textural evolution of the 'Gamayun' song correspond to the dramaturgy of the first movement of the Tenth Symphony, and Bernd Feuchtner is doubtless correct when he

[24] See Khentova, *Shostakovich*, ii, 492.

says that Shostakovich identified himself in both works with the role of a Prophet (the bird Gamayun and the monk Pimen in *Boris Godunov*).[25]

The Blok cycle has the subtitle 'Vocal-instrumental suite'; in fact it shows signs of a four-movement symphony. The first two songs, as it were introduction and first movement, are linked by the framing tonality of C minor. The third song, the dialogue between voice and violin, and the fourth in the form of a passacaglia, are as it were a slow movement. The fifth song functions as a scherzo. The sixth, with its motivic references to the first and second songs, represents a reprise and a finale. The seventh song then is an epilogue and apotheosis.[26] Corresponding to this arrangement by content is an instrumentation grouping by three duos, three trios and one quartet. In the many-levelled cyclic construction, in the pared-down musical language and in the death topos here indicated for the first time and even given a Christian aspect, the Blok cycle is a prototype for the Fourteenth Symphony, completed two years later.

Shostakovich clearly considered the Six Romances on Verses by English Poets so important that he reorchestrated them in 1971 for chamber orchestra and gave them a new opus number (Op. 140). Each of these songs carries, unusually for Shostakovich, a dedication. The new instrumentation also signified a memorial for dead friends, for his wife Nina Vasil'yevna, for his best friend in the 1920s and 1930s Ivan Sollertinsky, and for his especially close composer-colleague Vissarion Shebalin (dedicatees of the second, fifth and sixth songs, respectively). In certain respects the English Romances represent a synthesis in Shostakovich's output. It was perhaps for this reason and also because of the moral-ethical exhortation of the texts that Shostakovich took them into the sequence of his late works. In the second, folksong-like, simply formed song, 'V polyakh pod snegom i dozhdyom' (In the fields beneath snow and rain), we hear elements of nineteenth-century prisoner songs and more specifically the closing scene of *Lady Macbeth*. The third song, 'Makferson pered kazn'yu' (Macpherson before his execution), prefigures the second movement of the Thirteenth Symphony, 'Humour', as has often been pointed out in the Shostakovich literature;[27] the fact that Macpherson dances in the presence

[25] Feuchtner, 'Und Kunst geknebelt', 244.
[26] Khentova divides the cycle, rather unconvincingly, into segments; '"Gamayun" appears as the first conflict-like movement of a vocal symphony, "We were together" as a lyric scherzo, "The town sleeps" as a passacaglia, for the first time in his vocal works; "The storm" is the culmination of a symphonic development before the finale, a brightening, a return to peace' (*Shostakovich*, ii, 494).
[27] For details on this song and its meaning for Shostakovich's output, see Feuchtner, '*Und Kunst geknebelt*', 182, 192–4, 232.

of death maybe brings this song close to the 'Jewish' compositions – the Second Piano Trio, the cycle From Jewish Folk Poetry and the finales of the First Violin Concerto and Fourth String Quartet.

There is a direct link between the fifth and most important song (the 66th Sonnet of William Shakespeare) and the Michelangelo Suite. The sonnet identifies a theme which Shostakovich tackled again and again, at least from the time of the damning criticism of *Lady Macbeth*: the perversion of all values, to which only suicide would be an answer if it were not for friendship and love. For the sake of the text-declamation the musical language is reduced to a minimum – a pedal-point on G, a G major and a C major triad, and at the point in the text 'And strength by limping sway disabled, And art made tongue-tied by authority' a pointed disharmony by the movement to A♭ over the retained G pedal.[28] The last setting, on the counting verse 'The King of France went up the hill, / with twenty thousand men; / the King of France went down the hill, / and never went up again' (a variant of the children's verse 'The Grand Old Duke of York, / He had ten thousand men, / He marched them up to the top of the hill, / And he marched them down again') is only a joke on the surface. The tonality of E♭ major points to the middle section in the first movement of the Seventh Symphony and the Ninth of 1945, created in response to the victory celebrations; march rhythms and the 'Force motif' are acknowledged topoi in Shostakovich.

Already in the Alexander Blok cycle Shostakovich had consciously renounced the genre designation 'Romansi' – the Russian word for art songs – and substituted 'Stikhotvoreniya' – Poems. This kind of homage to the poetic word becomes the norm in the late cycles; even the child-like verses of Captain Lebyadkin are headed 'Stikhotvoreniya'. The theme of the Six Poems of Marina Tsvetayeva is the moral integrity of great artists – Marina Tsvetayeva herself, Alexander Pushkin (to whom the fourth and fifth poems are dedicated) and Anna Akhmatova (dedicatee of the sixth poem). At the same time Shostakovich chose and assembled the songs so that the cycle formed as it were an autobiography in notes.[29]

---

[28] Shakespeare's meaning is considerably attenuated in Pasternak's translation, but it seems not unlikely that Shostakovich was aware of the force of the original text.
[29] For details see Boris Tishchenko, 'Razmïshleniya o 142–m i 143–m opusakh' [Thoughts on Opus 142 and 143], *Sovetskaya Muzïka* (9/1974), 40–6, and Dorothea Redepenning, 'Autobiographische Reflexionen – Schostakowitschs Zwetajewa-Zyklus (Op. 143)', *Musica* (3/1990), 164–8.

THE LAST TWO CYCLES

The outward motivation for the Suite on Verses of Michelangelo Buonarroti[30] was the 500th anniversary of the artist's birth, which was also celebrated in the Soviet Union. The inner motivation was clearly Shostakovich's desire to pursue the ideas formulated in the Blok cycle, the English songs and the Tsvetayeva cycle. On 23 August 1974 he wrote with his characteristic understatement to Glikman:

> I can only judge Michelangelo with difficulty, but the most important things have become clear to me. And the most important things in these sonnets seem to me to be the following: wisdom, love, creation, death, immortality. The translations by A. M. Efros are not always successful. But Michelangelo's great achievement shines through even in so-so translations.[31]

During rehearsals in October 1975, Maxim Shostakovich mentioned to Nesterenko that his father considered this cycle as his Sixteenth Symphony,[32] a thought which seems reasonable given the many cross-connections with the symphonies, especially to the suite-like Fourteenth Symphony, which is also in eleven movements.

In its formal aspect the Michelangelo Suite is a stringently constructed cycle, which Soviet authors describe thus: the framework is the first and tenth songs, 'Istina' (Truth) and 'Smert' (Death). The second, third and fourth songs, 'Utro' (Morning), 'Lyubov'' (Love) and 'Razluka' (Separation), are textually linked, likewise the fifth, sixth and seventh, 'Gnev' (Anger), 'Dante' and 'Izganniku' (To an exile). A third group is formed by the eighth and ninth songs, 'Tvorchestvo' (Creation) and 'Noch'' (Night), the tenth song functions as a reprise, the eleventh, 'Bessmertiye' (Immortality) as an Epilogue.[33] That scheme will be challenged below.

Furthermore, there are some motifs or fragments of motifs which ensure cyclic unity. These are:

(a) Two rising fourths, or chains of fourths in general, which run leitmotivically through almost all the songs and which are a fundamental characteristic of Shostakovich's melodic technique (Ex. 9.3).

---

[30] For bass and piano, completed 31 July 1974, the orchestral version 5 November 1974; the Leningrad première took place on 23 December 1974, the Moscow première on 31 January 1975.

[31] The text was based on a Russian edition of 1964 – *Michelangelo: Life and Work*, compiled by V. Grashchenkov; Abram Efros's translations were made not from the Italian original but from a German paraphrase (cf. Hulme, *Dmitri Shostakovich: A Catalogue*, 334).

[32] See *ibid.*, 337.

[33] See Vasina-Grossman, *Kamerno-vokal'noye tvorchestvo*, 37ff., Levaya, 'Tayna velikogo iskusstva', 314–15, and Khentova, *Shostakovich*, ii, 567–8.

Shostakovich's song-cycles

Ex. 9.3 Michelangelo Suite, First movement, bb. 6–7, 14–15

Third movement, b. 1

Sixth movement, b. 1

Seventh movement, bb. 33–42

Eighth movement, bb. 17–19

Ninth movement, bb. 4–6

Tenth movement, bb. 59–63

Eleventh movement, bb. 32–7

Ya zhiv v te - be ch'im se - to - va - n'yam vnem - lyu

(b) A melodic figure consisting of a falling fifth or a falling third, usually with a rising minor second added, which in the second part of the cycle appears in free inversion (Ex. 9.4). This figure is also a topos in Shostakovich's melodic arsenal, for example (Ex. 9.5).

Dodecaphonic aspects also reinforce the cyclic construction. The instrumental passages in the first, third, fifth, sixth, eighth and ninth songs are

220 Dorothea Redepenning

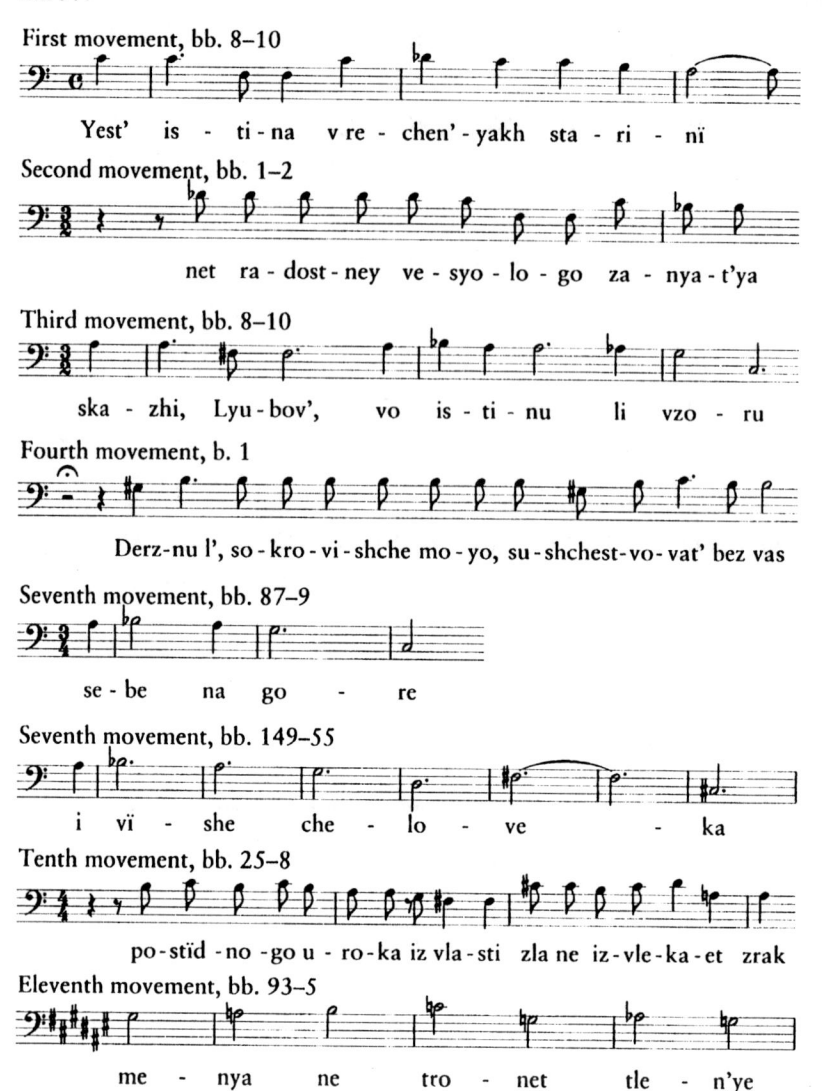

Ex. 9.4

First movement, bb. 8–10

Yest' is - ti - na v re - chen' - yakh sta - ri - nï

Second movement, bb. 1–2

net ra - dost - ney ve - syo - lo - go za - nya - t'ya

Third movement, bb. 8–10

ska - zhi, Lyu - bov', vo is - ti - nu li vzo - ru

Fourth movement, b. 1

Derz - nu l', so - kro - vi - shche mo - yo, su - shchest - vo - vat' bez vas

Seventh movement, bb. 87–9

se - be na go - re

Seventh movement, bb. 149–55

i vï - she che - lo - ve - ka

Tenth movement, bb. 25–8

po - stïd - no - go u - ro - ka iz vla - sti zla ne iz - vle - ka - et zrak

Eleventh movement, bb. 93–5

me - nya ne tro - net tle - n'ye

atonally conceived (they are not twelve-note); that also goes for the chord progressions in the second and fourth songs and the passagework in the eleventh song. The tenth song is a passacaglia over an eleven-note row repeated six times.

The cycle contains some allusions to early music. The vocal part in the second song, and the entire third song, are constructed in the manner of a

Ex. 9.5

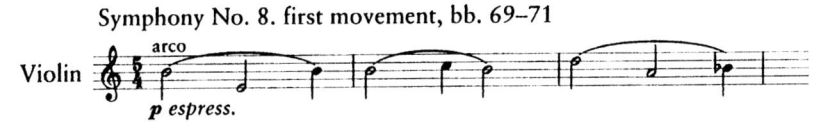

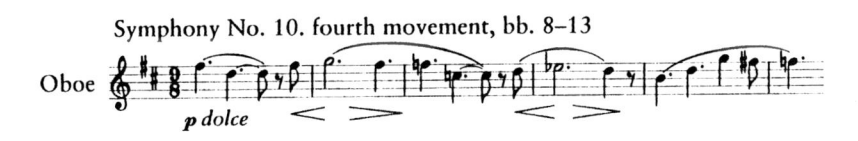

Symphony No. 8. first movement, bb. 69–71

Symphony No. 9. second movement, bb. 1–10

Symphony No. 10. fourth movement, bb. 8–13

Ex. 9.6 Michelangelo Suite, 'Istina', bb. 1–5

recitativo secco. The opening motto-motif, especially in its instrumentation for two trumpets, is also reminiscent of early music (Ex. 9.6).

This is a rudimentary two-voice writing, a kind of archaic heterophony. On the other hand, such eleven-note complexes (with no relation to the eleven-note row in the tenth song) are inconceivable without the example of dodecaphony. With such construction Shostakovich is possibly reacting also to Alfred Schnittke's conception of polystylisticism, which was much debated in the Soviet Union at the beginning of the 1970s.

Notwithstanding the motivic connections the cycle gives a remarkably heterogeneous and fragmentary impression. This comes, on the one hand, from the brittle texture, the unison and two-part writing maintained over long stretches, and the 'building-block' principle, as it were, in which the divisions and seams are obvious. On the other hand, the cycle is criss-crossed with reminiscences from Shostakovich's earlier

222   Dorothea Redepenning

works, which become clear as fragments of old memories thanks precisely to the fragmentary form. In the instrumental interludes of the first song Shostakovich quotes the rhythm (not the intervals) of the main theme from his First Violin Concerto (Ex. 9.7).

Ex. 9.7 Michelangelo Suite, 'Istina', bb. 14–18

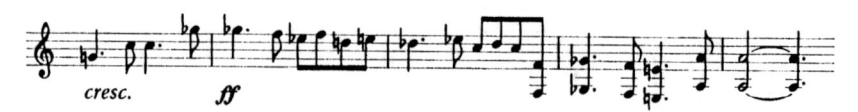

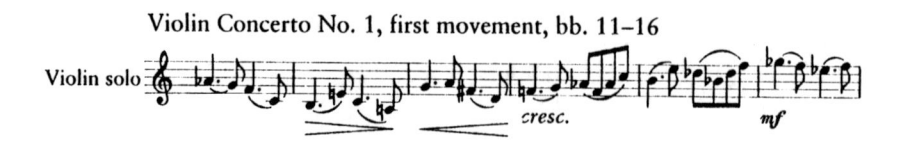

Violin Concerto No. 1, first movement, bb. 11–16

Ex. 9.8

Michelangelo Suite, second movement, bb. 10–14

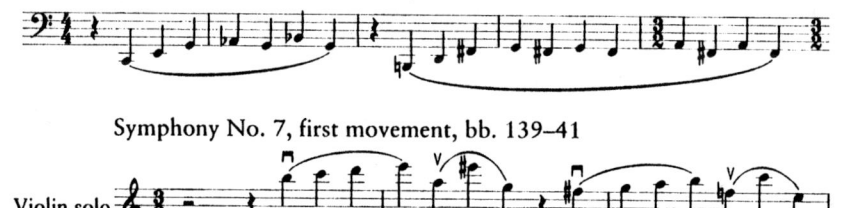

Symphony No. 7, first movement, bb. 139–41

In this way in 1948, condemned by the notorious 'Resolution on the Opera *The Great Friendship*' either to silence or falsehood, Shostakovich nevertheless spoke the truth.

The basic motif of the second song occurs in numerous works, with various intervals but always the same contour (Ex. 9.8).

The conclusion of this song, 'O skol'ko dela zdes' dlya ruk moikh!' (Oh, how much work there is for my hands here!), with its D♭ tonality, indeed with its clear tonality which in this context itself gives the impression of a quotation, is a reminiscence of the song 'O Delvig, Delvig!' from the Fourteenth Symphony. From the indirect reference to the Decembrist poet Wilhelm Küchelbecker, who sent the poem set by Shostakovich to his friend Anton Del'vig from exile, there arises a relation to the two songs dedicated to Dante.

Ex. 9.9

Michelangelo Suite, seventh movement, 'Izganniku', bb. 75–82

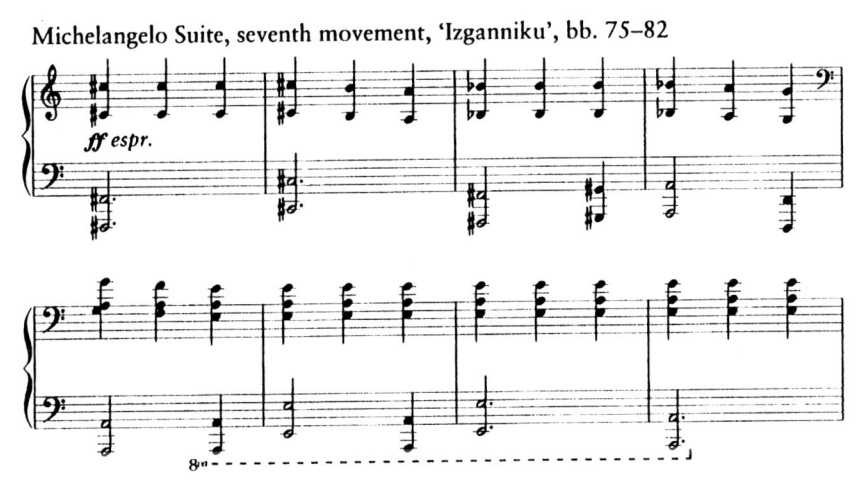

Symphony No. 11, first movement, bb. 75–81

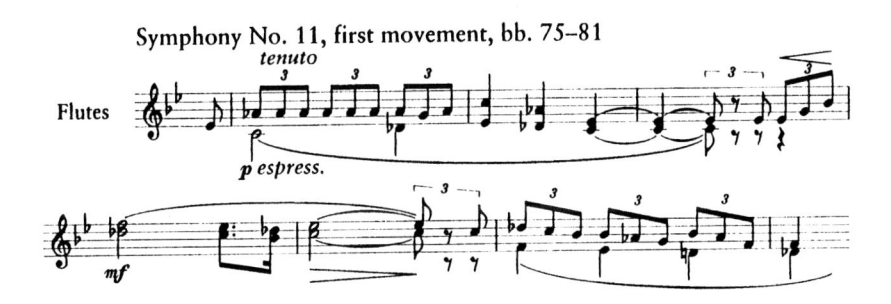

The semiquaver figuration in the third movement, 'Love', is given by Shostakovich to the flute in the orchestral version. Similar figurations may be found in the song 'Otkuda takaya nezhnost'?' (Whence such tenderness?) in the Tsvetayeva Cycle, and also in the Tenth Symphony (third movement, bb. 199ff., finale, bb. 46ff., bb. 246ff. and so on), in the Fifteenth Symphony (finale, bb. 64ff. and so on), even in the Sasha Chorny Satire 'Spring's awakening'.

The fifth song, 'Anger', with its layered note-repetitions and dotted rhythms, looks back to the song 'The storm' from the Blok cycle; moreover, the sharply accented interpolations and chords create a connection with the first movement of the Thirteenth Symphony, specifically to the passage about the boy from Białystok (bb. 66–170). The stylised march with the pregnant triplet rhythms in the sixth song, 'Dante', points to the first movement of the Eleventh Symphony; this relationship becomes still clearer in the seventh song, 'To the exile'. The theme in the Eleventh Symphony is itself a quotation of a prisoners' song, 'Slushay' (Listen!) (Ex. 9.9).

In the eighth movement, 'Creation', numerous motivic and timbral parallels make a connection with the fifth song, 'Anger', which is not inherent in the texts. Michelangelo's sonnets deal with anger over injustice in the world and with 'God's hammer' which is a spur to the sculptor. By linking these texts musically Shostakovich clarifies a central postulate of his creative morality: it is the task and duty of his art to accuse, to point out injustice, to proclaim truth. In this respect, as in the fifth song, there is a relationship to the first movement of the Thirteenth Symphony, and also to the fourth movement of the Eighth String Quartet – to the sharply accented *fortissimo* chords which frame the prisoners' song 'Zamuchon tyazholoy nevoley' (Tormented by heavy captivity) and the *Lady Macbeth* quotation – and also to the far from cheerful 'Serenade' from the Fifteenth String Quartet. Therefore, if we wish to subdivide the cycle, we should not make a division between the seventh and eighth songs, but see the songs 'Anger', 'Dante', 'To the exile' and 'Creation' as belonging to one group.

The ninth and tenth songs, 'Night' and 'Death', are related in subject matter and make a formal unit as a retrograde reprise of the second and first movements.[34] The contrary-motion quaver figurations in the ninth song point to the 'Nocturne' in the Fifteenth String Quartet. After the text 'lish' razbudi, ona zagovorit' (only wake up, she starts to speak) Shostakovich quotes in bb. 33–5 note for note the chorale-like string passage from the tenth movement of the Fourteenth Symphony, 'Death of a poet' (bb. 20–2 and 61–3). With this quotation the song gains two further aspects: the relationship between 'Night' and 'Death' and the reference to Rainer Maria Rilke, author of the poem about the 'Death of the poet'. The tenth song closes the cycle by a double reference back to the opening theme. The form of the passacaglia, to which Shostakovich time after time assigned serious and tragic subject matter, may represent a retrospective on all his passacaglias – from the interlude between the fourth and fifth scenes in *Lady Macbeth*, through the fourth movement of the Eighth Symphony, the third movement of the First Violin Concerto, the Blok setting 'The town is asleep', to the Tsvetayeva setting 'The poet and the tsar'.

In formal terms the eleventh movement, 'Immortality', is an epilogue. Malcolm MacDonald sees in the opening motif a quotation from the

---

[34] Only Tamara Levaya notices this ('Tayna velikogo iskusstva', 315).

finale of Beethoven's Fifth Symphony;[35] moreover, Shostakovich apparently used here a theme from his youthful opera on Pushkin's poem 'The gypsies'.[36] The triadic melody outline, high register and bright instrumentation, with celesta as symbol for eternity,[37] simplicity at all levels of musical construction and F♯ major as Shostakovich's key of love – all this makes for the greatest contrast to the preceding sorrowful tones. A similar tone-picture is found in the concluding bars of the Fifteenth Symphony (bb. 337ff.). In both these works the associations with toy-box music and ironic distance take on yet another aspect, which has nothing in common with naivety or irony: 'Immortality' means removal of time: 'Zdes' rok poslal bezvremenniy mne son' (here fate has sent me a timeless dream). Shostakovich achieves this by deliberately fashioning a repetitive music from his motifs and rhythms. Presumably unconsciously he thereby approaches several stylistic features of the American minimalists or the aesthetic of a 'Musique atemporelle' as developed since the 1970s above all by Corneliu Dan Georgescu.[38]

The Michelangelo cycle contains a multiplicity of allusions to earlier works of Shostakovich. We find something similar in the Fifteenth Symphony, the Fifteenth String Quartet, the cycle on Poems by Marina Tsvetayeva and the Viola Sonata. As a retrospective and conspectus of important earlier works these late compositions are a legacy in sound. The many references to great artists – Michelangelo, Dante, Shakespeare, Pushkin, the Decembrist poets, Rilke, Tsvetayeva, Akhmatova – may also signify a self-identification. These names stand for unshakable creative ethics and for the morality of art.

Shostakovich was by now an old man, marked by death. In summer 1973 he was staying in Washington, consulted specialists there, and was told finally that there was no hope of recovery.[39] From this point of view too, the late works, especially the Michelangelo cycle, are a testament, perhaps also a confession in notes.

[35] MacDonald, 'Word and music', 141.
[36] See Vasina-Grossman, *Kamerno-vokal'noye tvorchestvo*, 40; Levaya, 'Tayna velikogo iskusstva', 306; Hulme, *Dmitri Shostakovich: A Catalogue*, 11.
[37] Edison Denisov reports: 'He [Shostakovich] was faintly amused that in Mahler "eternity" was represented by a celesta'. Cited in Detlef Gojowy, *Dmitri Schostakowitsch* (Reinbek, 1983), 64.
[38] See his study, 'Considérations sur une "Musique atemporelle"', *Revue Roumaine d'Histoire de l'Art, Série Théâtre, Musique, Cinéma*, 16 (1979), 35–42.
[39] Malcolm MacDonald points this out in connection with the late song-cycles ('Word and music', 139).

How are we to understand the Four Poems of Captain Lebyadkin in this context? Formally they stand in relation to the Michelangelo cycle as the song about the French king to the Shakespeare sonnet in the English Romances; in terms of subject matter and music they are linked to *Rayok*, the Satires on Sasha Chorny's Poems, the *Krokodil* Romances and to the Preface. Captain Lebyadkin from Dostoyevsky's novel *The Devils* is one of the most distasteful figures in Russian literature, always drunk, brutal, cunning and calculating, without the ability to see the consequences of his actions, a man who proclaims the revolutionary and anarchic ideas of his time in primitive variants, a man without morals and as it were the folksy variant of the handsome, powerful Nikolay Stavrogin, who embodies a deliberate, misanthropic nihilism. Lebyadkin writes child-like poems which either offend or delight those around him. Shostakovich assembled and set these poems, with some interwoven prose-extracts. Terms such as 'satire' and 'parody' do not do full justice to the four songs;[40] rather the question is in what relation they stand to the Michelangelo cycle and even whether these caricatures of great art do not constitute a legacy, a negative legacy.

Shostakovich's statements concerning the Lebyadkin figure support such an assumption. He said to Yevgeniy Nesterenko: 'Of course Lebyadkin is a buffoon, but sometimes he can become sinister', and to Boris Tishchenko: 'Captain Lebyadkin is for the most part a buffoon, but it seems to me [also] an ominous figure',[41] and to Isaak Glikman: 'The figure of Captain Lebyadkin has much of the buffoon in him, but still more ominousness. It's turned out a very ominous piece of work.'[42]

Interpretations of the Lebyadkin songs point in different directions. Tamara Levaya sees in the Prelude to the fourth song, 'Svetlaya lichnost'' (A bright personality), a relationship to the beggar-monks in the Kromy scene at the end of *Boris Godunov*, and deduces that Shostakovich saw Lebyadkin's revolutionary ideas as extremely questionable. The sad fate of the 'Tarakan' (Cockroach) in the second song becomes in her view, 'a grotesque symbol of the disintegration of a personality (which is extremely important for the conception of the novel). Thus the idea shimmers through the Holy Fool character.' She sees the whole Lebyadkin cycle as:

linked in a paradoxical, negative way with the preceding cycles. The same complexity, the monographic style of narration with a principal hero in the

[40] Vasina-Grossman, *Kamernoye-vokal'noye tvorchestvo*, 28; Khentova, *Shostakovich*, ii, 572.
[41] Both cited in Khentova, *Shostakovich*, ii, 573.
[42] Letter of 23 August 1974, *Pis'ma k drugu*, 302.

Shostakovich's song-cycles

middle, the same themes of human life – love, social concerns, reflection on fate and death (also symptomatic is the motive of indifferent Nature which appears in 'Tarakan'). Only this is all debased into comedy, turned to jest, along the lines of an 'anti-world'.[43]

Even the construction of the cycle itself – with the suggestion of a four-movement symphony but a total renunciation of motivic interrelationship – is in Levaya's view the expression of an 'anti-'.

Bernd Feuchtner understands the Lebyadkin songs as a 'dark counterpart' to the Michelangelo cycle. With the stupid, impudent captain, Shostakovich made a monument to the culture-officials who tormented him all his life:

> Everything separated Shostakovich from the 'revolutionary' Lebyadkin. On the other hand he felt close to the Christian Michelangelo, who countered the negative phenomena of his time with a humanistic ethos and the ideal of Christianity. After half a millennium the times seemed to have lost nothing in darkness. Did he sense that it was religious longing that united him with the Christian Michelangelo? Christianity or Communism – in the latter case reality corresponded to the domination of the noble doctrine just as little as in the former. People like the coarse Lebyadkin played the great revolutionary and dragged the ideals into the mud. They bullied their way to the levers of power, and they misused this power with relish. In Lebyadkin Shostakovich found a prototype of the narrow-minded revolutionary, the kind he pursued all his life long with his sarcasm.[44]

Malcolm MacDonald suggests a third interpretation. He sees in Lebyadkin a fool or joker and places him in the line of the Fool from *King Lear* (whose songs Shostakovich set for a 1941 Leningrad production of the play), with Macpherson and the 'Humour' movement from the Thirteenth Symphony:

> This concern with jester-figures argues a certain degree of identification between composer and subject. So, when Shostakovich chose the lucubrations of Captain Lebyadkin for his last song-cycle, he may have felt more in common with his disagreeable mouthpiece than at first meets the eye.[45]

MacDonald exemplifies this thesis by placing the Prelude to the song about the 'Bright personality' alongside the movement 'A career', the finale of the Thirteenth Symphony, and adds the question:

> Is Shostakovich hinting here, in blandly merry music that underlies mock-serious words, that paying lip-service to Revolution and social justice without actually

[43] Levaya, 'Tayna velikogo iskusstva', 325–7.
[44] Feuchtner, *'Und Kunst geknebelt'*, 255–7.
[45] MacDonald, 'Word and music', 143–5.

doing anything about it, or taking any risks, is as cushy a way of having a career as any?[46]

In conclusion a fourth interpretation may be proposed: the Michelangelo cycle displays a reduction on all levels of musical construction. Between the bare melodic lines are introduced echoes of Shostakovich's great works, above all the symphonies. Michelangelo's words give these echoes the concrete meaning of a moral-ethical message – this is how Shostakovich wanted his oeuvre to be understood. The Lebyadkin cycle is worked out according to the same principle, but here primitivisms are added between the text and as accompanying figures, which likewise look back to Shostakovich's output. One could call them reminiscences of the 'Method of socialist realism'. Shostakovich set innumerable texts whose literary qualities are in no way inferior to Lebyadkin's revolutionary verses – for instance the popular songs and choruses of the 1940s and 1950s, the songs from the propaganda films, the oratorio *The Song of the Forests* and the cantata *The Sun Shines Over Our Motherland*. The concluding song about the 'Bright personality' – a strophic song with a folksy 'Ekh!' after each verse – is in the spirit of those mass-songs. Possibly the Lebyadkin cycle, like the Michelangelo cycle, is linked with Shostakovich's artistic biography – as a confession of aesthetic and moral sins.

[46] *Ibid.*

10

A debt repaid? Some observations on Shostakovich and his late-period recognition of Britten

ERIC ROSEBERRY

In the Red House at Aldeburgh hangs a portrait of Anton Del'vig, the poet to whom are addressed the lines by the Decembrist, Wilhelm Küchelbecker – lines set by Shostakovich in his Fourteenth Symphony, the work he dedicated to Benjamin Britten in 1969. A gift from Shostakovich to Britten, the portrait would seem to lend confirmation to what is surely implicit in the ninth movement of the symphony: that those lines of Küchelbecker served Shostakovich as a mouthpiece for a fraternal greeting to his English friend and colleague. In the desolate context of the symphony this setting stands apart on account of its emotional warmth and tonal stability; indeed, its calm, hymnal gesture of four luminous triads that dispel the angry twelve-note 'cluster' of the previous movement could almost be taken as a friendly salutation *à la manière de* Britten.[1] and the key – D♭ major – is the key of 'the world of high ideals' in Shostakovich's Twelfth String Quartet:[2]

> O Delvig, Delvig! What reward
> for lofty deeds and poetry? ...

[1] Britten's 'hymnal' triadic images include the setting of Keats's sonnet 'To Sleep' in the Serenade for Tenor, Horn and Strings, the four chords of the second act of *A Midsummer Night's Dream* and the famous interlude after the trial and Vere's aria ('I accept their verdict') in *Billy Budd*. The second stanza of the setting (No. 3) of 'Sokrates und Alcibiades' in the *Sechs Hölderlin-Fragmente* is a further memorable instance of a transforming 'clarification' through triadic harmony. As if taking a hint from Britten, Shostakovich's later music frequently employs this expressive device of triadic 'clarification'. See, for example, 'Night', No. 9 of the Suite on Verses of Michelangelo – a setting whose nocturnal beauty and calm suggest a response to Britten's perennial attraction towards images of sleep and darkness.

[2] See Hans Keller's reference to the official programme note accompanying the London première of the work in his article 'Shostakovich discovers Schoenberg', *The Listener* (10 August 1970), 494.

> Immortality is equally the lot
> of bold inspired deeds
> and sweet songs!
> Thus will not die our bond,
> free, joyful and proud!
> In happiness and in sorrow it stands firm,
> the bond of eternal lovers of the Muses.[3]

The high seriousness and cyclic sense of completion that Shostakovich brought to his work in the final years of his life coincide with an on-going, passionate admiration for Britten and his music, whose own accomplishments during the same period (the composers died within a year of each other) correspondingly proclaim a late, valedictory style. Britten's 'late period' reaches fruition in a single *chef d'œuvre* – the opera *Death in Venice* and its instrumental pendant, the Third String Quartet[4] – which may be said to match those monumental works of farewell to life and art in Shostakovich which occupied the Russian composer between 1969 and his death in 1975, such as the Fifteenth Symphony, the Fifteenth Quartet, the Suite on Verses of Michelangelo and the Sonata for Viola and Piano. (One may note in this connection the widely commented-upon 'autobiographical' aspect of Britten's last opera[5] and the several speculatively autobiographical programmatic explanations that have accompanied, for example, Shostakovich's Fifteenth Symphony and last string quartet.[6])

Rather than adopting the risky thesis of direct 'influence', I propose to examine certain aspects of Shostakovich's creative personality, biography, style and aesthetic in so far as they would seem to establish meaningful connections with Britten. I suggest that in Shostakovich's late work – notwithstanding a whole range of other allusions and homage-paying salutations – the music of Britten emerges as a significant catalyst. In

---

[3] Translation by Valeria Vlazinskaya accompanying HMV LP ASD 2633.
[4] Britten's Third Quartet follows the 'autobiographical' Eighth of Shostakovich in its use of self-quotations. These include not only the well-known quotations from *Death in Venice* at the beginning of the fifth movement, but also allusions to a prominent motif from the first movement of his Second String Quartet in the 'Ostinato' (see bb. 38 and 64).
[5] See, for example, Christopher Headington in his *Britten* (London, 1981), 138, in which he discusses Colin Graham's comment that 'of all his works, this one went deepest into Britten's soul'.
[6] Typical of this point of view are L. Danilevich on the Fifteenth Symphony in his book *Dmitri Shostakovich* (Moscow, 1980), 244, and Gerald Abraham in his BBC Radio 3 talk on the Shostakovich string quartets on 15 January 1977.

particular, it will be borne in mind that during the sixties, when the 'affair' between the two composers took off, so to speak, Shostakovich actually heard performed for the first time in Soviet Russia (amongst other things) Britten's *Peter Grimes*, *The Rape of Lucretia*, *Albert Herring*, *The Turn of the Screw*, *A Midsummer Night's Dream*, *War Requiem*, Cello Symphony and *The Poet's Echo*.[7] It is reasonable to suppose that the sound-images of these particular works were therefore present to a greater or lesser extent in his mind as he conceived his later works. And in admiring such works, in this delayed response to Britten's own long-standing devotion to Shostakovich, the Russian recognised a creative imagination that in many ways corresponded to his own. The main task, then, will be to assess the impact of Britten's music on Shostakovich in the late sixties and early seventies. This will be done in two ways. First, by showing how Shostakovich would have recognised in Britten a fellow traveller along a path he had already taken. And second, by suggesting ways in which Britten's example, particularly in the works fresh to Shostakovich's ears, may find its parallels in the later Shostakovich. But before this it will be necessary to give some account of Britten's admiration of Shostakovich and – despite their manifest individuality as creative artists – to look further at the evidence of a mutual compatability.

In a remarkably wide-ranging paper, Lyudmila Kovnatskaya has already set out many of the characteristics that unite the two composers,[8] despite the remoteness of their cultures and socio-political backgrounds and the fact that in Britten's case, to borrow a phrase from Philip Brett, his works are 'preoccupied with the social experience of homosexuality'.[9]

---

[7] *Peter Grimes* was given its USSR première in March 1964. The Cello Symphony was given its world première in Moscow on 12 March 1964. On 28 October 1965 *A Midsummer Night's Dream* was staged at the Bolshoy. The same month Britten appeared with the English Opera Group in a Russian tour with *Lucretia*, *Herring* and *Screw*. The first public performance (Vishnevskaya and Rostropovich) of *The Poet's Echo* was given on 2 December 1965. Britten had already played the work through to Shostakovich in September that year. (See Peter Pears in 'Armenian holiday, extracts from a diary', in Aldeburgh Festival Programme Book 1966, p. 73.) According to Vishnevskaya in her book of memoirs, *Galina* (London, 1984), 377, this private performance marked the beginning of the friendship between the two composers.

[8] Lyudmila Kovnatskaya, 'Britten and Shostakovich', revised version of a conference paper in Russian, 1990 (Aldeburgh Britten-Pears Library). The translations in this essay are my own.

[9] See Philip Brett, 'The authority of difference', *The Musical Times*, 134 (1993), 633–6. I am aware, of course, that perhaps even here there could be a parallel if one accepts the

Following Professor Kovnatskaya, I would wish to emphasise such things as their commitment to a socially 'useful' aesthetic (which, of course, in Shostakovich's case as a creative artist working in Soviet Russia was in part ideologically predetermined), their shared, deeply private, almost Chekhovian sensibilities,[10] and the impact of Civil War, Revolution and two World Wars on their outlook as they lived and worked through the first seven decades of the twentieth century. In the work itself the shared elements are the breadth of their 'Bach to Offenbach' eclecticism, the fundamental conservatism that stood behind an apparently modernistic start to their careers,[11] the importance of their 'applied' work for theatre and cinema, of certain shared and openly acknowledged musical influences from the past (Mahler and Berg!). More particularly there is the striking common attachment to baroque stylisations (especially passacaglia and fugue), a rich mixed-modal and tonally ambiguous language which, as it happens, is emblematised in a common use of the famous D–S–C–H motif,[12] a pronounced degree of motivic obsessiveness, and the crucial importance to their musico-dramatic work of the art of thematic transformation. Finally, if Shostakovich's engagement (in symphony, string quartet and concerto) with the sonata-cycle legacy was totally committed at all stages of his career, Britten's ambivalent relationship with it was none the less present to the end, not least in the dedication of his Third String

---

view that Shostakovich's sense of social isolation as a composer working in Soviet Russia, his resistances to what his society tried to enforce as the norm in artistic expression – 'happy endings', positive images, morally uplifting 'content', etc. – led him to speak an ambiguous, Aesopian language in almost every 'serious' composition he undertook.

[10] Kovnatskaya writes of the attraction of Chekhov for both Britten and Shostakovich, citing Britten's remark in *Sovetskaya Muzïka* (3/1965), 63, that his 'most cherished dream' was 'to create the kind of operatic form that would be the equivalent to a Chekhov drama'. Professor Kovnatskaya also cites Shostakovich on Chekhov in 1960 'Reading his writings, I often recognise myself; I think that in any of the situations in which he found himself, I should have reacted in just the same way as he did'.

[11] The high point of Britten's 'modernism' may be registered in *Our Hunting Fathers* – a work not at all to the taste of the English musical establishment in 1936. But for a refutation of Britten as a 'modernist' see Donald Mitchell in *The Britten Companion*, ed. C. Palmer (London, 1984), 37.

[12] In his *Dmitri Shostakovich: A Catalogue, Bibliography, and Discography*, 2nd edn (Oxford, 1991), 413, Derek Hulme suggests that the D–S–C–H motif in Britten's cantata *Rejoice in the Lamb* to the words 'But silly fellow is against me' may be an actual message of sympathy from Britten to Shostakovich in 1943. This seems far fetched. What is more to the point is that the motif, with its pair of interlocking minor thirds, is not uncharacteristic of Britten's musical language as a whole. Indeed, it forms the leitmotif of *Lucretia* where it is used with the same degree of obsessiveness encountered in Shostakovich's deployment of the motif as a personal motto in the Eighth String Quartet.

Quartet to Hans Keller, doyen of sonata-form theorists, and whose lectures at Aldeburgh were not without their creative influence on Britten.[13]

All the aspects enumerated above are an attempt to summarise and extend Kovnatskaya, who reminds us at the beginning of her paper that the two composers bequeathed a central body of work which falls into two quite distinct categories. Despite the fact that he composed in many genres, vocal and instrumental, Shostakovich is remembered above all for his work in what is predominantly the instrumental domain – as a symphonist and composer of string quartets. By contrast Britten is thought of primarily as a vocal/instrumental composer on account of his consistent commitment to the regeneration of opera in the twentieth century and – as it were complementing Shostakovich in his string quartets and chamber music – his extension of the Mahlerian domain of the orchestrally accompanied song-cycle and (in the tradition of Schubert, Schumann and Wolf) its counterpart with piano.

But in enlargement of Kovnatskaya's fundamental point here, in looking at the later work of these two composers we do encounter a marked, seemingly complementary interchange of roles in the appropriation of what has become thought of as their individual fields of expression. Through his association with Rostropovich, Britten for his part turned – in the Cello Symphony, the Cello Suites and Third String Quartet – to an intense cultivation of a purely instrumental field that he had appeared to neglect since his early American years. On the other hand Shostakovich, who had already turned (or rather *returned*) to vocal expression in the powerfully Musorgskian Thirteenth Symphony and *The Execution of Stepan Razin*, sustained his commitment in this direction. This he did through the Fourteenth Symphony with its significant dedication to Britten – a Mahlerian song-cycle symphony that in the context of the present discussion may be said to complement Britten's *Spring Symphony* and *War Requiem* – and the various song-cycles of these years, extending from the Seven Romances on Poems of Alexander Blok[14] to the monumental Suite

---

[13] See Britten's acknowledgment of the influence of Keller's 'Functional analysis' in the cadenza he wrote for Richter's performance of Mozart's Piano Concerto in E♭, K482 at Aldeburgh in 1967 (in the Aldeburgh Festival Programme Book for that year, p. 36).

[14] Britten, at the composer's personal request, gave the first performance of these Romances at the 1968 Aldeburgh Festival. It was Marion Harewood, writing in the programme book for that concert on 24 June 1968, who made one of the first comparisons between the two composers: 'Britten, like Shostakovich, has this inborn sense of craftsmanship, this unfailing sense of using instruments in an interesting, new and inevitable way. They are practical composers, who are prepared to write for special occasions and believe in

on Verses of Michelangelo. Although I am suggesting that Britten's example was a factor, it is not the purpose of this essay to investigate the psychological impulses operating upon Shostakovich's return to vocal musicodramatic composition or the significant socio-political factors in Soviet Russia at the time that facilitated such a reorientation. For practical purposes these questions will be set aside in favour of a consideration in due course of two consummatory works, the Fourteenth (vocal) and Fifteenth (instrumental) Symphonies.

The importance of the example of *Lady Macbeth* to a young composer who recognised in it the aims and eclectic methods he himself sought to pursue,[15] and the continuing fascination for him over the years (the great symphonies notwithstanding) of Shostakovich as a composer of string quartets and chamber music – all this is documented for us in the warm sixtieth birthday tribute that Britten paid to Shostakovich in 1966.[16] As Professor Kovnatskaya has pointed out, Britten's love of Russian music in general – in particular his life-long fascination with the Tchaikovsky ballet scores, his attraction towards Prokofiev and, to a more reserved extent, Stravinsky – is an acknowledged fact in the critical and biographical literature, and not hard to pinpoint in the music itself.[17] Shostakovich caught the ear of the youthful Britten in another work, the First Piano Concerto. This is a piece in which 'free association' and classicism combine in a kaleidoscope of impudent satire, slapstick, menace and images of strange nocturnal beauty – a mix already familiar to Britten through the poetry of W. H. Auden. As Donald Mitchell reminds us, the composition of certain works such as *Russian Funeral* (anticipating by

the importance of communicating with the audience. They like writing with particular artists in mind, and two of the artists in the concert – Rostropovich and Vishnevskaya – have had several pieces written for them by both composers. They are themselves excellent pianists, and perform frequently in public. And last, but not least, they have a genuine mutual admiration for each other as artists and human beings.'

[15] See Donald Mitchell, 'Britten on "Oedipus Rex" and "Lady Macbeth"', *Tempo*, 120 (March 1977), 10–12.
[16] This statement was translated from Britten's original English into Russian and appears in L. Danilevich (ed.), *Dmitri Shostakovich* (Moscow, 1967). A copy of Britten's original is in the Britten-Pears Library at Aldeburgh.
[17] Tchaikovsky (*The Sleeping Beauty*) stands behind *The Prince of the Pagodas* just as traces of the influence of the Stravinsky of *Oedipus Rex* and *Symphony of Psalms* may be detected in *Lucretia*. An intriguing instance of a passing salute to Prokofiev's *Romeo and Juliet* occurs in the brief sword fight scene in Act I scene 1.3 (Letter O) of *Gloriana*. For a more thoroughgoing example of the influence of Prokofiev and his toccata style (not to mention the influence of Poulenc and Ravel) see the first movement of the Piano Concerto, 1938.

more than twenty years the song 'Vechnaya pamyat" (Eternal memory) in Shostakovich's Eleventh Symphony) and the *Ballad of Heroes* document Britten's involvement with the aspirations of a politicised generation of artists and intellectuals who found themselves sympathetic to Communist ideals, just as the song-cycle *Our Hunting Fathers* provides potent musical metaphors for Britten's sense of outrage at the rising tide of fascism.[18] In 1937 Britten composed a piano concerto that not only proclaims a debt to Prokofiev (and Ravel), but in its supremely ironic finale (much misunderstood at the time) connects with a strain of expression that, as I have argued elsewhere, has since come to be identified as essentially Shostakovichian.[19] In the Mahlerian gestures of the first (funeral march) movement of his *Sinfonia da Requiem* and the portrayal of evil forces in the scherzo, with its grimacing distortions of 'straight' thematic material, he comes close to the language of Shostakovich's War Symphonies.[20] Indeed, both composers as children of their times share to a conspicuous degree a vein of expression that exploits images of violence, suffering and cruelty. Both *Grimes* and *Lucretia* provided potent images for a world deeply wounded by war. In this connection, Britten's passionate commitment to the idea of pacifism, his creative obsessions with the themes of innocence, childhood, beauty and the destructive forces invoked by them have their counterpart in Shostakovich's 'anti-fascist' stand in the War Symphonies and the sympathy he expresses for the victims of oppression in such works as the Second Piano Trio, the songs From Jewish Folk Poetry and the Eighth String Quartet. But his already not unextensive knowledge of Shostakovich's music apart, Britten's personal, creative encounter with musical life in contemporary Soviet Russia – with such leading personalities as Rostropovich (who introduced him to Shostakovich in London in 1959), Vishnevskaya, Richter and Shostakovich himself – had to wait until the sixties when the 'thaw' was making possible a whole series of cultural exchanges. It is at this stage, when Britten's style was fully formed – though as eclectic as ever[21] – that Britten's music moved into the foreground of Shostakovich's no less inquisitive aural field.

[18] See Donald Mitchell, *Britten and Auden in the Thirties* (London, 1981), 71–6.
[19] See my article 'Britten's Piano Concerto, the original version', *Tempo*, 172 (March 1990), 17.
[20] In his article 'Razdum'ya ob istoricheskom meste tvorchestva Shostakovicha' [Thoughts on the historical place of Shostakovich's creative work], *Sovetskaya Muzïka* (9/1975), 14, Lev Mazel' notes this as 'one of Shostakovich's greatest discoveries'.
[21] For example, the idea of the functional placing of the cadenza as a progressive transition from slow movement to finale in the Cello Symphony is surely indebted to Shostakovich in both his First Violin and Cello Concertos.

We have it on record as to what Shostakovich thought of what he heard. Writing in 1968, in the course of an acknowledgment of the impact of note-row and aleatory systems on the creative work of a country that, under Stalin, had previously been starved of such 'decadent' western importations ('everything is fine in moderation'), he offers a brief survey of the modern composers he loves:

> The English composer Benjamin Britten is extremely good. You asked me to say what direction I would like to see music taking today. Well, I would like to see more Brittens – Russian, English, German, old, young. . . . What I find attractive in Britten is his power and sincerity, the outward simplicity of his music and its deep, emotional effectiveness. Personally I do not like to listen to a work and remain unaffected by it: it should act on me and open up something new in the world and in myself. This is precisely what Britten does in all his works, from his operas and War Requiem to his quartets and romances based on the poetry of Pushkin. I think that anyone who takes music seriously ought to try to get to know Britten's works better; they are, by the way, played here fairly often.[22]

The *War Requiem*, I believe, makes a very appropriate starting point for an exploration of the aesthetic goals shared by Britten and Shostakovich. If opera and song-cycle were Britten's true *métier*, just as symphony and string quartet were that of Shostakovich, yet with Britten the term 'symphonic' is as applicable to his operas as the term 'operatic' is frequently applicable to Shostakovich in his symphonies. The fact is – and this is part of their innovatory conservatism – that both gave new meaning to the established generic forms through their very mixing of genres within them. In Britten's *War Requiem* we have a work that in its scale and formal planning, in the integration of its various themes and motifs, has every right to be considered as a choral symphony. As a 'mixed-genre' work, enfolding the intimacy of chamber music within the massive public statement, blending the concept of sonata-cycle with the idea of operatic 'scenes' and music to accompany documentary photography (and film-music techniques play their part in the *War Requiem* no less than in a work such as Shostakovich's Eleventh Symphony), conscripting the musico-dramatic means of the Bach Passions in the engagement of the Owen poems with the liturgy, Britten's *War Requiem* finds its parallel in the 'mixed-genre' symphonies of Shostakovich.

---

[22] *Dmitri Shostakovich: About his Life and Times* (Moscow, 1980; English translation, 1981), 286.

The *War Requiem*, moreover, is a work that is to some extent indebted to a great historical model shared by Britten and Shostakovich – that of Gustav Mahler.[23] Thus it 'embraces the world' in taking on board the suffering of humanity on an epic scale; it echoes the symbolic acoustic levels of Mahler's Eighth Symphony in its own deployment of spatial imagery; its multiple climaxes that erupt finally in the supreme climax of universal destruction in the 'Libera me' are after the Mahlerian example in such works as the finale of the latter's Sixth and the first movement of his Ninth Symphonies; it represents a huge expansion of the idea of song-cycle symphony embodied in *Das Lied von der Erde*. As in Mahler, it makes ironic play with meaning. Amongst its many ironic formulations – and Britten's inclusion of the Owen poems sets up a tension of subversive dissent with the liturgy of the Requiem that in the end leaves the message of the *War Requiem* ambiguous – there is the Offertorium. This is cast as a symphonic scherzo and trio, making use of the very Shostakovichian devices of thematic transformation and self-quotation. Consistent with the neobaroque model adopted by Britten in the *War Requiem*, we note that the movement is cast as a prelude and fugue – a form and texture which Shostakovich, in a number of important baroque stylisations, took seriously throughout his career. (Indeed, the model of Bach's '48' became the means of asserting his creative identity at a mid-way point in it through the Twenty-Four Preludes and Fugues in 1953.) If the *War Requiem* reaffirms the importance to Britten of baroque stylisation – a musico-dramatic 'theft' from the past that (via Stravinsky?) was evident enough as far back as *Lucretia* – in the Offertorium the very idea of fugue as a means of 'straight' musico-dramatic expression becomes ironised in the *pianissimo* repeat after the blasphemy of 'But Abraham would not so, and slew his son' in

---

[23] This is not to say that Mahler's music meant the same to each composer. Far from it. With Shostakovich, there was (via the influence of his friend Sollertinsky) a socio-ideological dimension to his respect for Mahler that, so far as I am aware, played no part in Britten's admiration. (For some light on the Mahler-Sollertinsky connection, see my thesis *Ideology, Style, Content, and Thematic Process in the Symphonies, Cello Concertos, and String Quartets of Shostakovich* (New York and London, 1989). That Shostakovich composed in the epic, artist-as-hero/narrator tradition of Mahler is obvious enough in his Fourth, Fifth and Fifteenth Symphonies. That, like Mahler, he was fond of quoting from vocal works (both his own and those of Mahler) is evident in the Fifth Symphony, just as (again like Mahler) he was capable of using extended song material for symphonic purposes, as in the Eleventh. Here again we have a sharp divergence from Britten, for whom the symphonic tradition was to be displaced by opera as a vehicle for self-expression.

238　Eric Roseberry

the 'Trio'. And here we come close to Shostakovich again. For if the *War Requiem* – though in no way to be interpreted as an atheistic statement – is, to say the least, somewhat subversive of orthodox Christian belief, then this too is not incongruent with Shostakovich's own essentially orthodox Marxian scepticism in matters connected with religious faith.

But to return to the concept of requiem, of the search for peace, eternal rest in the face of violence and death. This is a theme as close to Shostakovich's heart as it was to Britten's – in his 'War' symphonies, in the great requiem for the victims of the 1905 Revolution which is the Eleventh, in the chamber-orientated Fifteenth Symphony and much of the chamber music itself, where the idea of threnody becomes a dominant motif. Bearing in mind that for Britten Shostakovich spoke to him 'most closely and most personally' in his chamber music, I will refer briefly to the Second Piano Trio (performed for the first time at Aldeburgh in 1976, the last year of Britten's life) which remains one of his deepest, most tragic chamber works in a canon of elegies that includes the Seventh (dedicated to the memory of his first wife, Nina Vasil'yevna), Eighth ('Dedicated to the Victims of Fascism and War'), Eleventh, Twelfth (funeral-march dominated, despite the Beethovenian bravado of the final section), Thirteenth and Fifteenth String Quartets. Take, for example, the tritone as a tonal symbol common to both Shostakovich's Trio and Britten's *Requiem*. In the case of the Trio the tritone relationship B♭–E becomes a tonal device that links the grieving third movement with the ironic E major of the dance finale. (It is, by the way, a characteristic device in Shostakovich, ever since the First Symphony in fact, to construct a 'cyclic' finale that is in some way conditioned by the preceding movement(s).) The passacaglia lament of the third movement is based on a series of eight chords always starting out on B♭ minor, 'resolving' (as a 'false dominant') into the major-inflected home key of the fourth movement. Significantly, B♭ major–minor is the 'polarised', triumphant key at the climax of this despairing movement (see fig. 219 to fig. 245). And the passacaglia's same series of chords, now transformed into a wintry, cadenza-like flourish on the piano in strident opposition to E major, returns (fig. 282) at the climax – a crucial juncture, heralding the return of the original motto theme, at first passionately assertive, but dying away as a retransition into the compressed recapitulation and coda. From now on the tritone B♭ (= A♯)–E is a prominent inflection to the end, and through that coda the B♭ minor cortège passes for the last time (see also Patrick McCreless's chapter in the present volume). In its chilling emotional effect the equivocal implications of this cyclic gesture may be compared with the return of the tritone bells and the subdued chorale motif at the end of the *War Requiem*. Any raised hopes of an assured haven of peace and security are dashed by questions that cannot be banished. 'Happy endings' came no more easily to Shostakovich than to Britten.

Before moving on from the *War Requiem*, there is one further aspect of its craftsmanship that must be considered highly relevant to Shostakovich's aesthetic principles. This is the carefully sculpted balance, the elegant *classicism* of its forms and overall conception. To refer to the *War Requiem* – in view of its content – as an 'elegant' work may strike some readers as inappropriate, but it is in keeping with what may be defined as Britten's Mozartian aesthetic, his balancing of pleasure with pain, to find the *War Requiem* immensely satisfying in this respect. Such features are obviously a feature of Shostakovich's own 'simple' (at the formal level) communication with his audiences too – especially in the string quartets, where his love and respect for the formal conventions of the Viennese classical tradition are particularly in evidence. (But even his wildest and most discursive movements for large orchestra, such as the first movement and finale of the Fourth Symphony, pay their respects to the classical principle of recapitulation.) Moreover, the *War Requiem* echoes Shostakovichian practice in what might be referred to as its 'historically referential' dimension. For just as Shostakovich will allude to well-known motifs from the classical literature (for example, his passing allusions to Beethoven and Musorgsky[24] in the Twelfth String Quartet), so Britten in the *War Requiem* makes clear referential gestures towards the works which stand behind his undertaking, the B minor Mass of Bach and the Requiems of Mozart and Verdi.

If in its musico-dramatic techniques, its ironic layers of meaning and the precariously balanced tranquillity of its goal Britten's *War Requiem* follows a path parallel to that taken by Shostakovich in his War Symphonies and to be continued in the several deeply personal Requiems, whether with or without words, that he composed in memory of friends

[24] Beethoven, like Mahler, remained for Russians a symbolic figure in an ideological sense. As a symphonist, Shostakovich was well acquainted with Sollertinsky's ideas on the moral and ethical power of the Beethoven tradition, and indeed drew on it heavily in the creation of his Fifth. (See Chapter 1 of my *Ideology, Style, Content, and Thematic Process*.) For a concise documentation of the influence of Musorgsky, see Laurel Fay, 'Musorgsky and Shostakovich', in *Musorgsky: In Memoriam, 1881–1981*, ed. Malcolm H. Brown, Studies in Russian Music No. 3 (Ann Arbor, 1982), 215–26.

and 'the victims of fascism and war' throughout his creative life, then the opera *Peter Grimes* – which achieved great success in Russia in the 1960s – brings to mind some striking parallels in the biographies of both composers. Professor Kovnatskaya reminds us that for Britten, as for Shostakovich, international success came relatively early with a full-scale serious opera on a tragic theme in which the socially isolated and misunderstood hero/heroine commits suicide (by drowning) in the face of recognition of failure to realise unattainable personal ambitions (Grimes, the dreamer and butt of borough gossip, to achieve local respectability as a fisherman through marriage to Ellen, the school-mistress; Katerina, the respectable wife of an unsympathetic merchant, to stop at nothing – murder included – in order to marry the man she loves). The autobiographical content of each opera has been widely commented upon. In Shostakovich, it is manifest in the celebration of his own youthful sexuality (the opera is dedicated to his first wife, Nina Vasil'yevna) and the deep sympathy already felt for victims of official persecution – amongst whom he was shortly to be numbered himself. In Britten, it is manifest in the artistic sublimation of his own sense of being the social and sexual outsider. In the creative development of each composer, their 'grand' opera follows a first, humorous (if not exactly 'comic' – as Professor Kovnatskaya would have it) venture – with Britten *Paul Bunyan*, with Shostakovich *The Nose*. (And here it is important to distinguish between, on the one hand, the Britten–Auden 'morality' in the light-handed style of a 'guyed' American musical and Shostakovich's bold assault on the 'bourgeois' concept of opera in the avant-gardism of *The Nose*.)

The fate of each of these two great operas, however, could not be more strongly contrasted. In Britten's case it marked a return to native roots after a period of wandering, the finding of himself as a man and artist (not least through his partner, Peter Pears) and the beginning of his career as an opera composer. With Shostakovich, already at the pinnacle of fame at home and abroad, its official condemnation spelt alienation at home, the near-collapse of his career under Stalin's dictatorship, and the shift away from opera to purely instrumental symphony via the completion of the Fourth and the 'perestroyka' of the Fifth (see Richard Taruskin's chapter in the present volume).

Musico-dramatically considered, Britten's opera follows Musorgskian practice in *Boris Godunov* in its allocation of a collective role to the chorus, the people of the Borough. (How deeply Shostakovich must have responded to this as well as to other 'Musorgsky-isms' such as the bells in the 'Sunday morning' Interlude!) In each case the opera shows its indebtedness to, amongst other influences, Berg's *Wozzeck* – a work which both composers deeply admired. In each case, and following Berg, the opera makes use of the idea of symphonic interludes – purely orchestral statements that stand apart from the action on the stage. And in each case the composer turns to the baroque form of the passacaglia to make perhaps his most serious comment on the events portrayed at a crucial point of the opera (counterpart not so much to the passacaglia of Act I scene 4 as to the D minor Adagio between the last two scenes of *Wozzeck*).

As Professor Kovnatskaya points out at the end of her paper, the passacaglia is a musico-dramatic resource that each composer made his own in a whole succession of works. Shostakovich, taking his cue from Bach, reserved it almost invariably for the expression of high seriousness. Memorable examples of its use occur in the Preludes and Fugues, where, in the final Prelude and Fugue of each book, it fulfils a consummatory role. Another, different placing of the form occurs in the third movement of the first Violin Concerto where the high seriousness of its theme serves to establish a 'form within a form' through returning high on the horn in fast tempo at the end of the finale, a device that, as noted above, had already served the expressive goal of the elegiac Second Piano Trio. A further, grave example of its importance, this time in a vocal context, is in the Blok Romances where in 'The city sleeps' the calm undertow of the ground becomes an image of the sadness of Peter the Great's canal city of the North. (In her commentary Kovnatskaya justly notes that both composers show a strong attachment to *place* in their work – Suffolk, Aldeburgh, the sea, Venice, St Petersburg.) And in the elegiac, death-stricken finale of the Fifteenth Symphony, the development section is replaced by a large-scale passacaglia on a long-drawn out theme in Shostakovich's favourite chaconne rhythm that builds up to a catastrophic climax – a point to which I will return towards the end of this essay. As Professor Kovnatskaya puts it, what Bach was to Shostakovich, Purcell was to Britten. In his Second String Quartet, a commission for the 300th anniversary of the birth of Purcell, Britten constructed his long, climactic finale on the basis of the chaconne. The passacaglia was already well established around this time as a consummatory musico-dramatic device in Britten – both the Holy Sonnets of John Donne and *Lucretia* have resort to the form's capacity to effect a clinching concentration in underpinning a wide span of valedictory images. (According to a conversation Kovnatskaya had with Donald Mitchell, the example of the finale of Brahms's Fourth Symphony was not lost on Britten here.) In the recomposition of the third movement of his Piano Concerto and the finale of his Cello Symphony, not to mention the 'Ciaconna' of his Second Cello Suite, the finale of the *Nocturnal* for Solo Guitar and the setting (to a three-note 'ground' (B–C–B)) of Pushkin's 'Lines written during a sleepless night' at the end of *The Poet's Echo*, the form proves its worth for sustained, vividly contrasted unity in variety. And in his two children's operas, *The Little Sweep* and *Noye's Fludde*, the form continues to show its viability in dramatic situations as contrasted as a nursery crisis ('Help help she's collapsed!') and the rising of the flood. There is the denouement of *The Turn of the Screw* – the final triangular confrontation of the main protagonists – where the form is, literally, the strict finale of an opera that is itself composed on the variation principle. (Appropriately enough, I can only think of one opera, Purcell's *Dido and Aeneas*, where a formal ground ('When I am laid in earth') is comparably 'sited'.) Nor should it be overlooked that in the last movement of the Third String Quartet, Britten's last completed work, he takes his leave of the world in a stoic but touchingly lyrical passacaglia. Professor Kovnatskaya, defining the form according to the 'intonation' theory of the Russian tradition in musicology, considers the passacaglia a 'philosophic' concept in music.

If one were to evaluate the passacaglia in itself . . . then it realises the metaphor of a closed circle, life as a chain of metamorphoses within the boundaries of a fateful circle. Both Britten and Shostakovich are stamped with the cast of mind that is embodied in this idea of the form.

This essay has made reference to two works of Britten – *Peter Grimes* and *War Requiem* – which, in so far as Shostakovich knew and admired them in his late fifties and sixties, may have stirred in him a sense of kinship with his English friend and colleague in looking back both on his own life and creative preoccupations. But in what ways is it possible to discern the presence of Britten behind the works of Shostakovich that remained to be written? In what ways does the older composer appear to be absorbing the example of the younger? In looking now at two of Shostakovich's most important late works – the Fourteenth and Fifteenth Symphonies – it will be suggested that the influence of Britten lies as much in the remarkable *refinement* of Shostakovich's vocal-instrumental writing, in the frequent beauty of the sound itself, as in the kind of exchange of creative identities, vocal for instrumental and vice versa, that took place in this 'final period'.

The Fourteenth Symphony, as Marina Sabinina in her book on the symphonies has pointed out, represented a completely new departure for Shostakovich.[25] His previous vocal symphony, the Thirteenth, had followed the 'absolute' plan of the traditional four-movement cycle, but the Fourteenth is rooted in the concept of Mahler's song-cycle symphony, *Das Lied von der Erde* – a work for voices and instruments in several movements that grows out of a unifying expressive theme. As is well known, both composers knew and admired Mahler's *Das Lied* and to some extent adopted Mahler's method of grouping the setting of the poems according to the various stages of a symphonic cycle as established by Beethoven – expository first movement, scherzo, slow movement and finale, the musico-dramatic form by no means predetermined, but growing out of the 'questions' raised by the previous movements. Thus it is possible to group the movements of Shostakovich's vocal symphony according to the following plan:

Introduction and first movement Allegro: 1 'De profundis' and 2 'Malagueña'
Dramatic Scena (symphonic ballad cast in the style of a scherzo, with substantial instrumental development and 'Epilogue'): 3 (Duet) 'Lorelei'
Slow movement 1: 4 (Soprano) 'The suicide'
Scherzo 1: 5 (Soprano) 'On watch' leading without a break to
Transitional dialogue: 6 (Bass and Soprano) 'Look madam'
Slow movement 2: 7 (Bass) At the Santé prison
Scherzo 2: 8 (Bass) – The Zaporozhian Cossack's answer to the Sultan of Constantinople
Slow movement (Quasi Intermezzo) 2: 9 (Bass) 'O Delvig'
Epilogue (with thematic reference back (recapitulation?) to 1): 10 (Soprano) 'Death of the poet'
Coda: 11 (Soprano and bass duet) 'All-powerful is death'.

The continuity and symphonic pacing of Shostakovich's sequence – a matter of direct links or *attacca* confrontations – unites the musico-dramatic conception of this vocal symphony with that of his purely instrumental works. Here is the same fluidity and overlapping continuity that characterise, for example, the multi-movement Eleventh and Fifteenth String Quartets, a suite-like assembly of instrumental 'scenes' shaped into a larger coherence. (Britten's Cello Suites were possibly not un-influenced by this characteristic approach to form in Shostakovich.) As in Britten's *War Requiem*, the musico-dramatic scheme places individual confrontations

[25] See M. Sabinina, *Shostakovich: Simfonist* (Moscow, 1976), 400.

244   Eric Roseberry

with death in the context of a timeless perspective. It is the complementary antithesis to Britten's *Spring Symphony*, his symphony about life, anthologising its poems according to a similar symphonic plan of dramatic encounters and meditation. (Was Britten's *Spring Symphony*, indeed, a conscious model here?)

Shostakovich's symphony on death contains many sound-images that seem to echo and even pre-echo Britten: the snoring double basses (cf. the opening of *A Midsummer Night's Dream*); the rising fourths of 'Malaguena'; the beautiful clearing of sound in a magical, Lydian-inflected E♭ major in 'Lorelei' (the tonal symbolism may be Wagnerian, but the sonority is pure Britten); the two-part interweaving of vocal arioso and solo instrumental line (a favourite device in Britten) in 'The suicide', with its pre-echo of the Strawberry Seller's song in *Death in Venice*; the luminous simplicity of four simple triads in 'O Delvig'; the virtuoso handling of the string orchestra (one of Britten's favourite mediums) with its diversity of dark and brilliant sonorities. Brittenish too is the almost cinematic management of fluid transition and stark contrast in the symphony, a reminder of the influence of this area of 'applied' music on the compositional processes of both composers. And there is a new, surprising element of expression that Shostakovich (hitherto very much the 'realist' in his symphonies) seems to be taking over from Britten. Britten's fascination with ghosts (particularly as they are encountered in his two operas based on the two Henry James ghost stories: *The Turn of the Screw* and *Owen Wingrave*) now finds its response in Shostakovich – in the eerie, forlorn cry of 'The suicide' and its spine-chilling string sonorities, or the skeleton march-dance of 'On watch'. As will be seen, this invasion of Britten's special territory is present also, as we shall see, in the Fifteenth Symphony, whose twelve-note chordal motifs in slow movement and finale, ghostly celeste music and spectral marche-cum-danse macabre (cf. 'On watch' in the Fourteenth Symphony) relate to the images of its predecessor and would seem to lend weight to the alleged connection with Chekhov's ghost story *The Black Monk* in the Volkov–Shostakovich memoirs.[26]

The openly acknowledged influence of Musorgsky's *Songs and Dances of Death* apart, if there was any element of friendly creative rivalry in Shostakovich's undertaking of this unusual project, stimulated perhaps in part by what he knew of Britten's work in the field of the song-cycle, it has to be said at once, without seeking to make unfavourable comparisons,

[26] For a further discussion of this connection, see my extended programme note on the Fifteenth Symphony for the BBC Proms, Wednesday, 12 August 1992.

that Britten's own song-cycles do not compare in respect of symphonic breadth. Yet to ears more sympathetic with Britten's comparative conciseness and clarity of formal outline, the Fourteenth Symphony, with its acreage of vocal arioso-recitative and natural tendency to 'think big', even to sprawl, may appear to lose out in comparison. This work has to be taken as a large-scale vocal symphony, a blending of vocal, instrumental and operatic genres, a 'symphony', moreover, that is rich in motivic elements that have already become part and parcel of Shostakovich's language as a whole.[27] A wealth of experience – symphonic, vocal-operatic, chamber – stands behind 'Lorelei', for example. This is a through-composed ballad cast in the style of a large-scale symphonic scherzo that reaches its turning point, its apotheosis, at the moment when Lorelei looks down into the Rhine.

The Fourteenth Symphony confirms Shostakovich's thoroughgoing absorption of twelve-note (or near twelve-note) elements into his highly idiosyncratic, 'mixed-modal' style (see Yuriy Kholopov's chapter in the present volume) – an absorption as marked as it is in Britten, beginning with *The Turn of the Screw* and achieving an unprecedented degree of subtlety in the late operas, *Owen Wingrave* and *Death in Venice*.[28] To compare and contrast the two approaches to serialism of Britten and Shostakovich is a subject in itself; I will restrict myself here only to some general observations. As Erwin Stein was one of the first to observe, Britten's 'serialism' is but a part of an eclectic musico-dramatic language that owes allegiance to no such tradition, as Schoenberg's did. Commenting on a complex eleven-note chord in *Billy Budd* that, with the entry of the twelfth note, the pitch G becomes a dominant to the next section in C minor (fig. 72 in Act II scene 2, at Vere's words 'The mists have cleared, O terror, what do I see?' as he muses on Billy's fate and the judgement that is in his hands) Erwin Stein notes:

[27] For an attempt to document the characteristic motivic elements of Shostakovich's melodic style, see the chapter 'Notes towards an iconology of Shostakovich's instrumental music', in my *Ideology, Style, Content, and Thematic Process*, 322.
[28] For some discussion of twelve-note elements in these two operas, see John Evans, 'Owen Wingrave: a case for pacificism', in *The Britten Companion* (London, 1984), 227–37, and 'Twelve-note structures and tonal polarity in "Death in Venice"', in *Britten: Death in Venice*, ed. Donald Mitchell (Cambridge, 1987), 99–114. In this connection, see also Rosamund Strode in her 'A Death in Venice chronicle' (*ibid.*, 34), who notes that in mid-July 1972 Shostakovich visited Britten at Aldeburgh and on one occasion spent two hours alone in the library looking at the composition sketches of *Death in Venice*.

We have here in a nutshell the fundamental difference between Schoenberg's and Britten's harmonic conceptions. The chord with the highest possible tension which, indeed, did not exist before Schoenberg, and which by its structure bears no relation to any key, is made by Britten to function in a strictly tonal sense.[29]

As in *Budd*, so in Britten's later operas. Let two examples suffice: the twelve-note 'pile-up' of the *Screw* theme which functions as dominant to A with the entry of the final note E in *The Turn of the Screw*, and the way in which Owen's note, the pitch D, completes a twelve-note harmonic structure that 'resolves' the dissonance (with the 'dominant' A in the bass) on to its tonic in the portrait sequence at the beginning of *Owen Wingrave*. Similarly in Shostakovich twelve-note structures, whether harmonic, as in the build-up to the above-mentioned 'clearing' of 'Lorelei' as she gazes into the Rhine, three bars after fig. 47 in the Fourteenth Symphony (where E♭ is the resolving completion of a twelve-note complex), or melodic, as in the solo cello at fig. 53 of the second movement of the Fifteenth Symphony (where the cello line 'resolves' via its eleventh pitch, A, on to a D major chord), draw on Schoenberg's raising of the 'norm of dissonance' in a manner that nevertheless complies with the principles of traditional, functional harmony.

The traditional element of thematic shape, motif and motif repetition continues to hold in the twelve-note thinking of both composers, which nowhere adheres to the Schoenbergian strictness of deriving literally all its material from a single row. (Berg in his *Lyric Suite* rather than the 'athematic' Webern in his uncompromising Op. 28 String Quartet would seem to be the model here.) And although Shostakovich will use a particular motif to characterise, let us say, the ritornello theme of a particular *movement* (the rising fourth in 'Malaguena' or the falling minor third, for example, in 'both 'De profundis' and 'The suicide'), as already stated these motifs are made up out of intervallic characters that are consistent with Shostakovich's highly idiosyncratic musical language *as a whole*. The transference of themes or motifs from one movement to another to form a recognisable network of leitmotifs over the entire span of the symphony is not, as I understand it, a significant musico-dramatic feature in a symphony where, as always in Shostakovich, a certain chameleon-like mobility of motivic/thematic transformation keeps events in a permanent state of flux. The return of the 'De profundis' theme in

[29] See Erwin Stein, 'Britten against his English background', in *Orpheus in New Guises* (London, 1953), 154–5.

'The death of a poet' or the accelerando single note/chord-'cluster' motif first encountered in 'Malaguena' are exceptional 'fixed' events that recur as reminiscences rather than as structurally articulating devices. And thus this vocal symphony cannot be compared with other purely instrumental twelve-note works of Shostakovich (such as the Twelfth String Quartet or Fifteenth Symphony) where more thoroughgoing, openly traditional cyclic procedures obtain.

Yet one should not overlook the significance of a purely *timbral* system of symbols in the percussion here – the xylophone and celeste, for example – replacing the principle of the nineteenth-century motto-theme and echoing Britten's own use of the device in The Turn of the Screw (Quint's celeste), Nocturne (the C major 'sleep chord' on strings) and *Death in Venice* (Tadzio's A major vibraphone). Britten's twelve-note 'imagery' (as in Shostakovich, a recurring symbol not infrequently associated with death and sleep) can function as a structural principle, as in *The Turn of the Screw* and in the second act of *A Midsummer Night's Dream*, where in each case a twelve-note sequence (the one essentially melodic, the other harmonic) is the basis for variations. But in his two late twelve-note orientated operas, *Owen Wingrave* and *Death in Venice* (to say nothing of the Church Parables, where Schoenberg's 'unity of musical space' is realised on the basis of plainsong melodies that can function in a manner not unlike twelve-note rows), such large-scale commitment of twelve-note elements to a predetermined formal scheme would seem to be less in evidence. As in Britten, twelve-note thinking in Shostakovich goes hand in hand with an increasingly monodic tendency: the twelve-note 'monologues' of the late-period works have their counterpart in the melodic asceticism and spare textures of Britten's Church Parables (where, as already stated, the plainsong takes on the unifying properties of a row) and the heterophonic textures of *Death in Venice*. As regards thematic contour, Shostakovich's tendency to 'straggle', to use Professor Abraham's word, is of a different order from the more firmly shaped, symmetrical contours and mirror forms of Britten. In Shostakovich's works twelve-note 'themes' are as likely to assume an improvisatory character that changes shape, yields new continuations in the course of their ritornello-like recurrence, as assume the identity of an *idée fixe*. Such twelve-note themes as do retain a more or less fixed identity in the Fourteenth Symphony are invariably assigned to the orchestra and not to the voice, which is left free to pursue its arioso-recitative treatment of the text. Britten also invents themes with a strong triadic/tonal bent that scorn any suggestion of

248   Eric Roseberry

Schoenbergian orthodoxy in not flinching from note repetition[30] (again one is reminded of Berg). If, whether parodistic or serious in intent, these tend to be neater, more classically symmetrical than in Shostakovich (who becomes neat only in parodistic situations such as in 'On watch' and the scherzo of the Fifteenth Symphony) yet his characteristic attachment to the interval of the fourth in the construction of such shapes as the twelve-note theme of *The Turn of the Screw* – or its near neighbour, the passacaglia theme of the finale of the Second String Quartet – lends at times a certain kinship to their twelve-note 'thinking'. Such themes in Britten and Shostakovich may be derived from the famous rising-fourth horn theme of Schoenberg's First Chamber Symphony – itself influenced, no doubt, by the fourths of Mahler's Seventh.

'... much as I admire the Symphonies and the Opera [Britten is referring to *Lady Macbeth*] to me Shostakovich speaks most closely and most personally in his chamber music.' Britten's remark towards the end of his sixtieth birthday tribute to Shostakovich may be extended to the new, chamber-like textures not only of the Fourteenth but also of the enigmatic Fifteenth Symphony. For here, in a purely instrumental four-movement symphony that can be regarded as a last will and testament, is a work for large orchestra that to a quite remarkable extent incorporates intimate, soloistic elements almost without precedent in Shostakovich (the exception is the First Symphony – and this is perhaps no accident in view of the quasi-cyclic cross-references to that symphony in the Fifteenth: even the Wagner quotation from *The Ring* relates to a prominent motif from the finale of the First). This is apparent from the very outset (bells and mischievously prolonged flute solo) of the first movement, a scherzando sonata scheme, that, characteristically obsessional in its motivic play, continues to cavort in a prismatic display of soloistic activity in all departments, percussion not excluded. The slow movement, with its solo cello recitative-arioso, goes on to explore a number of solo timbres; trombone, violin, celeste, vibraphone, double bass speak in situations of the closest intimacy. The eerie scherzo with its rattle of bones (cf. the anapaest motif and *col legno* taps in the Thirteenth String Quartet) is no exception to this order of things. And the finale, epic though the slow build-up of the central passacaglia towards its catastrophic climax proves to be, inhabits a world of muted shades and intimate, elegiac intonations. The coda, through a

[30] A good example of such a theme is provided in 'The angel', No. 3 in *The Poet's Echo*.

frozen open-fifth pedal A on the strings, gives the final word to the 'other world' of percussion in its cyclic recall of motifs from all four movements.

As already noted, Shostakovich heard and admired Britten's chamber operas during a tour of Soviet Russia by the English Opera Group under Britten's direction in 1965. Britten's early *opera seria* and *buffa* diptych – the neobaroque, statuesque *Lucretia* and the satirical-social comedy of *Herring* – would have struck a sympathetic chord (did Shostakovich relish the Tristan-chord 'hiccup' at the wedding feast and the self-mockery of *Lucretia* on the cue of the policeman's 'Give me . . . a criminal case of rape'? – these are not un-Shostakovichian touches of boyish mischief). But perhaps the *Screw*, coming at a time when Shostakovich was evolving his own approach to twelve-note influence from the West, would have been of special interest. As a symphonist, Shostakovich could hardly have failed to admire Britten's formalisation of opera in the 'absolute' terms of variations on a twelve-note theme – a theme moreover built out of his own characteristic interval of the fourth (see the Fourth and Fifth Symphonies), nor would the exceptionally close motivic weave of the opera have failed to gain the approval of a creative imagination that could match such obsessional play with ease. As a composer whose personal melodic style, via the Eleventh Symphony and Eighth String Quartet, had developed through the absorption of symbolic quotations and cross-references, absorbed in such a way as to seem an organic part of the melody itself, he would have been fascinated with Britten's own use of quotation (the nursery rhymes as children's games) and genre allusion (church ritual (the Benedicite) as a kind of children's black Mass, or Quint-inspired Mozart piano improvisation) as a musico-dramatic resource. And, amongst the sonorites of the *Screw*, the 'other-worldliness' of the celeste seems to have haunted his imagination in the sound-symbolism of the Fifteenth Symphony and the last song of the Michelangelo Verses, 'Immortality', where the childish piping of a tune composed at the age of seven[31] becomes a spiritual symbol fading into eternity. Can the purely non-verbal dramaturgy of the Fifteenth Symphony suggest meaningful correspondences with this most symphonic amongst Britten's operas? In both there is the ever-present threat of death as, to quote the epilogue of the Fourteenth Symphony, it is 'on watch even in the hour of happiness'. This has nothing to do with the funeral-march genre of the second movement,

---

[31] See L. Danilevich, *Dmitriy Shostakovich* (Moscow, 1980), 256. As the author states, 'Krug zamknulsya' (The wheel has come full circle).

for the funeral march is a social genre, rooted in the idea of solemnity and respect for the dead. I mean rather the sensation one has in this symphony of 'children's games', of the 'toyshop', to use an image employed by Shostakovich in programme note and interview, of a playful innocence that would at times seem to be manipulated by some more sinister force. (Much the same feeling is conveyed in the 'playful' Ninth String Quartet of Shostakovich, a work that Britten found 'amazing'.) In the Fifteenth Symphony the mocking grimace, the cold, strange dissonance, the insubstantial timbre, such Quint-like manifestations are heard in the context of a more radiantly accessible human feeling.

Finally, to pick up a point made earlier in this essay, there is the resort to the clinching, consummatory form of the passacaglia in the closing stages of both works. In Britten's opera, the passacaglia is used in the final scene (Miles – 'Now my dear we're all alone') as a device that will carry the scene to its crisis-point. As this is approached, Quint's 'foreign' timbre and pitches strike here with something of the same terror as the return of Shostakovich's 'death chords' in the radiant A major context of the coda of the Fifteenth Symphony at fig. 146. In Shostakovich's symphony the passacaglia – a substitute for the normal symphonic development, and taking as its ground a near-twelve-note theme motivically derived from previous elements – is used in this final 'act' with the same sense of denouement. As in Britten's opera, it is the means by which we approach the final 'turn of the screw'. The climax is a ferocious dissonance (close to the retransitional dissonance in the first movement of the Fourth Symphony, which we have already revisited in the percussion coda of the scherzo). That chord, by association, is the cue in the ensuing abbreviated recapitulation for the cyclic return of the 'death chords' from the slow movement. The symphony then dissolves in a spectral, cyclic coda with its 'ghosts from the past' underpinned by the rhythm of the passacaglia on timpani. There is something Brittenish about this kind of negation of assertive, monumental rhetoric at the end of a deeply serious piece. We come across it also in the cyclic coda of Shostakovich's Second Cello Concerto. It is a fitting close to a large-scale symphony that has embraced to a remarkable degree the intimacy of chamber music in all four movements and which touches on a strange synthesis of the epic and the personal, the heroically assertive and the resigned, the playful and the macabre in Shostakovich's late, 'autobiographical' style. It is a style that, as I have argued here on the strength of purely musical evidence, could well have refreshed itself through his love-affair with Britten and his music.

The dedication of Shostakovich's Fourteenth Symphony to Benjamin Britten unites these two composers in a deeply symbolic way, calling to mind their common commitment to a humanist aesthetic and their high seriousness of expression, their sense of social mission as artists. The subject is death, and the contemplation of death is one of the great themes – if not the central theme of the western musical tradition. For Britten as a practical performing artist and creative thinker this meant Bach (in his passions and cantatas), Mozart (in his Requiem and dark G minor moods) and perhaps above all Schubert in his *Winterreise*, which in his everyday life Britten seemed to regard as a kind of purge when trivialities threatened. For Britten as a creative artist there can be little doubt that death gave life its meaning, its value – which is not to discount the perpetual stimulus to his imagination of images of darkness, the world of shadows, night, sleep and dreams. How many of his full-length operas end with a death – *Peter Grimes*, *The Rape of Lucretia*, *Albert Herring* (which celebrates a kind of death), *Billy Budd*, *Gloriana* (how tragic and deeply ironic is that overwhelming C minor funeral transformation of Essex's intimate lute song, 'Happy were we' at the end of the opera), *The Turn of the Screw*, *Curlew River* (the end of a journey in the discovery of a death), *Owen Wingrave*, *Death in Venice* – which makes *A Midsummer Night's Dream* (sombre though its imagery may be) rather exceptional, a diverting intermezzo in some dark procession.

For Shostakovich too death became a central preoccupation – and it is not hard to understand why, given the circumstances of his life and the sad history of his people. Not without good reason did the Yurodiviy's motif at the end of Musorgsky's *Boris*, the falling semitone, become a characteristic Shostakovichian leitmotif. The First Symphony, completed when he was a mere boy of nineteen, has no programme, but after the maskplay of the first two movements, the slow movement and finale become inextricably bound up with the destiny of a funeral march. The Second Symphony, despite its dutiful concluding hymn to Lenin, contains many a dark and grisly page, much violence of expression. *Lady Macbeth of Mtsensk*, with the tragic death by drowning of its heroine, is a successor to Berg's *Wozzeck* in its psychological portrayal of destructive, human passions, betrayals and lost ideals: the comparison with *Grimes* is inescapable. The list can be extended indefinitely – right up to the dark late period of the disillusioned, ailing composer of Volkov's memoirs. The last three symphonies, the Suite on Verses of Michelangelo, the cycle of late string quartets – all turn towards images of death.

As Professor Kovnatskaya has explained in her paper, Russian and Englishman grew up as close contemporaries in societies and cultural traditions very different from one another. Stalin's 'socialist realism', for example, had its nineteenth-century roots in a whole radical materialist philosophy of art that can make Darwinism or the fairy-tale medievalism of the Arts and Crafts Movement in England seem rather cosy in comparison. Yet through their common experiences as children of the twentieth century, they did not in the end find themselves so very far apart. This is perhaps all the more remarkable in the light of certain religious considerations. The Christian, essentially Anglican tradition that Britten adopted in a number of beautiful works, that he modified, changed, challenged even in the *War Requiem*, where peace and reconciliation rather than any conventionally religious notion of eternal life after death are surely the goal, could form no part of Shostakovich's outlook. However much he found himself at odds with Stalinist bureaucracy, obliged to don an ironic mask in having to live with an imposed cultural orthodoxy, Shostakovich in one important respect remained always in harmony with Marxist ideals. As a materialist, death was for him the end: he shared the stoicism of an atheist aesthetic, and we are not likely to learn of any secret Russian Orthodox Church Masses or Requiems that were hidden away in his bottom drawer. But this is not to say that he did not become a God-seeker, a moralist, a believer in a kind of spiritual immortality. In his later work – the finale of the Thirteenth Symphony, for example, or the eerie mockery of the severed head in *The Execution of Stepan Razin*, or the haunting close of the Michelangelo Verses – we find ourselves in the presence of an inspired and inspiring defiance of physical death. To reverse the words of Shakespeare's Mark Antony, he believed in 'the good that men do' living after them. In the words of the last of the Michelangelo settings:

> Now fate has sent to me untimely sleep,
> But I am not dead, although, laid in the earth:
> I live in you, whose plaints I listen to,
> Since friend and friend are mirrored in each other.
> I am as dead, but for consolation to the world
> I live with thousands of others in the hearts
> Of all those loving ones, and thus I am not dust,
> And in death, decay will not touch me.[32]

[32] Translation by Felicity Ashbee, 1977, in booklet accompanying EMI recording of Shostakovich song-cycles, SLS 5078.

And this, despite its undeniable ambiguities, is surely in part the message of Britten also, even in his most sombre pages. At the end of *Grimes* life has to go on; Albert Herring loses his innocence, his timid dependence on Mum, to whom, after a fashion, he has 'died', but ('Bounce me high, bounce me low') life has more to it than all that; Vere is 'saved' by Billy's sacrifice, even if, as Philip Brett has observed, 'the musical portrayal ultimately suggests a stronger impression of Vere's self-delusion and an implied criticism of the system he represents';[33] if, in a sense, the Wingraves 'win' through sending Owen to his death, yet that courageous death is also the triumph of the pacifist ideal over a military family's tradition of going to war; Aschenbach dies in pursuit of his aesthetic-physical ideal of beauty, but the radiant apotheosis speaks of spiritual transfiguration. So, in the case of both these composers, death becomes the gateway to ideals that we can cherish while we are still alive. More positive, perhaps, than the pale, lyrical *morbidezza* of a Schubert or a Chopin, more realistic than the macabre fantasies of a Berlioz, less fatalistic than the submission of a Tchaikovsky in his Sixth Symphony, less pessimistic than the infinitely sad farewells to life of a Mahler or the sunset nostalgia of a Delius, their sense of realism and high-mindedness, their commitment to life in the context of a deeply tragic sense of our mortality are worthy of our salute.

[33] See again that critic's 'The authority of difference'.

11

Shostakovich and Schnittke: the erosion of symphonic syntax

ALEXANDER IVASHKIN

In 1976 a collection of articles devoted to Shostakovich appeared in Moscow. It had been prepared during the composer's lifetime but was not published until after his death.[1] How often in those days was a collection of this sort full of 'official' eulogies of no use to anybody; but in this case there were just a couple of short articles which stood out from the common run – their authors were Boris Tishchenko, a pupil and friend of Shostakovich, and Alfred Schnittke, a composer who was destined to become the real spiritual successor of Shostakovich's music.

At that time Schnittke wrote in his short, two-page article:

It is now fifty years that music has been under the influence of Shostakovich. . . . In the twentieth century only Stravinsky was endowed with this same magic ability to subordinate everything coming into his field of vision to himself. . . . The Eighth and Fourteenth Quartets and the Fifteenth Symphony are the most original landmarks in time, where the past enters into new relations with the present, invades musical reality, like the ghost of Hamlet's father, and reshapes it. When in Shostakovich the images of his own musical past meet up in collages with images from the history of music an astonishing effect of objectivisation occurs, of introducing the individual to the universal, and it is in this way that the greatest task in the life of an artist is solved: to influence the world through confluence with the world [*vliyaniye na mir cherez sliyaniye s mirom*].[2]

Shostakovich's influence on the music of Russian composers embraced various dimensions. In the 1960s, for example, many simply borrowed his musical vocabulary, whereby they significantly devalued it. Many symphonies and concertos appeared in the style of Shostakovich. At the end of the 1960s and beginning of the 1970s there arose a feeling even of a sort

---

[1] Grigoriy Shneyerson (ed.), *D. Shostakovich: Stat'i i materialï* [Articles and Materials] (Moscow, 1976).
[2] Alfred Schnittke, 'Krugi vliyaniya' [Spheres of influence], *ibid.*, 223–4.

of weariness with this style drawing its pension in the works of his imitators, such as Moisey Vaynberg, Yuriy Levitin, German Galïnin, and even in the works of the most talented among them, Boris Tishchenko. Curiously Shostakovich himself rated the music of all these composers highly – because he saw in them a great deal in common with his own works. It probably seemed to him that the future development of music really ought to lie in that direction (a delusion typical of many composers). In actual fact, these works only served to kill off Shostakovich's music, to cover it over with a scab of numerous and bad copies.

Towards the end of the composer's life almost the same thing happened to Shostakovich's music as happened to the Russian language during the era of totalitarian Communist rule: the idioms of his musical language seemed to be emasculated and drained of their content. Just as nobody believed in Communist slogans, there were very few at the beginning of the 1970s who believed in the possibility of anything new in Shostakovich's music – it seemed that he was simply repeating himself and the others were repeating him. A certain amount of time was necessary for the hypnotic effect of Shostakovich's musical vocabulary (which could be felt in almost any piece of Russian music composed in the 1960s and 1970s) to pass and grow into a different, indirect influence, into a more objective perception of his music, from the side, as it were.

In Shostakovich's letters to Glikman[3] what is astonishing is the strange scantness of the language, just like officialese – in fact it is like reading reports written by Communist Party leaders. Undoubtedly this is partly dictated by his fear of censorship; but even so it was a characteristic trait of Shostakovich's behaviour in life and of his musical style. The meaning of his letters and of his music is not in the obvious banality of his vocabulary, but in its special hidden significance. In this sense Shostakovich needs interpretation. Without oblique reading of this sort his music, like his letters and statements, all turn out to have the same intonations. This peculiarity is undoubtedly a feature of that era and is intimately bound up with the Soviet way of life itself, with the attempt to reconcile 'life on the surface' with real, but concealed life. Therefore Shostakovich's imitators were both blind and deaf in borrowing his vocabulary – they neither saw nor heard anything in his music.

On the other hand, the period of imitation was evidently productive, for paradoxically the re-evaluation of Shostakovich's music took place

[3] *Pis'ma k drugu* [Letters to a Friend] (Moscow and St Petersburg, 1993).

considerably more rapidly than it would have done in different circumstances. As Mikhail Bulgakov wrote in *The Master and Margarita*, the Master has to be killed in order to be reborn into new life. It was precisely this necessary murder which was carried out by Shostakovich's diligent 'followers' while he was still alive.

After Shostakovich's physical death his music began to be perceived completely differently; first of all because its most typical features – rhythm and intonation – were, so to speak, moved outside the brackets of the musical present. From an object of imitation and current circulation they turned into a fact of history.

Shostakovich's music found genuine, although not immediately obvious, continuation in the works of Alfred Schnittke, who was actually not very well acquainted with Shostakovich and whose music Shostakovich knew very little about (the exception was Schnittke's oratorio *Nagasaki* of 1957, which is not a particularly typical composition of the then young composer but which Shostakovich rated highly).

How do Shostakovich's music and ideas find themselves reflected in Schnittke's music? More generally, are Shostakovich's works still something from which composers today can draw lessons? Finally, is Schnittke's music standing up to the rapid change of cultural context which is taking place in the Russia of the 1990s?

Shostakovich's most important idea is undoubtedly the 'big' symphony and the microcosm which it represents. Shostakovich was one of several twentieth-century composers who continued to compose symphonies, not simply by virtue of tradition but because the symphony (or concerto or quartet) was for them the most natural form of expression. Essentially it was a continuation of the great Romantic tradition, according to which the symphony, like the new-age novel, becomes not simply music but the process of solving particular problems by musical means. This relationship to the symphony was characteristic of Mahler and Sibelius. Each successive symphony was becoming just a new coil in the quest – for what was being written in fact was one large work, getting more or less closer to a heard ideal. Thus the symphony was something like an expanse of life and in any case a real time-reservoir and an interaction of different forces.

Schnittke's words to the effect that, 'Each embodiment of an idea is always also to some extent a limitation of that idea', are significant; they serve to confirm an on-the-whole Romantic conception of 'works' and of the symphonic cycle in particular. 'Everyone is trying to break through to a direct expression of a kind of pre-music, which they hear, but which has not yet been caught. . . . For other composers the ideal way out is the "non-embodiment" of the idea.'[4]

Actually the idea of writing a big symphony today (following the Shostakovich tradition) is paradoxically getting very close to the idea not to write music in the traditional sense of the word at all (cf. John Cage) or to write an anti- (post-)symphony, as Valentin Sil'vestrov does (he actually named his Fifth Symphony 'Post-Symphony'). So in either case one finishes up with the same result: the impossibility of logical, rational solutions within the text itself. Everything essential moves outside, as it were, beyond the limits of concrete musical composition itself and into that sphere of the 'delectable' where, according to Schnittke, the genuine music exists, needing only to be written down by the composer.

The impossibility of a 'pure' symphony, as a 'text', as a traditional product of creation, was already being felt by Shostakovich. In his last three symphonies he avoids this 'product' in different ways, and he tries to find other solutions, both in the area of composition (the Fourteenth Symphony) and in the sphere of the symbolism of the material itself, which creates its own correspondences 'on top of' the traditional skeleton of the symphony (Fifteenth Symphony). The limits of the symphony are thus being pushed out from within almost infinitely.

This impossibility of 'the symphony in earnest' is these days also clear to the younger generation of composers who sometimes deride Shostakovich and Schnittke for 'still' writing symphonies. But after investigation we shall see that in essence we are dealing with one and the same scepticism towards the traditional conception of the symphony, a scepticism which merely manifests itself in the music of different generations of composers in different ways.

Shostakovich and Schnittke prove the impossibility of a 'pure' symphony by the fact that they are pushing out its limits from within. At least four composers are following the same path as they are; they are all coevals of Schnittke who have developed in direct line with the Russian tradition – Giya Kancheli, Avet Terteryan, Arvo Pärt and Valentin Sil'vestrov. Each of them, having written a certain number of symphonies, has shown fairly convincingly that the symphony cannot exist as just a musical composition, but becomes a sort of 'meta-symphony' and is therefore deprived of any basis as a definite structural given. The symphony

---

[4] Schnittke, 'Na puti k voploshcheniyu novoy idei' [Towards the fulfilment of a new idea], in *Problemï traditsii i novatorstva v sovremennoy muzïke* [Problems of Tradition and Innovation in Contemporary Music] (Moscow, 1982), 106–10.

is, as it were, outgrowing its own logical framework. All the composers are actually 'opening' the symphony to the world, destroying its seemingly unshakable foundations, demolishing the in any case conventional boundaries between the music which exists primordially in Nature and what for many centuries was usually called 'the work of art'.

The post-Schnittke generation of composers – Vladimir Tarnopolsky, Alexander Knayfel' and Vladimir Martïnov – are not writing symphonies at all. They regard as unnatural even the act of turning towards this genre. However, at the same time their position relative to the symphonic 'conceptional' tradition is essentially similar to that of Shostakovich and Schnittke. This position has probably best been described (in a recent conversation in Moscow with the present author) by Vladimir Martïnov: 'The time allotted to Christian culture and, in particular, to the composition of music as such, is exhausted. In the twentieth century it is impossible realistically to feel oneself to be a creator of music.' Essentially this is a completely typical Schnittkian idea, even though it is presented in a different light. It is not the composer who is the creator of the music; he only picks up what exists around him and by virtue of the resources allotted to him embodies this in sounds.

In a certain sense that tradition of scepticism towards structural guarantees, the 'frameworks' of symphonies and, even more, towards the necessity of such guarantees, originates not just with Shostakovich, but even earlier, with Tchaikovsky. Never before Tchaikovsky's Sixth Symphony had musical history witnessed such a slow and catastrophic finale. The structural and logical formation had always been the most important function of the conclusion of a symphony, creating a full guarantee of closed form, or the symphony's microcosm. From Tchaikovsky onwards we see the beginning of the tradition of the indirect or false finale (the finale of the Fifth Symphony, for example) when the triumph is camouflaged and in actual fact turns out to be the complete opposite. Trying at first 'honestly' to erect the finale's construction on the basis of a folk song in the Fourth Symphony, Tchaikovsky rules out the idea of the final triumph in the Fifth, and in the Sixth refuses to complete the symphony as such altogether.

Formally speaking we can say that the symphony's slow movement (usually the middle movement) here acts as the finale. But in essence something more happens: the very idea of the finale collapses. 'The finale, which might have explained everything, no longer exists', says Schnittke. 'A finale like that in Tchaikovsky's Sixth Symphony, appears in the era of atheism when the certainty of belief in God has been lost.'⁵ The activity of a logical positive conclusion is replaced by reflection and self-destruction. From the point of view of musical form the structure, in practice, becomes open, irrational. A direct development of this tendency is found in Mahler – it is enough to remember the 'endless' finale Adagios of his last symphonies.

This irrationality finds a clear continuation in the symphonies of Shostakovich. We need only recall the finales of the Sixth, Ninth and Tenth Symphonies. The finales of these and many other cyclical compositions of Shostakovich are in actual fact scherzi. The composer, in exactly the same way as he does in his letters, puts on a mask and does not reveal his true thoughts on the surface; in any case, the final word remains allegorical. Shostakovich tries to avoid the final point. At the same time, real direct speech, the greatest sincerity and emotional force, can frequently be felt in his scherzi, for example in the scherzo of the Tenth Symphony. In actual fact the scherzo in Shostakovich becomes something significantly greater; the bitterness and sarcasm characteristic of Mahlerian burlesque-scherzi unite here with a finality and irrevocability of utterance which forces one to the assumption that the idea of finality, normally characteristic of the finale of a traditional symphony, is in Shostakovich moved to the scherzo, whilst the idea of the scherzo, as something rather allegorical, but in any case not final and conceptional, moves into the finales. Thus the finale ceases to be the finale in the classical and Romantic sense, and turns into a coda, into something which is morphological and symbolic in nature rather than syntactic, 'resultative'-structural.

In this connection one can briefly investigate the history of the coda as the transmitter of the irrational; starting with Mozart, with whom, after what is usually a very clear, well-balanced composition of the slow movements in his symphonies, concertos or sonatas, there followed an extra-structural irrational coda, which in fact washes away the whole of the preceding structure and, more importantly, transfers the listener's perception on to a completely different symbolic plane. It is not the logical proportionality of the composition or the development of the thinking in it which comes to the fore, but listening attentively to individual elements of what has already been heard and finding in them new emotional stimuli for some of the associations. From the point of view of the composition itself, as well as from the point of view of classical aesthetics, a coda of this sort is of no interest whatsoever.

⁵ Alexander Ivashkin, *Besedï s Al'fredom Shnitke* [Conversations with Alfred Schnittke] (Moscow, 1994).

So why did somebody like Mozart feel the need for endings of this type, which add precisely nothing new to what has already been said? I would suggest that it is because in any style of music there has to be an element which cannot be explained logically. An element which from the information point of view is surplus, irrational (which can be found to some extent in various styles), is at the same time the motor and the stimulus for subsequent new rational ideas. In his time V. I. Vernadsky justifiably remarked that irrational, intuitive discoveries in art as a rule pave the way for fundamental discoveries in science, and even direct them.[6] Thus the symbolic elements of baroque rhetoric have ceased to be symbolic for us, being perceived today purely musically and not creating any dissonance within the system. Time and change in the social situation as a whole are required in order for extramusical symbolic elements to 'germinate' into the musical language of the era and to become a fully-fledged part of its vocabulary, thus ceasing to be perceived as something foreign to the 'purest' music. Many elements of Olivier Messiaen's style – for example, the excessively slow tempi and disparateness of his language – which only recently seemed to be purely religious attributes of his music, are now, after the passage of just twenty or thirty years, perceived as organic elements of the musical language of the twentieth century. The same thing is happening to the music of Shostakovich. For example, his repetitive rhythmic patterns or the de-tensioned, seemingly strangely simple style of his works (the coda of the finale of the Eighth Symphony, the finale of the Viola Sonata). Thus the open twentieth-century forms, the many different peculiarities of modern musical forms – as, for example, the disintegration of the sonata allegro in the first movements of the First Symphony and the Fourth Violin Concerto of Schnittke – are the result of the development of the same tendency found in Mozart's codas or Gluck's slow balletic Adagios, which seem to slow down the flow of events in opera and transport us into an irrational sphere. And it is here that the seeds of the symbolic, metamusical approach are contained which will become characteristic of the twentieth century, starting from the late works of Shostakovich.

His late cycles are open – the idea of closedness is foreign to them in principle. Sometimes the composer introduces a direct and unambiguous image of time running away, ending a symphony with it (Symphony No. 15) or a concerto (the Second Cello Concerto). Occasionally, at the

[6] See V. I. Vernadsky, 'Nauchnaya mïsl' kak planetnoye yavleniye' [Scientific thought as a planetary phenomenon], in *Filosofskiye mïsli naturalista* [Philosophical Thoughts of a Naturalist] (Moscow, 1988).

end of a symphony, Shostakovich appears to draw aside real space, translating us from a gloomy everyday occurrence, with its awe-inspiring detailed chronicle of events, into the infinity of astral space. Sometimes, like Tchaikovsky, he ends the work with a big, unstructured Adagio (Viola Sonata), or, as an extreme case, completely turns the whole work, the entire cycle, into a huge, slow coda (Quartet No. 15).

This feature is directly continued in Schnittke's symphonies and the works of other composers. The coda acquires quite exceptional importance, becoming a generalised sign for the whole composition.

Codas in general embody the most important idea of the music of the eighties – its openness – revealing the real unity between Nature and Culture, between reality which has existed for ever and reality created by man. An entire movement of a cycle can become a coda – in the broad sense of that word – for example, the finale of the Third Violin Concerto and the Third Symphony of Schnittke, the finale of his *Faust* Cantata. In the music of Valentin Sil'vestrov the entire work becomes a coda, like Shostakovich's Fifteenth Quartet; for example, 'Postludes' (even the name is typical) for various instruments and ensemble, and his Fifth Symphony (1982) or 'Post-Symphony'.

In the music of Schnittke the most striking examples of codas which place the whole music into another dimension are the codas of the Fourth Symphony, the First and Second Concerti Grossi and the Epilogue of the ballet *Peer Gynt*. True, in all four works the coda is linked to the preceding material in different ways. In *Peer Gynt* and the Fourth Symphony it is a sort of summation, a condensed run-through of the principal themes, whilst in the Fourth Symphony it also has a symbolic programmatic character as well: Catholic, Russian Orthodox, Protestant and Judaic themes are first of all gone through in their pure form, reaching concord with one another in harmonic and consonantal sound. And although this coda is perceived by the ear as absolutely other than the preceding flow of music, in actual fact it is a sort of synopsis, a compressed nucleus of everything that has happened before. The same thing happens in *Peer Gynt*, except that here quotations of themes already heard pass by like recollections against a background of the continuous, vibrating, pure sound of the choir in D major, which is a new quality compared to the whole of the previous music of the ballet, and therefore symbolises a sort of breakthrough into a new dimension. In this sense the Epilogue of *Peer Gynt* has a great deal in common with the coda of Shostakovich's Thirteenth Symphony. The main difference between the unstructured metamusical codas of Shostakovich and Schnittke lies in the fact that in Shostakovich (in the same way as Mozart) the coda can occur completely independently of the rest of the material, whereas in Schnittke (in the same way as, say, Bach) the coda will still be latently or obviously correlated with the basic material of the work or have something in common with its beginning. Not without reason did Glazunov find elements of Mozartian talent in Shostakovich, whereas Schnittke, in his recent lecture to the students of the Hamburg Musikhochschule, pointed out that he had spent his whole life engaging with Bachian techniques and that, in his opinion, at least two centuries of European music were 'Bach-centred'.[7]

Continuing the list of differences in style between Shostakovich and Schnittke one should note the former's dislike for any purely formal ideas, and Schnittke's obvious penchant for them in such works as *Pianissimo* and the Third Concerto Grosso. For Schnittke this was not an end in itself, however, but merely a link in the search for the laws of the Ur-Alte; notable also is Shostakovich's speed of composition as against Schnittke's abundance of drafts and calculations (at least in the 1970s and the beginning of the 1980s).

Both composers use their monograms in different ways (although outwardly similarly). For Shostakovich it is more a symbol which is engraved during the music (although sometimes, as in the Eighth Quartet, a large stratum of the music is built on the monogram). For Schnittke monograms become a real building material, the same as a series. Without hesitation he builds the fabric of his Third Symphony on the monograms of German composers, uses the monogram of Gidon Kremer as the thematic material for his Fourth Violin Concerto, and even in the ascetic fabric of his Seventh Symphony he introduces the word 'Deutschland'. In Shostakovich the monogram remains unchanged as a rule, similar to a symbol, but in Schnittke it becomes the basis of intensive morphological modification. The rhythmic relief of Shostakovich's music is different from that of Schnittke.

Shostakovich employs ostinato and other forms of rhythmic inertia as a special 'supercharging' device, a sort of psychological pressure or pressurisation. Any sort of rhythmic inertia is alien to Schnittke, with the exception of those cases when it clearly demonstrates the idea of the absurdity of the musical unfolding itself – as, let us say, in the Allegro of

[7] Schnittke, Lecture on Polystylistics at the Hamburg Musikhochschule, 15 January 1993 (my summary).

the Fourth Violin Concerto. Schnittke's music is a blood relation of the more rational, but also more formal, experiments of the 1960s (when he himself was inclined towards such experiments); he is the heir and representative of the post-serial era and all its refined techniques, whereas Shostakovich's music reflects, directly or obliquely, the irrational, futuristic quest and ideas of the avant-garde of the 1910s and 1920s.

The codas of the First and Second Concerti Grossi of Schnittke in many ways repeat the material of the introduction of these works, creating, as it were, an extra-structural framework, the arch of the whole composition. When I asked the composer whether he composed this material beforehand, he categorically replied in the negative: 'This material must appear as an inevitable gift at the end of the composition'.[8] In fact the entire development of the symphony or concerto becomes an attempt to achieve the 'illumination' of the coda. In this sense, Schnittke's codas, in the same way as Shostakovich's codas, are a continuation of a typically Russian tradition, and not just a musical tradition. A work of art never exists as a fact of pure art; the listener enters into such works as a kind of medium in which he himself must make decisions to create, to act, to subject himself to experiments. The idea of the work, exactly in the same way as happens in life itself, opens out in the process of the experiment, the experience. Rephrasing the words of John Cage, one can compare, for example, the music of Shostakovich and Schnittke with the room in which a man lives, and the music of the 1960s western avant-garde with an ash-tray which he only uses occasionally.

The idea of the extra-structural, open coda which was revealed by Shostakovich and was developed by Schnittke, corresponds as closely as possible to such a feeling, and in the long run leads to growth in the duration of the works of composers of the younger generation in the 1980s. Even Shostakovich thinks, as a rule, in broad time-scales. Shostakovich's music is expansive and the drama of the form is created by the interaction of fairly large time-scale sections. This peculiarity becomes very characteristic of many composers of the next generation – Terteryan, Kancheli and above all Schnittke. The new understanding of time – prolongation (*dleniye*) – requires large dimensions to manifest itself. Thus Knayfel''s *Nika*, for seventeen double basses, lasts 2 hours 20 minutes, and his Agnus Dei for four players on various instruments, lasts 2 hours 30 minutes. A considerable time-span is also required for the meditative compositions of Vladimir Martïnov.

[8] Ivashkin, *Besedï*.

Of course the symphonies and concertos of Shostakovich and Schnittke are not as long as that. But an important feature can be seen in them which subsequently leads to a new understanding of time – the 'openness' of extra-structural codas and the idea of a through-composed cycle, or 'monocycle'. Thus, even the Second Cello Concerto of Shostakovich (1966) is in fact a single-movement concentric-type work with a coda which opens up the whole cycle to the outside. This tendency is continued in Schnittke's symphonies and concerti. Although the majority of them are not formally single-movement works (the Fourth Symphony, the Concerto for Piano and Strings, the Piano Concerto for Four Hands are examples of literally single-movement works) in fact the idea of a through-composed movement from beginning to end dominates (a similar conception can be found in Shostakovich's Fifteenth Quartet). It is sufficient to note that in Schnittke's symphonies and concerti the first movements which begin as normal sonata allegros collapse without reaching the recapitulation; and the idea of sequential development, so typical of the Classical and Romantic symphony and concerto, although it is in fact employed, is more often a negative image, a kind of 'bad infinity' or a stupid-mechanistic evil opposed to personality (for example, the first movement of the Fourth Violin Concerto). Conversely, the most positive and important images are found to be connected with those sections where there is no development, time stops and space moves apart (the finale – in actual fact the coda – of the Third Violin Concerto).

In all fairness it must be noted that the attitude to the idea of development in Shostakovich and Schnittke is different. Shostakovich related much more positively to this idea, particularly in the first movements of his symphonies, and we should recall, if nothing else, the grandiose design of the first movement of the Eighth Symphony, which is entirely based on through and gradual development. In his last works, incidentally, this bent for undeviating, single-minded development becomes less and less perceptible, and the flow of music goes along other, less direct, paths, subject to more important, although not so obvious, correspondences at the level of the *whole* cycle. In Schnittke, traditional symphonic development is always *only negative* by nature; for him the undeviating single-minded concept of 'development' is completely non-existent.

In his middle period Shostakovich still believes in the constructive function of development, whereas Schnittke does not believe in it at all. As has already been mentioned, Schnittke finds other rational supports to sustain the symphonic cycle, in the same way as Shostakovich does in his late period. These supports are connected more with baroque or serial thinking; they are more morphological than syntactical.

The whole tradition of symphonic thinking of Shostakovich and Schnittke is seen to be directed along a single channel which erodes the traditional, classical supports of the symphony, and in the long run the whole idea of syntactic conformities of movements and sections. Syntax is more and more eroded by morphology, by withdrawal into the *depths of the material itself*, by the search for different points of view upon it – as it used to be in the old variation form. In the same way that in a Russian icon our gaze must travel, and should slide from one object to another in order to take in the meaning of the image, the music of late Shostakovich and the works of Schnittke demand a mobile point of view from the listener which does not allow the sense of the whole to be seen except in its architectonics, or rather in the failure of architectonics to conform with classical models. In exactly the same way as in Dostoyevsky's novels, the final word sometimes proves to be the most simple and ingenuous – but is only perceived as such because everything that has gone before has indicated the necessity and the inevitability of such an ending. Let us recall the biblical epigraph to Dostoyevsky's *The Brothers Karamazov*:

Verily, verily, I say unto you, except a corn of wheat fall unto the ground and die, it abideth alone: but if it die, it bringeth forth much fruit.[9] (Gospel of St John 12: 24)

The *syntactical* idea of the symphony dies in order to give life to the *morphological* symphony, a symphony (not necessarily actually written in the form of a symphony) whose meaning lies in searching for *new reserves of the material itself*, and not in comparing clichéd idioms of the language in already well-known combinations.

Striving to find a new meaning for very simple elements of musical language is in general an attribute of Russian culture. We should remember that throughout its entire history Russian music has always 'made corrections' to the fate of European musical forms, first and foremost by bringing them closer to the variation principles which are much more characteristic of Slavic thinking than of Western thinking. As examples of this one could quote the forms used by Glinka, Rimsky-Korsakov and Tchaikovsky. In Russian music the variation principle has always signified less rationality, less abstractness of form, and greater penetration into the depths of the material itself, in search of its various inner resources.

[9] F. M. Dostoyevsky, *Polnoye sobraniye sochineniy* [Complete Collected Works] (Leningrad, *c*. 1976), xiv, 5.

Shostakovich developed this tendency to a large degree, particularly in his late works. In their extremely rarefied style (as, for example, the absolutely astonishing monody of the piano part in the Viola Sonata) the same articulation of the *root* values of musical speech occurs as was characteristic of both Russian poetry and Russian philology as long ago as the beginning of the twentieth century. Thus, let us say, in the poetry of Velimir Khlebnikov, Alexander Vvedensky and Daniil Kharms (and partly Nikolay Zabolotsky as well) the absurd correlations of syllables and words merely help to strike the spark of the new energy of meanings. The same thing happens in the prose and verse of Andrey Beliy. Shostakovich was perhaps the first person in twentieth-century Russian music to discover and make use of the new opportunities of the intonations and rhythms which seemed to be known to everybody. 'The ability to see the chasms above the banalities' (one of Webern's expressions) was characteristic of him in the highest degree; and moreover, by banalities, what is meant here is not the worn-out intonations themselves, but the worn-out context in which they are used, from which Shostakovich strips the deposit of rust, forcing people to hear the original, primordial roots rather than the idioms which had become established after decades of use.

In his music Schnittke is continuing this process of cleansing the simplest elements of the language, and building the drama of his compositions on them, instead of on the canons of form. In his compositions a large part is always played by major triads, chorale progressions and the overtone scale – givens always inherent in the symbolic aura of music and connected with its natural expressive resources. Schnittke's recent works – his Sixth and Seventh Symphonies – surprise by the same rarefied nature of their sound fabric as the late works of Shostakovich. The score of the Sixth Symphony (1992) contains almost no *tuttis* at all. The orchestra plays in groups and the actual texture of the music seems to be ascetically dry and abstract. At the same time it is impossible to listen to this music against an abstract rational design. The listener unwittingly senses the latent symbolism of the music, although he is not always able to be aware of what sort of symbolism it is. It is necessary to listen attentively, to penetrate into the musical material itself in order gradually to become accustomed to this at first glance strange, ascetically sparse texture. As an American critic justly remarked after the première of the Sixth Symphony in New York: 'When the last notes evaporated, I had the queasy feeling of having heard a Mahler symphony with most of its musical flesh torn away, leaving a gruesome skeleton dangling forlornly in a black space'.[10]

Shostakovich and Schnittke complete the process of modulation from the syntactical to the morphological symbolism of musical meaning. Their symphonies, just like Dostoyevsky's novels, are testing grounds leading to the elucidation of the simplest and most indisputable meaning. Here we are approaching the key problem of Shostakovich's and Schnittke's style: is there in fact a hidden or an overt symbolism of the musical elements, or is that an illusion engendered by the sick imagination of interested listeners, as well as by the local social situation in Russia when music (like the other arts) was obliged to replace the spiritual values of real life?

There is no doubt that the attitude to the music of Shostakovich and Schnittke has changed a great deal in recent years. Today we evaluate their music from objective positions, often not linking it with the social or cultural situation which has emerged. Even so, the feeling of symbolic polyvalency, an encoding, remains, which can be clearly seen in the American press reaction to the performance of Schnittke's Sixth Symphony. Perhaps this encipherment, occasionally obscurity, becomes even more noticeable in Schnittke's latest work, in the same way as occurred in Shostakovich's late work.

Schnittke's and Shostakovich's works require interpretation; they are not self-explanatory. It is not by accident that both composers have frequently hidden sound monograms and symbols in their compositions – D–S–C–H in Shostakovich, B–A–C–H and A–S–C–H, as well as the initials of various performers, in Schnittke. Neither is their common bent for allusion and the use of banal, but associatively rich, musical material, on the edge of triteness, accidental. In all this one can see a tendency to try to find additional meaningful and symbolic reserves not evident on the surface of the music.

The 'performer-coloration' of the vocabulary of the music of both composers is therefore not accidental. The intonational world of Shostakovich's and Schnittke's concerti is indissolubly connected with the special character of the expression, with the personalised and profoundly individualised statement of the soloist, who somehow opposes himself to the featureless and satanic social situation. This undoubtedly reflects the highly paradoxical role of personality and its connections with the social situation in the era of Communist dictatorship. After all, it is no secret

[10] Peter G. Davis, 'Uneasy-listening music', *New York* (28 February 1994), p. 125.

that it was the personal, the individual, the unique, which formed the core of the extremely intensive development of Russian culture during the oppression of Communist ideology. The most popular form of literature of those years – among the intelligentsia – were the so-called 'sborniki' (collections), a gathering together of articles by various authors, united extremely tenuously by a set of problems, but in actual fact comprising individual essays, mainly touching upon philosophical and social questions, using abstract or far from contemporary material. An ideal example of this type of literature was *Works on Sign Systems* published over many years by Tartu University under the direction of the remarkable Russian philosopher Yuriy Lotman. Under this distinctive title many brilliant articles on a whole range of topics from music to magic were published, and, moreover, the views of the authors were extremely individualistic and frequently opposed to one another. But at the same time it was obvious that we were dealing with a concentration and intersection of individual, high-voltage energies, or more accurately, with an original spiritual debate invisible to the ordinary eye. Soviet art was so hypertrophically individualistic because it was a substitute for real life, which did not exist for several generations of Soviet people, and under these conditions the part played by personality, bright and prophetic, increased considerably. This is also shown by the performance style of those years, towards which the music of Shostakovich and Schnittke was directed (a style which has somewhat lost its topicality today): the style of subjective, oratorical pronouncement, sometimes a sort of 'cult of originality'. The violin concerti of Shostakovich and Schnittke are simply designed for post-Romantic performance, for performance rhetoric, for the material to be sculpted by the hands of the soloist – it is not important what material figured in the music itself, whether it be a dramatic monologue of Shostakovich or Gidon Kremer's initials enciphered in notes as in Schnittke's Fourth Violin Concerto. The music of Shostakovich and Schnittke is inseparable from personality – its bright content and delivery – just as the music of, say, the Viennese classics depends a great deal on the accuracy with which it is read and does not need personal-subjective reading.

Of course today Romantic, dramatic or heroic performance pathos (appropriate to performances of the music of Shostakovich and Schnittke) is already regarded as having in many ways disappeared into the past and as being peculiar to a particular era. But it is not just a matter of pathos. The actual vocabulary of both composers reveals the 'depth of the velvet', the difference between the 'conceivable and the audible' (Schnittke's expression) which is enclosed not in the text itself but which somehow lies between the notes, filling the music with its tension. It is interesting that with the passing of time this vocabulary is changing, and changing quickly, from strikingly individual (characteristic of the style of the given composer) to universal; mankind is, as it were, appropriating the achievements of Shostakovich and Schnittke and losing 'current' interest in this music. As time passes, interest in this music will return; true it will be a different interest, not expecting any surprises – the music will be perceived as part of a sound-culture. In the process of this assimilation will the 'sub-marine', symbolic part, which was so important to the music of Shostakovich and Schnittke only yesterday, still remain? Yes, it will remain; for it is not directly connected with any of the social or psychological peculiarities of the age, but reproduces them, like a hieroglyph or a component of an architectural structure, in an extremely mediated form. The music of Shostakovich and Schnittke absorbs and augments historic meanings. We can sense the spiritual efforts of many generations in their symphonies without the experience of these generations being directly referred to, or restored. This experience is already given to us in the established vocabulary of Shostakovich's and Schnittke's music. Bachian rhetoric, Romantic phrases, idioms of the classics, vulgar melodies and Soviet songs appear in their music, and not just as various elements of styles. Nor are they perceived as such, rather as forming a new universal language. Future generations will probably not sense the sources or the roots, but even so they will receive mankind's 'cultural memory' enclosed in it ready made.

The music of Shostakovich and Schnittke preserves the link between music as a system of sounds and the system of symbols which, thanks to the experience of many generations, is encoded in music. This symbolic fund is preserved in their music permanently, regardless of how clearly we imagine its sources. In this sense the music of Shostakovich and Schnittke, in many ways engendered by the Russian tradition (and art for art, pure art, never existed in Russia), in actual fact turns out to be not just Russian, local, but general, universal.

Being closely linked with the Mahlerian tradition the music of Shostakovich and Schnittke somehow intensifies all the Mahlerian contrasts and articulates the ambivalence of his music. On the other hand, Shostakovich's musical language, and even more so Schnittke's, is both more abstract and sometimes (in their late works especially) even enigmatic. But it does not lose its significance or symbolism, proving that the true significance is not in the enciphered monograms or series, not in the political or social colour of the musical images, and not in the syntactical distortion of musical time, but in the very heart of this or that intonation – intonations intimately tied up with the experience of human self-expression and impossible in the pure, decorative, distilled form.

Shostakovich gave unique expression to the thoughts and feelings of those generations of Russian people whose fate it was to live under the yoke of totalitarian power. Schnittke is often called the 'man in between'. A very strong pulse of latent energy is undoubtedly inherent in both their musics, and common to both is extreme pessimism, embodied even in the nature of their musical forms – many works of late Shostakovich and Schnittke are 'dying', dissolving in the world, fading into the distance of time. All this is indisputably to do with time. Anyone who wants to listen to their music in future is by no means bound to feel all these concrete, time-connected, features. But he will undoubtedly absorb this intense energy of the flow of the music, make it part of his being, part of his thinking and part of his vocabulary. In the same way will come true the highest ideal of an artist's immortality, of which Schnittke wrote in his article on Shostakovich (already quoted at the beginning of this essay): 'To influence the world through confluence with the world'.

Index

Abbate, Carolyn, 158
Abraham, Gerald, 7, 230, 247
Abrams, Morris, 115
Adam, L. I., 82, 84, 91, 92, 98–100, 101, 103, 105
Agawu, V. Kofi, 28
Akhmatova, Anna, 217, 225
  Requiem, 39
aleatory, 236
Aldeburgh, 229, 233, 238, 241, 245
Alexander III, Tsar, 19
Alexandrov, Anatoliy, 27
Aranovich, S., 4
Armashevskaya, K., 195, 196, 197
Arts and Crafts Movement, 252
Asaf'yev, Boris, 1, 40, 80, 103
  Lost Illusions, 197
  Militsa, 197
  Solveg, 197
Ashbee, Felicity, 252
Ashkenazy, Abram, 21
Ashkenazy, Vladimir, 2
atheism, 259
Atovm'yan, Levon, 21, 177
Auden, Wystan, 234, 240

Bach, Johann Sebastian, 70, 74, 144, 232, 241, 262, 268
  B minor Mass, 239
  cantatas, 251
  '48' Preludes and Fugues, 237
  passions, 236, 251
Baker, Josephine, 195
Bakhmetev, Nikolay, 41
Balanchivadze, Andrey, 177
Barry, Malcolm, 25

Barshai, Rudolf, 2, 54
Bartlett, Rosamund, 15
Beethoven, Ludwig van, 15, 19, 31, 57, 68, 238
  Piano Sonata Op. 2 No. 2, 59
  Piano Sonata Op. 2 No. 3, 59
  Piano Sonata Op. 31 No. 2, 59
  Piano Sonata Op. 90, 59
  string quartets, 51, 116
  String Quartet Op. 59 No. 2, 115
  String Quartet Op. 95, 115
  Symphony No. 5, 45, 115, 225
  Symphony No. 9, 10–11, 28, 29, 43, 119–20
  Violin Sonata in A ('Kreutzer'), 213
Beliy, Andrey, 266
Beliy, Viktor, 20
Belyayev, Mitrofan, 42
Belyayev, Viktor, 78, 80
Benderoff, Sonia, 169
Benois, Nicolas, 185
Berg, Alban, 4–5, 15, 232, 248
  Lyric Suite, 246
  Wozzeck, 4, 151, 241, 251
Berlioz, Hector, 253
  Symphonie fantastique, 48, 115, 116
  Harold in Italy, 115, 116
Bernandt, Grigoriy, 78
Bernstein, Leonard, 42
Bershadskaya, Tatyana, 87, 88–90, 107
Billington, James, 28
Bizet, Georges, 189
'black box' principle, 65
Bobrovsky, Viktor, 84, 91, 99–101, 103, 110, 158

271

Bogdanov, 183
Bogdanov-Berezovsky, Valerian, 190
Bogdanova, Alla, 152, 155, 157, 191
Booth, Wayne, 30-1
Borodin Quartet, 113
Brahms, Johannes, 35, 144
  Symphony No. 3, 115
  Symphony No. 4, 241
Braun, Joachim, 31
Brazhnikov, Maxim, 77
Brett, Philip, 231, 253
Brezhnev, Leonid, 46
Britten, Benjamin, 7, 229-53
  Albert Herring, 231, 249, 251, 253
  Billy Budd, 229, 245, 246, 251
  cadenza to Mozart Piano Concerto in E♭, K482, 233
  cello suites, 233, 242, 243
  Cello Symphony, 231, 233, 235, 242
  church parables, 247
  Curlew River, 251
  Death in Venice, 230, 244, 245, 247, 251, 253
  Gloriana, 234, 251
  Holy Sonnets of John Donne, The, 241
  Little Sweep, The, 242
  Midsummer Night's Dream, A, 229, 231, 244, 247, 251
  Nocturnal, 242
  Noye's Fludde, 242
  operas, 233, 236
  Our Hunting Fathers, 232, 235
  Owen Wingrave, 244, 245, 247, 251, 253
  Paul Bunyan, 240
  Peter Grimes, 231, 240-1, 242, 251, 253
  Piano Concerto, 234, 235, 242
  Poet's Echo, The (words by Pushkin), 231, 236, 242, 248
  Prince of the Pagodas, The, 234
  Rape of Lucretia, The, 231, 232, 234, 237, 241, 249, 251
  Rejoice in the Lamb, 232
  Russian Funeral, 234
  Sechs Hölderlin-Fragmente, 229
  Serenade for Tenor, Horn and Strings, 229
  Sinfonia da Requiem, 235
  Spring Symphony, 233, 244
  string quartets, 236
  String Quartet No. 2, 230, 241
  String Quartet No. 3, 230, 232-3, 242
  Turn of the Screw, The, 231, 242, 244, 245, 246, 247, 248, 249-50
  War Requiem, 231, 233, 236-9, 242, 243, 252
Bredersen, Yuriy, 200, 201
Brown, Malcolm Hamrick, 31, 40, 78, 164, 239
Brown, Royal, 164, 167
Bruckner, Anton
  symphonies, 116
Bubnov, Andrey, 171, 198
Bulgakov, Mikhail, 53, 54, 198
  Master and Margarita, The, 256
Burda, V., 82, 84, 86, 91, 92, 94, 101-3, 109
Bychkov, Semyon, 2

cadenza, 235
Camus, Albert, 6
Cage, John, 257, 263
canon, 121-2, 128, 130-2
Carpenter, Ellon, 6, 7, 8-9, 66, 79
Catoire, Georgiy, 80
Chabukiani, Vakhtang, 192, 196
Chekhov, Anton, 15, 232, 244
Chelyapov, Nikolai, 21, 22, 25
Cherubini, Luigi, 151
Chesnakov, V. P., 194
Chopin, Fryderyk, 253
  Fantasy in F minor, 97
Chorny, Sasha, 212
Christianity, 227, 238, 252, 258, 261
Chung, Myung-Whun, 167
classicism (Viennese), 239, 268
coda, 51-2, 259-63
Communism, Communist Party, 14, 38, 47, 161, 208, 210-12, 227, 235, 255, 267-8
cyclic form, 113-36

Daniel, Yuliy, 46
Danilevich, Lev, 76, 230, 234, 249
Dante [= Dante Alighieri], 222, 225
Danuser, Hermann, 212

Index

Daragan, Dina, 206
Dargomïzhsky, Alexander
  'The Titular Councillor', 213
Darwinism, 252
Davis, Peter, 267
Decembrists, 208, 222, 225, 229
Degen, A., 197
Delius, Frederick, 253
Del'vig, Anton, 222, 229
Denisov, Edison, 225
'Dies irae', 214
Diletsky, Nikolay, 77
dissidence, 3, 46-7
Dmitriyev, Vladimir, 176
Dobrïkin, E., 212
Dolmatovsky, Yevgeniy, 207, 208
Dolzhansky, Alexander, 66, 76, 82, 91, 92-7, 98, 101, 103, 106, 108-11, 112
Dostoyevsky, Fyodor, 24, 265, 267
  Brothers Karamazov, The, 265
  Devils, The, 226
  Raw Youth, A, 56
doublespeak, 38
Downes, Edward, 162
Drïbachevsky, Galina, 4
Drukt, A., 85-6, 88, 89-90, 107
D-S-C-H monogram, 232, 262
Dubinsky, Rostislav, 113
Dudintsev, Vladimir
  Not by Bread Alone, 46
Dunayevsky, Isaak, 26, 27
  Marsh entuziastov, 39
Dzerzhinsky, Ivan, 22
  The Quiet Don, 26

Efros, Abram, 218
Emerson, Caryl, 56
English National Opera, 153
English Opera Group, 231, 249
Entelis, Leonid, 27, 34
Erenburg, Il'ya
  Thaw, The [Ottepel'], 212
Evans, John, 245
expressionism, 37

Fadeyev, Alexander, 34, 38
Famintsïn, Alexander, 78-9
Fanning, David, 6, 8, 13, 31, 45, 46, 66, 70-1, 117, 144, 145, 208

fascism, 129, 235, 238, 240
Fay, Laurel, 4, 6, 7, 14, 27, 137, 149, 179, 184, 239
Fedin, Konstantin, 211
Fedosova, Eleonora, 87, 91, 94, 103, 106-11, 112
Feuchtner, Bernd, 208, 215, 216, 227
finales, 34, 37, 38, 258-9
Fischer, Erik, 157
Fish, Stanley, 31
Five-Year Plan, First, 18, 19
form, 7-8
formalism, 22, 190
formalism, Russian (literary theory), 28
Franck, César
  Symphony in D minor, 116
Frisch, Walter, 115
Fuchs, Johann Leopold, 78
fugue, 57
funeral march, 116

Gachev, Dmitriy, 54
Gachev, Georgiy, 54, 55
Gadamer, Hans-Georg, 30
Gagarin, Yuriy, 207
Galïnin, German, 255
Garbuzov, Nikolay, 80
Gauk, Alexander, 191, 195, 202
Genina, Liana, 6, 13, 55
Georgescu, Corneliu Dan, 225
Gerlach, Hannelore, 212
Gladkov, Fyodor
  Cement, 26
Gladkovsky, Arseniy, 198
glasnost', 3, 4, 17, 40, 53, 55
Glazunov, Alexander, 40, 202, 262
Glière, Reinhold, 19, 182
  Red Poppy, The, 93
Glikman, Isaak, 1, 32, 39, 40, 54, 168, 169, 178-84, 187, 210, 213, 218, 226, 255
Glinka, Mikhail, 78, 265
  A Life for the Tsar, 78
Gluck, Christoph, 260
Glumov, Alexander, 32
Gnesin, Mikhail, 19
Gogol, Nikolay, 74
  Marriage, The, 213
Gojowy, Detlef, 145, 225

Golovina, 173
Gorbachov, Mikhail, 17, 18, 20, 47
Gorky, Maxim, 20
Gorodinsky, Viktor, 21, 25
Graham, Colin, 230
Grant, General Ulysses, 48
Grashchenkov, V., 218
Gres, Semyon, 201
Grigor'yeva, Alla, 206
Grigorovich, Yuriy, 203
Grieg, Edvard, 197
Gromov, Mikhail, 24
grotesque, the, 116

Hanna, George, 45, 113
Hanslick, Eduard, 157
Harewood, Marion, 233
Haydn, Joseph, 57
  Creation, The, 199
Headington, Christopher, 230
Hitler, Adolf, 51
Howe, Irving, 56
Hulme, Derek, 113, 207, 212, 218, 225, 232

idée fixe, 119, 247
Ilemichev, P. M., 204
intonation theory, 40, 52, 242
Iokhelson, Vladimir, 21, 32
irony, 30-1
Ivanovsky, Alexander, 192, 193
Ivashkin, Alexander, 7, 15, 259
Ives, Charles, 15

James, Henry, 244
'Jewish' music, 130, 132, 136
Jelagin, Juri, 19, 32, 36
John, Nicholas, 186

Kabalevsky, Dmitriy, 182
Kaltat, Lev, 170
Kancheli, Giya, 257, 263
Kandelaki, Vladimir, 177
Kann, E., 176
Kaplan, E. I., 194
Karklin, Lyudvig, 82, 86-7
Kastalsky, Alexander, 80
Katayev, Valentin
  I am the Son of Labouring Folk, 31
Katonova, Svetlana, 191

Kazenin, I., 177
Keats, John, 229
Keldïsh, Yuriy, 19
Keller, Hans, 119, 229, 233
Kerman, Joseph, 51
Kharms, Daniil, 266
Khentova, Sof'ya, 5, 27, 32, 34, 35, 36, 38, 49, 52, 57, 75, 206, 212, 213, 215, 216, 218, 226
Khlebnikov, Velimir, 266
Khodasevich, Valentina, 194, 196
Kholopov, Yuriy, 6, 8, 9, 77, 81, 86, 112, 245
Khrennikov, Tikhon, 23, 182
  Into the Storm, 32
Khrushchov, Nikita, 35, 46, 48, 210-11
Khubov, Georgiy, 25, 36-40, 42, 48, 51, 52
Kim, M. P., 198
Kiselyov, Mikhail, 190
Klimovitsky, A. I., 15
Knayfel', Alexander, 258
  Nika, 263
Knodel, Arthur, 27
Köchel, Jürgen, 212
Kolleritsch, Ludwig, 15
Kon, Felix, 19
Kon, Yuzef, 84, 86
Kopelev, Lev, 47
  To be Preserved Forever, 47
Kopp, Karen, 3, 7
Korchmaryov, Klimentiy, 201
Korotich, Vasiliy, 47
Kosachova, Rimma, 192
Koval', Marian, 191
Kovnatskaya, Lyudmila, 15, 231, 232, 233, 234, 240, 241, 242, 252
Kozlov, Ivan, 212
Kozlova, M. G., 42
Kramer, Lawrence, 115, 119
Kremer, Gidon, 262, 268
Kremlyov, Yuriy, 25
Kröplin, Ekhart, 145, 152, 155
Küchelbecker, Wilhelm, 222, 229
Kurilko, M., 193
Kushnaryov, Khristofor, 81, 103-4

Lakond, Wladimir, 169
Laptev, Konstantin, 183
Lavrovsky, Leonid, 192, 195

Layton, Robert, 158
Lebedinsky, Lev, 4–5, 20, 199, 208, 210
leitmotif, 13, **137–59**, 246
Leliva, 173
Lenin [= Ulyanov], Vladimir, 20, 251
Leskov, Nikolay, 162
Levaya, Tamara, 206, 218, 224, 226–7
Levitin, Yuriy, 5, 20, 255
linear polyphony, 144–5
Liszt, Franz
  Faust Symphony, 119–20
Longman, Richard, 7
Lopukhov, A., 190, 195
Lotman, Yuriy
  Work on Sign Systems, 268
Lunacharsky, Anatoliy, 198
L'vov, Nikolay, 78
L'vov-Anokhin, B., 196
Lyubinsky, Zakhar, 197
Lyukom, Yelena, 192

MacDonald, Ian, 2, 18, 45, 49–54, 113, 117, 126–7
MacDonald, Malcolm, 214, 224, 225, 227
Mahler, Gustav, 1, 15, 68, 232, 233, 237, 253, 269
  Das Lied von der Erde, 41–2, 237, 243
  symphonies, 28, 116, 256, 259, 266
  Symphony No. 5, 45
  Symphony No. 6, 237
  Symphony No. 7, 248
  Symphony No. 8, 237
  Symphony No. 9, 237
Malko, Nikolai, 1
Markov, P., 170
Marschner, Heinrich, 151
Martïnov, Ivan, 25, 48, 117
Martïnov, Vladimir, 258, 263
Marx, Adolf Bernhard, 8, 58, 67
Mason, Colin, 116–17
mass song, 19
Mayakovsky, Vladimir, 198
Mazel', Leo (Lev), 1, 5, 51, 52, 76, 84, 91, **96–8**, 235
Mazo, Margarita, 17, 78
McCarthy, Joseph, 53
McCreless, Patrick, 6, 7, 13

McQuere, Gordon, 79, 80
Méhul, Etienne, 151
Mel'gunov, Yuriy, 78–9
Melik-Pashayev, Alexander, 170, 176–7
Messiaen, Olivier, 15, 260
Meyer, Krzysztof, 2, 5, 15
Michelangelo [= Michelangelo Buonarroti], 218, 225
Mikhaylov, Lev, 184
Mikheyeva, Lyudmila, 1, 163, 178
Millington, Barry, 117
Minkus, Léon
  Bayadère, La, 193
  Don Quixote, 193
Mitchell, Donald, 232, 234, 235, 241, 245
mode, 8–9, 10, 11, 66, **76–112**
Molotov [= Vyacheslav Skryabin], 22, 182
monograms, 262
Morgener, Jörg [= Jürgen Köchel], 162
Mosolov, Alexander,
  Dam, The, 199
Moyseyev, M., 198
Mozart, Wolfgang Amadeus, 57, 59, 249, 251, 259–60, 262
  Piano Concerto in E♭, K482, 233
  Requiem, 33, 239, 251
Mravinsky, Yevgeniy, 35, 45
Mungalova, Ol'ga, 192, 196
Muradeli, Vano
  Great Friendship, The, 190, 222
musicologists, 1, 2, 16
Musorgsky, Modest, 19, 145, 212, 233, 239, 240
  Boris Godunov, 34, 149, 185, 216, 226, 240, 251
  songs, 211–12
  Songs and Dances of Death, 211, 244
Myaskovsky, Nikolay, 19, 45, 67, 86–7

Nagarov, I., 198
Nattiez, Jean-Jacques, 117
Nazi death camps, 113, 126, 128, 136
Nechayev, Vasiliy, 27
Nemirovich-Danchenko, Vladimir, 169, 170, 171–2, 176–9
neoclassicism, 26, 57
Nesterenko, Yevgeniy, 214, 218, 226

Newcomb, Anthony, 115, 119
Nielsen, Carl, 10
    Symphony No. 2, 11
    Symphony No. 5, 10
Niemöller, Klaus, 57, 192
Nikolayev, Leonid, 1
Norris, Christopher, 3, 25, 214

O'Brien, Justin, 6
O'Connor, T. E., 198
Odoyevsky, Prince Vladimir, 78
Olesha, Yuriy, 53
Offenbach, Jacques, 232
Ordzhonikidze, Givi, 35, 76, 152
Orfeyev, Serafim, 95
Orlov, Genrikh, 27, 35, 38
Orlov, Yuri, 46, 48, 49
Orlova, Yelena, 86
Ostretsov, Alexander, 48, 52, 168–9
Ostrovsky, Nikolai
    How the Steel was Tempered, 32
Ottaway, Hugh, 117
Owen, Wilfred, 236, 237

pacifism, 235
Palmer, Christopher, 232
Panfyorov, Fyodor
    Ingots, 26
panikhida, 40–2
    vechnaya pamyat' [*Eternal remembrance*], 40–1
Pärt, Arvo, 257
passacaglia [basso ostinato], 57, 72, 120, 121, **125–6**, 127–32, 136, 146, 168, 216, 220, 224, 238, 241–2, 248, 250
Pasternak, Boris, 54, 212, 217
Patterson, Annabel, 30
Pears, Peter, 231, 240
Pechkovsky, Nikolay, 190
perestroyka, 17–23, 24, 25, 32, 53, 55
Personality Cult, the, 4
Peter the Great, Tsar, 241
Petersen, Peter, 151
Petritsky, A., 197
Pilnyak, Boris, 54
    Mahogany [*Krasnoye derevo*], 198
Plantinga, Leon, 117
Pokrovsky, Boris, 153
Pokrovsky, N., 198

polystylisticism, 221
Pospelov, P. N., 210–11
Poulenc, Francis, 234
Pountney, David, 153
Pravda, 20, 22, 184
    'muddle instead of music', [*sumbur vmesto muzïki*], 22, 25, 33, 35, 53, 161, 176–7, 182, 190, 205, 217
Preys, Alexander, 162, 165, 171
Prokofiev, Sergey, 20, 42, 45, 67, 85, 118, 183, 234, 235
    Pas d'Acier, Le, 199
    Romeo and Juliet, 204, 234
    Semyon Kotko, 31–2
Prokoll (Production Collective), 19
Protopopov, Vladimir, 77
Prout, Ebenezer, 61
Pugni, Cesare
    Esmeralda, La, 193
Purcell, Henry, 241
    Dido and Aeneas, 242
Pushkin, 26, 43–5, 207, 208, 215, 217, 225, 236, 242

quotations, 5, 57, 61, 66, 74, 249

Rabinovich, David, 45, 113, 117, 206
Radamsky, Sergey, 171–2, 175
Radziyevsky, N., 197
Rakhmaninov, Sergey
    Bells, The, 199
    'Spring waters', 212
Ravel, Maurice, 234, 235
Rayskin, Iosif, 183
Redepenning, Dorothea, 7, 13, 217
Restagno, Enzo, 15
Réti, Rudolph, 119
Rezvoy, Modest, 78
Richter, Sviatoslav, 235
Rilke, Rainer Maria, 224, 225
Rimsky-Korsakov, Nikolay, 23, 40, 79, 265
Rittikh, M., 190
Rodzinski, Artur, 169
rondo form, 59, 62–8, 121
Roseberry, Eric, 1, 7, 15, 113, 237, 244, 245
Rossini, Gioachino
    Barber of Seville, The, 189

Index

Rostropovich, Mstislav, 167, 212, 233, 234, 235
Rozhdestvensky, Gennadiy, 189, 206
Rushdie, Salman, 24
Russian Association of Proletarian Musicians, The (RAPM), 19, 20, 25, 32, 199, 201–2, 203

Sabinina, Marina, 152, 243
Sadie, Stanley, 151
Sakharov, Andrey, 47
Samosud, Samuil, 22
Sapozhnikov, S., 191
Schenker, Heinrich, 9, 11, 13, 118, 119, 134, 144
Schmidt, Ole, 10
Schnittke, Alfred, 7, 15–16, 221, 254–70
  Concerto grosso No. 1, 261, 263
  Concerto grosso No. 2, 261, 263
  Concerto grosso No. 3, 262
  Concerto for Piano and Strings, 264
  Concerto for Piano Duet, 264
  Faust Cantata, 261
  Nagasaki, 256
  Peer Gynt, 261
  Symphony No. 1, 260
  Symphony No. 3, 261, 262
  Symphony No. 4, 261, 264
  Symphony No. 6, 266–7
  Symphony No. 7, 262, 266
  Violin Concerto No. 3, 261, 264
  Violin Concerto No. 4, 260, 262, 263, 264, 268
Schoenberg, Arnold, 58, 119, 229, 246, 247, 248
  Chamber Symphony No. 1, 248
Schoenbohm, Siegfried, 162
Schubert, Franz, 115, 233, 253
  Winterreise, 251
Schumann, Robert, 117, 233
  Symphony No. 2, 115, 119–20
Schwartz, Harry, 182
Schwarz, Boris, 31
Serafimovich, Alexander
  Iron Flood, The, 26
Sereda, V., 82, 87, 91, 92, 94, 99, 103, 104–5, 109–10, 112
Sergeyev, Konstantin, 192, 196
Serov, Alexander, 78

Shakespeare, William, 33, 217, 225, 226
  Julius Caesar, 252
  Lear, 227
Shapiro, Mikhail, 185
Shaporin, Yuriy, 184
Shashkov, 183
Shaydur, Ivan, 77
Shebalin, Vissarion, 216
Shemyakin, Andrey, 4
Shneyerson, Grigoriy, 254
Shostakovich, Dmitri, Works
  Alone, 189
  Aphorisms, Op. 13, 23
  Bolt, The, 189, 190
  Cello Concerto No. 1, 210, 235
  Cello Concerto No. 2, 103, 250, 260
  Cello Sonata, 189
  chamber music, 233
  concertos, 232
  Declared Dead (Uslovno ubitïy), 179
  Execution of Stepan Razin, The, 106, 211, 233, 252
  film scores, 228
  Five Romances on Texts from the Magazine *Krokodil*, 211, 213–14, 226
  Five Romances on Verses of Yevgeniy Dolmatovsky, 207
  From Jewish Folk Poetry, 207–8, 217, 235
  Four Poems of Captain Lebyadkin, 211, 217, 226–8
  Four Pushkin Monologues, 207
  Four Romances on Poems by Pushkin, 43–5, 205–6, 207
  Four Songs to Words by Dolmatovsky, 206
  Golden Age, The, 7, 14, 189–204
  Golden Hills, 189
  Gypsies, The, 225
  'Jewish' works, 113, 126
  King Lear, Op. 58a, 227
  Krïlov Fables, 14, 206
  Lady Macbeth of Mtsensk District, The (revised as *Katerina Izmaylova*), 6–7, 13, 14, 15, 21, 23, 25, 32, 53, 54, 73, 92, 93–4, 97, 98, 108–9, 137–59,

160–88, 189, 190, 205, 206, 208, 210, 211, 215, 216, 217, 224, 234, 251
Limpid Stream, The, 22, 189, 190
New Babylon, The, 189
Nose, The, 56, 74, 153, 189, 240
Passer-By, The (*The Counterplan*), 189
Piano Concerto No. 1, 57, 97, 189
Piano Quintet, 73, 92, 97, 113
Piano Sonata No. 2, 61–5, 92, 95–6, 97
Piano Trio No. 2, 13, 66, 72, 97, 113–36, 210, 217, 235, 238–9, 241
popular songs and choruses, 228
Preface to the Compete Edition of My Works, 211, 214–15
Preludes for Piano, 62, 189
Preludes and Fugues for Piano, 96, 237, 241
Rayok, 212, 213, 226
Satires (*Pictures from the Past*) [to words by Sasha Chorny], 211, 212–13, 223, 226
Seven Romances on Poems of Alexander Blok, 211, **214–16**, 217, 218, 224, 233, 241
Six Poems of Marina Tsvetayeva, 211, 217, 218, 223, 224, 225
Six Romances on Verses by English Poets, 207, **216–17**, 218
Six Romances on Words by Japanese Poets, 206
Song-cycles, 13–14, **205–28**
Song of the Forests, The, 206, 228
string quartets Nos. 1–8, 116, 230, 232, 233
String Quartet No. 1, 25, 62, 117
String Quartet No. 2, 57, 97
String Quartet No. 3, 66
String Quartet No. 4, 116, 217
String Quartet No. 5, 66
String Quartet No. 6, 66, 72, 116
String Quartet No. 7, 72, 73, 99, 105, 106, **110–11**, 238
String Quartet No. 8, 55, 61, 66, 72, 73, 117, 146, 187, 208, 210, 224, 230, 232, 235, 238, 249, 254, 262

String Quartet No. 9, 55, 250
String Quartet No. 10, 55
String Quartet No. 11, 238, 243, 251
String Quartet No. 12, 75, 229, 238, 239, 247, 251
String Quartet No. 13, 75, 238, 248, 251
String Quartet No. 14, 251, 254
String Quartet No. 15, 106, 224, 225, 230, 238, 243, 244, 251, 261, 264
Suite on Verses of Michelangelo Buonarroti, 211, **218–25**, 226, 227, 228, 229, 230, 233–4, 249, 251, 252
Sun Shines Over Our Motherland, The, 207, 228
symphonies, 228, 232
Symphony No. 1, 72, 238, 248, 251
Symphony No. 2, 72, 73, 252
Symphony No. 3, 72
Symphony No. 4, 26, 50, 72, 189, 237, 239, 240, 249
Symphony No. 5, 2, **9–12**, 24–56, 59–60, 61, 62, 65–6, 68, 69, 72, 92, 97, 98, 99, 118, 189, 205–6, 215, 237, 239, 240, 249
Symphony No. 6, 27, 57, 63, 66, 72, 92, 97, **109–10**, 259
Symphony No. 7, 48, 49, 52, 62, 67, 68, 72, 92, 96, 97, 109, 149, 178, 217
Symphony No. 8, 62, 66, 67, 68, 70, 72, 97, 149, 210, 224, 260, 264
Symphony No. 9, 66, 97–8, 217, 259
Symphony No. 10, 14, 31, 45, 66, 68, 70–1, **99–101**, 105, 210, 215, 223, 259
Symphony No. 11, 96, 223, 224, 235, 236, 237, 238, 249
Symphony No. 12, 213
Symphony No. 13, 208, 211, 214–15, 216, 223, 227, 233, 251, 252, 261
Symphony No. 14, 54, 75, 211, 216, 218, 222, 224, 229, 234, 242, **243–7**, 248, 249, 251, 257
Symphony No. 15, 223, 225, 230, 234, 237, 238, 242, 247, **248–50**, 251, 254, 260

'Symphony No. 16', 218
Two Romances on Verses by
  Dolmatovsky, 207
Violin Concerto No. 1, 72, 116,
  146, 217, 222, 224, 235, 241
Viola Sonata, 106, 225, 230, 260,
  261, 266
Violin Sonata, 75, 107-8
'War Symphonies', 235, 238, 239
Shostakovich, Galina (daughter of
  DS), 181
Shostakovich, Irina (third wife of DS),
  189
Shostakovich, Maxim (son of DS),
  181, 218
Shostakovich, Nina (née Varzar, first
  wife of DS), 178, 206, 216
Shteynberg, Anna, 26
Shul'gin, N., 171
Sibelius, Jean, 256
Siciliani, Francesco, 183
Sil'vestrov, Valentin, 257
  Postludes, 261
  Symphony No. 5, 261
Simpson, Robert, 158
Sinyavsky, Andrey, 46
Skrebkov, Sergey, 82, 84, 91, 98-9,
  103, 105
Skryabin, Alexander, 5
  Piano Sonata No. 9, 68
  Piano Sonata No. 10, 48
Smirnov, V., 197
Smolich, Nikolay, 170, 171-2, 176
Sobolov, Leonid, 211
socialism, 18, 27
socialist realism, 25, 32-3, 49, 157,
  160, 214, 228
Sokal'sky, Pyotr, 78
Sokhor, Arnol'd, 82, 85, 86, 87
Sokol'sky, Matias [= Matias
  Grinberg], 176, 177
Sollertinsky, Ivan, 1, 113, 128, 163,
  168, 200, 201, 216, 237, 239
Solzhenitsïn, Alexander, 47
sonata rondo [form], 66
sonata form, 29, 66, 68-72, 120-1,
  122, 128, 131
song forms, 58, 59, 60-2
Soudakova, L., 162
Souvchinsky, Pierre, 27

Sovnarkom (Council of People's
  Commissars), 21
Spencer, Stewart, 117
Spohr, Ludwig, 151
Sposobin, Igor', 61, 98
Stalin [=Iosif Dzugashvili], 2, 6, 18,
  19, 20, 25, 26, 28, 46, 49, 50,
  51, 54, 55, 56, 80, 161, 176,
  190, 198, 211, 236, 240, 252
Stalinism, 23, 46-7, 53, 56, 129, 252
Starokadomsky, Mikhail, 168
Startsev, A., 201
Stasov, Vladimir, 42
Stein, Erwin, 245-6
Steinberg, Maximilian, 23, 40
Stolyarov, Grigoriy, 162, 163, 168, 170
Strauss, Leo, 30
Stravinsky, Igor', 28, 31, 40, 50, 157,
  200, 201, 237
  Chroniques de ma vie, 40
  Histoire du Soldat, L', 127
  Oedipus Rex, 234
  Petrushka, 74, 127
  Poetics of Music, 27
  Pogrebal'naya pesn', 40
  Rite of Spring, The, 189
  Symphony of Psalms, 178, 234
Strode, Rosamund, 245
Stupnikov, I., 197
symphony, 256-61

Taneyev, Sergey, 79
Taruskin, Richard, 2, 3, 4, 6, 7, 9, 10,
  18, 28, 206, 240
TASS (Telegraphic Agency of the
  Soviet Union), 22
Tchaikovsky, Pyotr, 19, 28, 57, 68,
  79, 199, 200, 201, 202, 234,
  258, 261, 265
  Queen of Spades, The, 214
  Symphony No. 4, 45, 48-9, 258
  Symphony No. 5, 45, 258
  Symphony No. 6, 48, 68, 210,
    253, 258-9
  Yevgeniy Onegin, 185, 213
Tebosyan, A., 103, 105-6, 111, 112
'Terror, The Great', 36, 47
Tereshkovich, M. A., 22
Terteryan, Avet, 257, 263
'Thaw, The', 4, 212, 235

thematic transformation, 7–8, 116
Tiftikidi, N. F., 95
Tishchenko, Boris, 75, 217, 226, 254, 255, 268
Tolstoy, Count Alexey, 27, 28, 31, 32, 33, 36, 39, 48, 50, 214
Tolstoy, Lev, 213, 214
Tolstaya, Tatyana, 47
Treitler, Leo, 119
Trotsky, Leon [= Lev Bronsteyn], 20
Trutovsky, Vasiliy, 78
Tsïtovich, T., 190
Tsvetayeva, Marina, 217, 225
Tukhachevsky, Mikhail, 42
twelve-note music, 74–5, 219–21, 236, 246–8, 249, 250
Tyulin, Yuriy, 80, 82, 83–4, 90, 91–2, 98, 103–4, 106
Tyut'manov, I., 84

Ulam, Adam, 46
Ulanova, Galina, 190, 192, 195, 196, 202
Union of Soviet Composers, 17, 18, 20, 21, 22, 25, 36
Uspensky, Viktor, 80
Ustinov, Andrey, 46

Varzar, Nina, *see* Shostakovich, Nina
Vasina-Grossman, Vera, 206, 207, 218, 225, 226
Vaynberg, Moisey, 184, 255
Vaynonen, N., 195, 196, 197
Vaynonen, Vasiliy, 192, 194, 195, 196, 197, 200
'Vechnaya pamyat'' (revolutionary song), 235
Vel'ter, Nadezhda, 172–3
Verdi, Giuseppe
    Aida, 42
    Requiem, 33, 239
Vernadsky, V. I., 260
Vert, N., 198
Vigilyev, E., 197
Virta, Nikolai, 37
    Loneliness, 32, 37
Vishinsky, Andrey, 53
Vishnevskaya, Galina, 167, 185–6, 212, 231, 234, 235

Vishnevsky, Vsevolod
    Optimistic Tragedy, An, 34
Vlazinskaya, Valeria, 230
Volkov, Solomon (*Testimony*), 4, 5, 31, 34, 38, 45, 47, 49, 118, 242, 251
Vvedensky, Alexander, 266
Vyantskus, Antanas, 85

Wagner, Richard, 117, 157, 158, 242
    Götterdämmerung, 210
    Parsifal, 151
    Ring des Nibelungen, Der, 151, 248
    Siegfried, 158
    Tristan und Isolde, 151, 249
Webern, Anton, 266
    String Quartet Op. 28, 246
Whittall, Arnold, 151
Wilson, Elizabeth, 2, 5, 153, 210
Wolf, Hugo, 233
Wolzogen, Hans von, 157
Wolter, Günter, 3

Yakobson, Leonid, 192, 194, 196, 200
Yakubov, Manashir, 7, 14, 212
Yavorsky, Boleslaw, 79, 80, 93, 112
Yershov, Ivan, 193, 202
Yevtushenko, Yevgeniy, 47, 187
Yezhov, Nikolai, 24, 39, 42
Yordan, Ol'ga, 192, 195
Youmans, Vincent
    'Tea for Two' [*Tahiti Trot*], 191, 202
Yudin, Gavriil, 172–3
yurodivïy [Holy Fool], 118
Yusfin, A., 87
Yuzhak, Kira, 81

Zabolotsky, Nikolay, 266
Zaderatsky, Vsevolod, 57, 192
Zagursky, Boris, 182
Zamyatin, Yevgeniy, 53, 54
Zhdanov, Andrey, 20, 212
Zhilyayev, Nikolay, 62
Zhitomirsky, Daniil, 5, 76, 199
Zhuravlenko, P., 190
Zieliński, Tadeusz, 61
Zinoviev, Grigoriy, 22
Zoshchenko, Mikhail, 53

Printed in the United States
58162LVS00002B/444